GUM

Grammar, Usage, and Mechanics

Conventions of Standard English

ZB Zaner-Bloser

Grade Level Consultants

S. Elaine Boysworth
Lincolnton, North Carolina

Linda Crawford
Calhoun, Georgia

Martha Swan Novy
Florissant, Missouri

Heather Stanton
Colorado Springs, Colorado

Jaqueline Xavier
Cleveland, Ohio

Illustration: Tom Kennedy, Tracy Greenwalt

ISBN: 978-1-4531-1211-3

Zaner-Bloser, Inc.
1-800-421-3018
www.zaner-bloser.com

Printed in the United States of America

5 6 7 8 9 10 11 27950 20 19

ZB Code 16

Table of Contents

Unit 1 Sentence Structure

Looking Back: Innovations That Changed History

Unit 2 Sentence Structure

Beasts & Critters: Sea Creatures

Unit 3 Parts of Speech: Nouns, Pronouns, and Adjectives

Unforgettable Folks: People Who Overcame Challenges

Unit 4 Parts of Speech: Verbs, Adverbs, Prepositions, and Conjunctions

The World Outside: Cycles in Nature

Unit 5 Usage

Grab Bag: Cultural Snapshots

Unit 6 Grammar

Timeless Tales: Folktale Characters

Unit 7 Mechanics

Great Getaways: Islands and Near-Islands

Appendix

Unit Pretests

Extra Practice

Unit Posttests

The development of agriculture / changed human society forever.

        a   **b**

Which part (*a* or *b*) of this sentence tells whom or what the sentence is about? _____

Which part (*a* or *b*) tells what happened? _____

Every sentence has a subject and a predicate. The **complete subject** is made up of a noun or pronoun and words that tell about it. The subject tells whom or what the sentence is about. The **complete predicate** is made up of a verb and words that tell what the subject is, has, or does.

See Handbook Sections 11, 12

Practice

Underline the complete subject in each sentence once. Underline each complete predicate twice.

1. Prehistoric humans were hunter-gatherers for millions of years.

2. Small groups of people traveled around to the areas with the most plentiful plants and animals.

3. Earth's climate changed suddenly about eleven thousand years ago.

4. The familiar foods were often not available.

5. Some people experimented with agriculture in the Middle East, Asia, and Mexico.

6. People in these areas grew plants from wild seeds.

7. Nutritious grains were grown by these farmers.

8. They kept animals for their milk, wool, and meat.

9. The new farmers built permanent dwellings near their fields.

10. Some of these farmers lived in an area called the Fertile Crescent.

11. Humans considered land their property for the first time.

12. Some of the arid regions in Egypt and Sumeria had fertile soil.

13. Farmers developed complex irrigation, or watering, systems there.

14. Irrigation required the labor and cooperation of many people.

15. Extra food was produced as a result of irrigation.

16. Food production no longer required every person's effort.

17. Some people became craftspeople, soldiers, or merchants instead of farmers.

18. The abundant food supply enabled more people to live in villages.

19. These developments led to the establishment of the first civilizations.

Croplands in ancient Egypt were irrigated with water from the Nile River.

Apply

Add a subject or a predicate to each phrase to make a sentence. Underline the complete subject in each sentence you write. Circle the complete predicate in each sentence.

20. hunted bison and mammoth _____

_____

21. agriculture _____

_____

22. grew barley and wheat _____

_____

23. the world's earliest civilizations _____

_____

24. flocks of sheep _____

_____

Reinforce

Complete subjects and predicates may be very short (*Dogs / bark.*) or very long. Short sentences can make a passage seem spare and direct. They tend to focus the reader's attention on actions and events. Long sentences can create a smooth flow that carries the reader along from idea to idea while providing clear descriptive or explanatory information.

Notice the differences between these two passages by famous authors. Draw a slash (/) between the complete subject and the complete predicate in each sentence.

His face was sweaty and dirty. The sun shone on his face. The day was very hot.

—Ernest Hemingway, from *In Our Time*

The curious things about her were her hands, strange terminations to the flabby white arms splattered with pale tan spots—long, quivering hands with deep and convex nails.

—Dorothy Parker, from "Big Blonde"

On another piece of paper, write a paragraph of your own about meeting an unusual or interesting person. Try making the subjects and predicates in your sentences very short. Then rewrite your paragraph, adding words and phrases to make the subjects and predicates long. Now compare the two paragraphs. Which version do you prefer?

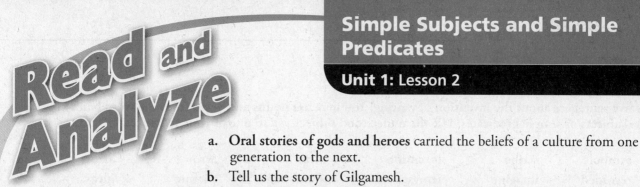

Read and Analyze

a. **Oral stories of gods and heroes** carried the beliefs of a culture from one generation to the next.

b. Tell us the story of Gilgamesh.

The complete subject of sentence *a* is in boldfaced type. Circle the most important word in the complete subject. Underline the verb that tells what the subject did.

Can you find a subject at the beginning of sentence *b*? _____

Circle the word below that fits as the subject of sentence *b*.

Gilgamesh   you   tell   story

The **simple subject** is the most important word or words in the complete subject. It is a noun or pronoun and tells whom or what the sentence is about. The subject of a request or command (an imperative sentence) is usually not named. The person being spoken to, *you*, is the **understood subject**. The **simple predicate** is the most important word or words in the predicate. It is a verb. The simple predicate tells what the subject did or what was done to the subject. The simple predicate may also be a form of the verb *be*.

See Handbook Sections 11, 12

Practice

Circle the simple subject in each sentence. If the understood subject is *you*, write *you* on the line. Underline the simple predicate.

1. The people of Sumeria developed a writing system more than 5,000 years ago. _____

2. Find the Euphrates River on a map. _____

3. Ancient Sumeria included the fertile lands near this river. _____

4. Some Sumerians owned large quantities of goods. _____

5. A record of these goods was often necessary for business purposes. _____

6. Sumerians drew marks or symbols on wet clay tablets for their records. _____

7. Some people became experts at the use of symbols. _____

8. These scribes could draw symbols for objects easily. _____

9. Ideas presented the scribes with a much greater challenge. _____

10. Draw a symbol for *life* or *freedom*. _____

11. Your drawing must be understandable to other people. _____

12. Guess the Sumerian scribes' solution to this problem. _____

13. *Ti* meant both "arrow" and "life" in the Sumerian spoken language. _____

14. Clever scribes used a picture of an arrow as the symbol for both words. _____

15. Symbols eventually represented sounds such as *ti* instead of objects such as *arrow*. _____

16. People could then write any word in the Sumerian language. _____

The early symbol for *fish* changed over time.

Name _____

Apply

Write five sentences about the invention of writing. You may use nouns and verbs from the word bank as simple subjects or simple predicates. Use the understood subject *you* in one of your sentences.

symbols	scribe	invention	draw	wrote	arrow
recorded	imagine	represented	Sumerians	picture	ideas

17. _____

_____

18. _____

_____

_____

19. _____

_____

20. _____

_____

21. _____

_____

Reinforce

A symbol that stands for a sound in a puzzle is called a *rebus*. For instance, a picture of an eye can stand for *I* in a rebus. Solve the rebus puzzles below to find the simple subject of each sentence. The first one has been done for you.

22. The 🌅 + 🔑 pulled a wagon full of vegetables. ___donkey___

23. My favorite C + ☀️ is winter. _____

24. The 🧢 + 10 of the ship commanded the crew to raise anchor. _____

25. One ✒️ + 🖐 will buy you a gumball. _____

Read and Analyze

_____ Clocks and calendars are very important in modern life.

_____ They wake us up, measure our working hours, and inform us of holidays.

Write _S_ next to the sentence with two or more simple subjects. Write _P_ next to the sentence with two or more simple predicates.

A **compound subject** is two or more subjects joined by a conjunction (_and, or_).
A **compound predicate** is two or more verbs joined by a conjunction.

See Handbook | Sections 11, 12

Practice

Each sentence below has either a compound subject or a compound predicate. If a sentence has a compound subject, circle the two or more nouns that are the simple subjects. If a sentence has a compound predicate, underline the two or more verbs that are the simple predicates.

1. The concept of time fascinates and perplexes humans.

2. Prehistoric men and women probably saw time as a circle.

3. These early people observed and noted regular changes in the sky.

4. The sun rose and set every day.

5. Spring, summer, fall, and winter occurred in the same sequence over and over.

6. People in several regions studied and recorded these yearly cycles.

7. The Sumerians, Mayas, and Chinese invented calendars independently.

8. Calendar-makers carved marks in stone or tied knots in string.

9. These early calendars predicted the times for harvests and indicated the days for festivals.

10. The sun and stars seem to change their position in the sky over the course of a year.

11. The moon moves across the sky and seems to change shape.

12. Ancient peoples observed and celebrated these celestial events.

13. Many ancient temples and monuments face the dawn or the North Star.

14. The sun's yearly cycle and the cycle of the moon are out of step with each other.

15. This confused most ancient astronomers and caused inaccuracies in some calendars.

16. Modern astronomers and physicists occasionally add leap seconds to a year for greater accuracy.

This calendar stone shows the days of the Aztec month.

Apply

Combine each pair of sentences to form one sentence that has either a compound subject or a compound predicate.

17. The world's first mechanical clock was made in China. The world's first mechanical clock showed changes in

the phases of the moon. _____

_____

18. The Buddhist monk I-Hsing designed a mechanical clock. Then he built this clock. _____

_____

_____

19. Gears controlled the clock's movements. Shafts controlled the clock's movements, too. _____

_____

_____

20. Water in a stream turned a water wheel. This water made the clock function. _____

_____

_____

21. A bell announced the time. A drum announced the time. _____

_____

Reinforce

It is possible to have both a compound subject and a compound predicate in the same sentence.
(*The boys and girls splashed and swam together.*) However, both parts of the compound subject must
be performing both actions of the compound predicate. Avoid sentences like this one: *The wolves and
frogs howled and croaked.* This sentence might make the reader think that the frogs howled and the
wolves croaked.

On the lines below, rewrite the incorrect sentence as two separate sentences. Write *C* beside the sentence that
uses compound subjects and predicates correctly.

22. The sun and moon light up the day and shine at night. _____

_____

23. Ice and snow come in winter and make travel difficult. _____

_____

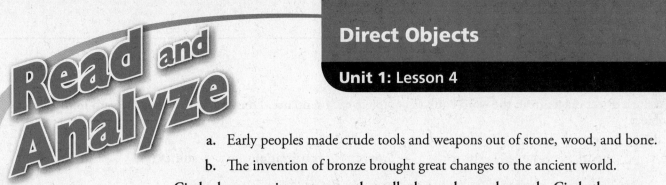
a. Early peoples made crude tools and weapons out of stone, wood, and bone.

b. The invention of bronze brought great changes to the ancient world.

Circle the nouns in sentence *a* that tell what early peoples made. Circle the noun in sentence *b* that tells what the invention of bronze brought.

The **direct object** is the noun or pronoun that receives the action of the verb. Only action verbs can take a direct object. A **compound direct object** occurs when more than one noun or pronoun receives the action of the verb. To find the direct object, say the verb and then ask "What?" or "Whom?" For example, to find the direct object of sentence *b*, ask "The invention of bronze brought what?" Answer: It brought *changes*.

See Handbook Section 21

Practice

Circle the direct object in each sentence. If there is a compound direct object, circle each noun or pronoun that is a direct object.

1. Craftspeople first produced bronze in about 3800 B.C., in Sumeria.

2. These craftspeople melted copper in a kind of furnace.

3. They accidentally mixed arsenic and other minerals with the copper.

4. This combination produced a stronger metal.

5. Eventually, metalworkers combined copper and tin into bronze.

6. Sumerian metalworkers could form this new metal into almost any shape.

7. Craftspeople in Egypt and other nearby areas soon learned the secret of bronze production.

8. People made durable tools, weapons, and statues out of bronze.

9. Farmers tilled fields with bronze-tipped plows.

10. They could cultivate larger areas with these efficient plows.

11. Soon Middle Eastern civilizations needed new sources of tin.

12. This stimulated trade with distant regions.

13. People from widespread cultures exchanged ideas as well as goods.

14. The expansion of trade also encouraged the expansion of empires.

15. Nations conquered other nations for their tin.

16. Over time, however, the Iron Age overcame the Bronze Age.

17. Iron replaced tin as the main metal.

Tools like this bronze-tipped sickle made life a little easier for ancient farmers.

Name _____

Apply

Write a direct object from the word bank to complete each sentence. Draw an arrow from the verb to the direct object.

model	horse	trick	bronze	civilization	stories	Trojans

18. The Mycenaeans used _____ for weapons and sculptures during the Bronze Age in Greece.

19. In about 1200 B.C., some disastrous event destroyed their _____.

20. Greeks in later times told _____ about the heroic deeds and amazing palaces of their Bronze Age ancestors.

21. In one of these legends, the Greeks played a clever _____ on their enemies, the Trojans.

22. They built a huge wooden _____ of a horse, and some soldiers hid inside.

23. The Trojans brought the _____ inside their walled city.

24. In the middle of the night, the Greek soldiers climbed out of their hiding place and defeated the _____.

Reinforce

An action verb that takes a direct object is a *transitive* verb. An action verb without a direct object is an *intransitive* verb. Many action verbs may be either transitive (*Mr. Garcia runs the store.*) or intransitive (*Mark runs fast.*), depending on whether they are used with a direct object. You will learn more about transitive and intransitive verbs in Lesson 38.

In the following sentences, write *transitive verb* on the line if there is a direct object. Write *intransitive verb* if there is no direct object.

25. Sculptors work very hard. _____

26. Sculptors work soft clay into figures. _____

27. They make molds from the clay figures. _____

28. Molten bronze pours easily. _____

29. The sculptor pours molten bronze into the mold. _____

30. This material hardens to make a permanent model of the sculpture. _____

Read and Analyze

In today's society, people give **clerks money** in exchange for food and other necessities.

Which boldfaced noun tells what people give? _____

Which boldfaced noun tells *to whom* they give it? _____

An **indirect object** is a person or thing to whom something is given, told, or taught. The indirect object is a noun or pronoun, and it comes before the direct object. To test whether a word is an indirect object, move it after the direct object and put the word *to* or *for* in front of it. Example: *People give money to clerks.*

See Handbook Section 21

Practice

First underline the direct object in each sentence. Then circle the indirect object.

1. In ancient times, farmers traded others their crops in exchange for different foods or useful things.

2. For example, a farmer might have offered a neighbor some beans.

3. The neighbor might have offered the farmer some plums from her garden in exchange.

4. But what if a plum gave the farmer a stomachache?

5. The farmer might have traded a cousin the other plums for some cucumbers.

6. Then the farmer might have traded a friend some cucumbers in exchange for a chicken.

7. This complicated system caused people problems.

8. China probably brought the world the first monetary system.

9. Money provided people a convenient method of exchange.

10. People give money its value.

11. Merchants will trade you goods for money.

12. Paper money gives the public a lightweight medium of exchange.

13. Enough money will buy you almost any product.

14. History teaches us lessons about how the value of money can change.

15. In times of economic disaster, people have given merchants

    wheelbarrows full of paper money in exchange for a few days' food.

16. Many people today give cashiers a plastic card to complete a purchase.

The earliest coins were shaped like small tools.

Name _____

Apply

Rewrite each sentence, changing the underlined phrase into an indirect object.

17. Mary's grandfather showed his collection of old and rare money to us. _____

_____

_____

18. He told a story about the use of rice as money in seventeenth-century Japan to Mary. _____

_____

_____

19. He showed a playing card that was used as money in colonial Canada to me. _____

_____

_____

20. I made a thank-you card with drawings of coins on it for him. _____

_____

_____

Reinforce

Write a word from the word bank to give each sentence an indirect object. Then use the numbered letters to form the mystery word.

coins	Mary	us	her	me	him

21. Mary's grandfather gave _____ _____ the idea of starting my own coin collection.
                                      4

22. I traded _____ _____ _____ a summer of yard work for some old coins.
                1

23. Mary's grandfather taught _____ _____ his methods for coin collecting.

24. He never gives the _____ _____ _____ _____ _____ a scrub or a polish.
                        2   3

25. One year later I showed _____ _____ _____ _____ the coin collection her grandfather had inspired.
                                              5

Mystery word: _____ _____ _____ _____ _____
              1   2   3   4   5

Read and Analyze

Movable type is a **method** of printing with letter stamps.

Each letter is **separate**.

Circle the boldfaced noun that tells more about who or what the subject is.
Underline the boldfaced adjective that tells what the subject is like.

A **predicate noun** follows a linking verb and tells more about who or what the subject is. A **predicate adjective** follows a linking verb and describes the subject.

See Handbook Section 12

Practice

Draw a box around the linking verb in each sentence. Circle each boldfaced word that is a predicate noun. Underline each boldfaced word that is a predicate adjective.

1. First developed in 1045, movable type was a Chinese **invention**.

2. The inventor was **Bi Sheng**.

3. This type of printing was not **practical** in China at the time, however.

4. Chinese characters were too **numerous**.

5. Movable type was more **useful** in Europe.

6. Before the development of movable type, most European books were handmade **copies** of manuscripts.

7. Scribes were the experienced **writers** of these books.

8. Handwritten books were unique **works** of art.

9. The pages were **beautiful**, with elaborate decorations in the margins.

10. Unfortunately, these books were **expensive** and **scarce**.

11. The first European printer was **Johannes Gutenberg**.

12. 1456 was the **year** of his innovation.

13. The Roman alphabet is a **set** of 26 characters.

14. The model for Gutenberg's printing press was a **press** for grapes or cheese.

15. Its output was 300 **copies** per day.

16. Soon books and pamphlets were **available** to many more people.

17. New ideas became the **property** of everyone, not just the rich.

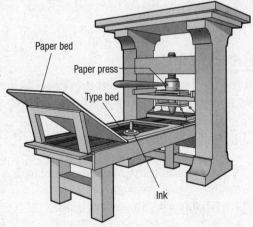

Paper bed
Paper press
Type bed
Ink

The printing press helped spread new ideas across the world.

Apply

Write a predicate noun or a predicate adjective to complete each sentence.

18. My favorite book is _____.

19. The main character in the book is _____.

20. This character's personality seems _____

_____.

21. The setting for that mystery book is _____

_____.

22. The mood of the story seems _____

_____.

23. Even the illustrations appear _____.

24. The villain changes in the story and becomes _____.

25. Whenever I read this book, I feel _____.

26. The author of this new adventure story has become _____.

27. The most important problem in the novel's plot is _____.

28. When I saw the cover of the book, I thought it looked _____.

29. Of all the books I've read, this one remains _____.

Reinforce

In the modern world, word processors help spread the written word. But sometimes words are mistyped. Circle the predicate noun in each sentence below. Unscramble that word to find a word that makes sense.

30. His best feature was his slime. ____ ____ ____ ____ ____

31. Manuela's tasty pies prove that she is a fine brake. ____ ____ ____ ____ ____

32. My favorite flowers are sores. ____ ____ ____ ____ ____

33. A distance of 5,280 feet is a lime. ____ ____ ____ ____

34. Of all our field trips, my favorite place was the diary. ____ ____ ____ ____ ____

35. He ran as hard as he could, and his last jump was his greatest peal. ____ ____ ____ ____ ____

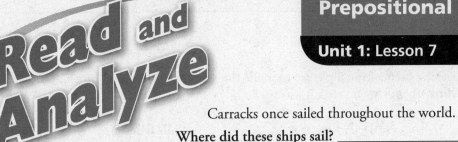
Carracks once sailed throughout the world.

Where did these ships sail? _____

> A **prepositional phrase** can tell how, what kind, when, how much, or where. A prepositional phrase begins with a **preposition**, such as *in, over, of, to,* or *by*. It ends with a noun or pronoun that is the **object of the preposition**. The words between the preposition and its object are part of the prepositional phrase. A prepositional phrase can appear at the beginning, middle, or end of a sentence.

See Handbook | Section 20

Practice

Underline each prepositional phrase. Circle the preposition that begins each phrase. Draw a box around the object of the preposition. There may be more than one prepositional phrase in each sentence.

1. In the fifteenth century, European shipbuilders built three-masted carracks with triangular sails.

2. The new design of these ships made long voyages easier.

3. The rudder and the compass, two inventions from China, helped sailors navigate and steer.

4. Europeans wanted silk and spices from Asia, and sailors began searching for better trade routes.

5. Seeking a new western route to Asia, Christopher Columbus landed on unfamiliar land.

6. Columbus thought the land was part of Asia, but others soon realized that

    this land to the west was an uncharted continent.

7. Soon sailors from many European countries were voyaging

    across the Atlantic.

8. In a few years, the invasion of the Americas had begun.

9. Corn, potatoes, and other nutritious crops from America were brought

    to Europe, and many European farm animals were brought to America.

10. People from different cultures exchanged ideas and customs.

11. The highly effective constitution of the Iroquois League would impress

    Benjamin Franklin and George Washington in later years.

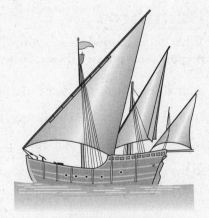

Improved ships and navigational methods brought widely separated cultures together.

12. This league comprised five Native American groups in the New York region.

13. The establishment of European colonies had terrible results for many Native Americans, however.

14. Thousands of Native Americans died in battle, and even more died from European diseases.

15. Africans were enslaved and brought in chains to the American colonies.

16. Many cultures and ways of life were lost to the world forever.

Apply

Rewrite each sentence. Add at least one prepositional phrase to make the sentence give more information. Use phrases from the word bank, or think of your own.

for the U.S. Constitution	from Native Americans	in their fields
of Native American nations	about new agricultural methods	of a democratic government
from European crops	in many regions	such as corn and potatoes

17. Native American groups developed innovative agricultural methods. _____

_____

_____

18. Their crops were different. _____

_____

19. Europeans learned. _____

_____

20. The Iroquois League provided an example. _____

_____

Reinforce

What animal introduced to America by the Spanish became important to Native Americans? Underline each prepositional phrase. Then follow the directions through the maze to trace out the answer. (21–36)

Start at the square. Go to the star. Go through the fish to the heart. Go from the heart to the letter A. Loop around the flower. Stop at the tree. Go to the number 1. Follow a curved route to the triangle. Draw a line to the sun. Follow the path through the letter B and through the circle. Stop at the diamond. Loop to the number 2. Follow a curved route to the moon.

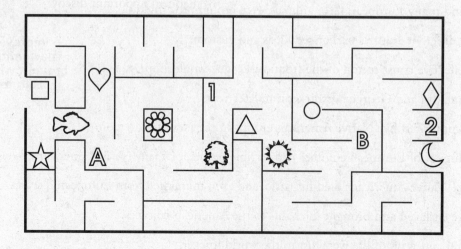

Read and Analyze

Modern photography began **in the 1830s.**

Photographs gave people a new view **of the world.**

Which of the boldfaced prepositional phrases gives more information about a noun? _____

A prepositional phrase can modify, or tell more about, a noun or pronoun. Prepositional phrases that modify nouns or pronouns are called **adjectival prepositional phrases**. An adjectival prepositional phrase usually comes after the noun or pronoun it modifies.

See Handbook | Section 20

Practice

Underline each adjectival prepositional phrase. Circle the noun it tells about. A sentence may have more than one adjectival prepositional phrase. Be careful! Not all the prepositional phrases in these sentences modify nouns or pronouns.

1. The man in the cloak holds a small box.

2. One side of the box has a hole in it.

3. He chooses an interesting scene near him and points the hole there.

4. Light rays enter the tiny hole in the dark box.

5. Inside the box the rays create a perfect miniature image of the scene.

6. This special dark box, a camera obscura, was an invention of the 1500s.

7. However, scientists in that era lacked knowledge of chemical processes.

8. Without that knowledge, film for the camera obscura could not be invented.

9. In the 1720s, Johann Schulze, a scientist from Germany, made an important discovery.

10. Exposure to light turns some chemicals dark.

11. Schulze's discovery made the invention of photographic film possible.

12. The images inside the camera obscura could be captured and preserved.

13. Louis Daguerre, often called the inventor of photography, publicized his photographic process widely.

14. But William Henry Talbot's process became the model for modern photography.

15. Using Talbot's process, a photographer could create many copies of a single photograph.

16. By 1888, a Kodak camera from George Eastman made photography accessible to anyone.

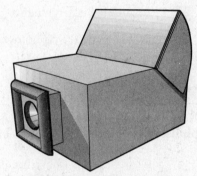

Artists often used images in a camera obscura to help them make sketches of large objects.

Name _____

Apply

Choose an adjectival prepositional phrase to complete each sentence. Write the phrase in the blank.

for close-up photography	with a telephoto lens	of José's photographs
of light	from his camera	near his home
as a photographer	of a baseball game	of his best picture
of a robin's nest		

17. José dreams of a career _____.

18. Last winter he bought a digital camera _____.

19. He borrowed a lens _____ from his uncle.

20. José experimented with different levels _____.

21. He took photographs _____ with the telephoto lens.

22. He climbed up a tree and took pictures _____ with the close-up lens.

23. José uploaded the digital files _____ to a photo processing website.

24. Most _____ turned out sharp and clear.

25. José ordered enlargements _____ and gave them to his mother and his uncle.

26. José plans to take a photography course at the community college _____.

Reinforce

Read this short letter written by Abraham Lincoln during the Civil War. Note how he used prepositional phrases to convey his sympathy. List the eleven adjectival prepositional phrases in this letter.

   Dear Madam, I have been shown in the files of the War Department a statement of the Adjutant-General of Massachusetts that you are the mother of five sons who have died gloriously on the field of battle. I feel how weak and fruitless must be any words of mine which should attempt to beguile you from the grief of a loss so overwhelming. But I cannot refrain from tendering to you the consolation that may be found in the thanks of the Republic they died to save. I pray that our heavenly Father may assuage the anguish of your bereavement, and leave you only the cherished memory of the loved and lost, and the solemn pride that must be yours to have laid so costly a sacrifice upon the altar of freedom.

—Abraham Lincoln, *Letter to Mrs. Bixby*

27. _____

28. _____

29. _____

30. _____

31. _____

32. _____

33. _____

34. _____

35. _____

36. _____

37. _____

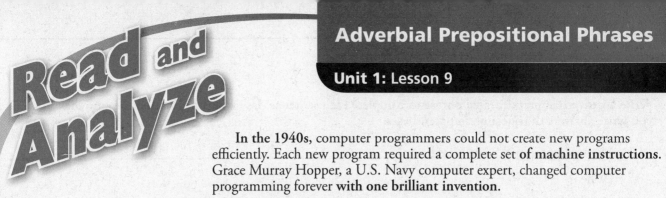

In the 1940s, computer programmers could not create new programs efficiently. Each new program required a complete set **of machine instructions**. Grace Murray Hopper, a U.S. Navy computer expert, changed computer programming forever **with one brilliant invention**.

Which of the boldfaced prepositional phrases tells *when* about a verb?

_____

Which tells *how* about a verb? _____

Which does not modify a verb? _____

A prepositional phrase can modify, or tell more about, a verb, an adverb, or an adjective. These prepositional phrases are called **adverbial prepositional phrases**. Many adverbial prepositional phrases tell when, where, how, or how long something was done.

See Handbook | Section 20

Practice

Underline each adverbial prepositional phrase. Circle the verb or verb phrase it modifies. A sentence may have more than one adverbial prepositional phrase.

1. Rear Admiral Grace Hopper developed the first computer compiler in 1952.

2. Machine instructions were gathered within the compiler.

3. Programmers could now use the same routine in many different programs.

4. Hopper's bosses had not encouraged her in her efforts.

5. Automatic programming seemed impossible to them.

6. Hopper was irritated by such old-fashioned thinking.

7. In the computer industry, changes come fast.

8. Hopper contributed a great deal to computer science.

9. In the 1950s, she developed COBOL, described as the first user-friendly computer programming language.

Grace Murray Hopper

10. Businesses used COBOL for data processing.

11. In 1964 Hopper received the Society of Women Engineers Achievement Award.

12. She was given the award because of her original computer programming systems.

13. Hopper first joined the United States Naval Reserve during World War II.

14. She retired in 1966, but she accepted a new assignment one year later.

15. In 1986 Hopper, then eighty years old, retired again.

16. Throughout her long and brilliant career, Grace Hopper made important contributions to computer science, business, and national security.

Apply

Write an adverbial prepositional phrase to complete each sentence. Use your imagination. Be sure the phrase you write answers the question in parentheses.

17. My new laptop will be delivered _____.

    (When?)

18. I will carry my new laptop _____. (Where?)

19. A laptop user controls the cursor on the screen _____.

    (With what?)

20. I have been studying computer science _____.

    (For how long?)

Reinforce

Poets commonly use adverbial prepositional phrases in descriptions. Underline the adverbial prepositional phrases in the excerpt below. Be careful not to mark phrases that begin with *to* and end with a verb. (21–26)

> She dwelt among the untrodden ways
>
>   Beside the springs of Dove;
>
> A maid whom there were none to praise,
>
>   And very few to love.
>
> A violet by a mossy stone
>
>   Half hidden from the eye!
>
> Fair as a star, when only one
>
>   Is shining in the sky.
>
>   —William Wordsworth, from "Lucy"

Now write a short poem of your own that includes at least two adverbial prepositional phrases. Circle these prepositional phrases.

_____

_____

_____

_____

_____

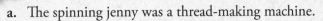
a. The spinning jenny was a thread-making machine.

b. The spinning jenny, a thread-making machine, helped bring about the Industrial Revolution.

Underline the phrase in sentence *b* that tells who or what the spinning jenny was. What punctuation marks separate this phrase from the rest of the sentence?

_____

An **appositive** is a phrase that follows a noun and identifies it. If an appositive is nonrestrictive—if it is not essential to the basic meaning of the sentence—it is set off from the other parts of the sentence by commas.

See Handbook Section 24

Practice

Underline the appositive in each sentence. Circle the noun it identifies.

1. The Industrial Revolution, a vast change in working methods, began in England in the 1750s.

2. Before 1750 most people lived in rural areas where they farmed or participated in domestic industry, work done in the home.

3. Clothing and other goods were either made at home or made by craftspeople, trained workers who crafted each item by hand.

4. The Industrial Revolution began in towns where textiles, woven cloths, were produced.

5. English colonies in America began producing large quantities of cotton, a cheap and useful alternative to wool.

New machines changed the way people worked and lived in industrialized countries.

6. Inventors created complex machines, the spinning jenny and others, which enabled spinners to make thread faster.

7. To keep up with the growing supply of cotton thread, inventors created power looms, machines for weaving thread into cloth quickly.

8. These new machines were housed in textile mills, cloth factories whose machines were powered by water or steam.

9. People moved from the hinterlands, the distant rural regions, into cities to work in factories.

10. Many people, children as well as adults, endured dangerous conditions in the factories.

11. Luddites, gangs of unhappy workers, resisted these changes and smashed machines in the new factories.

12. New working methods, methods opposed by the Luddites, brought changes in politics and education.

13. Young unmarried women, the bulk of the workers in many textile factories, were able to have some financial independence for the first time.

14. The middle class, mainly merchants and professional people, grew and gained political power.

15. Education, once the privilege of the rich, became available to many more young people.

Apply

Combine each pair of sentences to form one sentence. Change the underlined sentence into an appositive.

16. <u>The steam engine was a very important invention.</u> The steam engine was first used mainly in factories. _____

_____

_____

17. <u>John Fitch was a silversmith and clockmaker.</u> John Fitch built a boat powered by steam in 1787. _____

_____

_____

18. <u>Fitch's creation was a small, uncomfortable boat.</u> Fitch's creation was never popular. _____

_____

19. Two other inventors later built more successful steamboats. <u>Robert Fulton and Nicholas Roosevelt each built</u>

<u>steamboats that were successful.</u> _____

_____

20. Peter Cooper built the *Tom Thumb* in 1830. <u>The *Tom Thumb* was the earliest steam-powered railroad train.</u>

_____

Reinforce

All of the appositives covered so far have been separated from the rest of a sentence by commas. These appositives just give more information about the nouns they describe. But some appositives should not be set off by commas. If an appositive is vital to the meaning of the sentence, it should not be set off by commas.

| Example | Sarah Joseph, <u>my friend from camp</u>, sent me a letter. |

(The appositive *my friend from camp* is not essential to the sentence; it tells more about Sarah Joseph and should be set off by commas.)

My friend <u>Sarah Joseph</u> went to camp with me. (The appositive *Sarah Joseph* is necessary to explain which friend is meant.)

Add commas if they are needed around the appositives in the following sentences. Write *C* for correct if no commas are necessary.

21. My cousin Li is the oldest of all my cousins. _____

22. Li the oldest of all my cousins graduated from high school yesterday. _____

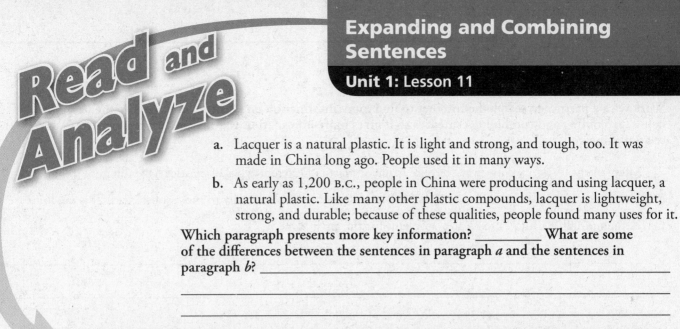

a. Lacquer is a natural plastic. It is light and strong, and tough, too. It was made in China long ago. People used it in many ways.

b. As early as 1,200 B.C., people in China were producing and using lacquer, a natural plastic. Like many other plastic compounds, lacquer is lightweight, strong, and durable; because of these qualities, people found many uses for it.

Which paragraph presents more key information? _____ **What are some of the differences between the sentences in paragraph *a* and the sentences in paragraph *b*?** _____

_____

_____

Sentences that include details, descriptive words, and words with precise meanings **give more information**. Sentences that combine connected facts or ideas **make clear important relationships**. Just adding more words to a sentence doesn't make it more effective, however. When you write, **expand or combine sentences** to help readers better understand what you are discussing.

See Handbook Sections 13, 16, 19, 20, 22

Practice

Draw a star on the line by the paragraph in each item that more effectively presents key information.

1. ___ Lacquer was used for utensils in ancient China. It was also used for furniture, storage containers, pillows, shoes, bows, and shields.

   ___ In ancient China, lacquer was used to produce long-lasting kitchen utensils that were easy to clean. Furniture, storage containers, and even pillows and shoes had lacquered surfaces. Lacquer was also used to make implements of war, such as bows and shields, more effective.

2. ___ Lacquer comes from lacquer trees. Workers collect the sap. They get only a little from each tree. Then they must wait five to seven years to tap the tree again.

   ___ Natural lacquer is obtained from a certain type of tree, which grows in China (but not Europe). Workers tap the tree trunks and collect the sap. Many trees are required for regular production, because each tree produces only a small amount of lacquer, and trees can be tapped every five to seven years only.

3. ___ Lacquering an object is a slow process. Coat after coat is applied to the object's surface and allowed to dry. Next the object is painted; then it is cleaned and polished.

   ___ It takes a very long time to apply lacquer to an object and then paint it and clean it and polish it. First, a coat of lacquer is applied to the surface of the object. Then the lacquer is allowed to dry. Then another coat is applied, and another, and another. When enough coats have been applied, it is painted and then cleaned and polished. Finally it is ready to be used.

Name _____

Apply

Work with a partner to search the Internet to find more information on plastics. Then rewrite the paragraph below, expanding and combining sentences so it gives more information and makes clear important relationships.

Many of the objects we use every day are made of plastic. Different types of plastics have different qualities. Most types can be molded into shapes. Plastic objects do not react chemically to most substances. This quality makes them durable. But it also creates problems for the environment.

_____

_____

_____

_____

_____

_____

_____

_____

_____

_____

_____

Reinforce

Rewrite a paragraph from a report or story you have written recently. Expand and combine sentences so the paragraph helps readers better understand what you are discussing.

_____

_____

_____

_____

_____

Read and Analyze

Read these four kinds of sentences.

We are totally lost! What can we do?

Calm down. I have a map.

Write the end mark that follows the command. _____

Write the end mark that follows the sentence that shows excitement. _____

Write the end mark that follows the question. _____

Write the end mark that follows the statement. _____

A **declarative sentence** makes a statement and ends with a period. An **interrogative sentence** asks a question and ends with a question mark. An **imperative sentence** gives a command and ends with a period or an exclamation point. An **exclamatory sentence** shows excitement and ends with an exclamation point. Begin every sentence with an uppercase letter.

See Handbook Section 10

Practice

Add the correct punctuation mark to each sentence. Then label it *declarative, interrogative, imperative,* or *exclamatory.*

1. A map is a sketch of a particular area _____

2. Who first decided to try to communicate the location of places by making a drawing _____

3. Where have the earliest maps been found _____

4. One of the oldest was discovered at the site of Nuzi, in northern Iraq _____

5. Show me its location on this map of the Middle East _____

6. Is that map more than 4,000 years old _____

7. Look at this picture of a silk map from the second century B.C _____

8. It is one of the two oldest maps found in China _____

9. What a large area of southeastern China it shows _____

10. The map is drawn to scale, and it shows the locations of the mountains and rivers _____

11. It's amazing how the mapmaker could create such an accurate map _____

12. In modern times mapmakers have depended on aerial photographs _____

13. Did you know that Pacific Island people made accurate maps using sticks, shells, and string _____

14. These maps showed wind and wave patterns as well as the locations of islands _____

15. What a comfort it must have been to sailors to have one of these maps on a journey across the open ocean _____

Nuzi, an ancient city, was located eight miles southwest of Kirkuk.

SYRIA

Kirkuk

Nuzi

IRAN

IRAQ

Baghdad

SAUDI ARABIA

Persian Gulf

Apply

Rewrite each sentence so it is the type of sentence indicated in parentheses.

16. You should read this article about city maps created in ancient Mesopotamia. (imperative)

_____

17. Researchers have found a map of a city beside the Euphrates River. (interrogative)

_____

18. Does this map date back to the fifteenth century B.C.? (declarative)

_____

19. It must have been exciting for researchers to observe remnants of the temples, walls, and other features

represented on the map. (exclamatory)

_____

_____

20. Were maps used by the ancient Greeks to plan military campaigns? (declarative)

_____

21. Is it fascinating to look at detailed maps of the ocean floor? (exclamatory)

_____

22. I'd like you to do research on the technologies that scientists use to map underwater regions. (imperative)

_____

Reinforce

Not only do poets choose uncommon words and unusual images to capture readers' attention, they also employ unexpected sentence structures. In the verse below, the poet does not use declarative sentences to present a description of an approaching storm—she uses a sentence type normally used for other purposes.

Think of the storm roaming the sky uneasily
like a dog looking for a place to sleep in,
listen to it growling.
　　　　　—Elizabeth Bishop,
　　　　　from "Little Exercise"

What type of sentence does the poet use in this verse? _____
What does she tell the reader to do? _____

Review

Subjects and Predicates

Underline the complete subject in each sentence. Circle the simple subject. If the understood subject is *you*, write *you* on the line.

1. Some inventions change almost everyone's life. _____

2. Imagine a world without cell phones! _____

3. The hours after school would be long and quiet. _____

Underline the complete predicate in each sentence. Circle the simple predicate.

4. The United States needed a cheap replacement for rubber during World War II.

5. The stretchy stuff bounced well.

6. Some stores sell his compound as Silly Putty.

Draw one line under each compound subject. Draw two lines under each compound predicate.

7. Levi Strauss invented blue jeans and became world-famous.

8. Miners and cowboys needed durable clothes in the old West.

9. Strauss designed and made overalls out of denim, a heavy cloth.

Objects, Predicate Nouns, and Predicate Adjectives

Circle the term in parentheses that correctly describes the boldfaced word in each sentence.

10. The ice cream cone is an American **invention**. (predicate noun/direct object)

11. Two vendors at the 1904 St. Louis World's Fair created **it**. (predicate adjective/direct object)

12. People at the fair were **hungry** for snacks. (predicate noun/predicate adjective)

13. An ice cream vendor needed more **dishes**. (direct object/indirect object)

14. He was becoming **desperate**. (predicate adjective/direct object)

15. A nearby waffle vendor gave **him** some rolled waffles. (direct object/indirect object)

Appositives

Underline the appositive in each sentence.

16. H. Cecil Booth, an inventor of the late 1890s, lay on the floor and inhaled dust through a cloth as an experiment.

17. The secret, finding the right kind of filtering bag, would be his path to success.

18. His messy experiment resulted in a suction cleaning machine, the vacuum cleaner.

19. Some people today use a new type of cleaning device, a vacuum cleaner without a dust bag.

Prepositional Phrases

Underline the prepositional phrase or phrases in each sentence. Circle the preposition. Draw a box around its object.

20. For many years, zippers and buttons were the main fasteners in the garment industry.

21. A mountain climber in Switzerland invented Velcro.

22. Prickly burrs clinging to his clothing gave him an idea.

23. Pairs of prickly cloth strips could substitute for zippers!

24. Some shoes, especially for children, are fastened with Velcro.

Circle each adjectival prepositional phrase. Underline each adverbial prepositional phrase. Draw a box around the word each phrase modifies.

25. The invention of the Frisbee was a happy accident.

26. The creator of this toy was the Frisbie Pie Company.

27. The Frisbie Pie Company was located in Bridgeport, Connecticut.

28. Their pies were sold in round metal pans.

29. The family name was etched across the bottom of these pans.

30. Students at Yale University saved the pie pans.

31. They flipped these metal pans to one another.

32. The pans sailed gracefully through the air.

33. The students' name for this new game was "Frisbie."

Sentences

Expand and combine these sentences to tell more and make clear relationships.

34. Early peoples made calendars. These calendars were useful.

_____

35. Ancient peoples learned how to make bronze. They made bronze-tipped plows.

_____

Add the correct punctuation mark to each sentence. Then label it *declarative, interrogative, imperative,* or *exclamatory.*

36. Imagine living in a home with no artificial illumination, no heating or air conditioning, and no indoor plumbing _____

37. What incredible changes homes underwent between 1890 and 1920 _____

38. Before 1890, homes were not pleasant places to spend time in, especially in the summer and the winter

_____

39. How did the development of home appliances change the nature of life at home during this period

_____

Spelling Practice

Designing the first rocket to send people into space must have been a tremendous challenge. There certainly was no room for error!

Underline the two words in the sentences that have double consonants.

Spelling Patterns: Double Consonants

Words such as *banner, equipped,* and *accomplish* have **double consonants**. Some words have consonants that were doubled when endings were added. Other double consonants are the result of prefixes being absorbed into words. For most words with double consonants, pronounce only one consonant sound.

Word Sort

Use the words below to complete the word sort.

exaggerate	assess	communicate	surrender	possibility	accommodate
aggressive	embarrass	impression	alliance	apparent	unnecessary

One set of double consonants	Two sets of double consonants

Pattern Practice

In each pair of words, one word is spelled incorrectly. Write the correctly spelled word and circle the double consonants.

1. asess assess _____

2. immense imense _____

3. professional proffesional _____

4. allegiance alegiance _____

5. proccesion procession _____

6. interupt interrupt _____

7. embarass embarrass _____

8. accommodate acommodate _____

Write the word from sentences 1–8 that best completes each sentence.

9. There was a(n) _____wave rolling straight toward the boat.

10. The telephone call could _____ my piano lesson.

11. Uncle Jay has been a(n) _____ basketball player for years.

12. Is the vacation house large enough to _____ both families?

13. Matt turns a deep red when you _____him.

14. The parade included a _____ of horses and riders.

15. Leah showed her _____ to her friends by going with them.

Use the Dictionary

Write the word from above that matches each definition. Use a print or an online dictionary if you need help.

16. to make room for _____

17. to determine the status of something _____

18. loyalty to something _____

(you) | Diagram | sentences

See Handbook **Section 40**

A **sentence diagram** is a picture of a sentence that shows how the parts of a sentence fit together. Diagramming sentences can help you understand how the words in a sentence are related.

Diagramming Subjects and Verbs

A short sentence consisting of a simple subject and a simple predicate is diagrammed this way:

Gold melts.   Gold | melts

Look at the structure of the diagram. Based on its structure, complete these sentences:

1. The simple subject and simple predicate go on a _____ line.
   horizontal/vertical

2. A _____ line divides the subject and predicate.
   horizontal/vertical

3. The subject goes to the _____ of the vertical line, and the predicate goes on the
   left/right
   _____ side.
   left/right

Use what you have learned to diagram these sentences. Include only the simple subject and the simple predicate. Ignore all the other words in the sentences.

4. The miners rested.

5. A storm approached.

6. Rain fell.

Diagramming Adjectives and Articles

An adjective (describing word) or an article (*a, an, the*) goes on a slanted line below the word it modifies. Look at the way this sentence has been diagrammed.

The weary miners rested.   miners | rested
                             The   weary

Now diagram these sentences.

7. A violent storm approached.

8. Torrential rains fell.

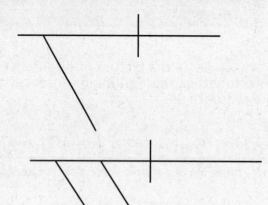

9. The wild rivers flooded.

Diagramming Direct Objects

A direct object (a noun that receives the action of the verb) is placed on a horizontal line to the right of the verb. Notice how the diagram changes when a direct object is added.

Few miners discovered **gold**.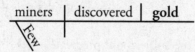

How is the vertical line that separates the direct object and the verb different from the vertical line that separates the subject and predicate?

_____

_____

Use what you have learned to diagram the simple subjects, simple predicates, adjectives, articles, and direct objects in these sentences.

10. One miner found a huge nugget.

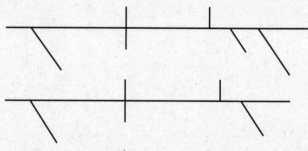

11. Warm rains melted the snow.

12. Icy water filled the reservoir.

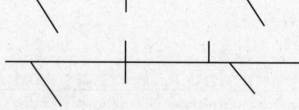

Now diagram these sentences on another sheet of paper.

13. Heavy rains eroded the hillsides.

14. The floods uncovered more gold.

15. Surprised miners staked new claims.

16. The eager men led difficult lives.

17. Some miners left their families.

18. Many miners lost their lives.

19. A few miners found immense wealth.

20. The majority met great disappointment.

Writing Sentences

These sentences need your help. Rewrite each one so it is clearer and makes better sense.

1. With triangular sails and three masts, European shipbuilders built large ocean-going ships. _____

   _____

2. Growing demand fueled an explosive growth of exploration and trade, in Europe, for treasures from distant

   lands. _____

   _____

3. Silk dresses and spices were comfortable to wear and made food taste better.

   _____

   _____

4. Soon, more people in Europe that only the extremely wealthy could previously afford began to acquire goods.

   _____

   _____

5. Brave captains sailed the tall ships to distant lands, and then these captains traded European goods for silks

   and spices. _____

   _____

All the sentences in a paragraph relate to a single topic. A paragraph should have a topic sentence, at least two supporting sentences, and a concluding sentence. Notice these kinds of sentences in this model paragraph.

topic sentence
(states the main idea
you are making)

supporting sentences
(give details to support
your main idea)

concluding sentence
(summarizes the paragraph
or restates the topic sentence)

Electric roller skates would be a useful invention, and they would be fun to use, too. Electric skates, or "electroblades," would give people a cheaper, safer way to travel. Running on rechargeable batteries, electroblades would save energy and reduce air pollution. People using electroblades would save money because electroblades would cost a lot less than cars. Since fewer people would be driving cars, there would also be fewer auto accidents. **Because skating is fun, people would actually enjoy traveling to work or school!**

Writing a Paragraph

The sentences you repaired on page 39 can be reordered to make a paragraph. Decide which sentence is the topic sentence, which are the supporting sentences, and which is the concluding sentence. Reorder the sentences, and write the paragraph on the lines below.

_____

_____

_____

_____

_____

_____

_____

Think of a new invention that would make your life easier, safer, or more comfortable. Write a paragraph explaining why you think this invention would be useful. Be sure to include a topic sentence, two or more supporting sentences, and a concluding sentence.

_____

_____

_____

_____

_____

_____

_____

_____

_____

Read your paragraph again. Use this checklist to make sure it is complete and correct.

☐ My paragraph has a topic sentence.

☐ My paragraph has at least two supporting sentences.

☐ All my sentences are clear and make sense.

☐ I have used prepositional phrases correctly.

☐ My paragraph has a concluding sentence.

Proofreading
Practice

Read this passage about patents and find the mistakes. Use the proofreading marks to show how the mistakes should be fixed. Use a dictionary to check and correct spellings.

Proofreading Marks

Mark	Means	Example
✀	delete	This machine is is broken, too.
∧	add	This machine broken too.
≡	make into an uppercase letter	this machine is broken, too.
/	make into a lowercase letter	This Machine is broken, too.
⊙	add a period	This machine is broken, too⊙
sp	fix spelling	This macheen is broken, too.

My Idea for a Great Invention

You have just put the finnishing touches on your marvelous new invention, electric in-line skates. Before you send your skates to the assembly line, however, consider this question: What's to prevent other people from stealing your design and copying your invention. The answer is that you can obtain leagle protection for you idea from the united states Patent and Trademark Office.

In simplest terms, a patent is an agreament between the inventor and the rest of the nation. When the government issues a patent, it grants an inventor all rights to manufacture and profit from his or her invention. Once you have a patent for your electric in-line skates. No one can copy your idea exactly. Obtaining a patent isn't complicated, but it does take time, usually more than two years

the Patenet and Trademark Office or PTO recieves about 100,000 patent applications every year. Each application is carfully evaluated by the staff at the PTO. First, officials must make sure that the invention hasn't already been patented by someone else. They must also decide weather the invention deserves a patent. It has to be entirely new, Not a variation of something that already exists. The invention must also be useful.

You don't need to put off production. While you are awaiting a response, however. Your skates can make their Debut in malls everywhere even if you haven't received your patent. Just make sure to put the notation *patent pending* somewhere on the product. These words arent a legal guarantee, but they our usually enough to discouradge other people from producing exact copies of your invention.

Proofreading
Checklist

You can use the checklist below to help you find and fix mistakes in your own writing. Write the titles of your own stories or reports in the blanks at the top of the chart. Then use the questions to check your work. Make a check mark (✓) in each box after you have checked that item.

Titles

Proofreading Checklist for Unit 1

Does each sentence have a subject and a predicate?				
Have I used appositives correctly?				
Have I used prepositional phrases to make my writing more precise?				
Have I varied the length and type of sentences to add variety to my writing?				
Do all my sentences state complete thoughts?				

Also Remember…

Does each sentence begin with an uppercase letter?				
Does each sentence end with the right end mark?				
Did I use a dictionary to check and correct spellings?				
Have I used commas correctly?				

Your Own List

Use this space to write your own list of things to check in your writing.

Community Connection

In Unit 1 of *Grammar, Usage, and Mechanics,* students learned about **different types of sentences** and **sentence structures** and used what they learned to improve their own writing. The content of these lessons focuses on the theme **Innovations That Changed History**. As students completed the exercises, they learned the stories behind some of the most influential creations in history—and some of the strangest. These pages offer a variety of activities that reinforce skills and concepts presented in the unit. They also provide opportunities for the student to make connections between the historical material in the lessons and innovative, productive activities going on today in the community.

Innovation Next Door

Identify a factory or manufacturing company in or near your community that produces something interesting or especially useful. Then arrange to visit it during working hours to see for yourself how the products are made. You might begin by contacting your chamber of commerce and asking for the names of some local factories or plants. Here are some questions you might try to answer about the place you select:

- What is the most interesting or important product manufactured here? What is innovative about it? What is its function?
- What raw materials are needed to produce the product? Where do these come from?
- What sequence of steps is involved in making the product? What is innovative about this process?
- Where is the finished product sold?
- Who are potential buyers of the product?
- How is the product transported?

Write answers to these questions in complete sentences. Check to make sure that each sentence has a subject and a predicate. Then use the questions and answers to prepare an oral or written report.

All-Star Inventors

Learn more about great inventors of the past and present by writing a business letter to the Inventors Hall of Fame. The Inventors Hall of Fame is housed at Inventure Place in Akron, Ohio. It contains exhibits and displays about George Washington Carver, Thomas Edison, Alexander Graham Bell, and many other inventors. Here's the address:

Inventure Place
221 South Broadway
Akron, Ohio 44308-1505
(330) 762-4463

Ask for information about one of these topics:

- Inventors from your city or state
- The origins of one of your favorite products or devices
- The life and work of an inventor you admire

HINT: To review the format of a business letter, see **G.U.M. Handbook** Section 34.

Bright Ideas

Close your eyes and imagine an invention that would make life in your community easier, safer, or more fun. Draw a sketch of your invention. Then write a description of what it would do and how it would work. Use prepositional phrases to help readers understand where and when your invention would be used. Use appositives to give more information about your invention.

Example	My invention is a magnetic repulsion system, a device for preventing auto accidents. This system uses electromagnetism to deflect oncoming vehicles. It can be installed in any auto or truck. A car equipped with this system can sense when another vehicle is on a collision course with it. When the system senses that a collision may occur, it activates an extremely powerful electromagnet in the part of the car that may be hit. The magnetic force produced is so great that it deflects the other car and prevents a direct collision.

Patent Pending

Learn more about the process of obtaining a patent for an invention. Use this form to help you gather information and organize notes.

United States Patent and Trademark Office

Address: _____

Telephone Number: _____

Website: _____

Questions I Want to Ask: _____

_____

My Findings

Types of Patents:

    1. _____

    2. _____

    3. _____

Cost of Obtaining a Patent: _____

Process of Obtaining a Patent:

    1. _____

    2. _____

    3. _____

    4. _____

    5. _____

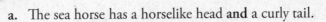

a. The sea horse has a horselike head **and** a curly tail.

b. The sea horse resembles a horse, **but** it is a true fish.

Cross out the boldfaced conjunction in each sentence.

Which sentence could be punctuated as two separate sentences? _____

A **simple sentence** is made up of a subject and a predicate and expresses only one complete thought. It is an *independent clause*. A **compound sentence** is made of two closely related independent clauses. The two clauses can be joined by a comma and a coordinating conjunction (*and, but,* or *or*) or by a semicolon (;).

See Handbook Sections 8, 13, 22

Practice

Write *S* next to each simple sentence. Write *CD* next to each compound sentence. Circle the comma and conjunction or the semicolon in each compound sentence.

1. Most sea horses are less than six inches long, but the Eastern Pacific sea horse can be fourteen inches long. _____

2. Sea horses are covered with knobby, bony armor; few predators will eat them. _____

3. Sea horses are not strong swimmers. _____

4. They live in warm, shallow water in the shelter of sea grass beds. _____

5. Like a monkey's tail, a sea horse's tail can grasp things; scientists call this kind of tail *prehensile*. _____

6. Sea horses must grasp stems of sea grass with their tails, or currents might sweep them away. _____

7. A sea horse sucks plankton through its tube-shaped mouth. _____

8. A sea horse's eyes swivel independently; it can spot prey in any direction. _____

9. Sea horses change color in response to their surroundings. _____

10. The sea horse looks strange, but its appearance is not its most unusual feature. _____

11. Virtually unique in the animal kingdom, the male sea horse can become pregnant. _____

12. At the full moon, the female sea horse lays eggs in the male sea horse's brood pouch. _____

13. The brood pouch is like a kangaroo's pouch, and the male sea horse nurtures the eggs inside it. _____

14. Sea horses are monogamous; they remain with the same mate throughout the breeding season. _____

15. After about two weeks, tiny sea horses emerge from the pouch. _____

Some sea horses can have as many as 300 babies at a time!

Apply

Rewrite each pair of simple sentences as one compound sentence.

16. Sea dragons are related to sea horses. They look even stranger. _____

_____

17. They live among leafy seaweed. Their bodies have developed leaflike appendages. _____

_____

18. Sea dragons are perfectly camouflaged. Most predators wouldn't eat this bony creature anyway.

_____

_____

19. Male sea horses bear young. So do male sea dragons. _____

_____

20. Male sea dragons have no brood pouch. They are still able to nurture eggs. _____

_____

Reinforce

Use clues from the Practice and Apply sections to complete the puzzle.

Across

2. Ocean vegetation
4. Remaining with one mate
5. A tail capable of grasping
6. Any animal that hunts other animals for food

Down

1. Tiny ocean life
2. A fish that resembles a horse
3. Water that moves in a pattern

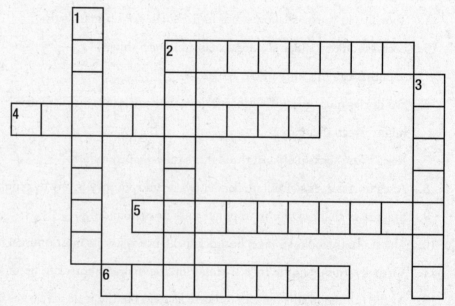

Now use two of the words in the puzzle to write a compound sentence.

21. _____

_____

Read and Analyze

Although California sea otters are mammals, <u>they usually spend their entire lives in the water.</u>

Look at the two parts of this sentence. Which part makes sense by itself? _____

    a. the boldfaced part   **b.** the underlined part

An **independent clause** is a group of words with a subject and a predicate that makes sense by itself. A **dependent clause** has a subject and a predicate, but it does not express a complete thought by itself. It needs—or is dependent on— an independent clause. Often a dependent clause begins with a subordinating conjunction such as *although, because, if, as,* or *when*. When a dependent clause begins a sentence, it is separated from the independent clause with a comma.

See Handbook Sections 8, 13, 22

Practice

Draw one line under each independent clause. Draw two lines under each dependent clause. Circle the subordinating conjunction that begins each dependent clause.

1. When sea otters sleep, they roll themselves in a floating blanket of kelp.

2. A sea otter usually dives to the bottom if it becomes hungry.

3. When it has found a clam or a sea urchin and a flat rock, it brings them back to the surface.

4. The otter floats on its back while it prepares its lunch.

5. As the otter holds the rock on its chest, it bangs the clam or sea urchin against the rock.

6. After the shell breaks open, the otter has a tasty meal.

7. Otters smile as they eat.

8. Because shells often have sharp edges, an otter carefully holds its lips away from its teeth in a grin.

9. Whales, walruses, sea lions, and dolphins can thrive in icy ocean water because they have a thick layer of insulating blubber under their skin.

Sea otters use rocks as tools to break open shells.

10. Although sea otters have no blubber, their dense, luxurious fur keeps them warm.

11. As an otter grooms its fur, tiny insulating air bubbles are trapped among the hairs.

12. An otter would freeze to death if it did not groom itself regularly.

13. People once hunted sea otters because their fur is so warm and soft.

14. When a 1911 treaty finally put an end to the slaughter, sea otters had almost become extinct.

15. Although they have been an endangered species for many years, sea otters are making a comeback.

Apply

Draw a line to match each dependent clause with an independent clause. Then write the new sentences you have created on the lines. Be sure to add punctuation.

Dependent Clauses	Independent Clauses
although otters are no longer threatened by hunting	orphaned baby sea otters are sometimes washed ashore
if there were a major oil spill	more otters survive in the wild
since otters eat fish	they face other threats
when storms hit the California coast	hundreds of California sea otters might die in the muck
when human volunteers teach orphaned pups how to live in the ocean	fisheries see them as competitors

16. _____

_____

17. _____

_____

18. _____

_____

19. _____

_____

20. _____

_____

Reinforce

On the lines below, write three funny or unusual dependent clauses. (Example: "After the octopus waved goodbye,") Trade papers with a partner. Complete your partner's sentences by writing an independent clause to go with each dependent clause. Take your own paper back and read the independent clauses your partner wrote.

21. _____

_____

22. _____

_____

23. _____

_____

Read and Analyze

a. Although octopuses once had a reputation as horrible monsters, most of these shy animals are not dangerous to humans.

b. Octopuses are the smartest invertebrates; they are as intelligent as house cats.

c. The Greek root *oct-* means "eight"; because octopuses have eight legs, the inclusion of this root in their name is appropriate.

Cross out the comma in sentence *a* and the semicolon in sentence *b*. Which sentence begins with a clause that would *not* be a sentence if a period were added to it? _____

Which sentence could become two separate sentences if a period were added to the end of its first clause? _____

Next, cross out the semicolon in sentence *c*. Could the two parts of the sentence become two separate sentences? _____

Now look at the two clauses that are separated by the comma. Could these clauses become two separate sentences if a period were added at the end of the first clause? _____

A dependent clause must be joined with an independent clause to make sense. A sentence made up of an independent clause and a dependent clause is a **complex sentence**. A sentence made up of two independent clauses and a dependent clause is a **compound-complex sentence**.

See Handbook Sections 8, 13, 22

Practice

Write *CD* next to each compound sentence, *CX* next to each complex sentence, and *CCX* next to each compound-complex sentence. Then circle each dependent clause and underline each independent clause.

1. Because octopuses have no backbone, scientists call them invertebrates. _____

2. Octopuses are good hunters; they have a hard, beaklike mouth and eight legs with suckers. _____

3. Although octopuses have eight legs, they do not use them for swimming; instead, they use jet propulsion for locomotion. _____

4. Octopuses take in water and squirt streams of it from their saclike bodies, and this propels them through the ocean. _____

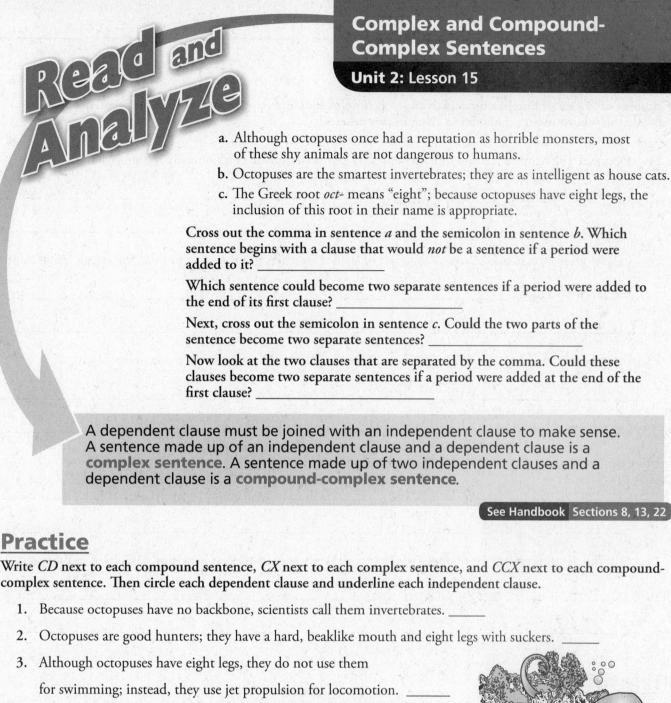

5. If an octopus loses a leg, it can grow another. _____

Because octopuses are flexible, they can squeeze through crevices.

6. An octopus might grab its prey with its legs, or it might drop down on top of its prey like a net. _____

7. Though the octopus is a hunter, it is hunted by other creatures, too; seals, dolphins, and humans kill and eat octopuses. _____

8. A threatened octopus squirts out a cloud of black ink, and this cloud can confuse an attacker because it is shaped like the octopus itself. _____

9. Scientists call octopuses, squid, and nautiluses *cephalopods*; this word means "head-footed." _____

10. Scientists chose this name because the legs of these animals seem to grow from their heads. _____

Name _____

Apply

Combine each pair of simple sentences to create a complex sentence or a compound-complex sentence. Include the subordinating conjunction given in parentheses.

11. (because) The nautilus has two hundred tentacles and a spiral shell. It is not easily recognized as a

relative of the octopus. _____

_____

12. (when) Dinosaurs roamed Earth. Thousands of shelled creatures like the nautilus filled the seas; a few of those

species survive today. _____

_____

13. (because) Its hard shell protects it from water pressure. The nautilus can survive at extreme depths.

_____

_____

14. (although) There are many chambers in a nautilus shell. The animal lives only in the outermost one.

_____

_____

15. (as) The nautilus pumps gas in or out of the inner chambers of its shell. It lowers or raises itself in the water.

_____

_____

Reinforce

A skillful author can communicate a great deal of information in a single compound-complex sentence.

Read the passage below and underline the compound-complex sentence in it. How many independent clauses does this sentence contain? _____ How many dependent clauses does it contain? _____

As the boat bounced from the top of each wave, the wind tore through the hair of the hatless men, and as the craft plopped her stern down again the spray slashed past them. The crest of each of these waves was a hill, from the top of which the men surveyed for a moment a broad tumultuous expanse, shining and wind-riven.

—Stephen Crane, from "The Open Boat"

Now find your own examples of compound-complex sentences in a story or textbook chapter you are currently reading. List at least three on another sheet of paper. Circle each independent clause and underline each dependent clause in these sentences.

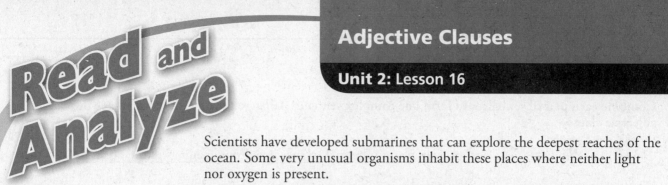

Scientists have developed submarines that can explore the deepest reaches of the ocean. Some very unusual organisms inhabit these places where neither light nor oxygen is present.

Draw one line under the dependent clause that gives information about the submarines that have been developed. Circle the first word in this clause. Draw two lines under the dependent clause that gives information about the places where the unusual organisms live. Draw a box around the first word in this clause.

An **adjective clause** is a **dependent clause** that describes a noun or a pronoun. An adjective clause can begin with a **relative pronoun,** such as *that, who, whom,* or *which;* or it can begin with a **relative adverb,** such as *when, where,* or *why.*

See Handbook Sections 8, 13, 17g, 19

Practice

Underline the adjective clause in each sentence. If the first word in the clause is a relative pronoun, circle that word. If the first word in the clause is a relative adverb, draw a box around that word.

1. Imagine a visit to a place where bizarre creatures emerge from the black depths.

2. Explorers of regions below a depth of 1,000 feet found fish and other organisms that have adapted to the extreme conditions.

3. Many have huge eyes and mouths as well as organs that glow in the inky darkness.

4. The reasons why some deep-sea creatures glow have to do with the value of trickery.

5. The deep-sea angler has a glowing plume that dangles over its mouth.

6. The plume, which resembles a tiny marine creature, attracts prey.

7. The angler attacks at the moment when the unsuspecting hunter has come too close for an escape.

8. The umbrella mouth gulper eel has a mouth that expands for huge bites.

9. This two-foot-long creature can devour fish that exceed it in size.

10. The ocean depths include regions where oarfish grow to lengths of 35 feet.

11. Sailors who encountered these long, odd-looking fish called them "sea serpents" and made up frightening tales about them.

12. You can probably think of reasons why the sight of a sixty-foot-long giant squid up from the depths would have struck fear into the hearts of sailors!

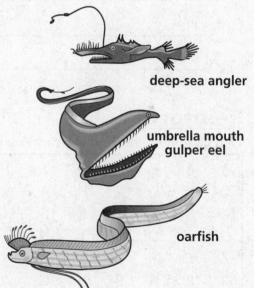

deep-sea angler

umbrella mouth gulper eel

oarfish

Apply

Combine each pair of sentences to form one complex sentence. Change the underlined sentence into an adjective clause.

13. Bizarre undersea "gardens" grow in places. <u>Thermal springs flow from openings in the ocean floor in these places.</u> _____

_____

14. The scientists found ten-foot-long bright red worms in those places. <u>These worms bloomed from the tops of white tubes.</u> _____

_____

15. Huge clumps of the worms grew around spots. <u>Warm water streamed from volcanic rifts there.</u> _____

_____

_____

16. The scientists also found foot-wide clams with bright red meat. <u>The meat was colored by hemoglobin.</u>

_____

_____

Reinforce

Find six words in the puzzle. Write them where they fit in the blanks.

A	A	E	Z	W	X	J	N	F	M	J
Q	N	D	X	H	A	S	M	P	N	P
W	G	E	C	R	B	K	Q	L	B	R
G	L	O	W	I	N	G	X	U	N	E
Z	E	M	V	X	F	L	W	M	V	D
R	R	H	B	Y	G	Z	R	E	C	A
T	Z	J	N	P	S	X	P	C	X	T
Y	A	T	T	R	A	C	T	S	Z	O
P	R	K	M	S	Z	V	S	H	L	R
S	X	L	Q	D	H	B	D	J	K	S

Across

__ __ __

__ __ __ __ __ __ __

__ __ __ __ __ __ __ __ __

Down

__ __ __ __ __

__ __ __ __ __

__ __ __ __ __ __ __ __

Use the words you found to make a complex sentence. Include an adjective clause that begins with *that*.

17. _____

_____

Read and Analyze

An 8,000-pound elephant seal sleeps wherever it wants.

Underline the dependent clause that tells where an elephant seal sleeps. Does this part of the sentence make sense by itself? _____

An **adverb clause** is a dependent clause that tells about a verb, an adjective, or an adverb. Adverb clauses tell where, when, why, or how much. They often begin with a subordinating conjunction such as *than, although, because, if, as, as if, while, when,* or *whenever*.

See Handbook Sections 8, 13, 22

Practice

Underline the adverb clause in each sentence.

1. Before they adapted to life in the sea, seals were land animals similar to otters and bears.

2. When seals' ancestors moved to the water, changes to their bodies occurred from generation to generation.

3. Now flippers paddle where paws once stepped.

4. Although seals still have all the bones for four legs, only the ankle and foot bones protrude from their barrel-shaped bodies.

5. A seal's shape improves its speed in the water because currents flow smoothly past its streamlined body.

6. As seals developed their swimming ability, they gave up most of their agility on land.

7. However, eared seals, or sea lions, move more quickly on land than true seals do.

8. While eared seals can walk on their flippers, true seals must wriggle on land with a caterpillarlike motion.

Fur seals were hunted for their coats, but now they are protected.

9. If they must find food or evade a predator, some seals can dive down to 2,900 feet below the surface.

10. Seals need sharp vision because there is little light in the ocean's depths.

11. Although they spend most of their time in the water, true seals come to beaches for the breeding season.

12. Seals often breed where they were born.

13. Mother seals nurse their pups while males compete for beach territory.

14. Male elephant seals on breeding beaches look as if they are immense slugs.

15. After the new pups have been weaned, the seals return to the sea.

Apply

Combine each pair of simple sentences to form one complex sentence. Use the word in parentheses to change the underlined sentence into an adverb clause.

16. (because) <u>Seals' eyes look much like human eyes.</u> The Scottish have made up legends about seal-people,

    or selkies. _____

    _____

17. (although) <u>Selkies wear seal skins.</u> They look like humans underneath. _____

    _____

18. (since) <u>Selkies can't swim in their natural form.</u> They must wear a fish or seal skin. _____

    _____

19. (whenever) <u>The moon is full.</u> Selkies shed their skins and dance on the beach in human form.

    _____

    _____

20. (If) <u>A human steals a selkie's skin.</u> The selkie will be in that human's power. _____

    _____

21. (When) <u>The selkie gets its skin back.</u> It will return to the sea. _____

    _____

Reinforce

In this activity, you will distinguish among adverbs, adverb phrases, and adverb clauses. Draw a line from each sentence to the correct description of the boldfaced word or words.

22. The selkie danced
    when the moon was full.   adverb (one word)

23. The selkie danced
    gracefully.   adverb phrase (no verb)

24. The selkie danced
    after midnight.   adverb clause (has a verb)

25. Their flippers paddle
    through the water.   adverb (one word)

26. Their flippers paddle
    where paws once stepped.   adverb phrase (no verb)

27. Their flippers paddle
    agilely.   adverb clause (has a verb)

a. The marine iguana is the only lizard **that spends much of its life in the ocean.**

b. This reptile, **which lives only on the Galapagos Islands,** feeds on marine algae.

In which sentence does the boldfaced clause give essential information? _____

In which sentence does the boldfaced clause give information that is not essential to the sentence? _____

What punctuation marks are used to set off this clause from the rest of the sentence? _____

A **restrictive clause** is a dependent clause that is essential to the message its sentence conveys; it gives critical information about the noun it modifies. A **nonrestrictive clause** is a dependent clause that is not essential to the message its sentence conveys; if this clause were left out, the sentence would still convey its message effectively. A nonrestrictive clause is set off from the rest of its sentence by one or two commas, depending on its placement in the sentence.

See Handbook Sections 8, 17g

Practice

Read each sentence. Draw a line under the dependent clause and circle the noun it modifies. Write *RC* if it is a restrictive clause and *NC* if it is a nonrestrictive clause.

1. The Galapagos Islands are volcanic islands that rise from the seafloor 600 miles off the western coast of South America. _____

2. This archipelago, which belongs to Ecuador, has many unusual species of animals. _____

3. The isolation of these islands limited the diversity of life forms there until the time when mariners reached the islands and introduced nonnative species. _____

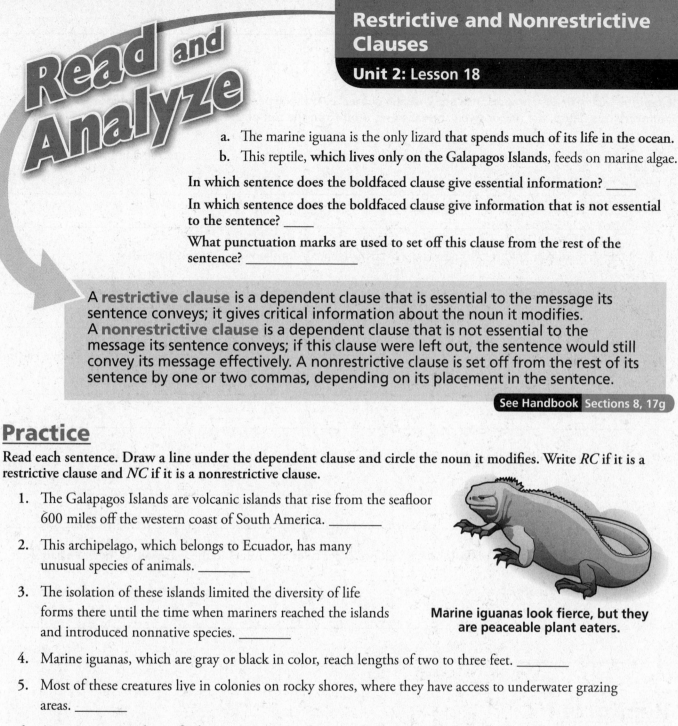

Marine iguanas look fierce, but they are peaceable plant eaters.

4. Marine iguanas, which are gray or black in color, reach lengths of two to three feet. _____

5. Most of these creatures live in colonies on rocky shores, where they have access to underwater grazing areas. _____

6. A marine iguana that is feeding can remain underwater for as long as an hour. _____

7. While feeding, they ingest much salt, which, if retained, would disrupt their bodily processes. _____

8. These creatures excrete the excess salt through a gland connected to their nostrils; they then sneeze away the salt that collects around the nostrils. _____

9. The waters where these iguanas feed are very cold. _____

10. The iguanas, which are cold-blooded, experience a dramatic drop in body temperature while feeding. _____

11. After feeding, these iguanas swim back to land and bask on rocks in the sun; the warmth of the sun, which shines on most days in the Galapagos, raises their body temperature to comfortable levels. _____

12. Like most creatures that live on the Galapagos Islands, the marine iguana has only a few natural predators. _____

Name _____

Apply

Combine each pair of sentences into one complex sentence. If the dependent clause in the sentence is a nonrestrictive clause, use one or two commas to set it off from the rest of the sentence.

13. Feral pests invade the marine iguanas' territory. They are a threat to the survival of these unusual creatures.

_____

_____

14. Human visitors hike through rocky areas. Marine iguanas sun themselves in these areas.

_____

_____

15. Marine iguanas have seldom needed to flee from predators. They do not react to people walking among them.

_____

_____

16. Some humans disturb the marine iguanas' nests. These humans cause harm to the population.

_____

_____

17. Ecuadorean government officials have developed strict rules for visitors to the Galapagos. These officials want to protect native species.

_____

_____

Reinforce

Write a paragraph about a wild creature you consider especially interesting. Include at least one sentence with a restrictive clause and one sentence with a nonrestrictive clause.

_____

_____

_____

_____

_____

Read and Analyze

a. Dolphins are relatives **of whales and porpoises.**

b. Scientists classify all three **as cetaceans.**

c. Dolphins have a snout **that looks like a beak.**

d. **Because dolphins feed their young milk produced in the mother's body,** scientists classify dolphins as mammals.

Which sentences above contain boldfaced phrases? _____ Which contain boldfaced clauses? _____ In which sentences do the boldfaced words tell more about a noun? _____ In which sentences do the boldfaced words tell more about a verb? _____

> A **phrase** is a group of words that functions as a part of speech. For example, a prepositional phrase can function as an adjective by modifying, or telling more about, a noun. A phrase does not contain a subject-verb combination. A **clause** is a group of words that contains a subject-verb combination. A dependent clause—a clause that cannot stand alone as a sentence—functions as a part of speech also. For example, it can function as an adverb by modifying a verb.

See Handbook Sections 13, 17g, 20

Practice

Look at the boldfaced group of words in each sentence. Circle the word or words it modifies. Then identify the structure and function of those words by writing *adjective phrase, adverb phrase, adjective clause,* or *adverb clause.*

1. Dolphin species vary **in size.** _____

2. Adults **in one species** are less than five feet in length and weigh about 100 pounds. _____

3. The bottle-nosed dolphin, **which is perhaps the most-familiar species,** can exceed 12 feet in length and weigh up to 1400 pounds. _____

4. Many people love this creature **because it appears to be smiling.** _____

5. There are other reasons **why these dolphins are favorites.** _____

6. **In many situations,** dolphins show friendliness toward people. _____

7. Common dolphins, **which are smaller than bottle-nosed dolphins,** are also friendly and playful. _____

Bottle-nosed dolphins range from New Zealand to Japan, and South Africa to Norway.

8. These cetaceans sometimes swim **beside ships** for miles. _____

9. **If you sail across the ocean in a temperate region,** you may see a school of common dolphins. _____

10. You can recognize a common dolphin by the dark band **around its eyes.** _____

Name _____

Apply

Combine each pair of sentences into a single sentence. If the sentence you create contains an adjective phrase, an adverb phrase, an adjective clause, or an adverb clause, underline it and write which it is. (You need to mark only one of these in each sentence.)

11. The orca is the largest species of dolphin. The orca is also known as the killer whale.

_____

_____

_____

12. Striped dolphins have black stripes. These are visible on their sides.

_____

_____

_____

13. You might see a dolphin leap out of the water and spin on its side. Then you are watching a

spinner dolphin. _____

_____

_____

14. All species of dolphins have a streamlined shape. This shape allows them to move easily through the water.

_____

_____

_____

15. Muscular tail fins propel a dolphin. It moves through the water swiftly.

_____

_____

_____

Reinforce

On another sheet of paper, write four sentences about cetaceans. Include an adjective phrase in one sentence, an adverb phrase in another, an adjective clause in another, and an adverb clause in the remaining sentence. Be prepared to tell what word or words each phrase or clause modifies.

a. Crabs use their claws **to defend themselves.**

b. Crabs belong **to the crustacean family.**

Look at each boldfaced phrase. In which phrase is *to* followed by a verb? _____

In which phrase is *to* followed by an article, an adjective, and a noun? _____

An **infinitive** is a phrase made up of the word *to* followed by the present form of a verb (*to defend*). Infinitives may act as adjectives, adverbs, or nouns. An **infinitive phrase** is made up of an infinitive and any other words that complete its meaning. In sentence *a* above, *to defend themselves* is an infinitive phrase.

See Handbook Section 25

Practice

Underline each infinitive phrase.

1. Scientists use the term *exoskeleton* to talk about a crab's shell.

2. Most crabs molt, or shed their rigid shells, in order to grow larger.

3. Just after molting, without a hard shell to protect them, crabs are very vulnerable.

4. The hermit crab finds an abandoned spiral shell to make its home.

5. When a hermit crab grows too large for its shell, it searches for another shell to occupy.

6. If a crab loses a leg, it is able to regenerate, or grow another.

7. Eyes perched high on stalks allow a ghost crab to watch for prey while the rest of its body is buried in sand.

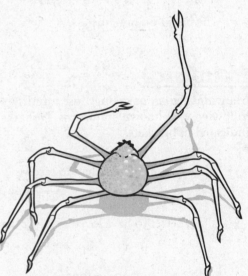

The giant spider crab is the world's largest crustacean.

8. The pea crab is tiny enough to live inside the shell of a live oyster.

9. On the other hand, you might need a twelve-foot-long ruler to measure an adult giant spider crab.

10. Because the giant spider crab normally lives at depths of around 1,200 feet, divers are rarely able to observe this amazing creature.

11. You might be surprised to find that some "crabs" are not crabs at all.

12. Many people assume horseshoe crabs to be crustaceans, but they are actually relatives of spiders and scorpions.

13. These creatures appear to have changed little since prehistoric times.

14. They were already ancient animals when dinosaurs began to prowl the earth.

15. Scientists hope the horseshoe crab will be able to survive for another 360 million years.

Name _____

Apply

Write an infinitive from the word bank to complete each sentence.

to lay	to grasp	to describe	to molt	to wait

16. Observers use the phrase "shaking hands" _____ the mating ritual
     of the Alaskan king crab.

17. A male king crab looks for a female who is preparing _____,
     or shed her skin.

18. He uses his powerful claws _____ her front legs tightly until
     molting occurs.

19. Only after molting is the female crab able _____ eggs.

20. The male crab may have as long as two weeks _____, but
     he hangs on nonetheless.

Reinforce

Many *aphorisms,* or sayings, use infinitives to name actions. Underline the infinitive phrases in the
following well-known aphorisms. Note that the last aphorism contains an understood infinitive,
indicated in brackets.

> "It is better to give than to receive."
> > —Anonymous

> "Tis better to have loved and lost than never to have loved at all."
> > —Alfred, Lord Tennyson

> "To err is human, to forgive divine."
> > —Alexander Pope

> "It is better to know some of the questions than [to know] all of the answers."
> > —James Thurber

Write an aphorism of your own, using an infinitive, to give your reader advice.

21. _____

_____

_____

_____

Armed with a deadly weapon, the scorpionfish swims calmly through tropical waters.

Circle the two verbs in the sentence above. Which verb has a subject just before it? _____

Which verb is part of a phrase with no subject? _____

Sometimes a verb does not act as the simple predicate of a sentence. A **verbal** is a word formed from a verb that plays another role in the sentence. One type of verbal is a **participle**. A participle may be a present participle (usually the present form + -ing: eating) or a past participle. Regular verbs form the past participle by adding -ed (armed). Irregular verbs change their spelling in the past participle (eaten, brought). A **participial phrase** is made of a participle and other words that complete its meaning. A participial phrase can act as an adjective. In the sentence above, Armed with a deadly weapon is a participial phrase describing the scorpionfish.

See Handbook Sections 18d, 25

Practice

Underline each participial phrase. Then circle the participle.

1. Even a very hungry predator will avoid a fish covered with venomous spines.

2. Fearing the effects of the poison, divers stay well away from this colorful fish.

3. The fish displaying colorful, feathery fins with stripes is a turkeyfish, one variety of scorpionfish.

4. Children visiting aquariums often watch this beautiful fish for many minutes.

5. The type of scorpionfish known as the lionfish is also admired for its beauty.

6. A scorpionfish displaying its stripes and colors is giving a warning to other creatures.

7. Not all scorpionfish have colors or stripes decorating their bodies.

8. A type of scorpionfish called the stonefish has no distinctive markings.

9. Resembling a rock, the stonefish attracts no attention.

10. Lying motionless on the ocean floor, it waits for a slow-moving fish.

11. Seeing only a gray lump, other fish swim into this creature's reach.

12. Divers exploring the ocean floor may mistake a stonefish for a rock.

A scorpionfish can be extremely dangerous.

13. Needle-sharp spines hidden beneath the stonefish's skin deliver a painful, dangerous sting.

14. Venom injected by the stonefish quickly circulates through the diver's body.

15. Fortunately, an antidote to stonefish venom is available in a number of cities near parts of the ocean inhabited by stonefish.

16. A sting victim taken quickly to a hospital has a good chance for survival.

Name _____

Apply

A participial phrase must be placed near the noun or pronoun it modifies, or it can create confusion for the reader. The participial phrase in each sentence below is misplaced. Rewrite each sentence so that it makes sense.

17. Known throughout the world for its teeming sea life, Alex and Shanna couldn't wait to dive at the

    Great Barrier Reef. _____

    _____

18. Hardened skeletons of dead water animals make up the coral in this reef called polyps. _____

    _____

19. Alex and Shanna hired an instructor not knowing how to scuba dive. _____

    _____

20. They gazed through their face masks at the astonishing creatures around them enjoying their new experience.

    _____

    _____

21. Covered with waving tentacles, Alex stared at a flowerlike sea anemone. _____

    _____

Reinforce

An absolute phrase consists of a noun or noun phrase followed by a descriptive word or phrase. Like a participial phrase, an absolute phrase may contain a verbal form ending in *-ing* or *-ed*. It may also contain an adjective, a noun, or a prepositional phrase.

Example

 noun phrase + verbal phrase

The fish displayed its fins, <u>the stripes warning other creatures of the danger.</u>

 noun phrase + adjective

The stonefish attracted no attention, <u>its body motionless.</u>

Underline the absolute phrase in each sentence below. Then discuss with a partner how that description makes the sentence interesting to read.

22. Its fins feathery and bright, the scorpionfish is gorgeous to look at.

23. Lila sat in the back of the boat, her scuba gear on the deck beside her.

24. We slowly toured the aquarium, our teacher stopping at important exhibits.

a. **Building a coral reef** takes many centuries.

b. Tiny animals create the reef by **depositing calcium carbonate**.

Circle the simple predicate in each sentence. Draw a box around each verb form ending in -*ing*. Is either -*ing* form part of a simple predicate? _____

Is the boldfaced phrase in sentence *a* the subject of the sentence, the direct object, or an object of a preposition? _____

Is the boldfaced phrase in sentence *b* the subject of the sentence, the direct object, or the object of a preposition? _____

A **gerund** is a verbal that acts as a noun. All gerunds are verb forms that end with -*ing*. A **gerund phrase** is made up of a gerund and the other words that complete its meaning. In the sentences above, *Building a coral reef* and *depositing calcium carbonate* are gerund phrases.

See Handbook | Section 25

Practice

Underline each gerund phrase. Draw a box around the gerund itself.

1. Swimming near coral reefs will acquaint you with many colorful fish.

2. The long blue teeth of the harlequin tusk fish are ideal for crushing the hard shells of clams.

3. Living among an anemone's poisonous tentacles might seem impossible.

4. The striped clownfish can do this because it is not harmed by the stinging of the anemone.

5. The beaklike mouth of the parrotfish is effective in grinding coral into sand.

6. This fine sand seems perfect for building sandcastles.

7. Spindly little spider crabs protect themselves by establishing homes inside hollow tube sponges.

8. A tiny cleaner shrimp attracts a reef fish by waving its long antennae.

9. Cleaner shrimp help reef fish by eating parasites off their skin.

10. Seeing the bright blue fringe on the four-foot-wide mouth of a giant clam is an unforgettable experience.

11. Diving around reefs is made dangerous by scorpionfish and other fish with venomous spines.

12. Swimming in the ocean with an open wound may be a dangerous thing to do.

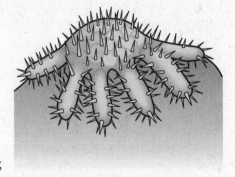

The crown-of-thorns starfish preys on living coral.

13. Sharks sometimes find prey by following the smell of blood.

14. Protecting live coral is a difficult task.

15. People harm coral by taking pieces as souvenirs.

16. Crown-of-thorns starfish have destroyed entire colonies of coral by devouring those tiny creatures.

Apply

Imagine you and your family are taking a vacation to an island in the South Pacific. Describe what you will do on this vacation by writing a gerund phrase to complete each sentence. The gerunds in the word bank may give you some ideas.

visiting	swimming	diving	photographing	eating	watching
catching	painting	protecting	helping	avoiding	seeing

17. I would enjoy _____.

18. _____ would be a new experience for me.

19. I would start each day by _____.

20. After breakfast I might try _____.

21. _____ would be fun for everyone in the family.

22. I would learn about coral reefs by _____.

23. Since I saw a documentary film on the tidewater pools, I think _____
_____ would be fun.

24. _____ is something that swimmers and divers should try to do.

25. _____ would be a great activity toward the end of the day.

Reinforce

Authors, poets, and filmmakers frequently use gerund phrases as titles of works. "Crossing the Bar" is one of Alfred, Lord Tennyson's best-known poems, and "Stopping by Woods on a Snowy Evening" is one of Robert Frost's most famous works. *Living Free* was a popular movie about African lions.

Look in a library and in the entertainment section of a newspaper to find five other works that have gerund phrases as titles. List these titles on the lines below.

26. _____

27. _____

28. _____

29. _____

30. _____

a. That creature is not a whale.

b. That creature is forty feet long, but it is not a whale.

c. Although that creature is forty feet long, it is not a whale.

d. Although that creature is forty feet long, it is not a whale; it is a whale shark.

Which sentence is made up of one independent clause? _____ Which sentence is made up of two independent clauses? _____ Which sentence is made up of one independent clause and one dependent clause? _____ Which sentence is made up of two independent clauses and one dependent clause? _____ Which of these sentences conveys the most information in an effective manner? _____

Simple sentences, compound sentences, complex sentences, and **compound-complex sentences** offer a writer a variety of ways of stating information and showing relationships. Choose sentence types that enable you to express your ideas clearly and show how they are related to one another.

See Handbook **Section 13**

Practice

Read each pair of sentences. Mark a star beside the one that more effectively expresses the idea and shows relationships. If the sentence you choose is a simple sentence, write *S* in the blank. If it is a compound sentence, write *CD*. If it is a complex sentence, write *CX*. If it is a compound-complex sentence, write *CCX*.

1. Because it has a huge mouth, a whale shark could swallow a person whole; it would never do so intentionally, however. _____

   The whale shark has a huge mouth, and it could easily swallow a person whole. _____

2. Whale sharks eat only small fish and plankton, so a human being is of no interest to them. _____

   Whale sharks eat small fish and plankton, not people. _____

3. A whale shark gets rid of big things in its stomach; it turns its stomach inside out to do this. _____

   If a whale shark accidentally swallows something large, it turns its stomach inside out; that process expels the large object or creature. _____

A whale shark weighs as much as an elephant.

4. How can such a large creature survive on a diet of tiny animals? _____

   Whale sharks are huge, but the creatures they eat are very small; so how is it that whale sharks can stay alive on a diet of that kind? _____

5. Whale sharks suck in plankton-filled seawater and then filter out the water. _____

   Whale sharks suck in huge quantities of plankton-filled seawater; they use bony plates in their mouths as strainers to separate the creatures from the water. _____

6. Baleen whales also have bony plates and eat in a similar way, but they are different creatures. _____

   Baleen whales may seem similar to whale sharks because they feed in the same way, but baleen whales are different because they are mammals and whale sharks are fish. _____

Apply

Combine each group of sentences to form one sentence. Choose a type of sentence that makes clear the relationships between ideas.

7. The whale shark prefers warm waters. The whale shark is found in temperate and tropical seas throughout the world. _____

    _____

8. Scientists know that whale sharks periodically swim long distances. Scientists suspect that whale sharks migrate at certain times of the year. Scientists do not have proof of this yet.

    _____

    _____

9. The whale shark has a streamlined body. It has a large flattened head. On its back it has a distinctive checkerboard pattern. This pattern consists of light spots and stripes on the fish's dark skin.

    _____

    _____

10. In the past, whale sharks were ignored by fishing crews. Recently, though, quite a few of these huge fish are being caught. Their flesh, oil, and fins are being sold.

    _____

    _____

Reinforce

Simple sentences need not be simplistic. A well-written sequence of simple sentences can communicate complex ideas in a dynamic manner.

Read this passage from a famous novel about a whale.

Go from Corlears Hook to Coenties Slip, and from thence, by Whitehall, northward. What do you see?—Posted like silent sentinels all around the town, stand thousands upon thousands of mortal men fixed in open reveries. . . Are the green fields gone? What do they here?

But look! Here come more crowds, pacing straight for the water, and seemingly bound for a dive. Strange! Nothing will content them but the extremest limit of the land. . .

—Herman Melville, from *Moby-Dick*

Imagine that you are a diver seeing a whale shark for the first time. Write a series of short sentences that give your impressions. Use another sheet of paper for your sentences.

Avoiding Fragments, Run-ons, Comma Splices, and Ramble-ons

Unit 2: Lesson 24

Rays are related to sharks, both have skeletons made of cartilage. Although rays look very different. Differences in appearance or the way animals look to the observer are not always significantly important to the classification of those animals that may seem so different from each other.

Circle the dependent clause that is missing an independent clause. Underline the sentence that is written incorrectly because it is made up of two independent clauses without a conjunction. Write *X* at the end of the sentence that uses a lot of words to say very little.

A **fragment** does not tell a complete thought. A **run-on sentence** is a compound sentence that is missing a comma and a conjunction. A **comma splice** is a run-on sentence that has a comma but is missing a conjunction. A **ramble-on** sentence is correct grammatically but contains extra words and phrases that don't add to its meaning. Avoid fragments, run-ons, comma splices, and ramble-ons in the final versions of your written work.

See Handbook Sections 8, 14, 22

Practice

Write *F* after each fragment. Write *RO* after each run-on. Write *CS* after each comma splice. Write *RA* after each ramble-on sentence.

1. Rays have wide, flat bodies and narrow tails, they are shaped almost like kites. _____

2. Rays flap their fins like a bird's wings they fly through the water. _____

3. Although their eyes are on the tops of their heads. _____

4. Mouths on the underside. _____

5. Rays cannot see their food, they must sense it with smell, touch, and electrosensors. _____

6. The low placement of the ray's mouth on the underside or bottom of its head makes the ray very well-suited for bottom feeding, or eating food off the sea floor, because its mouth is on the bottom near its food which is also there as well. _____

7. If a ray senses prey on the ocean floor. _____

8. The ray's flat body drapes over the prey its mouth sucks the animal up. _____

9. Poisonous spines along a stingray's tail. _____

10. Huge manta rays grow up to 20 feet across, these harmless animals eat only plankton. _____

11. A manta can jump six feet above the surface of the water it glides on its immense winglike fins. _____

12. Another fish in the ray family is the guitarfish, which was probably named in this way because it resembles that popular musical instrument known as the guitar, which has a shape somewhat similar to the shape of this fish. _____

Electric rays can attack with electric shocks of up to 200 volts.

Name _____

Apply

Rewrite the sentences from the Practice section that are listed below. Correct any fragments, run-ons, and comma splices. Shorten the ramble-ons. There is more than one way to correct each sentence. (13–19)

Sentence #2 _____

_____

Sentence #3 _____

_____

Sentence #5 _____

_____

Sentence #8 _____

_____

Sentence #9 _____

_____

Sentence #10 _____

_____

Sentence #12 _____

_____

Reinforce

This monster ramble-on sentence contains more than 50 words. Cross out unnecessary words, phrases, and clauses to make the sentence as short as possible. Write your revised sentence below.

Like sharks, most fish of the ray variety, including the manta ray, the stingray, and most other rays, are covered all over their bodies with toothlike scales, that resemble tiny teeth but are really scales, and which make the skin of these sharklike fish feel rough if you touch it with your hand.

20. _____

_____

Now try writing a monster sentence of your own. Start with a simple sentence, such as *The ray was swimming*. Add words, phrases, and clauses that add too much information for one good sentence. Then trade papers with a partner and trim each other's monster sentence.

21. _____

_____

_____

Review

Simple Sentences, Compound Sentences, Complex Sentences, Compound-Complex Sentences

Write *S* next to each simple sentence. Write *CD* next to each compound sentence. Write *CX* next to each complex sentence. Write *CCX* next to each compound-complex sentence.

1. Before anything lived on land, the seas were filled with creatures. _____

2. Trilobites were once the most numerous species on Earth, but they died out about

   300 million years ago. _____

3. These small bottom-dwellers had armored shells and many simple legs. _____

4. Because huge fish dominated the world about 400 million years ago, scientists call that period the

   Age of Fishes; its technical name is the Devonian Period of the Paleozoic Era. _____

5. Armor of heavy, bony plates protected these fish. _____

6. Sharks developed in this period, and modern sharks are very similar to those prehistoric sharks. _____

Dependent Clauses and Independent Clauses

Draw one line under the independent clause in each sentence. Draw two lines under the dependent clause.

7. When some fish with lungs emerged on land, they became the first amphibians.

8. Although most types of fishes with lungs died out millions of years ago, the modern lungfish

   still survives.

Adjective Clauses and Adverb Clauses

Underline the adjective clause in each sentence. Then circle the noun it modifies.

9. Plesiosaurs, which grew up to 46 feet long, were whalelike dinosaurs.

10. Some had necks that were double the length of their bodies.

Underline the adverb clause in each sentence.

11. When the dinosaurs dominated Earth, some took to the sea.

12. Many of these animals developed fins or flippers where they once had legs.

Gerund Phrases

Underline each gerund phrase.

13. Meeting a sea scorpion must have been an unpleasant experience for ancient sea creatures.

14. The sea scorpion's huge claws were ideal for grabbing prey.

Restrictive and Nonrestrictive Clauses

Draw a line under the dependent clause in each sentence. If it is a restrictive clause, write *RC* after the sentence. If it is a nonrestrictive clause, write *NC* after the sentence.

15. In the Canadian Arctic in 2004, a fossil of a fish that may have walked on land was discovered. _____

16. This creature, which has been named Tiktaalik, had a head like a crocodile; strong, bony fins; a neck; and nostrils for breathing air. _____

17. According to scientists who have studied the fossil, Tiktaalik may have used its fins like legs. _____

Phrases and Clauses

Read each sentence. Circle the word or words modified by the boldfaced phrase or clause. Then identify the boldfaced words as an *adjective phrase, adverb phrase, adjective clause,* or *adverb clause.*

18. Water temperatures in the ocean have changed **over time.** _____

19. The Devonian Period was a time **when the ocean was quite warm, with an average temperature of about 86°F.** _____

Underline each infinitive phrase. Circle each participial phrase.

20. The plesiosaur's long neck helped it to hunt food.

21. Stretching its long neck, the plesiosaur looked for prey.

22. Using its tail as a rudder, the mosasaur swam effectively.

Sentence Structures

Read each pair of sentences. Mark a star beside the sentence that more effectively expresses ideas. Then label that sentence *S* (simple), *CD* (compound), *CX* (complex), or *CCX* (compound-complex).

23. A mass extinction happened at the end of the Devonian Period. _____

   A mass extinction, which eliminated more than two-thirds of marine species, ended the Devonian Period; this was one of five mass extinctions that happened in prehistoric times. _____

24. This mass extinction may have been caused by global cooling, or it may have been the result of a reduction of carbon dioxide in Earth's atmosphere. _____

   Scientists are not sure of the reason why so many creatures died at one time; they have considered many possible explanations, which include global cooling, and also a drop in the amount of carbon dioxide in Earth's atmosphere, but they have not decided on which explanation is most likely. _____

Avoiding Fragments, Run-ons, Comma Splices, and Ramble-ons

Label each item as a fragment (*F*), a run-on (*RO*), a comma splice (*CS*), or a ramble-on (*RA*).

25. Ammonites were tentacled animals they lived in spiral shells. _____

26. Similar to the modern nautilus. _____

27. Ammonites changed through the ages, scientists use ammonite fossils to date rock layers. _____

28. Because the shells of the ammonites that lived in one period look very different from the shells of ammonites that lived in another period, scientists can look at the fossils of ammonites from each of these periods and notice the variations between them. _____

The increase in fish has led to more **competition** for food in this coral reef.

Write the base word of the word in bold type.

_____ Write a definition for the word in bold type.

_____

Adding Suffixes: *-tion, -ation*

The suffixes *-tion* and *-ation* can be added to the ends of words to change them to nouns. For example, the word *admire* becomes *admiration,* and the word *complete* becomes *completion.* The final e or *te* of the base word is dropped before these suffixes are added.

Word Sort

Use the words below to complete the word sort.

frustrate	combine	determine	decoration	elimination	decorate
education	eliminate	frustration	combination	educate	determination

Base words	Words with *-tion* or *-ation*

Pattern Practice

Replace the underlined word or words with a word that is a synonym.

educate	education	eliminate	elimination	introduce
introduction	admire	admiration	decorate	decorations

1. I'd like to <u>present</u> for the first time my friend Amy. _____

2. The great <u>respect</u> Julia had for her teacher was clear. _____

3. Avi's dream is to <u>teach</u> young people. _____

4. Mom said the <u>ornaments</u> on the dress were gaudy. _____

5. He ordered the <u>removal</u> of all school vending machines. _____

Add *-tion* or *-ation* to each base word given. Write the new word in the sentence.

6. During the game, Jen's _____ was evident. (frustrate)

7. He showed no _____ before jumping in the water. (hesitate)

8. Only two teams are left in the _____. (compete)

9. Oil and water are not a good _____. (combine)

10. Mr. Kim will oversee the _____ of the bridge. (complete)

11. Is there an _____ date on this can of soup? (expire)

12. Keri will speak at her high school _____. (graduate)

13. The referee made the _____ that the game should be delayed. (determine)

14. The losing team faces _____ from the tournament. (eliminate)

Use the Dictionary

Add *-tion* or *-ation* to each base word and write the new word. Check your spellings in a print or an online dictionary.

15. aspire + ation = _____

16. initiate + tion = _____

17. contemplate + tion = _____

Diagramming Compound Subjects

A sentence with a compound subject is diagrammed this way:

Whales and dolphins swim.

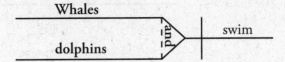

Diagram these sentences on the lines provided. (Refer to page 37 if you need help.)

1. Kevin and I saw two dolphins.

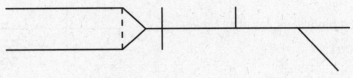

2. Roger and Ana spotted a whale.

3. The passengers and crew shouted.

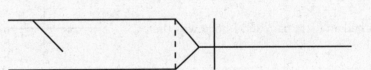

Diagramming Compound Predicates

A sentence with a compound predicate is diagrammed this way:

The whales leap and dive.

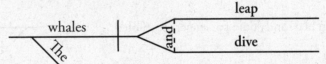

Try diagramming these sentences.

4. The dolphins chattered and whistled.

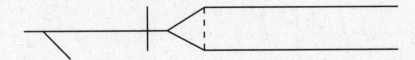

5. Onlookers pointed and yelled.

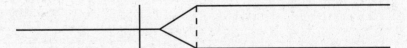

6. One child laughed and clapped.

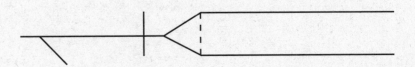

Diagramming Compound Sentences

A compound sentence is diagrammed this way:

One whale leaped, and another dove.

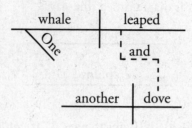

Try diagramming these compound sentences.

7. I carried binoculars, but they broke.

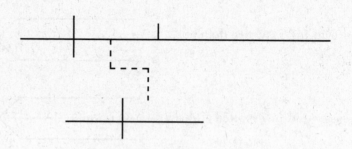

8. Ana had an extra pair, and I borrowed them.

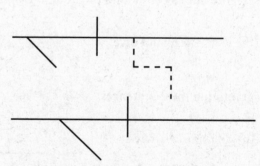

9. The ship lurched, and some passengers stumbled.

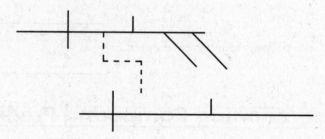

10. The stormy clouds parted, and the sun shone.

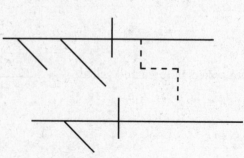

Writing Sentences

The writer of these sentences has tried to include too many ideas. Rewrite each sentence as two or three shorter, clearer sentences. Make sure each sentence you write is complete.

1. Due to the great energy they expend, otters eat tremendous amounts of food, so they spend most of their day diving for shellfish such as abalone and sea urchins, which they crack with the help of a rock which they lay on their stomachs and use as an anvil.

   _____

   _____

   _____

   _____

   _____

2. Otters seem to smile as they eat the meat from the shellfish they have broken when they hold their lips away from their teeth because the broken shells often have sharp edges.

   _____

   _____

   _____

   _____

   _____

There are four kinds of sentences—declarative, interrogative, imperative, and exclamatory. Any of these sentences may be simple, compound, or complex. Notice the different types of sentences in this model paragraph.

question

statements

complex sentence

command

exclamation

Have you ever wondered what life is like at the bottom of the ocean? Last month I had a chance to find out by studying it with my own eyes. I rode in a submersible to explore an oceanic trench off the Pacific Coast. *Because the bottom of the trench is so deep, no sunlight reaches the creatures there.* Several fish that I saw glow through a process called bioluminescence. **Imagine seeing an anglerfish use its glowing lure to attract prey.** *Wow, that was impressive!*

Writing a Paragraph

The sentences you repaired on page 75 can be used to make a paragraph. Decide what order the sentences should be in. Then revise at least two of the sentences so your paragraph has a variety of sentence types. Use the model on page 75 as a reference. Write the paragraph on the lines below.

_____

_____

_____

_____

_____

_____

_____

Imagine that you are an ocean diver. You have just returned from a dive during which you saw many unusual creatures. Write a paragraph about your experience. Vary the types of sentences you use, and include different types of phrases to add variety and interest to your paragraph.

_____

_____

_____

_____

_____

_____

_____

_____

Read your paragraph again. Use this checklist to evaluate your writing.

- ❏ Does my paragraph have a topic sentence?
- ❏ Have I used at least two of the four kinds of sentences?
- ❏ Have I included at least one compound or one complex sentence?
- ❏ Do my sentences have correct punctuation?
- ❏ Does my paragraph have a concluding sentence?

Proofreading
Practice

Read this passage about sperm whales and find the mistakes. Use the proofreading marks below to show how each mistake should be fixed. Use a dictionary to check and correct spellings.

Proofreading Marks

Mark	Means	Example
ℒ	delete	Sperm whales eats squid, sharks, and other fish.
∧	add	Sperm whales eat squid, sharks, and other fish.
≡	make into an uppercase letter	sperm whales eat squid, sharks, and other fish.
⊙	add a period	Sperm whales eat squid, sharks, and other fish
⌃	add a comma	Sperm whales eat squid, sharks, and other fish.
(sp)	fix spelling	Sperm whales eat sqid, sharks, and other fish.
/	make into a lowercase letter	Sperm Whales eat squid, sharks, and other fish.

Sperm Whales

Sperm whales are the largest toothed Whales in the world. a fully grown sperm whale. Can meshure anywhere from 38 to 60 feet in lenth and can be identified by its massive head.

groups of whales consisting primarily of females and there young travel through warm tropical waters. These groups are called pods. The young whales are raised not only by their mothers but by the other adults in the pod as well?

Young males leave the group by the time they are six they migrate to colder waters. They travel alone or with samll groups of other males. It is thought that the males leave their famly units so that there is less competition for food, they eat enormous quantities of food to satisfy their huge appetites. Adult males, called bulls, can be nearly one-third biger than the females.

After many years, when they are ready to mate, Bulls return to the warmer waters in which they were raised. They usually swim with many groups of female whales. Before they find an appropriate mate.

People of various societies have created storys legends and works of art featuring whales. Perhaps the most famous whale in literature is the male sperm whale that is the focus of the action in Herman melville's novel

Moby-Dick

Proofreading
Checklist

You can use the list below to help you find and fix mistakes in your own writing. Write the titles of your own stories or reports in the blanks at the top of the chart. Then use the questions to check your work. Make a check mark (✓) in each box after you have checked that item.

Proofreading Checklist for Unit 2

	Titles			
Have I used the correct punctuation at the end of each kind of sentence?				
Have I used a comma and coordinating conjunction or a semicolon to separate compound sentences?				
Have I avoided run-on sentences, comma splices, ramble-ons, and sentence fragments?				
Is each sentence an independent clause or an independent clause and a dependent clause?				
Have I combined sentences correctly?				

Also Remember…

Does each sentence begin with an uppercase letter?				
Did I use a dictionary to check and correct spellings?				
Have I used commas correctly?				

Your Own List

Use this space to write your own list of things to check in your writing.

Community Connection

In Unit 2 of *Grammar, Usage, and Mechanics*, students learned more about **different types of sentences and sentence structures** and used what they learned to improve their own writing. The content of these lessons focuses on the theme **Sea Creatures**. As students completed the exercises, they learned about some of the most impressive and unusual inhabitants of the world's oceans. These pages offer a variety of activities that reinforce skills and concepts presented in the unit. They also provide opportunities for the student to make connections between the material in the lessons and the community at large.

Local Fishes

Find out where the nearest saltwater aquarium is located. If possible, arrange to visit the aquarium. You might consider taking a younger family member with you and sharing with that person some of the things you have learned about the ocean in Unit 2.

Laws of the Sea

Because of its limited supply of fish and the presence of valuable minerals on and under the ocean floor, the question of who owns the world's oceans has become increasingly important. Learn about laws that govern the ocean. You might begin by finding out what the Law of the Sea Treaty, drafted in 1982 by the United Nations, suggests as fair use of the world's oceans. Find out which nations signed the treaty, which did not, and why. Summarize the information in a report.

Saving Water

Although some places have plenty of water for people to use however they want, many other places face a shortage of usable water. People there follow conservation rules so everyone will have the water they need for daily living. Organize a campaign to raise public awareness of the importance of water conservation in your school or neighborhood. Call your local water department and ask for water-saving tips. Make posters showing some of these suggestions and display them at school or in other places so people will be motivated to take part in your campaign.

Sea Dreams

Learn about job opportunities for people who love the ocean and the creatures that inhabit it. Such opportunities include careers in marine biology, marine geology, and underwater archaeology. Organizations that offer maritime careers include the Merchant Marines and the United States Coast Guard. Choose one occupation that interests you and learn more about it. Try to answer these questions:

- What skills are required to do this job?
- What preparation and training would I need for this job?
- Where is this training available?
- How long does it take to become proficient at this work?
- What is a typical working day like in this profession?

If possible, interview an adult you know who has a maritime job you might be interested in. Take notes during the interview, and share the results of the interview with your class. Use the planning guide on the next page to help you plan the interview and organize your notes.

Name _____

Interview Planner

Person I am interviewing:

Name _____

Age _____

Occupation _____

Number of years employed in that field _____

Date of interview: _____

Questions to ask:

1. _____
   _____

2. _____
   _____

3. _____
   _____

4. _____
   _____

5. _____
   _____

6. _____
   _____

7. _____
   _____

8. _____
   _____

Notes:

_____

_____

_____

_____

_____

_____

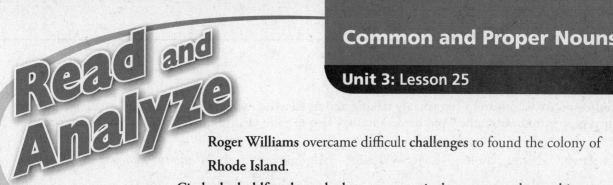

Read and Analyze

Roger Williams overcame difficult challenges to found the colony of Rhode Island.

Circle the boldfaced words that name particular persons, places, things, or ideas.

A **common noun** names any person, place, thing, or idea. A **proper noun** names a particular person, place, thing, or idea. Proper nouns must be capitalized. A proper noun made of more than one word (*Harriet Tubman* or *East Greenwood School*) is considered one proper noun.

See Handbook Section 15

Practice

Circle the proper nouns in the sentences below. Underline the common nouns.

Roger Williams founded Rhode Island on the principle of religious freedom.

1. Roger Williams was a minister who came to Boston with the Puritans in 1631.

2. The Puritans had come to America so they could worship freely.

3. They did not give that privilege to others in their colony, however.

4. They felt that their ideas were best, and they wrote laws saying everyone must hold the same beliefs they did.

5. Roger Williams disagreed.

6. He felt that all people should be allowed to worship as they wanted.

7. He also believed that the Native Americans owned the land and that the colonists had no claim to it unless they bought it fairly.

8. Williams's radical ideas about religious freedom and fairness to Native Americans got him into trouble, but he never went back on his convictions.

9. In October 1635, the government of Massachusetts banished Williams from the colony.

10. The government tried to send him back to England, but Williams fled through the woods to stay with the Narragansett.

11. The Narragansett welcomed Williams and helped him learn their language, Algonquian.

12. After a few months, Williams purchased land from these Native Americans.

13. The land was located at the head of the bay now known as Narragansett Bay.

14. On this site he founded a settlement he called Providence.

15. The settlement grew into the colony of Rhode Island, where religious freedom was the right of all people.

Name _____

Apply

Proper nouns specify whom and what you are talking about. Rewrite each sentence, and replace each common noun with a proper noun from the word bank. You may also need to change other words in your sentences.

| England | Narragansett | Roger Williams | Algonquian | *A Key into the Language of America* |

16. The minister became friendly with the local residents. _____

_____

17. He stayed with them and learned to speak their language. _____

_____

18. He later wrote a book. _____

_____

19. It was published in another country. _____

_____

Reinforce

Use information from Practice and Apply to complete the puzzle. Then circle the proper nouns you wrote.

Across

6. Native American group
7. Roger Williams's occupation
8. Settlers

Down

1. Strong beliefs
2. Group that went to Boston in search of freedom
3. A European island country
4. A special right
5. Another word for *liberty*

82

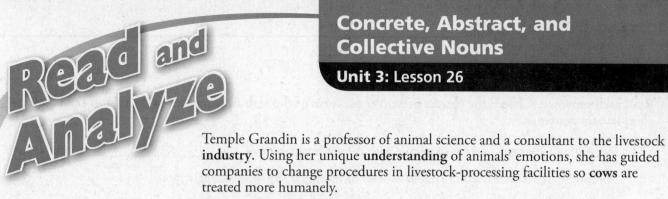

Temple Grandin is a professor of animal science and a consultant to the livestock **industry**. Using her unique **understanding** of animals' emotions, she has guided companies to change procedures in livestock-processing facilities so **cows** are treated more humanely.

Circle the boldfaced word that names a collection of companies. Draw one line under the boldfaced word that names things that can be seen, heard, and touched. Draw two lines under the boldfaced word that names an idea.

A **collective noun** names a group of people or things. In most cases, a collective noun that is singular in form should be treated as a singular noun for subject-verb agreement. A **concrete noun** names something you can see, touch, hear, smell, or taste. An **abstract noun** names an idea.

See Handbook Section 15

Practice

Read each sentence. Circle the boldfaced word that is the type of noun listed in parentheses.

1. When Temple Grandin was two years old, a **doctor** told her parents that she had the **condition** known as autism. (abstract noun)

2. The doctor said she should be placed in an institution, but Grandin's parents kept her with the **family** in their **home**. (collective noun)

3. Grandin's **behavior** was called weird by many of her **schoolmates**, but she showed that she had unusual talents. (concrete noun)

4. Although Grandin had difficulty interpreting the expressions and gestures of **people**, she demonstrated an amazing ability to recognize animals' signals of **emotion**. (abstract noun)

5. Grandin has had a lifelong **interest** in **cattle**; after receiving a bachelor's degree, she studied animal behavior in graduate school. (concrete noun)

6. Grandin used her **insights** into the thoughts and emotions of cows to help design new **machinery** for cattle-processing plants. (concrete noun)

7. Cattle remain much calmer in **plants** with this machinery because they experience far less **fear** and pain. (abstract noun)

8. Grandin has also helped **society** gain an **understanding** of the ways in which people with autism experience the world. (collective noun)

9. Grandin explains that many people with autism are extremely sensitive to **light**, sound, and touch, and she describes ways in which environments can be changed to cause less **discomfort** to people with such sensitivities. (concrete noun)

10. Grandin says that she, like many other people with autism, has the **ability** to remember sights in great detail; she believes that a person with this ability can make great contributions to a **group** planning physical facilities. (collective noun)

Temple Grandin was named one of the 100 most influential people in the world by *TIME Magazine* in 2010.

Apply

Read each sentence. Choose the correct present-tense form of the verb in parentheses. Write it in the blank to complete the sentence.

11. According to experts, a team of people with different capabilities _____ more creative

    solutions than does a team of people who all have similar capabilities. (generate)

12. Such a group _____ from the different perspectives of its members. (benefit)

13. An organization with creative problem solvers _____ an advantage over organizations without such

    people. (have)

Reinforce

Temple Grandin has overcome the challenge of being a person with autism and experiencing the world differently from the way most other people experience it. Think of someone you know who has overcome a challenge of some kind. Write a paragraph about this person's challenge and what she or he has done to overcome it. Use at least one abstract noun, one concrete noun, and one collective noun in your paragraph.

_____

_____

_____

_____

_____

_____

_____

_____

_____

_____

_____

_____

_____

_____

The **heptathlon** is one of the most demanding **contests** in **athletics**.
Circle the boldfaced nouns that name more than one person, place, or thing.

A **singular noun** names one person, place, thing, or idea. A **plural noun** names more than one. Most nouns add *-s* or *-es* to form the plural. A small number of nouns have **irregular plurals**. Some nouns change spelling in the plural form (*woman, women*). Some nouns have the same singular and plural form (*deer*).

See Handbook Sections 15, 29

Practice

Circle each singular noun. Underline each plural noun.

1. Seven different events compose the heptathlon, an Olympic competition for women.

2. Among all athletes who competed in this event in the last century, Jackie Joyner-Kersee demonstrated the greatest speed, strength, and leaping ability.

3. Joyner-Kersee set a world record in the heptathlon at the 1988 Summer Olympic Games.

4. She has recorded the six best scores in the history of this competition.

5. She won medals in the heptathlon in three consecutive Olympics, from 1984 to 1992.

6. Joyner-Kersee also won Olympic medals in another event, the long jump.

7. She set marks in the hurdles, too.

8. An all-around athlete, she even played professional basketball briefly.

9. A popular magazine named Joyner-Kersee the greatest female athlete of the century.

10. Joyner-Kersee achieved all these triumphs even though she has a form of asthma.

11. This disease affects the lungs; Joyner-Kersee sometimes had to be hospitalized after events.

12. For many athletes, retirement is the greatest challenge.

13. Joyner-Kersee has achieved success with her charity as well as in business.

14. The Jackie Joyner-Kersee Foundation has built athletic facilities for youths in her hometown of East St. Louis, Illinois.

15. This nonprofit organization also helps older men and women in that community.

Jackie Joyner-Kersee became one of history's greatest athletes.

Apply

Write the plural form of each singular common noun you identified in the Practice section. If a singular noun appears more than once, just write its plural once.

16. _____
17. _____
18. _____
19. _____
20. _____
21. _____
22. _____
23. _____
24. _____
25. _____
26. _____
27. _____

28. _____
29. _____
30. _____
31. _____
32. _____
33. _____
34. _____
35. _____
36. _____
37. _____
38. _____
39. _____

Reinforce

A collective noun names a group of people or things that act as one unit. *Class, flock,* and *orchestra* are collective nouns. Circle the words below that are collective nouns. Then use three of them in sentences.

| family | fleet | women | team | children |
| jury | events | committee | facilities | audience |

40. _____

_____

_____

41. _____

_____

_____

42. _____

_____

_____

Wilma Rudolph's triumph over a childhood disease made her a truly remarkable champion.

Circle the part of the boldfaced word that shows ownership.

A **possessive noun** shows ownership. **Singular** nouns add an apostrophe and -s to form the possessive (*worker, worker's*). Most **plural** nouns add an apostrophe after the -s to form the possessive (*workers, workers'*). Plurals that don't end in -s (*men, mice*) add an apostrophe and -s (*men's, mice's*) to show possession.

See Handbook Sections 7, 30

Practice

Underline each singular possessive noun. Circle each plural possessive noun. There may be more than one possessive noun in each sentence.

1. Wilma Rudolph's early childhood was made painful by a series of illnesses.

2. She got pneumonia and scarlet fever, and soon afterward she contracted polio, that era's most dreaded childhood disease.

3. That illness's effects left her with one leg paralyzed.

4. Wilma's mother had 19 children then, but she found time to get expert treatment for her young daughter's condition.

5. Every week she and Wilma traveled 50 miles by bus from Clarksville, Tennessee, to a hospital in Nashville to obtain doctors' help.

6. The Rudolphs, an African American family, had to sit in the back of the bus; Wilma Rudolph never forgot segregation's injustice.

7. Thanks to the treatments and to her mother's encouragement, Wilma began to improve.

8. In time she was able to walk with a brace's support, but she was determined to walk without it.

9. By junior high, Wilma no longer needed the brace, and she joined the girls' basketball team.

10. Her legs' muscles were now strong, and she starred in basketball.

11. This brilliant athlete's greatest triumphs would come in the sport of track and field; she first qualified for the United States Olympic Team in 1956, at the age of 16.

12. At the 1960 Olympics, Rudolph became the first American woman to win three gold medals, gaining recognition as the world's greatest woman sprinter.

13. The champion's homecoming parade in Clarksville was the first integrated event in the town's history.

14. Rudolph set world records in the women's 100- and 200-meter races and the 4 × 100-meter relay.

15. Working with young people after her Olympic triumphs, Rudolph became many youths' inspiration.

In 1961 Rudolph received the Sullivan Award, given each year to the top U.S. amateur athlete.

Apply

Rewrite each sentence, shortening the underlined section by using a possessive noun.

16. The biographies of many athletes include stories of their triumphs over physical problems. _____

_____

17. The strong swimming of Tom Dolan earned him gold medals in the 1996 and 2000 Olympics.

_____

18. An abnormally narrow windpipe provides Dolan with air at only 20 percent of the capacity of a

normal windpipe. _____

_____

19. The condition which Dolan has only made him train harder. _____

_____

20. The persistence of this swimmer brought him a world record and a gold medal in the men's 400-meter

individual medley. _____

_____

Reinforce

Circle six nouns hidden in the puzzle. Write each one in the column where it belongs. Then write the possessive form of each noun.

F	A	M	I	L	Y	C	D
Q	T	H	B	S	D	H	I
W	H	J	N	P	F	I	S
R	L	K	M	O	G	L	E
T	E	L	Q	R	H	D	A
Y	T	Z	W	T	J	R	S
P	E	X	R	S	K	E	E
S	S	C	T	S	L	N	B
D	M	V	W	O	M	E	N

Singular Nouns   **Possessive Forms**

21. _____   _____

22. _____   _____

Plural Nouns   **Possessive Forms**

23. _____   _____

24. _____   _____

25. _____   _____

26. _____   _____

Use one of the possessive forms you wrote in a sentence about Wilma Rudolph.

27. _____

_____

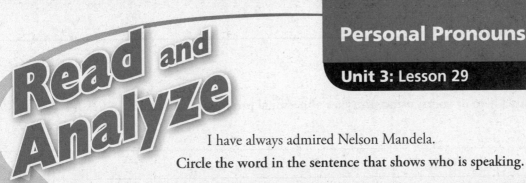

I have always admired Nelson Mandela.

Circle the word in the sentence that shows who is speaking.

A **pronoun** can take the place of a noun. **Personal pronouns** can be used to stand for the person speaking, the person spoken to, or the person spoken about. **First person** pronouns refer to the speaker (*I, me*) or include the speaker (*we, us*). **Second person** pronouns refer to the person being spoken to (*you*). **Third person** pronouns refer to the person, place, or thing being spoken about (*he, him, she, her, it, they, them*). **Remember to use this information when you speak, too.**

See Handbook **Section 17a**

Practice

Circle each personal pronoun. Write *1* if it is a first person pronoun, *2* if it is second person, or *3* if it is third person.

1. Do you know who Nelson Mandela is? _____

2. In 1994 he became the first black president of South Africa. _____

3. I am amazed by the obstacles Mandela overcame to reach the presidency. _____

4. From the 1940s through the 1980s, South Africa's laws took away most of black South Africans' lands and prohibited them from voting. _____

5. We learned in history class that this system was known as apartheid. _____

6. Nelson Mandela joined the African National Congress, a group that denounced apartheid and acted to try to end it. _____

7. The South African government imprisoned him for taking action against apartheid. _____

8. Although Mandela was a prisoner for 27 years, he never lost hope. _____

9. Mandela secretly wrote a book and helped other prisoners as they waged a struggle for better prison conditions. _____

10. You will be glad to know that international outrage finally led to Mandela's release. _____

11. Mandela negotiated the end of apartheid with South African President F.W. De Klerk, and together they were awarded the Nobel Peace Prize. _____

12. Nelson Mandela is a hero to me. _____

13. This great leader's courage is an example for all of us. _____

14. He proved to the world that oppression can be ended without widespread bloodshed. _____

Nelson Mandela helped end apartheid in South Africa.

Name _____

Apply

Write four sentences about a hero of yours, using the types of personal pronouns indicated.

15. first person: _____

_____

16. second person: _____

_____

17. third person singular: _____

_____

18. third person plural: _____

_____

Reinforce

The word *he* once was accepted as a universal pronoun that could refer to anyone, male or female, if a generalization about people was being made.

| Example | Early childhood experiences affect a person for **his** entire life. |

Now most writers try to avoid the use of universal *he*. Here are two ways the sentence above might be revised.

Solution #1:

Make the noun and the word it refers to plural.

Early childhood experiences affect people for their entire lives.

Solution #2:

Replace *his* with *his or her.*

Early childhood experiences affect a person for his or her entire life.

Try both of these solutions for replacing the universal *he* in these sentences.

The food a person eats affects his health.

19. _____

_____

20. _____

_____

Each student scheduled his choice of activity during gym class.

21. _____

_____

22. _____

_____

a. Kieran bought himself a book about the history of human flight.

b. He himself dreamed about becoming a pilot someday.

Circle the word in sentence *a* that indicates for whom Kieran bought the book about flight. Draw a line under the word in sentence *b* that emphasizes the identity of the person who wants to become a pilot.

Words such as *myself, herself, itself,* and *themselves* are **compound personal pronouns**. When a compound personal pronoun is used as an object in a sentence and refers back to the subject, that pronoun is called a **reflexive pronoun**. When a compound personal pronoun is used to emphasize the identity of the sentence subject, it is called an **intensive pronoun**.

See Handbook Sections 17c, 17e

Practice

Read the paragraphs below. Underline each compound personal pronoun that is used as a reflexive pronoun. Circle each compound personal pronoun that is used as an intensive pronoun. (1–10)

Since ancient times, we humans have imagined ourselves flying. Until recently, however, airplane pilots have not been able to lift themselves off the ground without the help of an engine.

In the 1970s engineer Paul MacCready dedicated himself to the dream of achieving human-powered flight. MacCready's first successful plane, the Gossamer Condor, had a wingspan of almost 100 feet but was made of extremely lightweight materials. In fact, the plane itself weighed only 70 pounds. In a test flight, cyclist Bryan Allen pedaled hard in the cockpit to spin the plane's propeller and lift himself and the Condor into the air for a flight of over a mile.

Paul MacCready and his team achieved the previously impossible goal of human-powered flight.

After the success of the Gossamer Condor, MacCready and his team set themselves a tougher challenge. They designed their new plane, the Gossamer Albatross, to be capable of transporting its pilot across the 22.5-mile-wide English Channel. Bryan Allen volunteered himself again to be both pilot and power source. Would you yourself be willing to flutter just above the ocean waves for that distance, being kept aloft only by your energetic pedaling? In an amazing feat of endurance, Allen pedaled nonstop and landed the Albatross on the other side of the channel safely. By doing so, Allen himself made flight history a second time.

The Gossamer Condor is on display at the National Air and Space Museum in Washington, D.C. I myself hope to visit the museum and see that historic plane someday.

Name _____

Apply

Rewrite each sentence, replacing the underlined word or words with a compound personal pronoun. Underline each reflexive pronoun you write. Circle each intensive pronoun you write.

11. My friend Jasmine bought <u>Jasmine</u> a model of the Gossamer Condor.

_____

12. We <u>the two of us</u> figured out how to put it together.

_____

13. I gave <u>me</u> three tries to get the plane airborne.

_____

14. My third try was successful; the plane rose up, flew a ways, and set <u>the plane</u> down on a patch of grass.

_____

15. Perhaps you <u>the person reading this</u> will fly a model plane successfully.

_____

Reinforce

When notable people give inspirational advice, they often use compound personal pronouns as they discuss the need for self-discipline and personal accountability.

Read these words of advice from the great humanitarian Eleanor Roosevelt:

You gain strength, courage, and confidence by every experience in which you really stop to look fear in the face. You are able to say to yourself, "I lived through this horror. I can take the next thing that comes along." . . . You must do the thing you think you cannot do.

—Eleanor Roosevelt from *You Learn by Living*

On the lines below, write a sentence telling whether you agree with these words. Then, on another piece of paper, write a paragraph about your opinion. Use at least one reflexive or intensive pronoun in your paragraph.

_____

_____

_____

_____

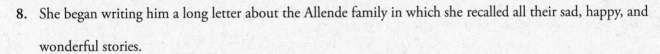

Isabel Allende **wrote** a **book** about **her** daughter, Paula.

Circle the boldfaced word that shows ownership or indicates a relationship.

To whom does it refer? _____

Possessive pronouns show ownership. The possessive pronouns *her, his, its, their, my, our,* and *your* can replace possessive nouns. (*Nancy's house is blue.*—*Her house is blue.*) The possessive pronouns *hers, his, theirs, mine, ours,* and *yours* can replace both a possessive noun and the noun that is a possession. (*Nancy's house is the blue house.*—*Hers is the blue house.*)

See Handbook | Section 17d

Practice

Circle the possessive pronouns. There may be more than one in a sentence.

1. My favorite author is Isabel Allende.

2. Who is yours?

3. Allende was an investigative journalist in her native country, Chile.

4. Its government was overthrown in the 1970s.

5. At that time her uncle, Salvador Allende, was the president of that country.

6. Many people lost their lives, and Isabel Allende was forced to flee.

Isabel Allende has lived on three continents.

7. In exile in Venezuela, Allende heard that her grandfather was very ill in Chile.

8. She began writing him a long letter about the Allende family in which she recalled all their sad, happy, and wonderful stories.

9. This long letter grew into her first great novel, *The House of the Spirits*.

10. My favorite of Allende's books, *Paula,* also had its beginning as a letter.

11. Allende was taking care of her daughter, Paula, who lay in a coma for a year as the result of an illness.

12. She wrote Paula a letter, relating in great detail the story of Paula's life and hers.

13. Allende hoped Paula would read the letter when she recovered from her coma, but Paula never regained consciousness.

14. Greatly saddened by Paula's death, Allende almost gave up writing her marvelous stories.

15. But instead she decided to create for her daughter the best memorial she could.

16. People all over the world have read Allende's book *Paula* and as a result keep her memory alive.

Name _____

Apply

Rewrite each sentence, replacing each group of underlined words with a possessive pronoun.

17. I really like <u>Cynthia Lord's</u> book *Rules*. _____

_____

18. <u>The book's</u> subject is a girl named Catherine, whose brother has a disability. _____

_____

19. Catherine learns that <u>people's</u> ideas of what is normal can vary. _____

_____

20. That red book over there is <u>the one belonging to me</u>. _____

_____

21. <u>The one belonging to you</u> is on the table. _____

_____

Reinforce

Circle the possessive pronouns in the riddles below. Then try to solve the riddles.
(Answers are given below.)

22. You can see mine, his, hers, and theirs, but you can never see yours.

23. Nobody wanted it. First it was hers, and then it was mine, and now it's yours.

24. The more you give yours, the more others give you theirs.

25. What is it, do you suppose? The more I take from mine, the bigger it grows.

Now write two of your own riddles using possessive pronouns and give them to a friend to solve.

26. _____

_____

_____

27. _____

_____

_____

(answers: 22: your back; 23: a cold; 24: friendship; 25: a hole)

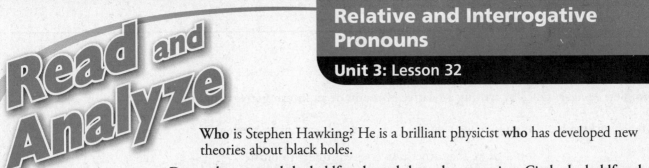

Who is Stephen Hawking? He is a brilliant physicist **who** has developed new theories about black holes.

Draw a box around the boldfaced word that asks a question. Circle the boldfaced word that refers to the noun just before it.

When the pronouns *who, whom, whose, which,* and *that* are used to introduce an adjective clause, they are called relative pronouns. A relative pronoun always follows the noun the adjective clause is describing. When the pronouns *who, whom, whose, which,* and *what* are used to begin a question, they are called interrogative pronouns.

See Handbook Sections 17g, 17h

Practice

Circle each relative pronoun. Underline the noun the adjective clause is describing. Draw a box around each interrogative pronoun.

1. Stephen Hawking has a disease that has left him almost completely paralyzed and unable to speak.

2. He taps out messages on a special computer, which communicates the messages
   with its synthesized voice.

3. What effects has this disability had on Hawking's work?

4. Stephen Hawking's brilliant mind is the only tool that he needs for the
   study of black holes.

5. Who knows the meaning of the term *black hole*?

6. Dying stars whose masses are great enough may collapse in on themselves.

7. They then form black holes, areas that may not allow the escape of any
   matter or energy, not even rays of light.

8. There are many theories that attempt to describe black holes.

9. Which did Hawking think up?

10. He developed the widely accepted theory that describes singularities.

11. What is a singularity?

12. It is the infinitely dense point that scientists believe lies at the heart of a black hole.

13. Hawking has also envisioned shrinking black holes, whose final explosions would release huge
    bursts of energy.

14. There are several physicists who disagree with this theory, however.

15. Who do you believe is correct, Hawking or his critics?

Stephen Hawking studied physics and mathematics at Oxford and Cambridge in England.

Apply

Complete each sentence by writing a relative pronoun or an interrogative pronoun.

16. Hawking has proposed many theories _____ cannot be proven.

17. _____ could prove that other universes exist next to ours?

18. Hawking has a theory _____ proposes the existence of wormholes.

19. _____ is a wormhole?

20. A wormhole is a tiny spot _____ connects one universe to another.

21. *A Brief History of Time*, _____ Hawking published in 1988, explains his ideas in relatively simple terms.

22. People _____ read this book may not understand all of Hawking's ideas, but they are likely to learn a great deal about the universe.

Reinforce

As you revise your writing, keep in mind these tips about the correct usage of relative pronouns:

1. *Who* is used only to refer to people.
2. *That* and *which* refer to things.
3. *Which* is generally used to introduce nonrestrictive clauses. These clauses are set off by commas and provide information about the noun they describe.
4. *That* is used to introduce restrictive clauses. These clauses are not set off by commas. They give information about a noun that is essential to the meaning of the sentence.

Circle the relative pronoun that is used incorrectly in each sentence. Then rewrite each sentence with the appropriate relative pronoun.

23. My favorite chapter of *A Brief History of Time* is the one which tells about black holes. _____

_____

24. In this section, Hawking describes what would happen to a person which flew a spaceship into a

black hole. _____

_____

25. The black hole's gravity, that is immensely powerful, creates forces that would compress and pull the spaceship

out of shape. _____

_____

26. People that watched the spaceship from a distance would see it fall more and more slowly into

the hole. _____

_____

Someone is coming across the ice!
Circle the word that refers to an unknown person.

Indefinite pronouns refer to persons or things that are not identified. Indefinite pronouns include *all, anybody, both, either, anything, nothing, everyone, few, most, one, no one, several, nobody,* and *someone.*

See Handbook Section 17f

Practice

Circle each indefinite pronoun in these sentences.

1. Does anybody know about the explorations of Sir Ernest Shackleton?

2. This British captain was the first one to locate the South Magnetic Pole.

3. In 1914 he led an expedition to cross Antarctica, a challenge no one had ever attempted before.

4. He set out in the sailing ship *Endurance* with a crew of 27, but soon everything went wrong.

5. The *Endurance* became trapped in ice far from the Antarctic shore, and there was nothing the crew could do to free it.

6. Everyone loaded the ship's supplies into lifeboats and began walking across the frozen sea, dragging the boats.

7. Shackleton and his crew walked 250 miles before they saw anything besides water and ice.

8. Finally the men reached a tiny island, but they found nothing to eat there.

Siberian ponies pulled heavy loads on one Shackleton expedition.

9. Winter was coming, and supplies were running out; Shackleton knew he had to do something to save his crew.

10. Someone had to seek help, so Shackleton and five crew members sailed away in a small lifeboat.

11. Everything was against these brave sailors: they faced huge waves and violent storms, and they had little water to drink.

12. After almost two weeks of sailing, somebody saw land!

13. Shackleton landed on the treacherous coast of South Georgia Island and climbed over a mountain before he found anyone able to rescue the rest of the crew.

14. Because of Shackleton's courage, everybody was saved.

15. Few could have done what Ernest Shackleton and his crew did.

Name _____

Apply

Complete each sentence by writing an indefinite pronoun.

16. It was more than forty years before _____ tried to cross Antarctica again.

17. A person who had been _____ of Shackleton's original team members backed a new expedition in 1957.

18. The new team traveled by dog sled and snowmobile; _____ were very useful.

19. _____ of the snowmobiles had to be connected together by cable.

20. That way, if _____ fell into a crevasse in the ice, the cable could be used for a rescue.

21. _____ went well on this expedition.

22. The team had several close calls, but _____ stopped them from traveling the 2,158 miles.

Reinforce

Circle the indefinite pronoun in each sentence. Then write the answer to each clue. Each answer appears in this lesson.

23. Thanks to his bravery, everyone on the expedition survived.

____ ____ ____ ____ ____ ____ ____ ____ ____
 10   12   2   7

24. Before Shackleton found it in 1908, no one had determined its location.

____ ____ ____ ____ ____
        8   5

____ ____ ____ ____ ____ ____
  6   13   9

____ ____ ____ ____
 4   11

25. All should agree that this was a good name for Shackleton's ship.

____ ____ ____ ____ ____ ____ ____ ____ ____
 3   14   1

Use the numbered letters to answer this question:

What was the name of the tiny island where most of Shackleton's crew awaited rescue?

____ ____ ____ ____ ____ ____ ____ ____ ____ ____ ____ ____ ____ ____
 1   2   3   4   5   6   7   8   9 10 11 12 13 14

The Two Fridas is a colorful, memorable painting.

Circle the two words that describe the painting. Draw a box around the short word that comes right before these words.

Adjectives describe nouns and pronouns. Some adjectives, like *colorful* and *memorable,* describe or tell what kind. Others, like *many* and *six,* tell how many. The **articles** *a, an,* and *the* are also adjectives.

See Handbook | Section 16

Practice

Circle each adjective that tells *what kind*. Underline each adjective that tells *how many*. Draw a box around each article. Finally, draw a star above the noun each adjective describes.

1. Frida Kahlo was an important modern painter.

2. As a young child in Mexico, much of her creative life was spent in bed; she had contracted polio, which

    left her with a weak right leg.

3. As a teenager, while a passenger on a bus, Kahlo was in a dreadful accident.

4. The terrible injuries left her in continuous pain.

5. Several months after the accident, Kahlo began painting.

6. Her vivid paintings, mostly self-portraits that dealt with feminist issues,

    expressed her pain as well as her joy in life.

7. In 1929 she married the famous muralist Diego Rivera.

8. Under his guidance she became a skillful painter.

9. Kahlo painted many portraits of herself over the years.

10. In one self-portrait, twisted roots grow from her body.

11. Another self-portrait shows her head on the body of a wounded deer.

12. In addition to her self-portraits, Kahlo created precise, detailed images of individual events on canvas.

13. Kahlo's paintings can evoke strong emotions.

14. Over the course of her short career, Kahlo made about two hundred paintings that told the story of her life.

15. As Kahlo gained importance as a leading Mexican artist, her paintings were classified as national treasures

    by the government of Mexico.

Frida Kahlo used images from traditional Mexican art in many of her paintings.

Name _____

Apply

Complete these sentences with adjectives from the word bank, or use your own words.

memorable	straight	happy	imaginative	zany
curly	strange	flowing	bright	blue
green	beautiful	pleasant	angry	a
brown	curious	frizzy	pale	an

16. If I were painting a self-portrait, it would be _____ _____ painting.

17. I would use _____ colors.

18. In the painting, I would have _____ hair.

19. My eyes would be _____.

20 I would have _____ _____ expression.

21. The background would be _____.

Reinforce

Circle four adjectives and four nouns in the puzzle. Then write each word in the correct group.

A	R	T	M	X	Z	T	P
A	P	U	U	T	L	E	R
Z	A	C	R	H	X	R	U
X	I	Z	A	E	H	R	S
B	N	E	L	X	Z	I	Z
G	T	I	I	Q	O	B	P
N	E	R	S	X	Z	L	K
T	R	Q	T	V	E	E	X
F	A	M	O	U	S	Q	T
A	C	C	I	D	E	N	T
P	S	E	V	E	R	A	L

Adjectives

22. _____

23. _____

24. _____

25. _____

Nouns

26. _____

27. _____

28. _____

29. _____

Now choose at least one noun and one or more adjectives from the puzzle and write a sentence about Frida Kahlo.

30. _____

_____

_____

This is a picture of Mary Patten.

That ship is a replica of the one she commanded.

Circle the word that modifies the noun *ship* and tells *which one*. Underline the word that stands for the noun *picture*.

This, these, that, and *those* are **demonstratives.** **Demonstrative adjectives** describe nouns and tell which one. **Demonstrative pronouns** take the place of nouns. *This* and *these* refer to a thing or things close by. *That* and *those* refer to a thing or things farther away. **Remember to use this information when you speak, too.**

See Handbook | Sections 16, 17i

Practice

Circle each demonstrative adjective. Underline each demonstrative pronoun. Draw a box around each noun the demonstrative modifies or replaces.

1. This is an old map of San Francisco Bay.

2. Fast-sailing clipper ships from New York once docked in that bay.

3. Those ships carried supplies to California during the Gold Rush, which began in 1849.

4. The sea route was 15,000 miles long, but clipper ships could cover that distance much faster than wagons could travel 3,000 miles overland to San Francisco.

5. In 1856 Captain Patten, of the clipper ship *Neptune's Car,* took his 18-year-old wife on this perilous journey.

6. That was not their first voyage together; she had traveled with him around the world and was an expert sailor.

7. Early in the trip, this brave young woman's husband became ill with tuberculosis.

8. That terrible disease was common in the nineteenth century.

9. The captain became too sick to command the ship, so a new commander had to be chosen from among those on board.

Mary Patten sailed a clipper ship around Cape Horn in the 1850s.

10. In that era, women were not expected to command ships, but no one on the ship besides Mary Patten knew how to navigate.

11. Soon after she took command, the ship entered the treacherous seas surrounding Cape Horn; this was the most dangerous part of the journey.

12. A series of terrible storms battered the ship; the crew had never seen gales like those before.

13. To avoid the storms, Mary Patten dared to sail into freezing Antarctic waters, and that risk paid off.

14. Patten guided the *Neptune's Car* to San Francisco, and the crew called her a hero for this achievement.

Apply

Rewrite each sentence, replacing the underlined words with a demonstrative pronoun or with a demonstrative adjective and any other needed words.

15. <u>The model I'm pointing to</u> is a replica of another clipper ship. _____

_____

_____

16. <u>The three masts shown in the model</u> would have risen one hundred feet above the deck. _____

_____

_____

17. <u>The mast closest to the front of the ship</u> is called the foremast. _____

_____

18. <u>The model across the room</u> is a replica of a five-masted ship from the late nineteenth century. _____

_____

Reinforce

Authors and speakers sometimes begin sentences with demonstrative pronouns for a dramatic or stirring effect. Circle the demonstrative pronouns in the famous quotations below.

This was their finest hour.

—Sir Winston Churchill (England, 1940)

These are the times that try men's souls.

—Thomas Paine (North America, 1776)

This is my own, my native land!

—Sir Walter Scott (Scotland, 1805)

Now research what the demonstrative pronoun refers to in each quotation. The place and time the quotation was said or written may give you a hint. Write your answers on the lines below.

19. _____

_____

20. _____

_____

21. _____

_____

a. Israeli-American violinist Itzhak Perlman is a **brilliant musical** performer.

b. Israeli-American violinist Itzhak Perlman is a **musical brilliant** performer.

c. He has been praised for his **sweet, elegant** tone and his **flawless, masterful** technique.

Read sentences *a* and *b*. Which sentence has the boldfaced adjectives in an order that sounds natural? _____

Read sentence *c*. What punctuation mark is used to separate each pair of boldfaced adjectives? _____

When you use more than one adjective to describe a noun, put the adjectives in an order that sounds natural. When you use **coordinate adjectives**—a pair of adjectives of a similar kind—to describe a noun, place a comma between the adjectives.

See Handbook Sections 8, 16

Practice

Underline the adjectives in parentheses that are written correctly.

1. Itzhak Perlman has been praised as the (living greatest/greatest living) violinist by many critics.

2. He has performed with (every major/major every) symphony orchestra in the world over his fifty-year career.

3. Perlman had to overcome a (serious physical/physical serious) disability in order to become a performer.

4. When he was four years old, Itzhak Perlman was stricken with polio, a (viral terrible/terrible viral) illness,

   and he lost the use of his legs.

5. Perlman overcame this challenge: he learned to walk using crutches, and became a (dedicated

   passionate/dedicated, passionate) student of the violin.

6. As a young teenager, Itzhak Perlman moved to the United States from Israel to study at the (exclusive,

   prestigious/exclusive prestigious) Juilliard School of Music in New York.

7. Perlman made his debut as an orchestra soloist when he was seventeen, and soon became famous for his

   (dazzling polished/dazzling, polished) playing.

8. Known for his warmth and kindness, Perlman has taught and guided (young many/many young) musicians.

9. He has introduced the (lyrical, affecting/lyrical affecting) sound of the violin to new generations through

   performances on TV's *Sesame Street* and on soundtracks for movies.

10. Perlman offers this (musical helpful/helpful musical) guidance: "The most important thing to do is really

    listen."

Name _____

Apply

Choose two adjectives from the word bank to complete each sentence. Be sure to use each pair of adjectives in a natural-sounding order. If the two adjectives are of a similar kind, use a comma to separate them.

quiet	dark	matching	different	formal
many	intricate	stirring	colorful	loud

11. Marching bands wear _____ uniforms.

12. These bands play _____ music at parades and athletic events.

13. Chamber music groups play _____ compositions.

14. The musicians in these groups often dress in _____ clothing.

15. Which of the _____ types of music are your favorites?

Reinforce

If you had the opportunity to learn to play an instrument, which one would you choose? Write a paragraph giving your choice of instrument, explaining why it appeals to you and telling what types of music you would play. Use a pair of adjectives with one of the nouns you include.

_____

_____

_____

_____

_____

_____

_____

_____

_____

_____

_____

Review

Kinds of Nouns

Underline the correct plural form in parentheses.

1. Most people's (lifes/lives) involve some sort of challenge.

2. Challenges make our (victorys/victories) sweeter.

3. There are (touches/touchs) of greatness in all of us.

Write whether the boldfaced word is a *common* noun or a *proper* noun.

4. When **Raden Kartini** was young, few Indonesian girls received an education. _____

5. Kartini rebelled against this restrictive **system**. _____

6. Kartini spent her life working for girls' **education**. _____

7. She founded a school for boys and girls in the town of **Japara**. _____

Read each sentence. Circle the boldfaced word that is the type of noun listed in parentheses.

8. In quite a few nations today, **girls** do not have equal **opportunities** to learn. (abstract noun)

9. Many nonprofit organizations work to give young women the **chance** to attend **schools** in these countries. (concrete noun)

10. A **team** might build a school or provide **books** and other learning materials. (collective noun)

Write the possessive form of this noun from the sentences above.

11. girls _____

Write the singular possessive form of these nouns from the sentences above.

12. Raden Kartini _____

13. Indonesia _____

Kinds of Pronouns

Circle each personal pronoun. Write *1* if it is a first person pronoun, *2* if it is second person, or *3* if it is third person.

14. I admire Raden Kartini. _____

15. Kartini wanted all women in Indonesia to have the same educational opportunities she had. _____

16. What would you have done in a similar situation? _____

Circle the phrase that tells what kind of pronoun the boldfaced word is.

17. Mount Everest, **which** is more than 29,000 feet high, is the tallest mountain in the world.

    relative pronoun   indefinite pronoun   interrogative pronoun

18. **What** are the climbing conditions on Mount Everest?

    compound personal pronoun   interrogative pronoun   possessive pronoun

19. **Its** steepness and dangerous crevasses make this mountain extremely difficult to climb.

    relative pronoun   compound personal pronoun   possessive pronoun

20. The air **itself** is so thin that climbers take oxygen to breathe.

    indefinite pronoun   reflexive pronoun   intensive pronoun

21. **Who** were Sir Edmund Hillary and Tenzing Norgay?

    possessive pronoun   interrogative pronoun   relative pronoun

22. They were the climbers **who** first scaled Mount Everest successfully.

    compound personal pronoun   possessive pronoun   relative pronoun

23. **No one** else had reached the top and returned alive.

    indefinite pronoun   interrogative pronoun   compound personal pronoun

24. A team set up camps on the lower slopes, but Hillary and Norgay continued on by **themselves**.

    reflexive pronoun   interrogative pronoun   intensive pronoun

25. Hillary and Norgay made **their** final camp almost 28,000 feet up the mountainside.

    relative pronoun   possessive pronoun   interrogative pronoun

26. **Both** then began the climb to the top.

    interrogative pronoun   indefinite pronoun   compound personal pronoun

Adjectives

Circle each adjective that tells *what kind*. Underline each adjective that tells *how many*. Draw a box around each article (*a, an, the*). Draw a star above the word each adjective modifies.

27. Kate Shelley lived near a remote bridge in Iowa.

28. During a fierce rainstorm a violent flood washed out the bridge.

29. Shelley knew that a train with many passengers would soon reach the bridge.

Demonstrative Pronouns and Demonstrative Adjectives

Circle each demonstrative adjective. Underline each demonstrative pronoun. Draw a box around the word each demonstrative modifies or replaces.

30. This teenager climbed across another bridge in the heavy rain to warn the train's engineer.

31. Kate Shelley was just in time; she saved many lives on that night.

32. This is the lantern Kate Shelley carried through the dark.

Ordering Adjectives

Underline the adjectives in parentheses that are written correctly.

33. Have you read any books about (brave young/young brave) heroes?

34. A person must make (swift sensible/swift, sensible) decisions in a dangerous situation in order to avert tragedy.

Spelling Practice

a. Trevor lost both legs in a **tragic** automobile accident.

b. This brave athlete still **wrestles** in a city league once a week.

Which sentence contains a boldfaced word with two silent consonants? _____

Spelling Patterns: Words With Silent Letters

Some words have silent letters that are not pronounced. For example, the *b* is silent in *crumb* and *plumber,* the *k* is silent in *kneel* and *knob,* and the *g* is silent in *align* and *resign.*

Word Sort

Use the words below to complete the word sort.

scenic	gnarled	wrestle	resign	honesty	descend
schedule	hustle	campaign	jostle	scenery	herb

Silent *t*	Silent *c*

Silent *h*	Silent *g*

Pattern Practice

| knoll | resign | scenic | gnarled | descend | schedule | gauge | guarantee | jostle | sought |

Write the word that goes with each definition. Then circle the silent letter or letters in each word. Do not circle silent *e*.

1. a promise or assurance _____

2. a small hill _____

3. to quit or give up _____

4. something that measures _____

5. to come down _____

6. to bump up against _____

7. a list of things to do _____

8. looked for _____

Write the word from above that best completes each sentence.

9. The _____ showed that we were running out of gas!

10. The old oak tree had ugly, _____ branches.

11. Diego _____ his friends in the huge crowd at the stadium.

12. I need a _____ that you will be on time for soccer practice.

13. We watched the hail mercilessly _____ on the house.

14. The rolling hills of the countryside were quite _____.

Use the Dictionary

Circle the correct spelling of each word. Use a print or an online dictionary to check your work.

15. The Memorial Day ceremony was a (solem/solemn) occasion.

16. These muffins are full of tasty (rasberries/raspberries).

Diagramming Understood *You*

Imperative sentences (commands) usually contain the understood *you* as the subject. When the subject is understood, write (*you*) in the sentence diagram, like this:

Light the candle.

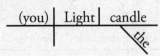

Try diagramming these sentences.

1. Set the table.

2. Light the fire.

3. Slice the cake.

Diagramming Possessive Pronouns

Look at the way the possessive pronouns *my* and *their* are diagrammed in these sentences.

My neighbors celebrated May Day.

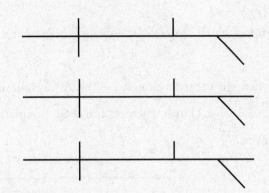

We decorated **their** garden.

Now diagram these sentences.

4. My sister made a salad.

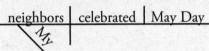

5. Alex brought his guitar.

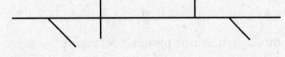

6. Your lasagna and my chili fed the group.

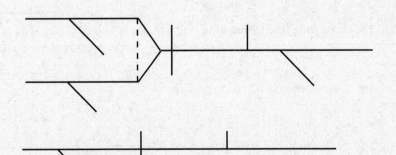

7. Our celebration pleased us.

Diagramming Demonstrative Pronouns

You have learned that the demonstrative pronouns *this, that, these,* and *those* take the place of nouns. Look at how the demonstrative pronouns in these sentences are diagrammed.

My grandfather carved **this**.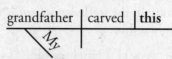

That demands courage.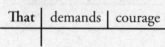

8. Based on these diagrams, which sentence below tells where to place a demonstrative pronoun in a sentence diagram? _____

   a. Always place it where the subject belongs.   **b.** Always place it where the direct object belongs.

   c. Put it wherever the noun it replaces would go.

Now diagram these sentences.

9. These need repair.

10. We ate those.

11. This works better and costs less.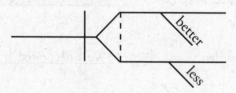

Diagramming Indefinite Pronouns

Indefinite pronouns include *anybody, somebody, both,* and *no one*.

12. Where do you think an indefinite pronoun belongs in a sentence diagram? _____

    a. where the subject goes   b. where the predicate goes

       c. wherever the noun it replaces would go

Try diagramming these sentences.

13. Everyone liked your song.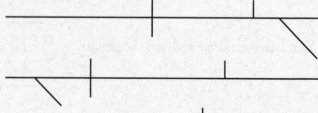

14. The music bothered no one.

15. Somebody ate my sandwich and drank my juice.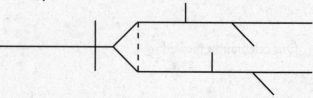

Writing Sentences

These sentences need help! Rewrite them so they give more information about Jackie Joyner-Kersee and her accomplishments. Refer to Lesson 27 if you need to.

1. Jackie Joyner-Kersee was a good athlete. _____
   _____
   _____

2. She was in the Olympics. _____
   _____
   _____

3. She won some medals and set some records. _____
   _____
   _____

4. She had an illness. _____
   _____
   _____

5. She did well after retiring. _____
   _____
   _____

When you write a paragraph, always include a topic sentence, two or more supporting sentences that add details about your topic, and a concluding sentence. Your reader will enjoy your paragraph more if you include colorful adjectives and use pronouns and possessives appropriately. Notice how this model paragraph is written.

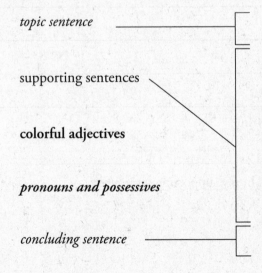

topic sentence

supporting sentences

colorful adjectives

pronouns and possessives

concluding sentence

My father is a hero to me because he was willing to risk everything to gain freedom. After the Vietnam War ended in 1975, life became very **difficult** for **many** people in Vietnam. Late in 1976 *my* father decided to escape. Crowded together with **twelve other** people in a **small wooden** boat, *he* endured a **dangerous** journey across the **stormy** South China Sea. After being picked up by a **fishing** boat, *he* came to the United States to start a **new** life. Here *he* has built a **successful** business, publishing a newspaper in Vietnamese. *My* father says *he* is **grateful** for the freedom of speech allowed in the United States. *I* am also very **glad** to be living in the United States. *I will always be grateful to my father for having the courage to seek freedom.*

Name _____

Writing a Paragraph

The sentences you revised on page 111 can be used to make a paragraph. Decide what order the sentences should be in. Write the paragraph on the lines below. Add other words, such as transition words, if necessary.

_____

_____

_____

_____

_____

_____

_____

Write a paragraph about one of your personal heroes. You might write about someone you learned about in Unit 3 or about another person. Refer to the model paragraph on page 111 if you need help. Be sure to include a variety of interesting adjectives. Use pronouns and possessives when appropriate.

_____

_____

_____

_____

_____

_____

_____

_____

Read your paragraph again. Use this checklist to evaluate your writing.

- ❑ Does my paragraph have a topic sentence?
- ❑ Have I included a variety of interesting descriptive words in my supporting sentences?
- ❑ Have I used pronouns and possessives appropriately?
- ❑ Do my sentences have correct punctuation?
- ❑ Does my paragraph have a concluding sentence?

Proofreading
Practice

Read this passage about sea turtle eggs and find the mistakes. Use the proofreading marks to show how the mistakes should be fixed. Use a dictionary to check and correct spellings.

Proofreading Marks

Mark	Means	Example
℉	delete	Sea turtles hidde their eggs in sand.
∧	add	Sea turtles hide their egg$\overset{s}{\wedge}$ in sand.
≡	make into an uppercase letter	s̲e̲a̲ turtles hide their eggs in sand.
◡	close up	Sea tur tles hide their eggs in sand.
(sp)	fix spelling	Sea tirtels hide their eggs in sand.
⊙	add a period	Sea turtles hide their eggs in sand⊙
/	make into a lowercase letter	Sea Turtles hide their eggs in sand.

Guardian of the Eggs

Georgias' Barrier Islands are among the few places in the united states where sea turtles can find open beach land to lay there eggs. these round eggs, about the size of table tennis balls, are wite and leathery. Its common on warm summer nights there to see a female turtle drag her self high onto the beach, dig a hole, deposit more than a 100 eggs, cover up the hole, and then slowly return to the ocean. These sea turtles that consistently brede along the southeastern koastline are called *loggerheads*.

By hiding her eggs. The mother turtle does all she can to protect her young. But without some extra help, many of the turtle eggs laid on them islandses wouldn't never hatch. Wild pigs and other animals dig up turtle eggs and eat them. Humans also dig up turtle nests It has taken speshel efforts by naturalists to protect the eggs.

Carol Ruckdeschel one of the turtle egg guardians on the Barrier Islands. each summer night for a number of years Ruckdeschel has patrolled the beachs, watching for turtles and driving off predators and human trespassers. Its not easy to stay awake ever nite for sevrel monthes, but Ruckdeschel believes that helping sea turtles excape extinction is worth missing sum sleep.

Proofreading
Checklist

You can use the checklist below to help you find and fix mistakes in your own writing. Write the titles of your own stories or reports in the blanks at the top of the chart. Then use the questions to check your work. Make a check mark (✓) in each box after you have checked that item.

Proofreading Checklist for Unit 3

	Titles			
Have I capitalized proper nouns?				
Have I written plural forms of nouns correctly?				
Have I written possessive forms of nouns correctly?				
Have I used correct forms of personal pronouns?				
Have I used possessive pronouns correctly?				
Have I used appropriate relative pronouns?				

Also Remember…

Does each sentence begin with an uppercase letter?				
Did I use a dictionary to check and correct spellings?				
Have I used commas correctly?				

Your Own List
Use this space to write your own list of things to check in your writing.

Community Connection

In Unit 3 of *Grammar, Usage, and Mechanics,* students learned about **different kinds of nouns, pronouns, and adjectives** and used what they learned to improve their own writing. The content of these lessons focuses on the theme **People Who Overcame Challenges**. As students completed the exercises, they learned about people who have overcome different kinds of challenges. These pages offer activities that reinforce skills and concepts presented in the unit. They also provide opportunities for the students to make connections between the materials in the lessons and the community at large.

Community Services

Find out what services for people facing challenges are available in your community. Look for rehabilitation programs, food distribution centers, shelters, immigrant resource centers, help centers for people with disabilities, and so on. Contact the organizations to find out what services they offer and whom they serve. Then create a descriptive list of helpful organizations. Make sure you include the name of each organization, its phone number and address, and how it helps members of your community. When you have finished, decide whether you think your community has services for all who need them or if other services should also be offered. Add your suggestions for new services to your list.

Any Volunteers?

Choose one organization in your community that helps people overcome challenges, such as a home for the elderly or a help center for wounded veterans. Visit or call the organization to find out about ways you might get involved with the organization as a volunteer. If possible, spend some time volunteering for the organization. Then write an advertisement to convince others to become volunteers for the organization. Include what services the organization offers, what jobs the volunteers do, and why volunteers are important. You may also want to invite a representative from the organization to talk to your class about community needs and the value of volunteers.

Local Heroes

Research people in your community, region, or state who have overcome challenges of various kinds. Use what you find out to create a scrapbook of local heroes. In your scrapbook, include a brief biography of each of the people you found. Or, choose two or three of the people and write a short report about each one.

Fundraising

Join a fundraiser, such as a walk-a-thon that raises money for a good cause. Answer each of these questions:

- What type of fundraiser will you join?
- How does the fundraiser work?
- What organization or group will the money go to?
- What is the target amount for funds raised?
- How many people will participate?
- How does the sponsoring organization get people interested in participating?
- Do the participants get any rewards for their participation? If so, what?

Write the details of the fundraising event in a report.

Name _____

A Special Person

Interview a family member, friend, or acquaintance about a challenge he or she had to overcome in order to achieve an important goal. Before holding the interview, write a list of questions that you will ask. Take notes during the interview to record the person's responses. After the interview, write a paragraph about the challenge the person faced and how he or she overcame it.

Work That Helps

Learn about and list some of the job opportunities available for people who want to help others overcome challenges. Look for jobs in education, medicine and science, and social work. Then learn more about one job that interests you. Find out what skills are required for the job, how to get the training required to do the job, and what the job responsibilities are. Use the planner that follows to help you find and organize the information.

Job Information

People/Organizations to call for information:

_____

_____

_____

_____

Information given:

_____

_____

_____

_____

Training needed:

_____

_____

_____

_____

Where to get the training/how long it takes:

_____

_____

_____

_____

Special skills needed/suggested:

_____

_____

_____

Job responsibilities:

_____

_____

_____

_____

Other information:

_____

_____

_____

Read and Analyze

The Sonoran Desert is one of the largest deserts in North America. Its weather patterns give this vast area a fifth season.

In the first sentence, circle the verb that links the subject of the sentence to words in the predicate that rename and describe it. In the second sentence, underline the verb that shows action.

An **action verb** shows action. It usually tells what the subject of a clause is doing, will do, or did. An action verb may include one or more helping verbs in addition to the main verb. A **linking verb** does not show action. It connects the subject of a sentence to a word or words that describe or rename the subject. Linking verbs are usually forms of *be*. Some common linking verbs are *am, is, are, was, were, been,* and *will be*. The verbs *become, seem, appear,* and *look* can also be used as linking verbs. A linking verb may also include one or more helping verbs in addition to the main verb.

See Handbook Sections 18a, 18c

Practice

Underline each action verb. Circle each linking verb. Be sure to include any helping verbs you find.

1. The Sonoran Desert is one of the hottest and driest areas in North America.

2. Seasons in the Sonoran Desert are different from the seasons in temperate climates.

3. The amount of rainfall determines the timing and nature of each season there.

4. Because the rainfall is so unpredictable, not everyone agrees on the number of seasons in the Sonoran Desert.

5. The Arizona-Sonora Desert Museum officially recognizes five seasons.

6. The annual cycle begins with the summer rainy season, from July through early September.

7. This period of heavy rainfall relieves the extreme heat of the previous two months.

8. It also provides much-needed water for desert plants and animals.

9. After the rainy season, temperatures become cooler and rainfall diminishes.

10. The fall season has begun; it typically lasts through November.

11. The winter months of December, January, and February are mostly sunny and mild, although they occasionally bring wind, rain, and cold temperatures.

12. Spring (mid-February through April) features mild temperatures and little rain.

13. This is the main flowering season for small plants, shrubs, and trees.

14. In a normal year, no rain falls during the foresummer drought months of May and June, and temperatures are high.

15. Plants and animals remain in survival mode during the drought months.

16. The return of the summer rains starts the cycle over; flora and fauna thrive in their desert home.

Name _____

Apply

Complete each sentence below with a verb from the word bank. On the line, write *A* if the verb you wrote is an action verb and *L* if the verb you wrote is a linking verb.

are	jump	captures	become
is	thrive	work	appears

17. The Sonoran Desert _____ home to many species of wildlife. _____

18. Many species of plants and animals _____ despite the scarcity of water. _____

19. On a hot, still day, the desert _____ to be empty, but in fact it is full of life. _____

20. There _____ more than 2,000 species of plants in the Sonoran Desert. _____

21. Thousands of harvester ants _____ in their underground tunnels. _____

22. Ants above ground _____ breakfast for a hungry horned lizard. _____

23. The lizard _____ the hapless insects with its sticky tongue. _____

24. Bighorn sheep _____ from ledge to ledge in the desert mountain range. _____

Reinforce

Some verbs, such as *appear, look, smell, feel, grow,* and *taste,* can be either action verbs or linking verbs, depending on how they are used in a sentence. You can test whether a verb is a linking verb by substituting a form of the verb *be* (*am, is, are, was, were,* or *been*) in its place. If the form of *be* makes sense, the verb probably is a linking verb.

In the sentences below, circle each boldfaced verb that is used as a linking verb. Underline each boldfaced verb that is used as an action verb.

25. I **grew** strawberries in my backyard.

26. They **looked** ready to pick.

27. I **smelled** one.

28. It **smelled** delicious.

29. I rinsed it off and **tasted** it.

30. It **tasted** better than the strawberries you buy at the store.

Some wasps **lay** their eggs on other insects.

Caterpillars **change** in their cocoons.

Which boldfaced verb says an action the subject did by itself? _____

Which boldfaced verb tells about an action the subject did to something else? _____

A **transitive verb** is an action verb that transfers its action to a direct object. (*Wasps lay eggs.*) An **intransitive verb** does not have a direct object. An intransitive verb shows action that the subject does alone. (*Caterpillars change.*) Many verbs can be either transitive or intransitive, depending on whether there is a direct object.

See Handbook Section 18b

Practice

Underline each transitive verb and draw a box around its direct object. Circle each intransitive verb.

1. Most insects grow in stages.

2. They begin their lives as eggs.

3. The number of eggs and their size, shape, and color vary from insect to insect.

4. Soon a juvenile insect, or larva, hatches.

5. Most larvae scarcely resemble the adults of their species.

6. Many live in very different habitats.

7. Mosquito larvae swim in the water.

8. Cicada nymphs devour roots underground for as long as seventeen years.

9. Some wasp larvae live inside the bodies of other insects.

10. Ants feed their colonies' larvae with great care.

11. Some beetle larvae imitate ant larvae for a free meal.

12. Larvae eat constantly for maximum growth.

13. Some enter a pupal stage before adulthood.

14. Some of a pupa's tissues dissolve inside its cocoon or shell.

15. The insect emerges from its cocoon as an adult.

16. In time, the female adult lays many eggs.

17. For many insects the entire cycle lasts only a few days.

18. A few insects have a seventeen-year life cycle.

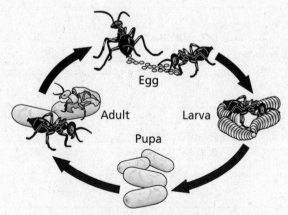

Egg

Adult

Larva

Pupa

Life Cycle of an Ant

Apply

Write a verb from the word bank to complete each sentence. Then label each transitive verb *T* and each intransitive verb *I*. Circle the direct object of each transitive verb.

begins	lay	live	have	attract	fly

19. Unlike larvae, adult insects often _____ beautiful wings. _____

20. After pumping blood through the new wings, they _____ for the first time. _____

21. Some adults _____ a mate with a scent or a flashing signal. _____

22. Most adult insects do not _____ very long. _____

23. They must _____ their own eggs quickly. _____

24. Then the life cycle _____ again. _____

Reinforce

Many verbs can be transitive or intransitive, depending on whether they are used with a direct object.

         D.O.
The butterfly *grew* wings inside its cocoon. (transitive)

The wings *grew* inside the cocoon. (intransitive)

Use the verbs *stopped* and *broke* in two sentences. In one sentence, use the verb as a transitive verb with a direct object. In the other, use it as an intransitive verb. Circle the direct object of each transitive verb.

25. stopped (transitive): _____

_____

_____

26. stopped (intransitive): _____

_____

_____

27. broke (transitive): _____

_____

_____

28. broke (intransitive): _____

_____

_____

Read and Analyze

Hot flames scorched the underbrush. _____

The underbrush was scorched by the hot flames. _____

Circle the simple subject in each sentence. Write *X* by the sentence in which the subject does something. Write *O* by the sentence in which something is done to the subject.

If the subject performs an action, the verb is said to be in the **active voice**. (*Hot flames scorched.*) If the subject is acted upon by something else, the verb is said to be in the **passive voice**. (*The underbrush was scorched.*) Many sentences in the passive voice have a prepositional phrase that begins with the word *by* and follows the verb.

See Handbook Sections 18g, 20

Practice

Circle the simple subject in each sentence. Draw a box around the simple predicate. Be sure to include helping verbs. Write *A* if the verb is in the active voice. Write *P* if it is in the passive voice.

1. Forest fires consume trees and other vegetation. _____

2. Many animals are killed by the raging flames. _____

3. But a fire's destruction clears the way for new life. _____

4. Small trees and sickly trees have been incinerated by the fire. _____

5. Strong, healthy trees have been saved from damage by their thick bark. _____

6. Sunlight pours through the open spaces between bare branches. _____

7. New grasses, wildflowers, and seedlings sprout in the ashes. _____

8. The number of plant and animal species in a forest may actually increase after a fire. _____

9. In a forest, small fires are sparked frequently by lightning. _____

10. Dead material on the forest floor is eliminated by these small fires. _____

11. Small fires rarely cause serious harm to a forest. _____

12. This natural cycle of destruction and rebirth has been upset by humans. _____

13. Until recently, firefighters fought all forest fires, large and small. _____

14. Flammable dead materials on the forest floor were not eliminated. _____

15. In a region with much dry brush and dead wood on the forest floor, a small fire can quickly grow into an inferno. _____

16. Soon the furious flames incinerate healthy adult trees. _____

17. Today, small natural fires generally are ignored by firefighters. _____

18. They battle only dangerous ones. _____

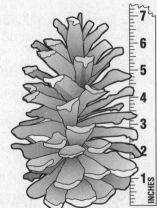

Some pinecones release their seeds only after a forest fire.

Apply

Look again at each sentence in the Practice section that has a verb in the passive voice. Rewrite each sentence so the verb is in the active voice.

19. _____
    _____

20. _____
    _____

21. _____
    _____

22. _____
    _____

23. _____
    _____

24. _____
    _____

25. _____
    _____

26. _____
    _____

Reinforce

> The active voice communicates action briefly and powerfully. Some writers believe that the passive voice should be used only when an action is done by an unknown or unimportant agent—for example, *The clock had been dropped.*

Read the passage below. Notice that all of the sentences are in strong active voice. Then underline each verb in the active voice in the excerpt. (27–37)

I kicked into the muscles of the horse. Once again it reared and snorted. Then it began to run. I didn't

know what to do. Instead of running across the field to the irrigation ditch the horse ran down the road to

the vineyard of Dikran Halabian where it began to leap over vines. The horse leaped over seven vines before

I fell. Then it continued running.

—William Saroyan, from "The Summer of the Beautiful White Horse"

Look over a story or a report you have written recently. Find a sentence with a verb in the passive voice. Rewrite the sentence so the verb is in the active voice.

38. _____

Every year, migrating geese pass over my community. In September I watched them on their southward journey. In spring the geese will fly north again.

Circle the verb phrase that tells about something that will happen in the future. Underline the verb that tells about something that happened in the past. Draw a box around the verb that tells about something that happens regularly or is true now.

A **present tense verb** indicates that something happens regularly or is true now. A **past tense verb** tells about something that happened in the past. Regular verbs form the past tense by adding *-ed* (*watch, watched*). The spelling of most irregular verbs changes in the past tense (*fly, flew*). A **future tense verb** tells what will happen in the future. Add the helping verb *will* to the present tense form of a verb to form the future tense (*pass, will pass*). **Remember to use this information when you speak, too.**

See Handbook Sections 18d, 18e

Practice

Circle the verb in each sentence. (Don't forget to include helping verbs.) Write whether the verb is in the *present, past,* or *future* tense.

1. About sixty percent of all birds migrate to warmer places in the winter. _____

2. This fall you will probably see many migrating birds. _____

3. The arctic tern holds the world record for long-distance yearly migration. _____

4. This hardy bird spends the summer months near the North Pole. _____

5. Each fall it travels to the continent of Antarctica. _____

6. In July of 1951 scientists banded an arctic tern in Greenland. _____

7. The bird traveled 11,000 miles in three months. _____

8. In October the scientists found it in South Africa on its way to Antarctica. _____

9. On their migrations, birds travel invisible routes called flyways. _____

10. Billions of birds fly these routes each year. _____

11. I live under one of North America's major flyways. _____

12. Next fall I will borrow some binoculars from my grandmother. _____

13. I will watch the birds on their way south. _____

14. I bought a field guide to Western birds last year. _____

15. I will record my observations carefully. _____

North Pole

Autumn migration

Spring migration

Antarctica

Twice a year, the arctic tern migrates from pole to pole.

Name _____

Apply

Write the past, present, or future tense form of a verb from the word bank to complete each sentence. Use a helping verb to form future tense verbs.

watch	take	have	go	photograph	swim

16. Many creatures besides birds _____ both a winter and a summer address.

17. Last year I _____ gray whales on their southern migration.

18. A gray whale typically _____ up to 16,000 miles on its way from the Arctic seas to Baja California.

19. Next year I _____ on a whale-watching expedition.

20. On an expedition last year my uncle _____ some gray whales.

21. I _____ my camera with me the next time I go whale watching.

Reinforce

Use these notes about a group of monarch butterflies to write a journal entry about phases of the monarchs' migration. Play the role of a scientist who has observed the monarchs. Use past, present, and future tenses in your entry.

- Monarchs—amazing insects (beautiful orange butterflies, black spots)
- Fall—fly to mountains in Michoacán, Mexico
- Spring—fly to Canada
- Journey begins in September in Canada, ends in Mexico in November (3,000 miles)
- Spend winter in Mexico—cover trees with a blanket of color
- Reproduce in spring—begin northward journey again

22. _____

_____

_____

_____

_____

_____

_____

_____

_____

Read and Analyze

Have you ever **watched** a meteor shower? A wonderful display of shooting stars **will appear** in the night sky in early August. You **can view** the Perseid meteor shower, an awesome celestial event, without a telescope or binoculars.

Circle the more important boldfaced verb in each sentence. Underline the remaining boldfaced verb that indicates the ability to do something. Draw a box around the remaining boldfaced verb that indicates how likely something is to happen.

The **main verb** is the most important verb in each clause or sentence. One or more **auxiliary verbs** (helping verbs) may come before the main verb. Some auxiliary verbs are **modal auxiliaries**—auxiliary verbs with special functions. The auxiliary verbs *may* and *might* can be used to ask or give permission. The auxiliary verbs *can* and *could* can be used to indicate ability. The auxiliary verbs *should* and *must* can be used to communicate a duty or an obligation. The auxiliary verbs *may, might, could, should,* and *will* can be used to indicate possibility—how likely something is to happen.

See Handbook Section 18c

Practice

In each sentence, circle the main verb and underline the auxiliary verb or verbs.

1. The Perseid meteor shower has occurred at the same time each year for many centuries.

2. With their knowledge of the orbital path of the comet Swift-Tuttle, astronomers can predict the date of this meteor shower each year.

3. This year as every year, Earth will pass through a stream of ice and dust fragments in the tail of Comet Swift-Tuttle.

4. These fragments will enter our planet's atmosphere at very high speeds.

5. Have you seen the bright trail of a meteor in the night sky in early August?

6. That trail was produced by the incineration of one of these fragments in that comet's tail.

7. You should check the NASA website for the dates of the next Perseid meteor shower.

8. Would you and your family enjoy this show?

9. If so, you must choose a viewing area far from artificial lights.

10. This area should offer an unobstructed view of the whole sky.

A meteor can create a bright streak in the sky as it burns up in Earth's atmosphere.

11. You and the others will need pads or portable chaise lounges, warm clothes, and blankets.

12. According to astronomers, your eyes may require as much as an hour for adjustment to the darkness.

13. Perhaps by dawn you will have seen more than 500 shooting stars!

14. The Perseid meteor shower can also be viewed inside homes, on computers with Internet access.

15. Live webcasts of the event will be presented on SPACE.com by NASA again this year.

Name _____

Apply

Use one of the modal auxiliaries in the word bank to complete each sentence.

might	can	should	may	will	must

16. You _____ be able to see a meteor shower this month.

17. To find out whether the time for a display is approaching, you _____ visit a website with a meteor shower guide.

18. If you are reading this in October, you _____ have the chance to see the Draconids or the Orionids.

19. The Leonids _____ provide a brilliant display in mid-November.

20. A dedicated skywatcher _____ try to see the Quadrantids in January and the Lyrids in April.

Reinforce

Write five sentences about how to prepare to watch a meteor shower. Use a modal auxiliary in each sentence.

_____

_____

_____

_____

_____

_____

_____

_____

_____

_____

_____

_____

Read and Analyze

Before I studied ecology, **I had** not **understood** the importance of each individual in a community of living things. Now **I have gained** a better understanding of how living things in an ecosystem affect one another. Before it dies, each organism **will have affected** other creatures, eating some or becoming food for others.

Circle the boldfaced verb phrase that tells about an action that began in the past and continues today. Draw a box around the boldfaced verb phrase that tells about actions that will be complete before a certain time in the future. Underline the boldfaced verb phrase that tells about actions that were completed by a certain time in the past.

The **present perfect** tense (*have gained*) shows action that started in the past and was recently completed or is still happening. The **past perfect** tense (*had understood*) shows action that was completed by a certain time in the past. The **future perfect** tense (*will have affected*) shows action that will be complete by a certain time in the future. To form perfect tenses, use a form of *have* with the past participle of a verb. **Remember to use this information when you speak, too.**

See Handbook Sections 18d, 18e

Practice

Circle boldfaced verbs in the present perfect tense. Underline boldfaced verbs in the past perfect tense. Draw a box around boldfaced verbs in the future perfect tense. (1–13)

Scientists **have discovered** ecosystems in very small places. Looking into the center of a bromeliad (broh MEE lee uhd), they found that a diverse group of animals **had established** a community there. Bromeliads are pineapple-like plants that trap water that **has fallen** into their leaves. This protected, watery environment is rich in nutrients. By the time it dies, a typical bromeliad **will have supported** thousands of tiny animals in the pools among its leaves.

For example, a tadpole swims in the water that **has collected** in the center of a bromeliad. The tadpole hatched yesterday from an egg a frog **had laid** a few weeks before. By the time the tadpole grows into a frog, it **will have eaten** many mosquito larvae. These larvae **have lived** on one-celled creatures floating in the water, which **have eaten** waste from frogs and other creatures. The cycle of food-web interactions **will have repeated** itself many times before the bromeliad dies.

A universe of creatures may live their entire lives in the tiny ecosystem in a bromeliad.

I **have** just **completed** a report on bromeliads. In the past I **had thought** ecology was boring. This report **has changed** my view.

Apply

Write the present perfect form (*has* or *have* + past participle), the past perfect form (*had* + past participle), or the future perfect form (*will have* + past participle) of the verb in parentheses to complete each sentence correctly.

14. For the last ten years I _____ bromeliad plants. (study)

15. Before I looked inside my first bromeliad, I _____ to find only a few bugs inside. (expect)

16. I was astonished by the number of creatures that _____ their homes inside. (make)

17. Over the past decade I _____ hundreds of tiny creatures under my microscope. (examine)

18. By the time my research is finally complete, I _____ thousands of animals. (count)

Reinforce

Authors usually write fiction as if a story's events happened in the past. Actions happening in the "now" of the story are written in the simple past tense. The past perfect tense is often used to indicate events that came before the time in which the story is taking place.

Notice the verb tenses used in this passage.

He felt that his luck was better than usual today. When he had reported for work that morning he had expected to be shut up in the relief office at a clerk's job, for he had been hired downtown as a clerk, and he was glad to have, instead, the freedom of the streets and welcomed, at least at first, the vigor of the cold and even the blowing of the hard wind.

—Saul Bellow, from "Looking for Mr. Green"

Read the passage again, and write the verbs. Then write whether each verb is in the past tense or the past perfect tense.

19. _____   _____

20. _____   _____

21. _____   _____

22. _____   _____

23. _____   _____

24. _____   _____

25. _____   _____

At midnight last night, Rick **was playing** a video game.

Now he **is snoring** loudly.

Soon his alarm clock **will be ringing**.

Circle the boldfaced verb phrase that tells about an action that is going on now. Underline the boldfaced verb that tells about an action that was happening for a while in the past. Draw a box around the verb phrase that tells about an action that will happen in the future.

Progressive forms of verbs show continuing action. The **present progressive** form of a verb consists of the helping verb *am, is,* or *are* and the present participle of that verb. (*I am watching.*) The **past progressive** form consists of the helping verb *was* or *were* and the present participle. (*They were listening.*) The **future progressive** form consists of the helping verbs *will be* and the present participle. (*You will be studying.*) **Remember to use this information when you speak, too.**

See Handbook Sections 18d, 18e

Practice

Read each sentence. If the boldfaced verb in it is a progressive form, write *P* on the line. If the boldfaced verb is not a progressive form, write *X*.

1. Birds that fly south in the fall **are listening** to their biological clocks. _____

2. Scientists **have shown** that many human activities are controlled by biological clocks. _____

3. Changes in body temperature called circadian rhythms **are waking** us up every morning and putting us to sleep every night. _____

4. These natural cycles can cause problems for people who **are trying** to work late at night. _____

5. Scientists **have reset** people's biological clocks successfully by having those people sit under bright lights. _____

6. Every night, biological cycles **are controlling** not only when we sleep but also how we sleep. _____

7. Before 1951, most people **believed** that the brain shut down during sleep. _____

8. That year, a scientist who **was studying** his son's sleep patterns made an important discovery. _____

9. For short periods while the boy **was sleeping**, his eyes moved back and forth quickly. _____

10. Scientists **have labeled** this phase of sleep REM (rapid eye movement) sleep. _____

11. During the night, you normally **move** from deep sleep to REM sleep and back several times. _____

12. Your eyes **are moving** constantly during REM sleep, and this is when most dreams occur. _____

13. Some scientists believe that REM sleep **helps** the brain with learning and emotional adjustment. _____

14. By age 70, most people **will have slept** for more than 200,000 hours. _____

15. Tomorrow at 8 A.M. I **will be sleeping** soundly. _____

16. By sleeping late, perhaps I **will be helping** my brain! _____

Name _____

Apply

Use a helping verb from the word bank plus a form of the verb in parentheses to complete each sentence. Each verb you write should be a progressive form.

am	was	were	will be

17. Last night I dreamed that I _____ through a huge swamp. (walk)

18. In the dream, a big mosquito _____ around my head. (buzz)

19. Its transparent wings _____ me. (tickle)

20. When I woke up, I _____ out loud. (laugh)

21. Now I _____ about my mosquito dream in a journal. (write)

22. If I have my way, tonight I _____ about something else! (dream)

Reinforce

Circle the progressive verb form in each clue. Then write the answers in the puzzle.

Across

2. Scientists are studying this state of deep sleep.

4. When you grow sleepy tonight, this rhythm will be influencing your energy level.

5. You will be doing this tonight.

7. When you look at this, you are checking the time.

Down

1. When you think, you are using this.

3. Some scientists are using bright lights to reset people's _____ clocks.

6. One scientist observed that these were moving rapidly at certain times as his son slept.

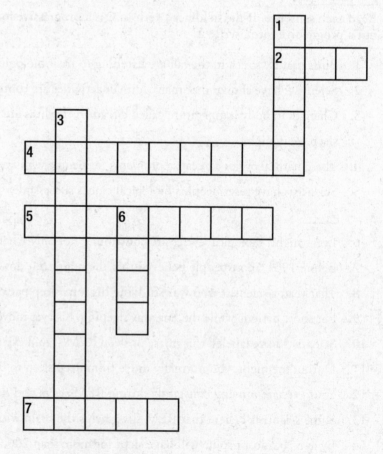

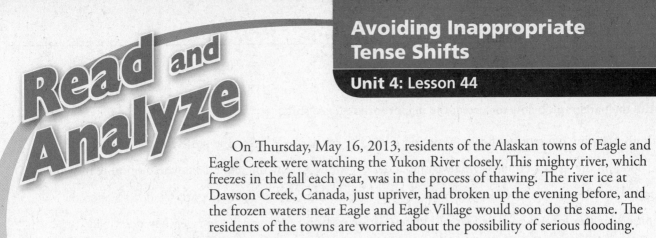

On Thursday, May 16, 2013, residents of the Alaskan towns of Eagle and Eagle Creek were watching the Yukon River closely. This mighty river, which freezes in the fall each year, was in the process of thawing. The river ice at Dawson Creek, Canada, just upriver, had broken up the evening before, and the frozen waters near Eagle and Eagle Village would soon do the same. The residents of the towns are worried about the possibility of serious flooding.

Which verb phrase in this paragraph shifts the time frame in a way that doesn't make sense? _____

How should the sentence be rewritten so it stays in the time frame that was established in the previous sentences? _____
_____

Choose **verb tenses** carefully so that the verb forms you use work together to indicate time accurately and consistently. When you describe events that happen in the same time frame, do not shift tenses. When you describe events that happen at different times, use verbs in different tenses to indicate the order in which the events happened.

See Handbook Section 18e

Practice

Read these paragraphs. If the verb in a sentence creates a time shift that doesn't make sense, mark an X through the verb and write the correct tense form of that verb on the line at the end of the paragraph.

The residents of those small towns had good reason to be concerned. The ice breakup on the Yukon in May of 2009 had caused severe flooding in the area. The historic native settlement of Eagle Village was totally devastated by ice and water; residents had to rebuild their village on a new site several miles away. The town of Eagle had also been flooded, and many buildings have suffered damage. River and weather conditions in mid-May 2013 are so similar to those in 2009 that the mayor of Eagle went door-to-door warning residents to prepare for the worst. _____

Residents' fears turned out to be well-founded. At 12:30 A.M. on Friday, May 17, an ice jam formed in the Yukon during breakup a few miles downstream from Eagle. The jam caused river water to back up and flood the town; the water carried ice chunks as big as trucks along with it. Seven buildings were knocked off their foundations, nine sheds were washed away, and many power poles were toppled. Fortunately, though, the ice jam breaks loose at about 5:30 A.M. on the 17th, and the flood waters quickly recede.

_____

Eagle residents generally were shaken but thankful. Although their town was a mess—huge chunks of ice covered the land and blocked the highway—no one is hurt. The damage was minor compared to that caused by the 2009 flood. Eagle Village, 12 miles away, suffers no damage. Other towns along the Yukon were not so lucky in 2013. Galena, a larger town downriver, was made uninhabitable by flood waters just days after Eagle's immersion. _____

Name _____

Apply

Rewrite the paragraph below to correct the inappropriate tense shifts.

Emily Schwing is a reporter for radio station KVAC in Fairbanks, Alaska. She posted a report about the Eagle flood on the Alaska Public Media website on May 19, 2013. Schwing had talked with a number of people in Eagle about the damage and clean-up efforts, and she is quoting several in her report. Claude Denver, the Response Manager for Alaska's Division of Homeland Security and Emergency Management, described "large pans of ice" that are lifted onto roads by the high water. David Helmer, an employee of Alaska Power and Telephone, talks about dealing with downed power lines to "keep [things] safe for the people in the area." Marlys House, the owner of a bed and breakfast, said that three feet of water had flooded her building's bottom floor. She explains that she and her husband "had to open the doors to let the water out," but it has caused no real damage, and the business would reopen soon.

_____

_____

_____

_____

_____

_____

_____

_____

_____

Reinforce

On another sheet of paper, write a report about a memorable event caused by a natural process. This could be an event you have experienced or one you have learned about. Start your report with a description of the situation before the natural process caused change. Next, describe the process and its immediate effect. Finally, tell what the results were and how people dealt with them. Choose verb tenses carefully so that the verb forms you use work together to indicate time accurately and consistently.

Read and Analyze

The current flows **swiftly**. Salmon must be **very** strong to swim **upstream** against it.

Which boldfaced word tells how the current flows? _____

Which tells where salmon swim? _____

Which modifies an adjective by telling how much? _____

Adverbs modify verbs, adjectives, or other adverbs. They tell **how, when, where,** or **to what extent** (*how much*). Many adverbs end in *-ly*. Other common adverbs are *fast, very, often, again, sometimes, soon, only, too, later, first, then, there, far,* and *now*.

See Handbook | Section 19

Practice

Circle each adverb. There is at least one adverb in each sentence.

1. Some animals almost always bear their young in their own place of birth.

2. Salmon hatch in streams, but they swim steadily to the ocean.

3. After several years at sea, salmon return instinctively to their native streams.

4. The journey upstream is extremely hard.

5. The water flows powerfully in the other direction.

6. The big fish swim forcefully against the current.

7. They leap high in the air over small waterfalls.

8. Finally they reach their birthplace.

9. There, females lay eggs, and males fertilize them.

10. Then the salmon collapse wearily.

11. Their lives usually end near their own birthplace.

12. Tiny salmon soon hatch and begin the cycle again.

13. Sometimes salmon cannot return to their birthplace.

14. Dams can block their journey upstream.

15. Specially built fish ladders in some streams can help salmon safely around obstacles such as dams and power plants.

16. Drought can temporarily turn a river into a dry, sandy path.

17. Salmon are eagerly sought by commercial fishing boats.

18. Bears thoroughly enjoy fishing in the salmon-rich streams.

19. Fortunately, hatcheries sometimes can restock streams that have been overfished.

Salmon battle upstream to lay eggs where they themselves once hatched.

Apply

Circle the adverb in each sentence that tells about the underlined word. Then write *how, when, where, how often,* or *to what extent* to tell what the adverb explains.

20. The ability of salmon to find their birthplace once <u>seemed</u> magical. _____

21. One scientist wisely <u>guessed</u> that smell might guide these fish. _____

22. He plugged the noses of salmon, and the fish were completely <u>unable</u> to find their streams of birth.

   _____

23. He next <u>exposed</u> hatching salmon to a certain chemical smell and let them go free in the water.

   _____

24. He spread the chemical smell in a stream, and all of his salmon <u>swam</u> there. _____

25. The sense of smell is extremely <u>important</u> to salmon. _____

Reinforce

Often, adverbs concisely convey information that would otherwise need to be stated in a series of prepositional phrases. Read the sentence below, and circle the eleven adverbs it contains. Remember, adverbs can modify other adverbs. (26–36)

   [The river] ran seemingly straight for a while, turned abruptly, then ran smoothly again, then met

   another obstacle, again was turned sharply and again ran smoothly.

                                    —Norman Maclean, from *A River Runs Through It*

Now rewrite the sentence, replacing as many adverbs as you can with phrases. Then work with a partner to decide which version—the original or your revision—seems clearer and easier to understand.

37. _____

   _____

   _____

   _____

   _____

   _____

   _____

   _____

Read and Analyze

During a storm, rainwater carries small particles **of** soil downhill **into** streams or storm drains.

Which boldfaced word begins a phrase that tells *when*? _____

Which begins a phrase that tells about a noun? _____

Which begins a phrase that tells *where*? _____

A **preposition** shows a relationship between the noun or pronoun that follows the preposition (the **object of the preposition**) and another word or group of words in the sentence. The preposition, its object, and the word(s) between them make a **prepositional phrase**.

See Handbook | Section 20

Practice

Underline each prepositional phrase. Circle the preposition and draw a box around its object.

1. The process of erosion changes the shape of the earth.

2. Water, wind, and ice break solid rock into small pieces.

3. These forces remove soil and rocks from hillsides.

4. After many centuries, a mountain may be reduced to a broad mound.

5. A swift stream can carve a path through a rocky landscape.

6. Creeks in the mountains carry eroded material downward to wide rivers.

7. During a flood, rivers deposit tiny grains of soil across low-lying farmlands.

8. Floods destroy homes, but they increase the fertility of the farmlands.

9. A river may spread soil near its mouth, across a triangle-shaped area.

10. The geographic term for such a region is a delta.

11. Some particles of eroded material eventually reach the ocean.

12. The sand grains on your favorite beach were probably transported to the sea by rivers.

13. They were possibly then carried along the shoreline by a current.

14. Finally some gentle waves carried the tiny grains onto the beach.

15. Rain in the mountains today may be moving grains of sand that someday will stick between your toes!

The force of water can change the shape of landforms.

Apply

Fill each blank with an appropriate preposition from the word bank, or use one of your own. You may use a preposition more than once.

of	with	by	among	from	between	in	on	under	along

16. Trees and other plants hold down soil _____ their roots.

17. When people cut down trees and remove bushes _____ hillsides, rains may carry away large amounts _____ soil.

18. Farmers have developed several methods _____ soil conservation.

19. Strip-cropping involves planting two different crops _____ alternating strips.

20. A soil-holding crop is planted _____ a strip of land _____ grain fields to reduce the amount of soil carried off _____ the wind.

Reinforce

Use the clues to help you complete the crossword puzzle with prepositions. Then circle the object (in the clues) of each preposition you wrote.

Across

1. We looked _____ the canyon to the other side.
3. It was thousands _____ feet wide.
4. Carolyn rose an hour _____ dawn and made hot oatmeal for our breakfast.
6. We decided to start hiking _____ seven A.M., while it would still be cool.
7. A narrow trail led _____ the edge down into the canyon.
8. We descended carefully _____ the canyon.

Down

1. _____ a long time, we reached the river at the bottom.
2. The canyon walls loomed _____ our heads.
5. We drank from our water bottles and splashed some water _____ our faces.
6. The sound of rushing water echoed all _____ us.

Now choose one or more prepositions from the puzzle and use them in a sentence about erosion.

21. _____

_____

Kiesha **and** Reiko went outside **because** they wanted to paint a picture of the moon in the night sky. They stared at the sky for hours, **but** they never did see the moon.

Which boldfaced word links two nouns? _____

Which links two independent clauses? _____

Which begins a dependent clause? _____

Coordinating conjunctions (*and, but, or*) connect words or groups of words (including independent clauses) that are similar. **Subordinating conjunctions** such as *although, because, since, if,* and *before* show how one clause is related to another. Subordinating conjunctions are used at the beginning of adverb clauses.

See Handbook Section 22

Practice

Underline each coordinating conjunction. Circle each subordinating conjunction.

1. The moon often lights up the sky, but sometimes it is not visible at all.

2. The moon's appearance changes nightly, and the times at which it is in the sky vary also.

3. The moon may look like a half circle one night, and a few nights later it may look like a crescent.

4. Over 29 1/2 days, the moon changes from a thin sliver to a full round disc and back again.

5. These changes, or phases, are called new, crescent, quarter, gibbous, and full.

6. People once associated the moon with unreliability because they saw it changing constantly.

7. The moon may have a reputation for unreliability, but it is actually very consistent.

8. Although the moon's appearance varies, it never turns different sides toward Earth.

9. As the moon revolves around Earth, one side permanently faces us.

10. Before lunar probes visited the moon, humans had never seen its far side.

11. The moon's phases occur because the sun's light hits different parts of its face.

12. If you look at a crescent moon through a telescope, you can see the dark part dimly lit by Earth's reflected light.

13. Because that dim light has been reflected by Earth, it is called earthshine.

14. When Earth passes between the sun and the moon, a lunar eclipse occurs.

15. In a partial lunar eclipse, Earth blocks part of the sun's light for a short period of time, and a portion of the moon temporarily becomes dark.

The Moon's Phases

Name _____

Apply

Complete each sentence with a conjunction from the word bank. Write *C* if you used a coordinating conjunction or *S* if you used a subordinating conjunction.

because	but	although	as	and

16. _____ Earth rotates, the moon's gravity pulls on the water in the oceans. _____

17. _____ the moon's gravity is too weak to pull water off Earth, it is strong enough to create bulges. _____

18. _____ Earth is constantly rotating, these bulges move steadily across the face of Earth. _____

19. The bulges of water create high tides _____ low tides. _____

20. Tides are highest during the new moon, when the sun _____ the moon pull the waters in the same direction. _____

21. There are also tides in the air, _____ they can be detected only with sensitive machines. _____

Reinforce

Subordinating conjunctions are commonly used in proverbs, aphorisms, and other wise sayings. In many of these, the subordinating conjunction introduces a clause that tells the conditions under which something is true.

Underline the subordinate clause in each wise saying below; circle each subordinating conjunction.

When the well's dry, we know the worth of water.

Don't throw stones at your neighbors', if your own windows are glass.

Three may keep a secret, if two of them are dead.

—Benjamin Franklin, from *Poor Richard's Almanac*

Now try your hand at writing a proverb, aphorism, or wise saying of your own that includes a subordinating conjunction.

22. _____

_____

_____

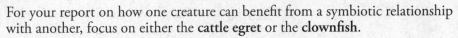

For your report on how one creature can benefit from a symbiotic relationship with another, focus on either the **cattle egret** or the **clownfish**.

Circle the word that joins the two boldfaced nouns. Underline another word that helps this word show how the nouns are linked.

Correlative conjunctions always appear in pairs. They connect words or groups of words and provide more emphasis than coordinating conjunctions. Some common correlative conjunctions are *both...and, either...or, neither...nor, not only...but (also),* and *whether...or.*

See Handbook Section 22

Practice

Circle the correlative conjunctions and coordinating conjunctions in these sentences. If a sentence contains correlative conjunctions, write *COR.* Write *X* if the sentence does not contain correlative conjunctions.

1. When two animal species not only live together but also have a very close relationship, we call them symbiotic. _____

2. Symbiotic relationships can be either parasitic, commensal, or mutual. _____

3. Parasites may hurt their hosts or even kill them. _____

4. In a commensal relationship, the host is neither hurt nor helped by its neighbor. _____

5. Mutual symbiotic relationships involve a cycle of give and take. _____

6. For example, both the cattle egret and the African buffalo benefit from their relationship. _____

7. A buffalo might be infested with skin parasites, but the egret cleans them off. _____

8. In return, the egret gets a tasty meal of both the parasites and the insects the buffalo kicks up from the grass. _____

9. The sea anemone's sting is not only painful but also deadly to most fish. _____

10. Only the clownfish is able to build up immunity to the sting and live in harmony with this dangerous predator. _____

11. The clownfish both lures prey for the anemone and chases away fish that might damage it. _____

12. In return, the anemone provides the clownfish with protection and scraps from its meals. _____

13. If you study either biology or environmental science, you may learn about lichens. _____

14. Lichens, gray-green organisms that live on rocks and trees, appear to be plants but are actually a combination of an alga and a fungus. _____

15. Neither the alga nor the fungus can survive alone. _____

16. The alga produces food for the fungus, and the fungus protects the alga from the drying effects of sun and wind. _____

Apply

Rewrite each sentence pair as one new, shorter sentence using the correlative conjunctions in parentheses.

17. Swollen-thorn acacia trees provide food for acacia ants. The trees provide a home for the ants. (not only/ but also) _____

_____

18. The ants protect the tree from harmful insects. They clear other plants away from it. (both/and)

_____

_____

_____

19. Swollen-thorn acacia trees benefit from their mutual relationship with acacia ants. Acacia ants benefit from the mutual relationship, too. (both/and) _____

_____

_____

20. Acacia ants may be the subject of my oral report. Perhaps clownfish will be the subject of my oral report instead. (either/or) _____

_____

_____

Reinforce

Circle the correct correlative conjunction in each clue. Use information from the lesson to label each symbiotic relationship.

21. (Both/Neither) the host creature and its neighbor benefit in this kind of relationship.

____ ____ ____ ____ ____ ____

22. The host may be (either/neither) hurt or killed in this kind of relationship.

____ ____ ____ ____ ____ ____ ____ ____ ____

23. The host is (either/neither) harmed nor helped in this kind of relationship.

____ ____ ____ ____ ____ ____ ____ ____ ____

Review

Verbs and Verb Tense

Circle each linking verb. Underline each action verb. Label each action verb as transitive (*T*) or intransitive (*I*).

1. Nature's most celebrated cycle is the yearly cycle of seasons. _____

2. Most temperate regions experience four seasons each year. _____

3. The seasons are spring, summer, fall, and winter. _____

4. With each new season, weather and temperatures change. _____

5. In autumn the days become shorter and cooler. _____

6. Winter brings early darkness and cold. _____

7. The days lengthen again in spring. _____

8. Summer is the hottest season in most areas. _____

Circle the main verb in each sentence. Underline each auxiliary verb.

9. You should protect your skin from the strong summer sun.

10. Ultraviolet rays will damage skin over time.

11. I have been using sunscreen regularly this summer.

Circle the word or phrase in parentheses that identifies the tense of each boldfaced verb.

12. In the Southern Hemisphere, summer **begins** in late December. (present/present perfect)

13. Many tourists **will visit** Australia next January. (future/future perfect)

14. Some already **have reserved** hotel rooms. (present/present perfect)

15. Here in the Northern Hemisphere, many of us **will be shoveling** snow in January. (present progressive/future progressive)

16. Last year snow **fell** throughout the Northeast in mid-April. (past/present)

17. During that snowstorm, we **were dreaming** of flying to South America for a long visit. (past perfect/past progressive)

18. A shipment of delicious grapes from Chile **had arrived** in our markets just a few days earlier. (past perfect/past progressive)

19. Chilean farmers **are growing** more fruits and vegetables each year for sale in the United States during our winter and spring months. (simple present/present progressive)

20. By the middle of next March, those farmers **will have harvested** most of their crops. (future perfect/future progressive)

In each sentence, mark an *X* through the verb that makes an inappropriate tense shift. Write the correct form of the verb on the line.

21.   My sister is growing tomatoes this summer; every weekend she sold them at a stand. _____

22.   Last Saturday I helped her at the stand, and she splits her profits with me. _____

Active and Passive Voice

Write *A* after the sentence with a verb in the active voice. Write *P* after the sentence with a verb in the passive voice.

23.   In the mountains, snow is melted by the warm sunshine. _____

24.   At the beach, sunbathers lie on towels and mats. _____

Adverbs and Prepositions

Draw a star above each boldfaced word that is an adverb. Circle each boldfaced word that is a preposition. Underline the prepositional phrase it begins and draw a box around its object.

25.   Knowledge of the cycle of seasons was **very** important to many ancient peoples.

26.   **In** some cultures, astronomers understood the relationships between the length of days and the progression

of seasons.

27.   These ancient scientists **also** learned to use the angle of the sun's rays to identify the longest and shortest

days of the year.

28.   **On** winter's shortest day, people celebrated the approach of spring.

Conjunctions

Circle each coordinating conjunction. Underline each subordinating conjunction. Draw boxes around the two parts of each correlative conjunction.

29.   Plants sense the changing seasons; they sprout, bloom, and drop their leaves according to the

seasonal cycle.

30.   Not only plants but also people can be affected by the seasons.

31.   If people continually feel sad in winter, they may have winter depression.

32.   A lack of sunlight can produce feelings of sadness, anger, or despair.

33.   Since the condition is brought on by reduced amounts of sunlight, doctors renamed it light deprivation

syndrome.

34.   Doctors use either medication or bright sunlamps to treat this condition.

Spelling Practice

Read and Analyze

One of the properties of plants is that they make their own food. Therefore, vegetables such as tomatoes are at the bottom of most food chains.

Circle the plural whose singular form ends in *y*. Underline the plural whose singular form ends in *o*.

Spelling Conventions: Plural Nouns

To form the plural of words ending in a consonant and *y*, change the *y* to *i* and add *-es*, as in *treaty, treaties*. To form the plural of some words ending in *f* or *fe*, change the *f* to *v* and add *-es*, as in *knife, knives*. To form the plural of some words ending in a consonant and *o*, add *-es*, as in *hero, heroes*.

Word Sort

Use the words below to complete the word sort.

potatoes	shelves	passersby	activities	mosquitoes	loaves
mix-ups	fathers-in-law	opportunities	thieves	boundaries	echoes

Consonant + o + -es	**f to v + -es**
y to i + -es	**Plural Compound words**

Pattern Practice

Write the plural form of each word.

1. grocery _____
2. potato _____
3. echo _____
4. shelf _____
5. wolf _____

6. property _____
7. thief _____
8. company _____
9. ability _____
10. editor-in-chief _____

Write the plural form of the word that best completes each sentence.

| boundary | treaty | echo | glossary | potato |
| copy | volcano | knife | mosquito | activity |

11. We should print two _____ of the instructions.

12. The chef has a very expensive set of _____.

13. Those _____ actually haven't erupted for centuries.

14. Conflicts are often resolved with the signing of _____.

15. The _____ of the park are shown on the map.

16. These woods are full of pesky _____.

17. My science and social studies books have helpful _____.

18. The _____ of our voices bounced off the walls of the canyon.

19. The festival included many _____ for small children.

Use the Dictionary

Some plurals are formed by dropping the endings of base words and adding the letter *a*. Write the plural forms of these words. Check your spellings in a print or an online dictionary.

20. datum _____

21. bacterium _____

22. criterion _____

Diagramming Linking Verbs

Notice the difference between these two sentence diagrams.

Hawks eat rodents.   Hawks | eat | rodents   *Rodents* is the object of the action verb, *eat*.

Hawks are predators.   Hawks | are \ predators   *Predators* is a predicate noun that follows the linking verb *are* and renames the subject, *hawks*.

Diagram these sentences yourself. Make a slanting line after each linking verb and a vertical line after each action verb.

1. Hawks are capable hunters.

2. Small animals fear them.

3. Young animals are frequent victims.

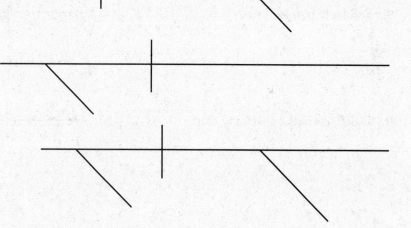

Diagramming Predicate Nouns and Predicate Adjectives

You have learned that a predicate noun follows a linking verb and renames the subject of the sentence. Notice the way a predicate noun is diagrammed.

The osprey is a **hawk**.   osprey | is \ **hawk** / The / a

You have learned that a predicate adjective follows a linking verb and describes the subject of the sentence. Here's how to diagram a predicate adjective.

Ospreys are **powerful**.   Ospreys | are \ **powerful**

Diagram these sentences on another sheet of paper.

4. Carp are bottom-feeders.
5. Many mature carp are orange.
6. That osprey is hungry.
7. Its cry is shrill.

Diagramming Adverbs

You have learned how to diagram sentences containing adjectives (page 37). Like adjectives, adverbs are diagrammed on slanted lines. An adverb is connected to the word it modifies. This model shows how to diagram an adverb.

The osprey circled the river **slowly**.

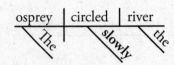

Diagram these sentences to show where the adverb belongs.

8. The big bird watched the water intently.

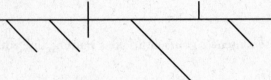

9. Suddenly it dove.

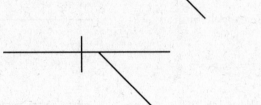

10. It deftly seized a glistening carp.

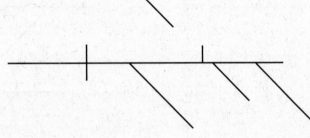

Some adverbs modify other adverbs. Notice how these adverbs are diagrammed.

Ospreys dive **very** swiftly.

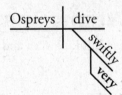

Use what you have learned to diagram these sentences on another piece of paper. Look back at this lesson to recall how to diagram action and linking verbs, adverbs, predicate nouns, and predicate adjectives.

11. Steelhead are large trout.

12. Many steelhead inhabit coastal streams.

13. Steelhead are migratory.

14. They are powerful swimmers.

15. I hooked a large steelhead once.

16. It fought desperately.

17. The steelhead was the uncontested victor.

18. It swam upstream.

19. I was disappointed, but I was impressed.

Writing Sentences

Revise each sentence written in the passive voice so that it is in the active voice. Revise each sentence in which the coordinating conjunction and the dependent clause are misplaced so that the sentence makes sense.

1. Although springtime is still months away, days grow longer after the winter solstice. _____
   _____
   _____

2. Because animals shed their winter coats, the air temperature grows warmer. _____
   _____
   _____

3. The cycle of the seasons is demonstrated by longer days, warmer temperatures, and renewed plant life.
   _____
   _____

4. As the landscape looks alive again, new buds form on trees. _____
   _____
   _____

5. Every year the winter solstice is celebrated by people in some cultures. _____
   _____
   _____

6. The longer, warmer days of spring are welcomed by most people. _____
   _____
   _____

A well-written paragraph has a topic sentence, at least two or three supporting sentences, and a concluding sentence. Your reader will understand your writing more easily if you use correct verb tenses, temporal (time-order) words, and clear linking words and phrases. Notice how this model paragraph is written.

topic sentence _____

temporal words

verb tense

transition sentence

concluding sentence _____

Every year my family celebrates the coming of summer with a camping trip. Last year we ***went*** to Yellowstone National Park in June. This year we ***will go*** to Crater Lake, Oregon. **Although sleeping out in the open is fun, what I like best about our camping trips is fishing.** My sister and I ***have caught*** trout, steelhead, and salmon in some of America's most beautiful streams. *Nothing beats wide-open spaces, clean air, and the smell of fish sizzling over the fire.*

Writing a Paragraph

The sentences you revised on page 147 can be used to make a paragraph. Decide what order the sentences should be in. If necessary, add linking or temporal words to make the sentences flow more easily. Write the paragraph on the lines below.

_____

_____

_____

_____

_____

_____

_____

Write a personal narrative about what you do at your favorite annual event. A personal narrative is a passage about a real experience you have had in which you refer to yourself as *I*. Make sure you use verb tenses correctly. Also, make sure you use clear linking and temporal words and phrases to help your reader follow changes in place, time, or idea. Use the paragraph at the bottom of page 147 as a model.

_____

_____

_____

_____

_____

_____

_____

_____

Reread your paragraph. Use this checklist to make sure it follows the style of a personal narrative.

❑ Does my paragraph have a topic sentence?

❑ Have I written in the first-person voice?

❑ Have I included temporal and linking words to create clear transitions that make my personal narrative easy to follow?

❑ Have I used verb tenses correctly?

❑ Does my paragraph have a concluding sentence?

Proofreading
Practice

Read this passage about a mini-ecosystem that exists inside an acorn and find the mistakes. Use the proofreading marks below to show how each mistake should be fixed. Use a dictionary to check and correct spellings.

Proofreading Marks

Mark	Means	Example
℘	delete	Many creatures maked their home inside an acorn.
∧	add	Many creatures make their home inside a acorn.
≡	make into an uppercase letter	many creatures make their home inside an acorn.
(sp)	fix spelling	Many creetures make their home inside an acorn.
⊙	add a period	Many creatures make their home inside an acorn
/	make into a lowercase letter	Many creatures make their home inside an Acorn.

More Than Just an Acorn

Would you beleive that the humble acorn is responsible for the survival of numerous creatures in the wild? If you don't. Just crack open an acorn. Inside you will find all kinds of creatures flourishing. Living off the acorn but also one another. Even before an acorn is full ripe, insects burrow or gnaw their way into its shell. Acorn weevils dig holes with their tiny, sharp teeth? After dining on the nutmeat. The females lay their eggs inside the shell. The eggs hatch, and the larvae had fed on the soft flesh within the acorn. Once the acorn falls to the ground, the now fully grown larvae emerge, squeezing through a whole they gnaw in the shell!

A whole host of creatures, looking for sustenance, may find their way into a fallen acorn. These creatures, as well as the parasites that live off them, make they're home inside it. They enter the shell through holes and cracks created by previous insect residents. Or by the fall from the tree. The nutmeat offer them nourishment, and the shell offers shelter from the sun the wind.

even decaying acorns attract a variety of creatures. Scavengers look for remains left by other insects Carnivores had gone from acorn to acorn looking for prey inside the shells Empty acorn shells serve as houses for both small insects, such as the tiny fungus beetle, and larger ones, such as the slug

Birds and animals hoard acorns for the winter by burying them in the soil. More than a few are forgotten. Some of the luckily survivors take root and grow into oak trees. in doing so they beginning a new cycle, and in time they will produce acorns that will sustain new generations of tiny creatures.

Proofreading
Checklist

You can use the list below to help you find and fix mistakes in your own writing. Write the titles of your own stories or reports in the blanks at the top of the chart. Then use the questions to check your work. Make a check mark (✓) in each box after you have checked that item.

Proofreading Checklist for Unit 4

	Titles			
Have I used colorful action verbs in sentences?				
Have I used the simple tense, the perfect tense, and the progressive verb forms correctly?				
Have I used adverbs and prepositions effectively?				
Have I used correlative conjunctions correctly?				

Also Remember…

Have I written complete sentences?				
Does each sentence begin with an uppercase letter?				
Have I included correct end punctuation?				
Did I use a dictionary to check and correct spellings?				

Your Own List
Use this space to write your own list of things to check in your writing.

Community Connection

In Unit 4 of *Grammar, Usage, and Mechanics,* students learned about **verbs, adverbs, prepositions,** and **conjunctions** and used what they learned to improve their own writing. The content of these lessons focuses on the theme **Cycles in Nature.** As students completed the exercises, they learned about things in the natural world that follow a cyclical pattern, from ocean tides to migration. These pages offer a variety of activities that reinforce skills and concepts presented in the unit. They also provide opportunities for students to make connections between the materials in the lessons and the community at large.

Animal Migration

Conduct research about animal migration in the United States to find out what animals, if any, pass through or near your community as they migrate. Follow these steps to aid your research:

- Find out if you live near any major paths of bird migration, especially one of the four main flyways (the Pacific, Central, Mississippi, or Atlantic flyway).
- Learn about the routes that are followed by other long-distance migrants, such as monarch butterflies or gray whales.
- Look for migratory patterns of animals indigenous to your region or state. Keep in mind that some animals migrate over relatively short distances. For instance, mule deer migrate between mountains in the summer and valleys in the winter.

If you discover that some animals come near your community during migration, find out when they are most likely to be nearby. If possible, try to see the animals as they pass through your area.

Unnatural Cycles

In imitation of nature, people have created cyclical systems to organize or regulate human activities. For example, the repeated green-yellow-red cycle of a traffic light is used to control the flow of traffic. List as many artificial cycles as you can; describe what purpose each one was invented to serve.

The Cycle of Life

Insects develop in one of three basic ways: through simple growth, incomplete metamorphosis, or complete metamorphosis. Research the life cycle of one insect from each of these three groups:

Simple growth: silverfish, springtail

Incomplete metamorphosis: grasshopper, roach, dragonfly, cicada

Complete metamorphosis: butterfly, moth, beetle, bee, ant

Develop a chart that illustrates the life cycles of the three insects you have chosen.

Who Works With Cycles in Nature?

Many occupations are affected by cycles in nature. Some examples include farmers, park rangers, snowplow operators, astronomers, biologists, and lifeguards.

Work with a partner to add some other jobs to your list. Then think of someone in your community who does one of these jobs, and arrange to interview her or him. Prepare your questions in advance. Use the planning guide on page 152 to help you plan the interview. Take notes during the interview, and share the results of the interview with your class.

Name _____

Interview Planner

Person I am interviewing:

Name _____

Age _____

Occupation _____

Number of years employed in that field _____

Date of interview: _____

Questions to ask:

1. _____
   _____

2. _____
   _____

3. _____
   _____

4. _____
   _____

5. _____
   _____

6. _____
   _____

7. _____
   _____

8. _____
   _____

Notes:

_____

_____

_____

_____

_____

You're going to have such fun in Hawaii. Don't forget **your** swimsuit!

Circle the boldfaced word that shows ownership. Underline the boldfaced word that means "you are."

The words *your* and *you're* sound alike but have different spellings and meanings. *Your* is a possessive pronoun and shows ownership. *You're* is a contraction made from the words *you* and *are*.

See Handbook Section 33

Practice

Read the conversation below. Circle the word in parentheses that completes each sentence correctly. (1–17)

"It's so great that (your/you're) aunt invited you to Hawaii," said Rita.

"(Your/ You're) really going to enjoy it."

"What did you like best about (your/you're) visit?" asked May.

"My favorite part was the luau we attended. You should definitely ask (your/you're) aunt to take you to a luau."

"I'm sorry, but I don't know what (your/you're) talking about," said May.

"A luau is a modern version of a traditional Hawaiian feast. Be sure to take (your/you're) appetite when you go!"

"I'll take (your/you're) advice. But what does the word *luau* mean?"

"It refers to the young tops of the taro root. They're always part of the feast.

Many Hawaiian luaus feature hula dancing.

The centerpiece of a luau is kalua pig. It's roasted in an imu, a hot pit dug into the ground and layered with stones and banana stalks. These days, (your/you're) given other food, too, such as fish or chicken."

"(Your/You're) making me hungry!" May exclaimed.

"Another traditional food is poi," Rita added. "That's a dish made of fermented taro root. I'm not sure (your/you're) going to like it, but you should try it anyway."

"What was (your/you're) favorite part of the luau?" May asked.

"I really enjoyed the hula dancing. Traditionally, it was performed as a way of telling history or praising a great Hawaiian leader. (Your/You're) not going to believe this, but I even tried some hula dancing myself!"

"(Your/You're) kidding!" exclaimed May. "Was it hard?"

"(Your/You're) really self-conscious at first, but then (your/you're) shyness goes away. You follow the leader, pay attention to the chant, and move (your/you're) hands and feet."

"So show me (your/you're) hula photos!" demanded May, smiling.

Name _____

Apply

Imagine that you are at the beach in Hawaii and a friend asks you these questions. Answer each question with a complete sentence. Use *your* or *you're* in each answer.

18. Am I wearing my snorkel correctly? _____
_____

19. Do you want to borrow my flippers? _____
_____

20. Do you think I'm a strong enough swimmer to try surfing? _____
_____

21. Do you think I'm going to be able to stand on the surfboard? _____
_____

22. Would you like to use my board? _____
_____

23. Have you seen my bottle of sunscreen? _____
_____

24. Am I getting sunburned? _____
_____

Reinforce

Words like *your* and *you're* that sound alike but have different spellings and meanings are called homophones.

Each sentence below uses one or more homophones incorrectly. Circle the misused word(s) in each one. Then write the correct word(s) on the line.

25. The son beet down on the beach. _____

26. The sand was hot on our bear feet. _____

27. The hula told a tail of the island long ago. _____

28. The pig was roasted in a whole in the ground. _____

29. We eight a lot of that tasty meet. _____

30. To of us went to here Hawaiian music. _____

31. The ukulele player inn the band was grate! _____

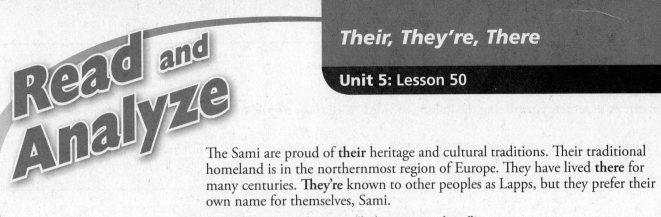

Read and Analyze

The Sami are proud of **their** heritage and cultural traditions. Their traditional homeland is in the northernmost region of Europe. They have lived **there** for many centuries. **They're** known to other peoples as Lapps, but they prefer their own name for themselves, Sami.

Which boldfaced word means "belonging to them"? _____

Which means "they are"? _____

Which means "in that place"? _____

The words **their, they're,** and **there** sound the same but have different meanings and spellings. *Their* is a possessive pronoun that means "belonging to them." *They're* is a contraction that means "they are." *There* is an adverb and usually means "in that place." *There* may also be used as an introductory word.

See Handbook Section 33

Practice

Circle the word in parentheses that correctly completes each sentence.

1. Today about half of the Sami people make (their/they're/there) homes in northern Norway.

2. (Their/They're/There) ancestors came to northern Scandinavia more than 8,000 years ago.

3. Sami people have herded, hunted, fished, and gathered berries (their/they're/there) for centuries.

4. (Their/They're/There) language is related to Finnish and Estonian.

5. The rugged, treeless lands of northern Norway may appear barren to outsiders, but (their/they're/there) home to abundant wildlife.

6. Reindeer flourish (their/they're/there); in winter they eat lichen, which is plentiful in Arctic regions.

7. The Sami have herded reindeer for a very long time; this animal has been (their/they're/there) most important single source of food and clothing.

8. The Sami divide (their/they're/there) year into eight seasons, all of which relate to reindeer activities.

9. Many Sami who do not herd reindeer make (their/they're/there) living from the sea.

10. (Their/They're/There) known as skillful seafarers, fishers, and hunters of seals.

11. (Their/They're/There) are also many Sami who are artists, farmers, writers, educators, and musicians.

Many Sami brides and grooms wear traditional Sami costumes.

12. Sami students can formally study (their/they're/there) traditional language in major Norwegian universities.

13. The Sami people of Norway now have (their/they're/there) own parliament.

Name _____

Apply

Rewrite each sentence, replacing the boldfaced words with *their, they're,* or *there.*

14. If you visit the town of Kautokeino at Easter, you may see many people in bright blue and red clothing

   in that place. _____

   _____

15. Long ago, the Sami wore these outfits as everyday clothing; today **these outfits** are worn only at festivals and

   special events. _____

   _____

16. Sami people are famous for **the Sami people's** unusual form of song, called *joik.* _____

   _____

17. These songs are sung and hummed without instrumental accompaniment; **these songs are** composed for many

   occasions, including courtship. _____

   _____

Reinforce

Find the mistakes in the dialogue in this cartoon. Then rewrite the dialogue, correcting the errors, on the lines below.

18. _____

   _____

19. _____

   _____

Russia is known throughout the world for **its** great composers, ballet dancers, and especially writers. **It's** not unusual for the works of Tolstoy and Dostoevsky to be listed among the greatest novels ever written.

Circle the boldfaced word that means "it is." Underline the boldfaced word that shows ownership.

Its and *it's* sound the same but are spelled differently and have different meanings. *Its* is a possessive pronoun; it means "belonging to it." *It's* is a contraction that means "it is" or "it has." The apostrophe takes the place of the missing letter(s).

See Handbook | Section 33

Practice

Circle the words in parentheses to complete these sentences correctly. (1–16)

(It's/Its) an understatement to say that Russia is a big country. (It's/Its) land stretches across eleven time zones. (It's/Its) population includes many peoples with distinct cultural backgrounds. (It's/Its) history is dramatic and turbulent. For centuries (it's/its) people were dominated by the Mongols of eastern Asia. (It's/Its) rather surprising that the great music, art, and literature of Russia are so much a part of the European tradition.

The link between the arts in Russia and the rest of Europe began in 1682. In that year Peter the Great became the czar, or ruler, of Russia. He was determined to make (it's/its) way of life more modern. Peter admired the arts of Europe and brought several of (it's/its) most skillful architects to Russia to create great buildings.

In the middle of the eighteenth century, European music became popular in Russia. Russian classical music reached (it's/its) height more than 100 years later. (It's/Its) likely that you have heard Peter Ilyich Tchaikovsky's music for the ballet *Swan Lake*. (It's/Its) played and broadcast almost everywhere. So is his music for another popular ballet, *The Nutcracker*.

Tchaikovsky composed the music for several ballets, including *Swan Lake*.

Ballet did not begin in Russia, but many of (it's/its) greatest choreographers and dancers have come from there. The Bolshoi Ballet of Moscow, Russia's capital, tours the world; (it's/its) considered to be one of the greatest classical ballet companies of our time.

At the heart of Russia's culture are (it's/its) great poet, Alexander Pushkin, and (it's/its) most celebrated novelists, Leo Tolstoy and Fyodor Dostoevsky. Tolstoy's *War and Peace* and *Anna Karenina* are long, complex books, as is Dostoevsky's *Crime and Punishment*. (It's/Its) not easy for readers to finish these books, but those who do are richly rewarded, for these writers are unmatched in their storytelling.

Name _____

Apply

Write *its* or *it's* to complete each sentence correctly. Remember to capitalize a word that begins a sentence.

17. Russia is also known for _____ superb playwrights.

18. _____ almost impossible to study theater without reading the plays of Anton Chekhov.

19. _____ rare for a great play to be considered both a comedy and a tragedy.

20. *The Cherry Orchard* has moments of comedy among _____ tragic events.

Reinforce

Charles Lutwidge Dodgson, who used the pen name Lewis Carroll, wrote two immensely popular fantasies, *Alice's Adventures in Wonderland* and *Through the Looking-Glass*. In these works, Dodgson, who was a mathematician by profession, presented characters who argue whether particular statements are nonsensical.

The passages below have been printed without apostrophes. Read each passage and add apostrophes to the contractions. Then work with a partner to decide whether what each character is saying makes sense.

"Take some more tea," the March Hare said to Alice, very earnestly.

"Ive had nothing yet," Alice replied in an offended tone: "so I cant take more."

"You mean you cant take *less*," said the Hatter: "its very easy to take *more* than nothing."

—*Alice's Adventures in Wonderland*

"Theres no use trying," she said: "one cant believe impossible things."

"I daresay you havent had much practice," said the Queen. "When I was your age, I always did it for

half-an-hour a day. Why, sometimes Ive believed as many as six impossible things before breakfast."

—*Through the Looking-Glass*

"The rule is, jam tomorrow, and jam yesterday—but never jam today."

"It must come sometimes to 'jam today,'" Alice objected.

"No, it cant," said the Queen. "Its jam every other day: today isnt any other day, you know."

—*Through the Looking-Glass*

"**Who's** familiar with the traditions of the Maasai people?" asked the speaker from Tanzania.

"Aren't the Maasai a people **whose** traditional way of life involves cattle herding?" responded Frank.

Underline the boldfaced word that means "who is." Circle the boldfaced word that shows ownership.

Who's and *whose* sound alike but are spelled differently and have different meanings. *Whose* shows ownership or possession. *Who's* is a contraction of "who is" or "who has."

See Handbook Section 33

Practice

Circle the correct word in parentheses.

1. "The Maasai, (who's/whose) traditional homelands are in Kenya and Tanzania, are known for strength and bravery," said the speaker.

2. "(Who's/Whose) willing to face a lion with only a few simple weapons?" she then asked the students.

3. "Young Maasai (who's/whose) job it is to guard the village's cows and goats must be alert for predators of many kinds," the speaker continued.

4. "(Who's/Whose) interested in learning more about Maasai life today?" she asked next.

5. "Many cultural programs in Tanzania are run by Maasai (who's/whose) goal is to educate visitors about the lives of Maasai people today," she explained.

6. "Aren't the Maasai the people (who's/whose) traditional diet includes only meat and milk?" asked Isabel.

7. "Yes, but now many Maasai eat *ugali,* which is made of corn meal," replied the speaker. "(Who's/Whose) eaten foods made of corn meal?"

8. "Anyone (who's/whose) eaten tamales has eaten corn meal," said Dexter.

9. "So the Maasai are a people (who's/whose) culture is changing?" asked Debra.

10. "(Who's/Whose) surprised to hear that some Maasai live very modern lives, while others continue to live in traditional ways?" asked the speaker.

11. "My friend Gerald, (who's/whose) a true Maasai warrior, has two daughters studying computer science in India," she explained.

12. "I believe that a people (who's/whose) children are well-educated have a bright future," she concluded.

Name _____

Apply

Write a question to go with each answer below. Use *who's* or *whose* in each question you write.

13. My sister is downloading photos of Maasai villagers. _____
_____

14. The man in the red cloak is a Maasai warrior. _____
_____

15. The tall woman's necklace has the most beads on it. _____
_____

16. Our family hopes to visit East Africa someday. _____
_____

17. My sister is going to study Swahili. _____
_____

18. Residents of Kenya, Tanzania, and other East African countries speak Swahili. _____
_____

Maasai children herd livestock and take care of younger brothers and sisters.

Reinforce

Look on the Internet or in a geographic magazine to find pictures of a people whose traditional way of life interests you. Write four questions about what the pictures show; use *who's* or *whose* in each question. Then show the pictures to a classmate and have him or her answer the questions.

19. _____

20. _____

21. _____

22. _____

Have you traveled **to** Brazil? You might hear samba music there. **Two** friends of mine can play samba drum beats. I'm learning a samba beat, **too.**

Which boldfaced word names a number? _____ Which means "in the direction of"? _____ Which means "also"? _____

The words *to, too,* and *two* sound the same but have different meanings and spellings. *To* can be a preposition that means "in the direction of." *To* can also be used with a verb to form an infinitive, as in the sentence *We like to play the drums. Too* is an adverb and means "also" or "excessively." *Two* means the number 2.

See Handbook Section 33

Practice

Circle the word in parentheses that correctly completes each sentence.

1. Have you listened (to/too/two) samba music?

2. If you travel (to/too/two) Brazil, you will surely hear this distinctive mix of three musical traditions.

3. For thousands of years, Brazil's indigenous Indians had chanted (to/too/two) rhythmic sounds of rattles, panpipes, and flutes.

4. In the 1500s, (to/too/two) other groups arrived in Brazil: Portuguese and Africans.

5. Portuguese settlers brought captured Africans to Brazil (to/too/two) work on plantations there.

6. The captured Africans would play the music of their homeland (to/too/two) lighten their spirits.

7. In time, they began playing European instruments, (to/too/two).

8. (To/Too/Two) of the instruments they picked up were tambourine and guitar; accordion was another.

9. Over the years, (to/too/two) uniquely Brazilian kinds of music resulted from the blend of these three cultures: samba and the more modern bossa nova.

10. (To/Too/Two) popular types of samba are hill samba and theme samba.

11. Hill samba is very exciting (to/too/two) hear; it is performed by a large group on drums and other percussion instruments.

12. During Carnival parades, colorfully clad dancers march (to/too/two) theme samba; theme samba has a lead singer, a chorus, and a percussion section.

13. There are many other types of samba, (to/too/two).

14. Samba has given rise (to/too/two) other forms of music, most notably bossa nova in the 1950s and 1960s.

15. Bossa nova is less percussive than most types of samba; it's more harmonious, (to/too/two).

Drums and other percussion instruments are the backbone of samba music.

Name _____

Apply

Write *too, to,* or *two* to complete each sentence correctly.

Brazil

Pacific Ocean

Atlantic Ocean

16. My family is going _____ Brazil next summer.

17. We're going to be there for about _____ weeks.

18. I'm not _____ sure where we're going yet.

19. Hopefully, we'll visit São Paulo; I'd enjoy visiting

    Rio de Janeiro, _____.

20. I might try _____ take a samba drumming workshop

    while I'm there.

21. I've been drumming for _____ years now.

22. Samba beats are still _____ tricky for me to play in public.

23. I want _____ learn to speak Portuguese, the language of Brazil.

24. I like _____ listen to recordings and repeat what I hear.

25. I do lessons in a workbook, _____.

Reinforce

To, too, and *two* are homophones; they sound the same but are spelled differently. These riddles are based on other homophones.

Question: How can you tell
when food goes bad?
Answer: Your nose knows.

Question: Why was the race rough?

Answer: The course was coarse.

Choose three of the following sets of homophones to create your own riddles. Write them on the lines below. Use a dictionary to check the meaning of any word you don't know.

to/too/two	course/coarse	bored/board	vain/vein	see/sea
scent/cent/sent	wail/whale	bolder/boulder	pair/pear	heel/heal

26. _____

_____

27. _____

_____

28. _____

_____

The Braemar Gathering is more famous **than** any other Highland games event. It is said to date back to the eleventh century. King Malcolm III ruled Scotland **then**.

Which boldfaced word is used to make a comparison? _____

Which is used to talk about time? _____

Than and *then* sound similar but are different words with different spellings and meanings. *Than* is a subordinating conjunction used to make comparisons, as in the sentence *Malcolm is younger than Derrick*. *Then* can be an adverb that tells about time. It can also mean "therefore."

See Handbook | Section 33

Practice

Circle the correct word in parentheses to complete each sentence.

1. I've never had more fun (than/then) I did at the Braemar Gathering last year.

2. We flew into Aberdeen and (than/then) drove to Braemar in the Scottish Highlands.

3. Highland games take place throughout the summer in Scotland; many tourists visit (than/then).

4. The Braemar games are more famous (than/then) Highland games held elsewhere.

5. They are much larger (than/then) Scottish games held here in the States.

6. People were wearing more patterns of plaid (than/then) I thought existed.

7. A boy presented Queen Elizabeth with a bouquet, and (than/then) the festivities began.

8. One band marched onto the field, and (than/then) another and another until the sound of bagpipes echoed through the hills.

9. (Than/Then) groups began performing traditional dances.

10. Each one was more impressive (than/then) the last.

The length and weight of a caber varies.

11. There were many more competitions (than/then) I expected.

12. First we watched the Stone Put, and (than/then) we watched the Tossing the Caber event.

13. One of the stones in the men's Stone Put event is much heavier (than/then) the shot in men's shot put.

14. In Tossing the Caber, each competitor runs with a very long piece of wood on his shoulder and (than/then) tosses it.

15. In my opinion, the Braemar Gathering is more fun (than/then) the Summer Olympics.

16. If you find yourself in Scotland on the first Saturday of September, (than/then) you should definitely make your way to Braemar!

Name _____

Apply

Write a sentence that follows each direction. Use *then* or *than* in each answer.

17. Compare two games you enjoy. _____

_____

18. Write simple instructions for beginning a game. _____

_____

19. Compare two kinds of music. _____

_____

20. Imagine you are watching a Highland games event. In order, tell about three things that you see. _____

_____

_____

21. Describe two things you would do to plan a trip to Scotland. _____

_____

22. Compare a kilt to traditional clothing from another culture. _____

_____

23. Name one event you attended last summer. _____

Reinforce

People often confuse words that sound similar. Decide which word from the word bank should be used in place of each boldfaced word. Then write the correct word on the line.

descent	formally	precede	accept	accent

24. I'm afraid I cannot **except** your invitation to the party. _____

25. An opening ceremony will **proceed** the first event. _____

26. His Scottish **ascent** was quite strong, so I had to listen carefully. _____

27. My father is of Scottish **decent**, but my mother is not. _____

28. Scotsmen wear kilts when they are **formerly** attired. _____

a. Some visitors say that there isn't no country friendlier than Thailand.

b. My aunt says that she never encountered an unfriendly person there.

Which sentence uses too many negative words? _____

Which uses negatives correctly? _____

A **negative** is a word that means "no" or "not." The words *no, not, nothing, none, never, nowhere,* and *nobody* are negatives. The negative word *not* is found in contractions such as *don't* and *wasn't.* It is a convention of standard English to use only one negative word to express a negative idea. Use the contraction *doesn't* with singular subjects. Use the contraction *don't* with plural subjects and with *I* and *you.* 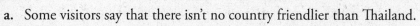 **Remember to use this information when you speak, too.**

See Handbook | Section 26

Practice

Underline the correct expression in parentheses to complete each sentence.

1. Because they value harmony, Thai people try not to make (no one/anyone) feel uncomfortable.

2. Traditionally, a stranger (isn't never/isn't ever) treated as an intruder.

3. Even if a family has very little food, they will (never/ever) let a visitor go hungry.

4. Most Thai residents practice Buddhism, which in general does not encourage (no/any) conflict.

5. Friendships are very important in this nation; a Thai person (won't/will) let nothing stand in the way of helping a close friend.

6. In Thai village life especially, nothing (is/isn't) more important than family.

7. It isn't (unusual/not unusual) for several generations of a family to live together in adjacent homes.

8. Young family members must (never/ever) be disrespectful of their elders.

9. Even among brothers and sisters, younger ones aren't (never/ever) permitted to disobey older ones.

10. Don't be surprised to see (no/a) young child leading a huge buffalo out of the village to graze.

11. In general, children in the United States do not have (no/any) responsibilities as significant as those that Thai children of the same age have.

12. Many Thai babies aren't given Thai official names by (no/a) parent; they receive a name from the village's religious leader.

13. Soon, though, the baby will be given a nickname, and family and friends will use this name, (not/not never) the official one.

14. Because so many Thai people are friendly and speak English, you shouldn't have (no/any) trouble learning more about Thai customs if you visit that nation.

Name _____

Apply

Rewrite each sentence so that it uses negatives correctly. There is more than one way to change each one.

15. No shopping mall isn't as interesting as the floating markets of Thailand. _____

_____

16. A friend told my dad and me that we shouldn't never pay the first price mentioned by no salesperson. _____

_____

17. Neither of us hadn't never gone shopping in a boat before. _____

_____

18. There isn't no space on neither bank of the canal that isn't occupied by no shop. _____

_____

19. I didn't want to buy no more than one purse or handbag, but the shops had so many cool ones that I couldn't

never make up my mind. _____

_____

20. We didn't feel no hunger, because we kept buying snacks from vendors with cookstoves on their boats!

_____

_____

Reinforce

Write a positive answer and a negative answer to each question about a Thai tourist experience.

21. Would you like to ride on an elephant for an hour?

(positive) _____

(negative) _____

22. Are vegetables with flames leaping from them your idea of a great meal?

(positive) _____

(negative) _____

23. Do you have any desire to sample very spicy food?

(positive) _____

(negative) _____

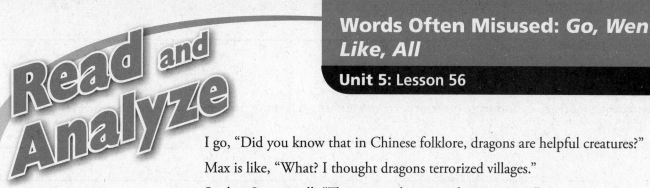
I go, "Did you know that in Chinese folklore, dragons are helpful creatures?"

Max is like, "What? I thought dragons terrorized villages."

So then Jenna is all, "Those are video game dragons, Max!"

Has this conversation been written in formal language or informal language?
_____ **Cross out the words that indicate that someone is speaking. Write *said* above the words you crossed out.**

Go and *went* mean "move(d)." *Is like* means "resembles something." *All* means "the total of something." In your written work and in polite conversation, avoid using *goes, went, (is) all,* or *(is) like* to mean "said." Also be careful not to insert the word *like* where it doesn't belong, as in the sentence *This is, like, the best day ever.* **Remember to use this information when you speak, too.**

See Handbook | Section 32

Practice

Cross out *go, went, all,* or *like* if these words are used incorrectly. (If a form of the verb *be* is part of the incorrect expression, cross it out also.) (1–13)

My sister and I were telling Max about our trip to Hong Kong. I go, "Would you like to hear about the dragon boat races?"

And Max is all, "What are the boats like?"

Jenna is like, "The boats are so impressive! Some of them are, like, one hundred feet long! They have a dragon head at the front of the boat and a tail at the end. A big one may carry, like, fifty paddlers, an oarsman, and a drummer who sets the pace."

Some dragon boats are one hundred feet long.

Then Max goes, "Who do the boats belong to—sports teams?"

I was all, "I think each boat belongs to a particular village or organization."

Jenna went, "People say that the boat races are held to remember a man named Qu Yuan who lived more than 2,000 years ago. He was, like, a great poet and also an advisor to the emperor. He tried to get the emperor to reform the government in order to bring peace to China."

And I went, "The emperor not only rejected Qu Yuan's advice but also told him to leave the kingdom forever! This made Qu Yuan very sad, so he went to the river to write. That was, like, the last time anyone saw him."

Then Max is all, "But what does that have to do with dragon boat races?"

Jenna went, "When Qu Yuan disappeared, people raced around in their boats looking for him. Today the dragon boats race around as if looking for Qu Yuan."

Name _____

Apply

Rewrite each sentence to eliminate incorrect expressions. There is more than one way to rewrite each sentence.

14. Jenna was like, "Let's have our own dragon boat race!" _____

_____

15. I go, "What do you mean?" _____

_____

16. Jenna goes, "We'll get some friends together and rent canoes at the lake." _____

_____

17. Max was like, "Canoes don't look like dragon boats!" _____

_____

18. But she goes, "We'll make dragon heads and tails out of papier mâché. _____

_____

19. Immediately Max was like, "I'll be the drummer in our canoe!" _____

_____

20. I shook my head and went, "We need you to help row the boat!" _____

_____

Reinforce

Many verbs, including *asked, answered, replied, added, exclaimed, remarked, suggested, began, continued, cried, whispered, grumbled,* and *yelled,* may be used to tell how a character is speaking. Using a variety of verbs for this purpose not only makes writing more interesting, it also has a dramatic effect on the mood of a direct quotation.

Choose verbs from the word bank to complete the sentence frame in six different ways. Notice how each verb gives the sentence a different mood.

muttered	shouted	gasped	boomed	wailed	sighed	mumbled	breathed
growled	thundered	hissed	grumbled	whispered	giggled	screeched	sniffed

21. "I know," he _____.   24. "I know," he _____.

22. "I know," he _____.   25. "I know," he _____.

23. "I know," he _____.   26. "I know," he _____.

Before a Japanese tea ceremony, the Tea Master carefully **sets** out utensils.

The guests will **sit** on mats, not in chairs.

I should **lie** down before the ceremony. I'm tired!

Would you hand me my guidebook? I **laid** it on the chair.

Which boldfaced word means "move your body into a chair"? _____

Which means "recline"? _____

Which boldfaced words mean "place or put something somewhere"?

_____ _____

Lie and *lay* are different verbs. *Lay* takes a direct object and *lie* does not. *Lie* means "to recline." *Lay* means "to put something down somewhere." The past tense form of *lie* is *lay,* and the past participle form is *lain.* The past tense form of *lay* is *laid,* and the past participle form is also *laid.* *Set* and *sit* are different verbs, too. *Set* takes a direct object and *sit* does not. If you're about to use *set,* ask yourself, "Set what?" If you can't answer that question, use *sit.* Also, remember that you can't sit anything down—you must set it down. The past tense form of *sit* is *sat,* and the past participle form is also *sat.* *Set* is one of the few verbs that does not change in past or past participle form. **Remember to use this information when you speak, too.**

See Handbook | Section 32

Practice

Underline the word in parentheses that correctly completes each sentence.

1. Get up, Miki! You have (laid/lain) in bed all morning.

2. I'm going to (sit/set) your breakfast here to entice you to get up.

3. The tea ceremony starts at noon, so we can't (sit/set) around all day!

4. Did you see where I (sit/set) the pamphlet about the ceremony?

5. I think I (lay/laid) it on the dresser.

6. It says that everyone at a tea ceremony must follow a strict etiquette; even where and how guests (sit/set) is important.

7. Before the ceremony, the host, or Tea Master, (sits/sets) out tea utensils.

8. The Tea Master will hand you a bamboo ladle of water; use it to wash your hands and rinse your mouth and then carefully (lie/lay) it down.

9. When guests arrive, they politely remove their shoes and (sit/set) them outside the door.

10. Remember, you can't just (lie/lay) down on the *tatami* mat.

11. You must (sit/set) with your legs folded neatly beneath you.

12. When the Tea Master (sits/sets) your *matcha*, or traditional powdered tea, before you, you must turn the bowl in this way in order to admire it.

In a Japanese tea ceremony, a skilled Tea Master prepares a powdered green tea.

Name _____

Apply

Rewrite each sentence using a form of *sit, set, lie,* or *lay.* There is more than one way to rewrite each sentence.

13. Miki placed her shoes outside the door. _____

_____

14. She bowed to the host and took a seat on the tatami mat. _____

_____

15. Her sister had told her to admire the food that was placed before her. _____

_____

16. The Tea Master placed the tea on a lacquered table. _____

_____

17. Miki wanted to recline on the mats, but I had warned her not to. _____

_____

18. Miki put her bowl down too quickly, and it knocked against the tray. _____

_____

19. She wished that she had placed it on the tray silently. _____

_____

20. On the bus back to the Tokyo Hotel, Miki told me to take a seat by the window. _____

_____

Reinforce

Even professional writers sometimes make mistakes with word choices. Look at the following examples from published works. Correct each sentence by replacing the boldfaced word.

21. From a book review: "Rosa roams afield while Julie **lays** and writes." _____

22. From a story about basketball players: "...they **laid** on the floor." _____

23. From an ad for swimsuits: "Choose from one or two pieces in all these exciting styles for the beach or

laying in the sun." _____

24. From a *National Geographic Adventure* mailer: "A croc hits you with his tail, then drags you to the bottom

and **lays** on you until you are drowned." _____

25. From an Associated Press report: "The six participants **laid** down on the hogan's earthen floor to sleep

around 4 A.M." _____

Read and Analyze

The Spanish **brang** many things from the New World back to Europe. They **took** many fruits and vegetables that they had never **seen** before.

Cross out the boldfaced word that is an incorrect verb form.

Many commonly used verbs are **irregular**; they do not add *-ed* in the past tense. Here are some of the verbs:

Present	Past	With *has, have,* or *had*
take	took	taken
see	saw	seen
grow	grew	grown
spring	sprang	sprung
bring	brought	brought
make	made	made

Remember to use this information when you speak, too.

See Handbook Section 18d

Practice

Circle the correct verb form in parentheses in each sentence.

1. Many foods enjoyed in Mexico today are foods that the Aztecs (eaten/ate) long ago.

2. Corn, or maize, (grew/growed) in abundance in the New World.

3. The Aztecs prepared it in a number of the same ways it is (ate/eaten) today.

4. They (beated/beat) it into flour and then used it to make tortillas and tamales.

5. Much as Mexicans do today, the Aztecs ate or (drank/drunk) *atole,* a corn flour porridge flavored with fruit or chilies.

6. Whole corn also (went/gone) into many Aztec dishes.

7. The Aztecs (took/taken) seeds from pumpkins and squash and used them in sauces.

8. Many travelers to Mexico have (saw/seen) *pipian verde* on menus.

9. This dish is (maked/made) with pumpkin seeds and another Aztec food, tomatillos, which are cousins of the tomato.

Maize has been a staple food in Mexico for hundreds of years.

10. Another food that grew in the Americas was cacao, the plant from which chocolate is made; the Aztecs (put/putted) cacao to good use.

11. The Aztecs (grinded/ground) up cacao beans and used them to prepare a cold chocolate drink.

12. Sugar was not (knowed/known) to the Aztecs, so they flavored this thick, rich drink with vanilla and various spices.

13. Many years later, a Mexican dish (brang/brought) together chocolate, chili, and spices: *mole poblano,* a rich dark sauce served over chicken.

Apply

Fill in the blank with a past tense form of the verb in parentheses.

14. I _____ *mole poblano* to Victor's birthday party. (bring)

15. My friend Raul _____ tamales. (take)

16. Because our arms were full, Ana _____ the door open for us. (hold)

17. We _____ music blasting in the backyard. (hear)

18. As we stepped onto the patio, we _____ brightly colored streamers everywhere. (see)

19. Victor's mother _____ colored lanterns. (light)

20. We _____ the food and gifts on a big table. (lay)

21. When Victor arrived, we all _____ a birthday song, *Las mañanitas*. (sing)

22. Victor _____ embarrassed from all the attention. (become)

23. The party _____ quite late. (go)

24. We waved *adiós* when we _____ the party. (leave)

Reinforce

Use forms of the verbs in the word bank to complete the crossword puzzle.

build	write	steal	drink	bring	take	know

Across

4. I _____ chocolate in Mexico last year.
5. English settlers _____ chocolate to the colonies.
6. I never _____ that the Aztecs drank chocolate.
7. The Spanish _____ Aztec gold and chocolate.

Down

1. The conquistadors _____ chocolate back to Europe.
2. I have just _____ a report on the Aztecs.
3. Last month I _____ a paper on the Maya.
5. The Aztecs _____ many impressive pyramids.

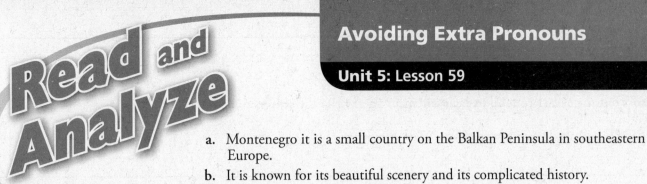
a. Montenegro it is a small country on the Balkan Peninsula in southeastern Europe.

b. It is known for its beautiful scenery and its complicated history.

Which sentence makes sense if you take out the word *it*? _____

A subject pronoun takes the place of one or more nouns in the subject of a sentence. Follow the conventions of standard English in your writing: do not use a subject pronoun right after the noun it stands for. **Remember this information when you speak, too.**

See Handbook Section 17b

Practice

Read each sentence. Draw a line through a subject pronoun if it is not needed.

1. My aunt she is a teacher in the city of Cetinje.

2. That city it is the former royal capital of Montenegro.

3. My aunt visits our family every other summer; she wants me to visit her this summer.

4. From her I have learned about Montenegro's history and culture.

5. The land it was divided into three principalities in the tenth century.

6. Each of these was populated primarily by Slavic people.

7. Stefan Vojislav he led a revolt in the middle of the eleventh century.

8. He and his supporters they unified the country and established its first great dynasty.

9. According to my aunt, Montenegro's first works of literature they were written during the eleventh century.

10. She has told me that the first book printed in the southern Slavic region was printed in Montenegro in the fifteenth century.

11. From the end of the fifteenth century to the beginning of the twentieth century, the Ottoman Turks they controlled the Balkan Peninsula.

12. The Montenegrins fiercely resisted Turkish rule, and they won great victories over Turkish forces at the end of the seventeenth century and again in the middle of the nineteenth century.

13. The Kingdom of Yugoslavia it was created after the fall of the Ottoman Empire in World War I; Montenegro became one of the parts of this nation.

Montenegro is one of Europe's smallest nations.

14. The people of Montenegro they voted to make themselves an independent nation in 2006.

15. I have visited Montenegro's website; it shows pictures of beautiful beaches on the Adriatic Sea and steep mountains crisscrossed by ancient trails.

16. I think I will send my aunt an e-mail today accepting her invitation to visit Montenegro next summer.

Apply

Cross out the extra pronoun in each sentence. Then write the sentence correctly.

17. The name *Montenegro* it means "black mountain."

_____

18. One beach on the Adriatic Sea it is eight miles long.

_____

19. Montenegro's mountains they are high and rugged.

_____

20. My aunt she drives the steep, twisting mountain roads confidently.

_____

21. My dad he is teaching me how to say, "Please slow down!" in the Montenegrin language.

_____

Reinforce

Europe currently has more than 35 nations. Choose one that you think you might want to visit. Do an Internet search to learn about its history, geography, and culture. Write the name of the country and three facts you discover on the lines below. Then, on another sheet of paper, write a brief report about this nation. Use subject pronouns correctly in your report.

_____

_____

_____

_____

_____

_____

_____

_____

_____

_____

a. The country of Jamaica is an island nation in the Caribbean, one of many islands in the Caribbean; like most of those islands, Jamaica has fertile soil and a climate that makes it an ideal place for growing food on farms.

b. Jamaica, an island nation in the Caribbean, has fertile soil and a climate favorable to agriculture.

Which sentence above communicates information more effectively? _____

Why? _____

Effective writers use the fewest words possible to convey facts and ideas clearly. When you write, first decide what information you need to communicate, and then state this information as simply and directly as you can. When you edit, identify and **eliminate unnecessary words and repetitive ideas.**

See Handbook Section 14

Practice

Draw a line through unnecessary words in the sentences below.

1. In the 1990s, the amount of food Jamaica imported from other countries increased sharply.

2. When a nation imports food, it must pay for it, because food costs money.

3. Jamaica is not a wealthy country, and the cost of importing so much food so people could eat it put a strain on its finances.

4. Ten years ago Jamaica's leaders recognized the problem and developed a plan to address it, even though they had other things to worry about.

5. The leaders started a campaign to encourage Jamaicans to do the right thing and grow food for themselves.

6. The slogan for the campaign, which is easy to remember, was "Grow what we eat, eat what we grow."

7. The nation's people have responded positively to the campaign; the amount of food being grown in Jamaica has increased steadily, with more being produced each year.

8. More and more rural land is being farmed, and many patches of land in cities are now currently under cultivation.

9. Hundreds of schools in the nation of Jamaica have established gardens in which students grow crops in the soil and even tend chickens.

10. At some of these schools, students are served meals made from the foods they have raised by working in the garden before, during, or after school.

Students in Jamaica are learning to grow crops in school gardens.

11. Not only has the homegrown food helped stop the growth of food imports, it has improved nutrition, which will help the people of Jamaica become healthier over time.

12. Instead of eating processed foods from abroad, Jamaicans are enjoying more fresh fruits and vegetables grown locally in their own country.

Name _____

Apply

Rewrite each sentence, eliminating the unnecessary words.

13. Several other nations in the Caribbean region are trying to increase agricultural production by growing more

    food. _____

    _____

14. In the tiny nation of Antigua and Barbuda, students have planted thousands and thousands of avocado,

    mango, and orange trees, all of which produce delicious, nutritious fruit. _____

    _____

15. In 2009 Antigua and Barbuda produced only 20% of its food; five years later, it was producing 50%, and

    importing much less food than before. _____

    _____

16. Haiti and the Bahamas are two other Caribbean nations in North America that have recently made

    investments in local agriculture. _____

    _____

    _____

Reinforce

Do you think it would be a good idea for people in your community to try to grow more food for local
consumption? On the lines below, list possible benefits and drawbacks of encouraging local agriculture. Then,
on another sheet of paper, write an essay telling why you favor or oppose a campaign to promote growing food
for local consumption. State your ideas simply and clearly; do not use unnecessary words.

Growing Food for Local Consumption

Benefits	Drawbacks

Review

Usage

Circle the word in parentheses that correctly completes each sentence.

1. If (your/you're) looking for interesting ways to celebrate the beginning of spring, here are some ideas.

2. If you go (to/too/two) India in the spring, you might see a Hindu festival called *Holi*.

3. Everyone (whose/who's) participating throws water and brightly colored powder.

4. Soon (their/there/they're) all covered with the colors of spring.

5. People in many parts of Europe show (their/there/they're) joy at the coming of spring by celebrating May Day on the first day of May.

6. Each community puts up (it's/its) own maypole and decorates it, and then people dance around the pole.

7. Many people decorate their homes with flowers on this day, (to/too/two).

8. The Japanese holiday called *Setsubun* is more (than/then) just a celebration of spring.

9. According to tradition, (it's/its) also a day to drive away evil spirits.

10. If you want to follow tradition, you put sardine heads and branches on (your/you're) door on this day.

11. (Than/Then) you throw beans in every corner of the house.

12. (Their/There/They're) are also several significant holidays that are celebrated near the end of spring.

13. (Your/You're) probably familiar with Memorial Day, which is celebrated on the last Monday in May.

14. (Its/It's) a legal holiday in most states and territories of the United States.

15. This holiday has special meaning for people (whose/who's) relatives lost their lives fighting for the United States.

16. (Whose/Who's) going to fly an American flag on Memorial Day?

17. If people fly a flag on Memorial Day, (their/there/they're) likely to fly it on June 14 as well.

18. They will fly the flag (then/than) because that day is Flag Day.

19. Let's buy a larger flag; this one is (to/two/too) small to be seen by passersby.

Circle each error. Write *C* on the line if the sentence is written correctly.

20. The Fourth of July is nearly here, and I haven't made no plans to celebrate yet. _____

21. I haven't never had as much fun as I did at last year's celebration. _____

22. I hope nobody gets hurt by fireworks this year. _____

177

Cross out each incorrect use of *go, went, like,* and *all.* (If the word *was* is part of the incorrect expression, cross that out also.) Write a correct word to replace the incorrect expression if a replacement is needed. Try not to use a word more than once as a replacement.

23. My brother Ali was like, "We need some new holidays. The ones we have are all really old."

    _____

24. I was all, "They're not all old. Presidents' Day is only about 40 years old." _____

25. Then Ali went, "Presidents' Day is not a new holiday. It's a combination of two old holidays, Washington's

    Birthday and Lincoln's Birthday." _____

26. I was, like, surprised to learn that Washington's Birthday has been celebrated as a holiday for, like, more

    than 200 years. _____

Lie and *Lay, Set* and *Sit*

Circle the correct word in parentheses to complete each sentence.

27. Last year for *Kamakura,* the Snow Cave Festival in Yohoto, Japan, Osamu built a snow cave and

    (sat/set) a hibachi inside.

28. After he had finished, he (lay/laid) a straw mat on the floor.

29. He invited his friends and family to (sit/set) inside and talk with him.

30. After they left, he (lay/laid) on the mat, covered himself with blankets, and went to sleep.

Irregular Verbs

Circle the correct form of the verb in parentheses.

31. *Loy Krathong,* or the Festival of the Floating Leaf Cups, has been (held/holden) in Thailand for more than

    six thousand years.

32. Tiny boats called *krathongs* are (built/builded) out of banana leaves, lotus, or paper.

33. Then people launch the boats, (litten/lit) by candles, on the river.

34. It is (thought/thinked) that a wish will come true if the krathong disappears before the candle goes out.

Eliminating Unnecessary Words

Read each sentence. Draw a line through any words that are not needed.

35. Henry he has studied the history of Odessa.

36. That city it was once part of Russia, but now it is in Ukraine.

37. Odessa, unlike many other cities, is not a very old city; as a matter of fact, it was established as a Russian

    port city in the year 1792 and given its name in the year 1795.

38. Henry wants to visit Odessa because his ancestors lived there, and he wants to go to the place where people

    in his family lived long ago.

Spelling Practice

Read and Analyze

In the late nineteenth century, the invention of the gramophone made it possible for people around the country to hear recordings of popular music.

Underline the word with two Greek word parts—one that means "letter" and one that means "sound." Write a definition for the word.

_____

Greek Forms: *gram, chron, phon(e), scope*

Word parts that come from the ancient Greek language can be found at the beginning, middle, and end of a word. The Greek form *gram* means "letter," as in *grammar.* The Greek form *chron* means "time," as in *chronic.* The Greek form *phon(e)* means "sound" or "voice," as in *phonics.* The Greek form *scope* means "to see," as in *telescope.*

Word Sort

Use the words below to complete the word sort.

anagram	microphone	telescope	synchronize	telegram	parallelogram
chronology	symphony	stethoscope	microscope	megaphone	chronicle

Greek form *gram*	Greek form *chron*

Greek form *phon(e)*	Greek form *scope*

Pattern Practice

Write the word that solves each riddle. Use a dictionary if you need help.

saxophone	microscope	chronicle	stethoscope
anagram	periscope	megaphone	earphones

1. I am something a cheerleader uses. What am I? _____

2. I am something on a submarine. What am I? _____

3. I tell the order of historical events. What am I? _____

4. I often make jazzy music. What am I? _____

5. I help you hear your heartbeat. What am I? _____

6. I am attached to your mp3 player. What am I? _____

7. I help you spy on the tiniest cells. What am I? _____

8. I am a puzzle involving letters. What am I? _____

Circle the word that is spelled correctly in each sentence.

9. Anna plays the flute in the community (symphonic/symfonic) band.

10. If we (syncronize/synchronize) our watches, we will meet on time.

11. There are (microscopic/microskopic) animals swimming in this water.

12. After reading my paper, Mr. Lopez said I must work on my (grammar/gramar).

13. These headaches have become a (cronic/chronic) problem.

14. This powerful (telescope/telescop) is located in the desert.

Use the Dictionary

Write *gram, chron, phon,* or *scope* to complete each word. Check your words in a print or an online dictionary.

15. epi_____   A short, clever saying or remark

16. _____ology   Events placed in the order they occurred

17. poly_____ic   Producing many sounds at once

Diagramming Prepositions and Prepositional Phrases

You have learned that many adverbial prepositional phrases tell *when, where,* or *how.* You have also learned that most adjectival prepositional phrases describe nouns. Note how the adverbial prepositional phrase is diagrammed in the first example. Then observe how the adjectival prepositional phrase is diagrammed in the second example.

We celebrate the harvest **in early October.**

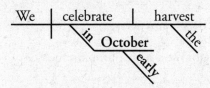

We serve fresh foods **from local farms.**

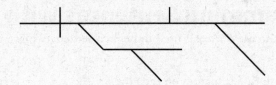

Where does the diagonal line for the preposition connect in the first example? Circle your answer.

    a. to the verb   **b.** to a noun

Where does the diagonal line for the preposition connect in the second example? Circle your answer.

    a. to the verb   **b.** to a noun

Diagram these sentences. Connect each adjectival prepositional phrase to the noun it tells about, and each adverbial prepositional phrase to the verb it tells about.

1. I invited thirty people to the party.

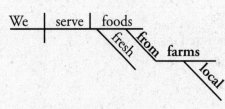

2. Margie brought a plate of sandwiches.

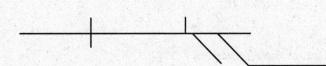

3. I bought twelve red hats with gold tassels.

4. We decorated the table with dried leaves.

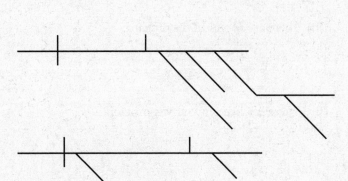

Name _____

Diagramming Indirect Objects

You have learned where to place a direct object in a sentence diagram. Here's how to diagram an indirect object. (The indirect object is in boldfaced type in this example.)

I sent my **cousin** an invitation.

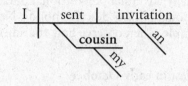

Try diagramming these sentences.

5. Giselle brought me a huge pumpkin.

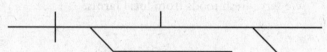

6. I lent Giovanni my binoculars.

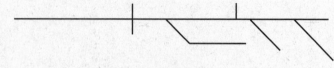

7. He gave me some lettuce seeds.

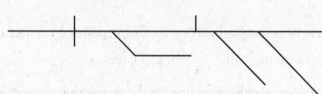

8. Colleen gave the muddy puppy a good bath.

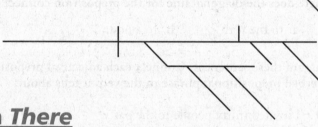

Diagramming Sentences with *There*

When the word *there* is used to begin a sentence, place it on a separate line above the subject.

There are ripe tomatoes on the vine.

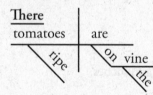

Diagram these sentences.

9. There are apples in the orchard.

10. There is a bee on your watermelon!

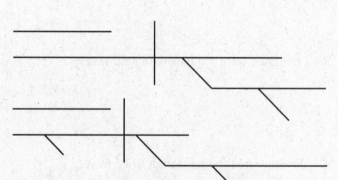

182

Writing Sentences

These sentences need your help. Rewrite each one so that homophones, problem words, and irregular verbs are used correctly.

1. Its no surprise that many celebrations of the Hopi people focus on rain and fertility.

   _____

   _____

2. No large rivers or lakes furnish water to they're high desert homeland. _____

   _____

3. According to traditional Hopi beliefs, *kachinas* bring good health and rain with them; no year can be a good

   year without these too things. _____

   _____

4. In some Hopi ceremonies, dancers wear costumes and masks representing sacred spirits that are knowed as

   kachinas. _____

   _____

5. The kachina ceremonies show that the Hopi are a people who's harsh environment has affected their

   culture. _____

   _____

6. Without rain, this people of the American Southwest wouldn't be able to raise no crops.

   _____

   _____

An informative paragraph's purpose is to inform readers. It should contain several important facts about a particular topic. The paragraph begins with an introductory sentence and ends with a concluding sentence. In between are sentences providing more information about the topic. Read this informative paragraph.

introductory sentence	*The short days and cold weather of winter seem to require special ceremonies.* The ancient Druids in Britain built huge bonfires and danced around them on the shortest day of the year. Members
sentences that give more information about the topic	of the Iroquois people put on masks and shook rattles outside their neighbors' homes for their midwinter ceremony. In the state of Oaxaca in Mexico, people carve sculptures out of odd-shaped radishes each winter. *These are only a few*
concluding sentence	*of the unusual winter traditions various cultures have developed.*

Writing a Paragraph

The sentences you repaired on page 183 can be reordered to make an informative paragraph. Decide which sentence is the introductory sentence, which sentences provide more information, and which sentence is the concluding sentence. Reorder the sentences, and write the paragraph below.

_____

_____

_____

_____

_____

_____

Write an informative paragraph about a culture you read about in Unit 5 or another culture that interests you.

_____

_____

_____

_____

_____

_____

Reread your paragraph. Use this checklist to make sure it is complete and correct.

- ❑ My paragraph contains an introductory sentence and a concluding sentence.
- ❑ My paragraph provides several interesting facts about a topic.
- ❑ I have used homophones and problem words correctly.
- ❑ I have used irregular verbs correctly.
- ❑ I have used negatives correctly.

Proofreading
Practice

Read this passage about Mongolia. Use the proofreading marks below to show how each mistake should be fixed. Use a dictionary to check and correct spellings.

Proofreading Marks

Mark	Means	Example
✗	delete	Mongolia's steppes ~~they~~ are grass-covered plains.
∧	add	Mongolia's steppes are grass-covered ∧. (plains)
≡	make into an uppercase letter	mongolia's steppes are grass-covered plains.
(sp)	fix spelling	Mongolia's steps are grass-covered plains.
⊙	add a period	Mongolia's steppes are grass-covered plains⊙
˅	add an apostrophe	Mongolias steppes are grass-covered plains.
/	make into a lowercase letter	Mongolia's Steppes are grass-covered plains.

Mongolian Cultural Traditions

Mongolia lays between Russia and china. The countrys landscape ranges from steep mountains to flat grassland. For thousands of years, Mongolians lived as nomads. Guiding herds of horses, sheep, camels, oxen, and goats to different grazing areas In the past century, cities and towns has sprouted throughout the country, and many Mongolians have sought jobs their. Others have chose to settle on farms. Some Mongolians, however, are still nomadic. They're portable homes are called *gers* or *yurts*.

Mongolians celebrate there nomadic warrior culture in a annual festival called *Naadam*. The festival is holded in the capital city of Ulan Bator, which is in the north central part of the country. The festival features three sports: horse racing, wrestling, and archery.

The Naadam Festival features another distinctive Mongolian tradition, "throat" singing. According to Mongolian Tradition, the oldest music was created by shepherds in western Mongolia. There isn't nothing like the music that comes from that region. Its also knowed in English as overtone singing because it requires the singer to produce too or more tones at the same time.

Mongolia is certainly a country who's cultural traditions are, like, distinctive!

185

Proofreading
Checklist

You can use the list below to help you find and fix mistakes in your own writing. Write the titles of your own stories or reports in the blanks at the top of the chart. Then use the questions to check your work. Make a check mark (✓) in each box after you have checked that item.

Titles

Proofreading Checklist for Unit 5

Have I used *your* and *you're* correctly?				
Have I used *their, they're,* and *there* correctly?				
Have I used *its* and *it's* correctly?				
Have I used *who's* and *whose* correctly?				
Have I used *to, too,* and *two* correctly?				
Have I used *than* and *then* correctly?				
Have I used correct forms of irregular verbs?				
Have I used *go, went, like,* and *all* correctly?				
Have I used negatives correctly?				
Have I eliminated all unnecessary words?				

Also Remember…

Does each sentence begin with an uppercase letter?				
Did I use a dictionary to check and correct spellings?				
Have I used commas correctly?				

Your Own List

Use this space to write your own list of things to check in your writing.

Community Connection

In Unit 5 of *Grammar, Usage, and Mechanics*, students learned how to **use words that are easily confused** when writing. The content of these lessons focuses on the theme **Cultural Snapshots**. As students completed the exercises, they learned about people in many parts of the world who have developed distinctive cultures. These pages offer a variety of activities that reinforce skills and concepts presented in the unit. They also provide opportunities for the student to make connections between the material in the lessons and the community at large.

Festival Calendar

Use the entertainment section of a local newspaper, fliers posted around your community, and other sources to find out what cultural events are happening in your community this season. Then create a calendar of cultural events to organize the information. If possible, arrange to go to one of the events with a friend or family member. You may also want to display your calendar in your school or community center for others to see.

Traditions

Interview an elderly person in your community who came to the United States from another country. Use his or her responses to write a report to summarize one or more important traditions in that culture. Make sure you correctly use words that are easily confused, such as *their* and *there*.

Party Time

Think about what kind of cultural celebration you would like to see in your community, and make a plan for organizing one. Try to answer these questions when making your plan.

- What culture or cultures will this event celebrate?
- What kinds of entertainment would the celebration feature? What individuals or groups would you invite to participate?
- Would the celebration have food, arts and crafts, or anything else? Whom would you have provide these things?
- When and where would the celebration be held?
- How would you advertise the celebration? Be specific.
- How much would you need to charge to offset the costs of putting on the event?

When you have finished working out your plan, develop a flier you could use to advertise the event. Include the important details about the event on the flier.

The Planning Stage

To hold a celebration, planners must make sure they follow local laws governing community events. Research the laws and rules you would need to comply with in order to hold a cultural celebration in your community. Make sure you also find out about any permits you would need. Use the Event Planner on the next page to help you organize what you learn.

Name _____

Event Planner

Phone number of City Hall: _____

Other numbers to call:

_____

_____

_____

_____

Whom to speak to:

_____

_____

_____

_____

Permits needed:

_____

_____

_____

Other laws/regulations to follow:

_____

_____

_____

_____

Notes

_____

_____

_____

_____

_____

_____

_____

_____

a. Laluah and Bonsu tricked Anansi.

b. **They** tricked **him**.

Which boldfaced word replaces the word *Anansi*? _____

Which boldfaced word replaces the phrase *Laluah and Bonsu*? _____

Which pronouns would you use in sentence *b* if Anansi tricked Laluah and Bonsu? _____ _____

Subject pronouns include *I, he, she, we,* and *they.* (Subject pronouns are in the *nominative case.*) Subject pronouns can be the subject of a clause or sentence. **Object pronouns** can be used after an action verb or a preposition. Object pronouns include *me, him, her, us,* and *them.* (Object pronouns are in the *objective case.*) The pronouns *it* and *you* can be either subjects or objects. **Remember to use this information when you speak, too.**

See Handbook | Section 17b

Practice

Circle the correct pronoun in parentheses. Write *S* if you circled a subject pronoun. Write *O* if you circled an object pronoun.

1. My aunt used to tell (I/me) stories about Anansi. _____

2. (She/Her) says Anansi is the central folktale character of the Ashanti people of West Africa. _____

3. The stories (they/them) tell about (he/him) teach moral lessons. _____ _____

4. In some stories Anansi is a spider, and in others (he/him) is a man. _____

5. Anansi is called a trickster character because (he/him) is always trying to swindle others. _____

6. Anansi is sometimes clever and sometimes foolish, but either way, another character usually gets the better of (he/him). _____

7. (I/Me) remember a story in which Anansi says (he/him) wants to start a business but not do any work. _____ _____

8. Anansi's wife tells her friend Laluah about Anansi's plan, and (she/her) tells her husband, Bonsu. _____

9. Bonsu tells (she/her) that (he/him) will trick Anansi into doing all the work instead. _____ _____

10. It's not surprising that (he/him) succeeds in tricking Anansi. _____

Anansi tales are popular in the West African nation of Ghana.

11. Anansi's wife tells (he/him) at the end of the story that when (he/him) digs a hole for someone else, (he/him) will fall into it himself. _____ _____ _____

12. My friend Vanessa and I have started telling stories about Anansi when (we/us) baby-sit. _____

13. (We/Us) think (they/them) help kids learn the consequences of trying to cheat others. _____ _____

14. Telling these stories is fun for (we/us), too. _____

Name _____

Apply

Rewrite each sentence. Replace each boldfaced phrase with a pronoun. Circle the subject pronouns you write. Draw a box around the object pronouns.

15. **Anansi tales** have been carried all over the world by people of African descent. _____
_____

16. As new storytellers have told **Anansi tales, the tales** have changed in some ways. _____
_____

17. For example, **Anansi** has had his name changed to "Aunt Nancy" in some Caribbean countries. _____
_____

18. **The plants and animals in a story** might change from African ones to those found in the Caribbean or in

North or South America. _____

_____

19. **The message of the stories** has remained the same, however. _____
_____

20. **Anansi** always tries to take advantage of **other people or animals in the forest**, but **others** usually teach **Anansi**

a lesson in the end. _____

_____

Reinforce

Forms of personal pronouns in English have changed over the years. Until the sixteenth century, the word *thou* was used as a subject pronoun to indicate the person being spoken to, and the word *thee* was used as the object form. Since that time, people have used the word *you* as both a subject and an object pronoun to indicate the person being spoken to. Yet many writers continued to use *thou* and *thee* well into the eighteenth century.

Read the following passage. Circle each pronoun that is no longer commonly used. Then write the modern English pronoun that would be used instead of each of these archaic pronouns.

ROMEO: By a name
I know not how to tell thee who I am:
My name, dear saint, is hateful to myself,
Because it is an enemy to thee;
Had I written it, I would tear the word.

JULIET: My ears have not yet drunk a hundred words
of thy tongue's uttering, yet I know the sound:
Art thou not Romeo, and a Montague?

ROMEO: Neither, fair maid, if either thee dislike.
—William Shakespeare, from *Romeo and Juliet*

21. _____

22. _____

23. _____

24. _____

25. _____

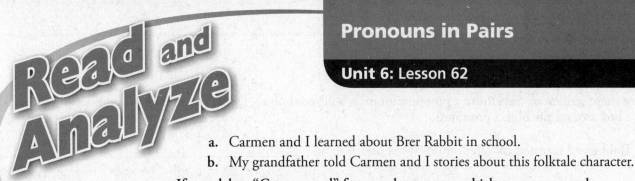

a. Carmen and I learned about Brer Rabbit in school.

b. My grandfather told Carmen and I stories about this folktale character.

If you delete "Carmen and" from each sentence, which sentence sounds correct? _____

Use a **subject pronoun** in a compound subject. Use an **object pronoun** in a compound direct object, a compound indirect object, or a compound object of a preposition. If you are unsure which pronoun form to use, say the sentence with only the pronoun part of the compound. For example, *He told stories to Carmen and I* becomes *He told stories to I.* You can hear that *I* should be replaced with *me.* **Remember to use this information when you speak, too.**

See Handbook Section 17b

Practice

Circle the correct pronoun in each pair. Write *S* if you chose a subject pronoun and *O* if you chose an object pronoun.

1. Last week Carmen, Bobby, and (I/me) visited my grandparents. _____

2. Bobby had asked me to arrange the visit because (he/him) and Carmen hoped Grandfather would tell them about Brer Rabbit for their school folklore project. _____

3. Carmen knows a lot about Anansi the Spider, and our teacher had told Bobby and (she/her) that Brer Rabbit stories are similar to Anansi stories. _____

4. (She/Her) and Bobby explained that enslaved African Americans developed the Brer Rabbit stories. _____

5. Grandfather told Grandmother and (we/us) that he heard Brer Rabbit stories when he was little. _____

6. (He/Him) and Grandmother talked about the ways Brer Rabbit outsmarts more powerful animals. _____

7. Grandfather told Carmen, Bobby, and (I/me) that these stories helped enslaved people think about outsmarting slaveholders. _____

8. Carmen asked Grandfather to tell a Brer Rabbit story that (she/her) and Bobby had never heard. _____

9. Grandfather told Grandmother and (we/us) about Brer Rabbit and Brer Fox. _____

10. (He/Him) and Brer Rabbit were always trying to trick each other. _____

11. Bobby took notes as Grandfather told Carmen and (he/him) that Fox caught Rabbit with some tar. _____

12. Grandmother and (I/me) said we had heard this story many times before. _____

13. Everyone listened to Grandmother and (I/me) as we told how Brer Rabbit got stuck to the Tar Baby. _____

14. Grandfather turned to Carmen and asked Bobby and (she/her) what Brer Fox did to Brer Rabbit. _____

15. Grandmother and (I/me) said Brer Rabbit tricked Brer Fox into throwing him into the briar patch. _____

16. Carmen laughed and said (she/her) and Bobby could guess the ending: Brer Rabbit got away easily since he had been born and raised in the briar patch. _____

Apply

Rewrite these sentences. Substitute a pronoun for each boldfaced noun. Circle the subject pronouns you write. Draw a box around the object pronouns.

17. **Bobby** and Carmen collected stories about Brer Rabbit. _____

_____

18. Grandmother and Grandfather told Bobby and **Carmen** most of the stories. _____

_____

19. Ramona and **Carmen** read other stories in a book. _____

_____

20. Ramona discovered lots of stories about Brer Fox and **Brer Rabbit**. _____

_____

21. Bobby, Carmen, and **Ramona** gave an oral report on folktales to the class. _____

_____

22. **The students** and the teacher were especially interested in the Tar Baby. _____

_____

23. The story of how **the Tar Baby** and **Brer Rabbit** met made everyone burst out laughing. _____

_____

24. Bobby and **Carmen** acted out a few stories. _____

_____

25. Everyone gave **Bobby** and Carmen a big round of applause. _____

_____

Reinforce

When *I* and *me* are used in a pair with a noun or another pronoun, the pronouns *I* and *me* should always come last (*Grandfather and me,* NOT *me and Grandfather*).

Circle the choice that completes each sentence correctly.

26. (I and Carmen/Carmen and I) presented what we had learned about Brer Rabbit to the class.

27. The class had lots of questions for (Carmen and me/me and Carmen).

28. (Me and Carmen/Carmen and I) answered all the questions we could.

29. The questions we couldn't answer gave (Carmen and me/me and Carmen) a great idea.

30. (Bobby, I, and Carmen/Carmen, Bobby, and I) are going to start up a folktales club at school.

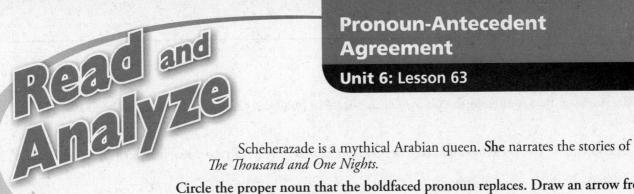

Scheherazade is a mythical Arabian queen. **She** narrates the stories of *The Thousand and One Nights*.

Circle the proper noun that the boldfaced pronoun replaces. Draw an arrow from the pronoun to that name.

An **antecedent** is the word or phrase a pronoun refers to or takes the place of. The antecedent always includes a noun. When you write a pronoun, be sure its antecedent is clear. A pronoun must also **agree** with its antecedent. An antecedent and pronoun agree when they have the same number (singular or plural) and gender (male or female). For example, *women*, a plural noun naming females, would never be the antecedent of *he*, a singular masculine pronoun.

Remember to use this information when you speak, too.

See Handbook Section 17c

Practice

Circle the antecedent of each boldfaced pronoun.

1. *The Thousand and One Nights* is a famous piece of Arabic literature. **It** was written around A.D. 1500.

2. There are about 200 folktales in this collection. **They** originally came from Arabia, Egypt, India, Persia, and other countries.

3. The first story tells of a cruel king. **He** does not trust women.

4. Each evening the king marries a new bride. Then, the next morning, he executes **her**.

5. The wise and beautiful Scheherazade volunteers to marry the king. **She** has a plan to stop his cruelty.

6. On the night of the wedding, Scheherazade's sister asks the king if Scheherazade can tell a story. **He** gives his permission.

7. Scheherazade begins telling the king a story, but she does not finish **it**.

8. The king has to spare Scheherazade's life if **he** wants to find out how the story ends.

9. The next night, Scheherazade finishes the story. Then right away **she** tells the beginning of another story.

10. Scheherazade's stories tell about genies, princesses, and talking animals. **They** are wonderful fairy tales.

The story of Aladdin's lamp is in *The Thousand and One Nights*.

11. Every night, Scheherazade tells stories to her husband, and every morning **he** lets her live so that she can finish them.

12. Scheherazade tells stories for one thousand and one nights. By this time, the king has fallen in love with **her**.

13. Scheherazade's stories are so entertaining that **they** save her life.

14. Jean Antoine Galland made it possible for people in France to enjoy *The Thousand and One Nights*. **He** translated **it** into French in the early 1700s.

15. English translations of these tales were not generally available until the 1880s. **They** were prepared by Sir Richard Francis Burton, who was a famous explorer as well as a skillful translator.

Name _____

Apply

Write the pronoun that could take the place of each phrase in boldface. Capitalize a word that begins a sentence.

16. The stories in *The Thousand and One Nights* are hundreds of years old, but people still enjoy telling and listening to _____ today.

17. One of the most popular stories tells of **a poor boy named Aladdin.** _____ finds a genie in a magic lamp.

18. When Aladdin rubs the lamp, **the genie** appears. _____ grants Aladdin's wishes.

19. Aladdin later meets **a princess** and falls in love with _____.

20. **A cartoon film version of Aladdin's tale** was released in the early 1990s. _____ quickly became one of the most popular films ever shown.

21. **Sinbad the Sailor** also appears as a character in some of these stories. Incredible things happen to _____ during seven long sea voyages.

22. **Real Arab sailors** regularly sailed as far as China in the Medieval period (about A.D. 500–1500). Some scholars think the character of Sinbad was based on _____.

23. Another popular character in *The Thousand and One Nights* is **Ali Baba.** _____ finds a sealed cave filled with treasure.

24. To open **the treasure-filled cave,** Ali Baba stands in front of _____ and says the magic words.

25. Unfortunately, the treasure belongs to **forty thieves.** _____ will do anything to protect it.

Reinforce

Ante means "before." A pronoun's antecedent should come before the pronoun so that the reader knows for sure what noun the pronoun replaces. Rewrite the paragraph below so that every pronoun has a clear antecedent. There is more than one correct way to do this. You'll want to replace some pronouns with nouns, but remember that using pronouns with clear antecedents helps the flow of your writing.

She tells about him in the story "Ali Baba and the Forty Thieves." In it, Ali Baba hides from them. While hidden in the tree, he overhears them opening it with the password "open sesame." He later says the password himself and is able to enter their treasure cave and take it for himself. They try to kill him, but he gets away with it in the end. It has remained a favorite tale for centuries, and several exciting movie versions of it have been made.

_____

_____

_____

_____

_____

_____

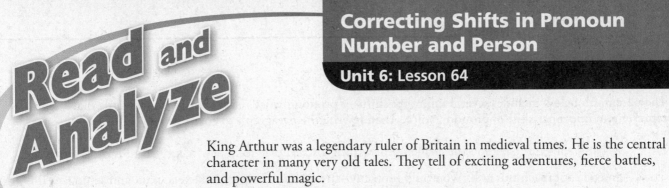

King Arthur was a legendary ruler of Britain in medieval times. He is the central character in many very old tales. They tell of exciting adventures, fierce battles, and powerful magic.

Circle the words that the pronoun *he* replaces. Draw a line under the word *They* replaces.

Pronouns must agree with their **antecedents** in number (singular or plural) and gender (male or female). When you use a pronoun to establish a point of view, be careful not to shift to a pronoun of a different number and person.

See Handbook | Sections 17a–c

Practice

In each sentence, circle the pronoun form that agrees with its antecedent. Then underline the antecedent.

1. The mythical Arthur character may have been based in part on a real British leader of the early sixth century. (He/They) led warriors to victory in battles against German invaders.

2. The first collection of King Arthur tales was created in the early twelfth century. Over time (he/they) have been told and retold not only in Britain but throughout the world.

3. Geoffrey of Monmouth was the author of this collection. Scholars believe (he/it) gathered some tales of Arthur from storytellers and made up others himself.

4. Geoffrey's tales featured such vivid characters as Uther Pendragon, Arthur's father; Merlin the Magician; and Guinevere, Arthur's wife. (They/It) also told of a magic sword known as Excalibur.

5. Later in the twelfth century, the French writer Chrétien de Troyes wrote more tales about King Arthur. (It/They) featured romantic adventures in addition to military exploits.

6. Chrétien de Troyes introduced the character Lancelot, who served Arthur gallantly but became (his/their) rival for the affections of Guinevere.

7. Other European writers added to the store of Arthurian adventures, and (he/they) also created alternate versions of earlier tales.

King Arthur is the subject of many legends.

8. Geoffrey's tales present Arthur as a mighty warrior who vanquished foes through skill and bravery, but Chrétien de Troyes and other continental writers depict (him/them) as a passive character who allowed the Knights of the Round Table to prove their valor in battle.

9. One tale told consistently is the story of how Arthur proved himself to be the rightful heir to the throne of Britain: he pulled the sword Excalibur out of a stone in which (it/they) had been magically embedded, which legend said that only the future king could do.

10. Poets, novelists, and filmmakers continue to use Arthurian legends as their subject matter today. (Its/Their) themes of loyalty, bravery, and civility are appreciated by audiences in every era.

Apply

The paragraph below includes several improper shifts of pronoun voice. Circle the word or words that represent an improper shift of pronoun voice. Then rewrite the paragraph to correct these shifts.

What if someone gave you the challenge of writing a screenplay for a new King Arthur movie? How would someone approach this task? We would probably start with the basics: characters, plot, and setting. With King Arthur as the focus, much of the work has already been done for us. The characters in Arthurian legends are bold, colorful, and memorable. You also have a head start on your plot. Many exciting events involving Arthur have already been imagined and written down. Once the screenwriter has skimmed a few volumes of tales about Arthur and his knights, she can select her favorites, add a little imagination, and stitch everything together into a riveting plot. Planning locations might be the easiest part of the process. Screenwriters can flip through a United Kingdom travel guide or visit some online travel sites. All they need to find is an acre of forest for surprise encounters, a lush field for jousting, and a castle with a room big enough to hold a large round table. Before you know it, you'll have a fully developed screenplay ready to be made into the greatest King Arthur film ever!

_____

_____

_____

_____

_____

_____

_____

_____

_____

_____

Reinforce

On another sheet of paper, write a script for a 30-second TV commercial for a new King Arthur movie. Use at least two personal pronouns in your commercial. Circle them and underline their antecedents.

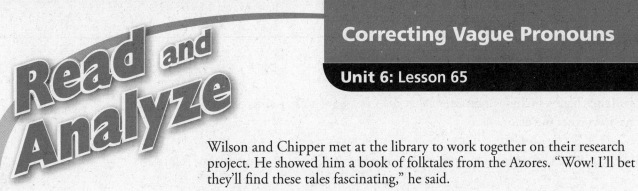

Wilson and Chipper met at the library to work together on their research project. He showed him a book of folktales from the Azores. "Wow! I'll bet they'll find these tales fascinating," he said.

Can you tell from these sentences who showed whom the book of folktales? _____

Do these sentences make clear who might find the tales fascinating? _____

Can you tell who is speaking in the third sentence? _____

Mark an X through each pronoun that does not have a clear antecedent.

Each **personal pronoun** and each **demonstrative pronoun** you use should have a **clear antecedent**. If you see that you have written a sentence with a pronoun that does not refer clearly to an antecedent, you should rewrite the sentence.

See Handbook Sections 17a–c, i

Practice

Draw an arrow from each boldfaced pronoun to its antecedent. Underline the antecedent. If a boldfaced pronoun does not have a clear antecedent, mark an X through it.

1. The library has books with folktales from different parts of the United States and also has collections of tales from other lands, but Jennifer is only interested in **those**.

2. Jennifer and Jill brought **their** tablets to the library and took notes about **them**.

3. Chipper read "Why Dogs Sniff" in the book *The Islands of Magic;* **he** recommended **it** to his friends.

4. Wilson waved to Chipper as **he** went to look at some books of folktales Jennifer and Jill had found.

5. "Have **you** read any of these books?" **he** asked.

6. "Yes," **she** replied, "the ones in this book are quite unusual."

7. **She** handed **him** *Tales of the Enchanted Islands of the Atlantic,* by Thomas Wentworth Higginson.

8. "I recognize that name!" said Jill, and **she** explained that Thomas Wentworth Higginson had led the first officially constituted unit of African American soldiers into battle in the American Civil War.

9. "I wonder if that Higginson and the author of this folktale collection are the same person," said Chipper.

10. "Why don't **you** use **your** tablet to look **it** up?" Chipper continued.

11. **She** did as Chipper suggested and found that the Civil War colonel was the author of the folktale collection.

12. "Why would a famous soldier be interested in **that**?" **he** wondered.

13. "I'll answer **your** question by reading from the preface," said Jill, and **she** opened the book to page vii.

14. Jill read aloud to **them** from the preface: "No one has yet made . . . use of the wondrous tales that gathered for more than a thousand years about the islands of the Atlantic deep."

15. "Higginson must have loved the folktales and wanted to give others the opportunity to enjoy **them**, too," said Wilson.

Name _____

Apply

Each sentence below includes a pronoun that does not have a clear antecedent. Rewrite each
sentence to correct the error.

16. When Jill talked with her aunt that evening, she mentioned several books of folktales.

_____

_____

17. Jill's aunt lives between Akron and Youngstown in northeastern Ohio; Jill has never had a chance to visit it.

_____

_____

18. Jill's aunt collects recordings of folktales by famous storytellers, and Jill is especially interested in them.

_____

_____

19. Jill and her aunt talked with Jill's parents, and they made plans for a visit by Jill to Ohio.

_____

_____

20. After Jill and her aunt finished their conversation, she e-mailed her a link to a website for folktale

enthusiasts.

_____

_____

Reinforce

Think of a favorite folktale that you would enjoy telling to a group of younger students. On another sheet of
paper, write your retelling of this tale. Make sure the personal pronouns and demonstrative pronouns you use
have clear antecedents. Read your final draft aloud to an audience.

Read and Analyze

Some folk heroes are based on people **who** actually lived. _____

John Henry was a real African American worker about **whom** many folk songs and stories have been written. _____

Underline the clause in each sentence that includes *who* or *whom*. Which boldfaced word is a subject? _____ Which boldfaced word begins a clause that is the object of a preposition? _____ After each sentence, write whether *who* or *whom* is a subject or an object.

Use *who* as the **subject** of a sentence or a clause. Use *whom* as the **object** of a verb or a preposition. **Remember to use this information when you speak, too**.

See Handbook | Sections 17b, 17h

Practice

Underline the clause in each sentence that includes the words in parentheses. Decide whether the word in parentheses will be a subject or an object. Circle *who* or *whom* to complete each sentence correctly.

1. John Henry is a folk hero (who/whom) is legendary for his strength of body and will.

2. He was one of a group of workers (who/whom) a railroad company had hired to dig a tunnel in the 1870s.

3. The workers, (who/whom) had to be very strong, used heavy sledgehammers to pound drills into solid rock.

4. They were followed by other workers (who/whom) put sticks of dynamite into the holes to blast a tunnel through the rock.

5. John Henry could swing a hammer harder and faster than any of the other men with (who/whom) he worked.

6. One day a man (who/whom) had built a steam-powered drill came to the work site.

7. He claimed it could dig a hole faster than twenty workers (who/whom) used regular hammers.

8. The workers were worried: if the steam drill was so fast, (who/whom) would need workers to pound drills anymore?

9. To (who/whom) could they turn?

10. John Henry was the only one (who/whom) was willing to accept the challenge of competing against the steam drill driver.

11. The winner would be the one (who/whom) drilled a hole faster.

12. (Who/Whom) won the contest? John Henry did, but he died soon after.

John Henry beat a machine in a race.

13. According to legend, John Henry died of exhaustion, but the people (who/whom) witnessed the contest said he was crushed by falling rock.

14. The workers made a hero of John Henry, (who/whom) they buried with a hammer in his hand.

15. John Henry, (who/whom) came to symbolize the workers' struggle against machinery that could replace them, has been the subject of both stories and songs.

Name _____

Apply

Complete a question to go with each statement. Be sure to end each sentence with a question mark.

16. The folktale character John Henry was based on a real person. On whom _____

    _____

17. The real John Henry was an African American worker. Who _____

    _____

18. He was working with other laborers to build the Big Bend Tunnel and the Ohio Railroad. Who _____

    _____

19. Songs and stories have been written about him. About whom _____

20. John Henry was given the task of competing with a mechanical steam drill. To whom _____

    _____

21. John Henry won the race. Who _____

22. Workers especially admired him. Who _____

23. For many, he is an important American hero. For whom _____

    _____

Reinforce

Circle *who* or *whom* to complete each quotation correctly.

No man is an island . . . never send to know

for (who/whom) the bell tolls; it tolls for thee.

                                    —John Donne

He (who/whom) learns but does not think is

lost. He (who/whom) thinks but does not learn is

in great danger.

                                    —Kong Qiu (Confucius)

I am only a public entertainer (who/whom)

has understood his time.

                                    —Pablo Picasso

If your lips would keep from slips,

Five things observe with care:

To (who/whom) you speak; of (who/whom)

    you speak;

And how, and when, and where.

                                    —William Edward Norris

No! the two kinds of people on earth that I mean

Are the people (who/whom) lift and the

people (who/whom) lean.

                                    —Ella Wheeler Wilcox

Now write your own saying using *who* or *whom*.

24. _____

    _____

Jewish **tales** of a helpful **monster** have been told and retold for centuries.

Circle the boldfaced noun that is the simple subject of this sentence. Is this noun singular or plural? _____ Underline the helping verb that agrees with the subject. What form of this verb would be used if the simple subject of this sentence was *tale*? _____

The **subject** and its **verb must agree**. Add *s* or *es* to a verb in the present tense when the subject is a singular noun or *he, she,* or *it*. Do not add *s* or *es* to a verb in the present tense when the subject is a plural noun or *I, you, we,* or *they*. The verb *be* is irregular. Singular forms of *be* are *is, am, was*. Plural forms are *are* and *were*. Be sure the verb agrees with its subject and not with the object of a preposition that comes before the verb. **Remember to use this information when you speak, too.**

See Handbook | Section 18f

Practice

Circle the simple subject in each sentence. Then underline the correct form of the verb in parentheses.

1. Stories about the golem (is/are) still told and read today.

2. According to legend, the body of a golem (is/are) made of clay and dust.

3. Only a person very learned in the ways of magic (is/are) able to bring the clay golem to life.

4. These monsters, human in form, (is/are) very strong but unable to speak.

5. One of the most famous golem stories (is/are) "The Golem of Prague."

6. At the time in which this tale is set, the sixteenth century, Jewish people (was/were) terribly persecuted in many parts of eastern Europe.

7. In the story, the rabbi of Prague, a religious leader known for his great knowledge, (creates/create) a golem to guard his people.

8. This protector of the Jews (roams/roam) the streets of the city at night, stopping crime.

9. Some parts of the story (is/are) humorous.

10. The wife of the rabbi (asks/ask) the golem to carry water from the well to fill a washtub.

11. The obedient golem (carries/carry) buckets of water so fast that the tub is soon overflowing.

12. (Is/Are) the persecutors of the Jews brought to justice with the help of the golem?

13. Yes, a plot to make false accusations against the Jewish residents (is/are) revealed by the golem, who has been disguised as a night watchman.

14. The king, hearing news of the cruel plot, (issue/issues) an order protecting the Jewish people.

15. When the help of the golem is no longer needed, the rabbi (turns/turn) the giant back into clay.

16. According to legend, the clay form of the golem still (lies/lie) hidden, waiting to be brought to life if needed.

In legends of the golem, a clay figure comes to life.

Name _____

Apply

Circle the simple subject in each sentence. Then write the correct form of the verb in parentheses to complete the sentence.

17. A book of folktales _____ the power to entertain adults as well as children. (have)

18. A favorite story of my parents _____ "Strongheart Jack and the Beanstalk," an early

    version of the story we know as "Jack and the Beanstalk." (be)

19. In this version, a hot desert filled with cactus plants _____ the first thing Jack sees

    when he reaches the top of the beanstalk. (be)

20. Then a yellow turtle in a pond _____ Jack to answer a riddle. (challenge)

21. A calico cat named Octavia _____ Jack defeat the giant. (help)

22. The prisoners in the giant's castle _____ very happy to be free. (be)

23. Any story about giants _____ my brother. (scare)

24. One of my assignments in art class this week _____ to mold a clay figure. (be)

25. _____ the name *golem* a good one for a large clay figure? (be)

Reinforce

Folktales are one way wisdom has been passed from one generation to the next. *Aphorisms,* brief truths about human behavior, are another.

Read these three aphorisms from Benjamin Franklin. Underline the correct verb form in each. Then write a brief explanation of each saying's message.

26. The cat in gloves (catch/catches) no mice. _____

    _____

27. A word to the wise (is/are) enough, and many words won't fill a bushel. _____

    _____

28. They that can give up essential liberty to obtain a little temporary safety (deserve/deserves) neither liberty nor

    safety. _____

    _____

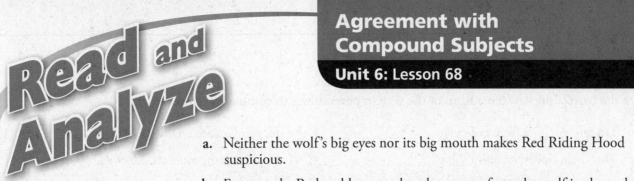
a. Neither the wolf's big eyes nor its big mouth makes Red Riding Hood suspicious.

b. Fortunately, Red and her grandmother escape from the wolf in the end.

Circle the compound subject in each sentence. Underline the verb in each sentence. Which sentence has a verb that goes with a singular subject? _____

A **compound subject** and its verb must agree. If a compound subject includes the conjunction *and,* the subject is plural and needs a plural verb. If a compound subject includes *or* or *nor,* the verb must agree with the last item in the subject. **Remember to use this information when you speak, too.**

See Handbook Sections 11, 18f

Practice

Look at the compound subject in each sentence. Draw a box around the conjunction. Then underline the correct verb in parentheses.

1. Lin and Rick (collect/collects) information about wild canine characters in folktales.

2. Wolves, foxes, and coyotes (is/are) all closely related to dogs.

3. A wolf or a coyote (act/acts) more like a dog than a fox does.

4. Native American cultures and European cultures (has/have) very different ideas about wild canine characters.

5. When a fox or a wolf (appears/appear) in a European fairy tale, it is usually the villain.

6. "Little Red Riding Hood" and "The Three Little Pigs" (is/are) two good examples.

7. Neither Red Riding Hood nor the pigs (regrets/regret) the evil wolf's death.

8. Although the real animals may be similar, the evil fairy tale wolf and the coyote of Native American tales (is/are) totally different from each other.

9. Native American stories and a favorite Mexican folktale of mine (portrays/portray) Coyote as a lovable trickster figure.

10. Greed, arrogance, or selfishness (gets/get) Coyote into trouble.

11. Fox, Bear, or other animals (laughs/laugh) at his misadventures.

12. But neither injury nor even death (stops/stop) Coyote.

The Coyote character lived in a legendary time before humans.

13. The power to come back from the dead and the power to create anything he can imagine (belongs/belong) to Coyote.

14. This laughable fool or powerful creator (is/are) one of the most complicated characters in Native American folklore.

Apply

Write the correct present tense form of the verb in parentheses to complete each sentence.

15. Lin and Alvin, a friend of hers, _____ the story of Coyote's name best. (like)

16. The Great Spirit, or Spirit Chief, _____ to rename all the animals. (decide)

17. Coyote and all the other animals _____ to line up first thing the next morning for their new names. (agree)

18. *Grizzly Bear* or *Salmon* _____ to Coyote as a new name. (appeal)

19. Coyote's ambition and cunning _____ him think of a scheme for being first in line: he'll stay up all night. (help)

20. Boasts and selfish wishes _____ from the mouth of Coyote almost all that night. (pour)

21. Finally, either laziness or just plain exhaustion _____ Coyote, and he falls asleep. (overwhelm)

22. While Coyote sleeps, the real Grizzly Bear and the real Salmon _____ their own names. (choose)

23. By the time the tired Coyote wakes up, neither *Grizzly Bear* nor *Salmon* _____ a possibility for a new name. (remain)

24. Coyote and his old name _____ to stick together. (have)

Reinforce

Use information in this lesson and in earlier lessons in this unit to fill in the puzzle. Each answer will be part of a compound subject. Then circle the correct verb in parentheses to complete each clue.

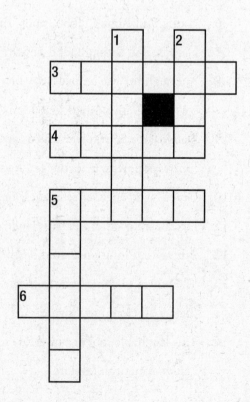

Across

3. Aladdin, Ali Baba, and ___ the Sailor (is/are) all characters in *The Thousand and One Nights*.
4. Either the steam drill driver or John ___ (wins/win) the race.
5. The *Great Spirit* and the *Spirit* ___ (is/are) both Native American names for the same deity.
6. Wolves and ___ (is/are) often villains in European fairy tales.

Down

1. Bonsu and ___ the Spider (goes/go) fishing together, and they try to trick each other.
2. Brer Rabbit and the Tar ___ (sticks/stick) to each other.
5. Either Brer Rabbit, Anansi, or ___ (makes/make) a good example of a trickster character.

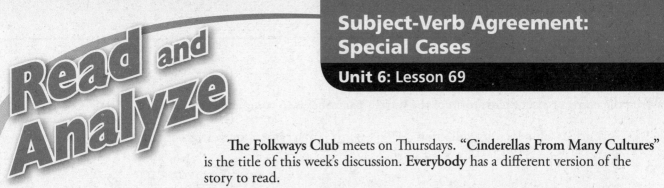

The **Folkways Club** meets on Thursdays. "Cinderellas From Many Cultures" is the title of this week's discussion. **Everybody** has a different version of the story to read.

Look at the boldfaced subjects of these sentences. Circle the proper noun that refers to a group of people but does not end in *s*. Underline the story title. Draw a box around the indefinite pronoun. Do the verbs that follow these subjects agree with singular subjects or with plural subjects? _____

The **subject** and its **verb must agree**. There are special rules for certain kinds of subjects. **Titles** of books, movies, stories, or songs are considered singular even if they end in *-s*. (*"The Three Little Pigs"* is my little brother's favorite story.) A **collective noun,** such as *collection, group, team, country, kingdom, family, flock,* and *herd,* names more than one person or object acting together as one group. These nouns are almost always considered singular. (*Katie's team wins every game.*) Most **indefinite pronouns,** including *everyone, nobody, nothing, something,* and *anything,* are considered singular. (*Everyone likes pizza.*) A few indefinite pronouns, such as *many* and *several,* are considered plural. (*Many like spaghetti.*) **Remember to use this information when you speak, too.**

See Handbook Sections 17f, 18f

Practice

Underline the simple subject in each sentence. Then circle the correct form of each verb in parentheses.

1. "Cinderella and the Little Glass Slipper" (is/are) a story with a fascinating history.

2. Almost every culture (has/have) a collection of folktales it passes from generation to generation.

3. Many (seems/seem) to have their own version of a Cinderella story, in which a poor, mistreated girl wins the love of a prince.

4. My favorite folktale collection (include/includes) versions of this tale from Russia, Appalachia, Egypt, and Vietnam.

5. "Mufaro's Beautiful Daughters" (is/are) a version from Zimbabwe.

6. "Boots and the Glass Mountain" (comes/come) from Norway.

7. Something (is/are) unique about each version of the story.

The footwear in the Cinderella stories reflects different cultures.

8. Cinderella's footwear (is/are) sometimes made of glass, sometimes of fur, and sometimes of gold.

9. In some versions, Cinderella makes friends with the birds, and a flock (helps/help) her with difficult chores.

10. *Grimm's Fairy Tales* (includes/include) the grisly German version, in which Cinderella's sisters cut off their toes to try to fit into her shoe.

11. But everyone easily (recognizes/recognize) each of these stories as a Cinderella story.

12. In almost every version, Cinderella's family (mistreats/mistreat) her.

13. A prince finds the slipper of a beautiful, mysterious woman, and the whole kingdom (tries/try) it on for size.

14. Nobody (fits/fit) into the slipper but Cinderella.

15. When the prince and Cinderella marry, the whole country (rejoices/rejoice)—except Cinderella's family.

Name _____

Apply

Write the correct present tense form of the verb in parentheses to complete each sentence.

16. An ancient Chinese story collection _____ the earliest known version of the Cinderella story. (include)

17. The beautiful Yeh-hsien's wicked stepmother _____ her dress in rags and do dangerous chores. (make)

18. Yeh-hsien has a magic fish who _____ in a nearby pond, but her stepmother kills the fish. (live)

19. The pile of magic fish bones _____ Yeh-hsien's wishes, giving her gorgeous clothes to wear to a festival. (grant)

20. "Wishbones" _____ one title for the story. (be)

21. Unlike many versions of the Cinderella story, no royal men _____ the festival. (attend)

22. But, just as in other versions, one of Yeh-hsien's golden slippers _____ lost as she hurriedly leaves the festival. (get)

23. The richest merchant in the land _____ Yeh-hsien's lost golden slipper after the festival. (find)

24. No one _____ more beautiful than Yeh-hsien when she tries on the slipper. (look)

25. In the end, the beautiful Yeh-hsien _____ the merchant. (marry)

Reinforce

Flock and *herd* are not the only collective nouns that can refer to a group of animals. Groups of certain kinds of animals can be named by special collective nouns. Some of these nouns may be familiar to you, but others are used very rarely.

Match the collective nouns below with the animal groups they refer to. Write the correct letter in the blank.

a. cats	d. zebras	g. jellyfish	i. grasshoppers
b. lions	e. dogs or wolves	h. bees	j. ants
c. seals or whales	f. fish		

26. school _____   29. swarm _____   32. army _____   34. pack _____

27. cloud _____   30. zeal _____   33. clutter _____   35. pod _____

28. pride _____   31. fluther _____

Now use one of these collective nouns in a sentence. Remember that a collective noun is singular even when it is followed by a prepositional phrase. (*A herd of horses is coming toward us.*)

36. _____

_____

a. Always getting into trouble, Juan Bobo is a classic "noodlehead" character.

b. When telling stories to children, Juan Bobo tales are popular in Puerto Rico.

Who is getting into trouble in sentence *a*? _____

Does sentence *b* say exactly who is telling stories? _____

Verbal phrases must always refer to, or modify, a noun or a pronoun in the main part of a sentence. **Dangling modifiers** are phrases that do not clearly refer to any particular word in the sentence. Dangling modifiers make your writing unclear, so avoid them. When you begin a sentence with a verbal phrase such as *When telling stories to children,* make sure that the question "<u>Who</u> is telling?" is answered clearly in the first part of the rest of the sentence.

See Handbook Sections 25, 31

Practice

Underline the verbal phrase that begins each sentence. If the phrase is a dangling modifier, write *dangling* on the line. If the phrase is used correctly, circle the word it modifies and write *C* on the line.

1. While doing the housework, Mama often calls Juan Bobo to help her with the chores. _____

2. Needing his help, Juan Bobo only wants to play. _____

3. Doing everything wrong, even easy tasks spell disaster. _____

4. Needing water for the dishes, Mama asks Juan Bobo to fill buckets of water at the stream. _____

5. Not wanting to carry heavy buckets, baskets are chosen instead. _____

6. Woven from strips, the baskets are not waterproof. _____

7. Dripping through holes in the baskets, Juan Bobo walks home.

   _____

8. Arriving at the house, no water is left. _____

9. When leaving for church, Mama asks Juan Bobo to stay home and

   take care of the pig. _____

10. Listening to the pig's squealing, Juan Bobo thinks it must want to go

    to church, too. _____

11. Dressing the pig in Mama's new dress, the sight is

    hilarious. _____

12. Letting the pig go free, the people laugh or shriek. _____

13. Rolling in the mud with its snout in the air, Mama's dress is ruined. _____

14. Seeing the pig in her dress and shoes, Mama could not have been angrier. _____

15. Reading a Juan Bobo story, laughter is unavoidable. _____

Juan Bobo creates chaos and produces laughter in stories.

207

Apply

Use the noun in parentheses to rewrite each sentence correctly and avoid the dangling modifier. There is more than one way to rewrite each sentence.

16. While creating chaos for everyone else, trouble is sometimes made for himself as well. (Juan Bobo)

_____

_____

17. Warning him to be polite, Juan Bobo is taken to Señora Soto's house for lunch. (Mama) _____

_____

18. Trying not to sneeze, his head shakes from side to side. (Juan Bobo) _____

_____

19. Seeing Juan Bobo shake his head, it is assumed that he doesn't want any beans and rice. (Señora Soto)

_____

_____

20. Not wanting to scratch an itchy mosquito bite, a squeal of frustration is heard. (Juan Bobo) _____

_____

21. Hearing the squeal, the assumption is made that Juan Bobo doesn't like fried bananas either. (Señora Soto)

_____

_____

22. Going home hungry, it is very disappointing. (Juan Bobo) _____

_____

Reinforce

Introductory verbal phrases delay the message a sentence has to communicate. A writer might avoid introductory verbal phrases in a business letter in order to make the message more direct. Sometimes, though, writers want to delay the message of a sentence while they create an image or give important information.

Read the passage below; notice how the long introductory verbal phrase evokes Johnny Appleseed's long journey and the trees he planted.

> Planting the trees that would march and train
>
> On, in his name to the great Pacific,
>
> Like Birnam Wood to Dunsinane,
>
> Johnny Appleseed swept on.
>
> —Vachel Lindsay, from "In Praise of Johnny Appleseed"

Now look for a sentence beginning with a long verbal phrase in a book you are reading. On another sheet of paper, explain why the writer might have decided to construct the sentence this way.

a. Credited to Mother Goose, many generations of American children have listened to nursery rhymes.

b. Many generations of American children have listened to nursery rhymes credited to Mother Goose.

Which sentence makes clear who or what is credited to Mother Goose? _____
Why? _____

_____

A **verbal phrase** should be placed near the word or phrase it modifies. **Misplaced modifiers** are words or phrases that do not appear near the words they modify. Misplaced modifiers make your writing less clear; when you proofread your work, look for misplaced modifiers and revise sentences to eliminate any you find.

See Handbook Sections 25, 31

Practice

Underline the verbal phrase in each sentence. If the phrase is misplaced, draw an arrow from the phrase to the place in the sentence where it should be placed.

1. Published over the past three centuries, the name Mother Goose has appeared on collections of nursery rhymes.

2. Although she often appears surrounded by folktale characters in illustrations, Mother Goose herself is a character in only one rhyme.

3. Scholars have various theories on the origins of this figure, researching the history of nursery rhymes.

4. Some experts think that Mother Goose may be a representation of a storyteller unknown to us today.

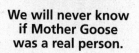

We will never know if Mother Goose was a real person.

5. Called "Goose-Footed Bertha," the original Mother Goose might have been Queen Bertha of France.

6. An alternate theory is that Mother Goose has her origin in New England, popularized in the Boston area.

7. A Boston woman, Elizabeth Goose, supposedly collected traditional rhymes in a book called *Mother Goose's Melodies.*

8. Fitting this description, no one has ever found a book.

9. Mother Goose is most likely a made-up character, though she has seemed real to many generations of children and adults, according to many experts.

10. Illustrators drawing Mother Goose have given her a consistent, recognizable appearance.

11. Surrounded by children or characters from folktales, most illustrators have drawn Mother Goose as an elderly woman in a long dress and an outlandish hat.

12. In some pictures she is riding on a huge goose, appearing on book covers.

Apply

Insert each phrase in parentheses into the sentence it follows. If the phrase is a nonrestrictive phrase, use one or more commas to set it off from the rest of the sentence.

13. The Mother Goose rhyme "Rock-a-Bye-Baby" may have been inspired by a Native American custom.

   (sung to infants by generations of parents) _____

   _____

   _____

14. At one time, some Native American peoples would safely hang babies' cradles from trees.

   (growing near their homes) _____

   _____

   _____

15. The writer of this rhyme may have been a pilgrim who came to America on the *Mayflower*. (according to

   some historians) _____

   _____

   _____

16. This rhyme might be the earliest poem on the North American continent. (written in English) _____

   _____

   _____

Reinforce

Poets often order words and phrases in unusual ways to create more vivid images in readers' minds.
Read these first lines of a poem by the twentieth century poet E. E. Cummings:

> All in green went my love riding
> on a great horse of gold
> into the silver dawn.
>
>   —"All in green went my love riding"

On another sheet of paper, rewrite these lines as a sentence with standard word order.
Then compare your version to the poet's. How does his word order intensify the image
of a horse and rider at dawn?

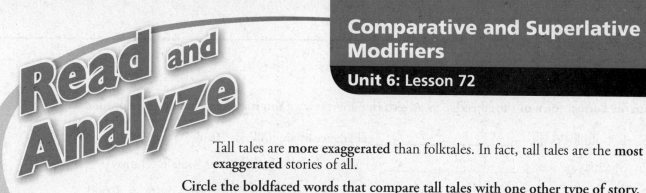

Tall tales are **more exaggerated** than folktales. In fact, tall tales are the **most exaggerated** stories of all.

Circle the boldfaced words that compare tall tales with one other type of story. Underline the boldfaced words that compare tall tales with more than one other type of story.

The **comparative form** of an **adjective** or **adverb** compares two people, places, things, or actions. Add -*er* to short adjectives or adverbs to create the comparative form. Use the word *more* before long adjectives and adverbs (generally three or more syllables) to create the comparative form (*more exaggerated*). The **superlative form** compares three or more people, places, things, or actions. Add -*est* to create the superlative form. Use the word *most* before long adjectives and adverbs to create the superlative form (*most exaggerated*). Use *better* and *less* to compare two things. Use *best* and *least* to compare three or more things.

Remember to use this information when you speak, too.

See Handbook Section 27

Practice

Think about how many things are being compared in each sentence. Then underline the correct form of the adjective or adverb in parentheses.

1. (More often/Most often) than not, folktale characters have qualities that make them different from others.

2. Rapunzel's hair grows (longer/longest) than any ordinary person's hair ever grows.

3. Snow White's troubles arise from the fact that she is "the (fairer/fairest) of them all."

4. Tom Thumb gets his name because he is (shorter/shortest) than his father's thumb.

5. Thumbelina is the (smaller/smallest) of all: she is only half as big as a thumb.

6. Folktale giants, of course, are (taller/tallest) than normal.

7. In one English story, the (meaner/meanest) giant in the land captures three sisters and plans to eat them.

8. Molly Whuppie, the (younger/youngest) of the three, is very clever.

9. She is (smarter/smartest) than the giant, and she tricks him and steals his gold.

10. After Molly tricks him, the giant keeps watch (more carefully/most carefully) than before.

11. He captures her when she returns to steal his ring, but she tricks him again, even (more cleverly/most cleverly) than the first time.

12. The folktale giant known (better/best) is Paul Bunyan, the legendary North American lumberjack.

13. Stories about Paul Bunyan's adventures on the frontier are the (more outrageous/most outrageous) tall tales I have ever heard.

14. According to legend, Bunyan cleared all the trees from North Dakota and South Dakota, and, even (more incredible/most incredible) than that, he created all five Great Lakes.

15. He dug the lakes to provide water for his blue ox, Babe, who was much (larger/largest) than any real ox.

Name _____

Apply

Write the correct form of the adjective or adverb in parentheses. (You may need to add *more* or *most*.)

16. Is Goldilocks the _____ character in any folktale? (rude)

17. She may be the _____ of all: she breaks the baby bear's chair. (clumsy)

18. She wants her porridge to be _____ than the father bear's porridge. (cool)

19. She wants her porridge to be _____ than the mother bear's porridge. (hot)

20. She eats all of the baby bear's porridge because she thinks it is the _____ of all. (good)

21. If I were a bear in a folktale, I would lock my cottage _____ than those bears did! (carefully)

Reinforce

Some adjectives are *absolute*: either they describe a thing or they do not. They cannot properly be put into the comparative form. For example, a plant is either dead or alive; it does not make sense to say "That plant is the *deadest*."

Read each of the sentences below. Think about the italicized adjectives. Decide whether putting that adjective in the comparative or superlative form in which it appears is logical and correct. If it is not logical and correct, rewrite the sentence so it gives accurate information.

22. Paul Bunyan is the *most unique* character in American folklore. _____

_____

23. Snow White's stepmother seems even *more wicked* than Cinderella's stepmother. _____

_____

24. The clothes made for the emperor in Hans Christian Andersen's tale "The Emperor's New Clothes" are the

most invisible clothes any emperor has ever worn. _____

_____

25. "Rumpelstiltskin" is one of the *most difficult* fairy tale names to spell. _____

_____

26. Goldilocks thought that the baby bear's bed was the *most perfect*. _____

_____

Review

Subject Pronouns and Object Pronouns

Circle each boldfaced word that is a subject pronoun. Underline each boldfaced word that is an object pronoun.

1. I am doing a report on animal characters in folktales.

2. Keesha is working with **me** on the report.

3. **We** are going to act out some stories.

Circle the correct pronoun or pronouns in parentheses.

4. Keesha and (I/me) are going to act out the story of Coyote and Horned Toad.

5. (Her and I/She and I) have made masks for our performance in the school folktale contest.

6. I hope first prize will go to Keesha and (I/me).

Pronoun-Antecedent Agreement

Underline the antecedent or antecedents of each boldfaced pronoun.

7. Coyote gets mad at Horned Toad and swallows **him** whole.

8. Trapped inside Coyote, Horned Toad begins kicking and scratching **him**.

9. Keesha is playing Horned Toad, so **she** will hide behind me and pretend to be inside my stomach.

Mark an *X* through each pronoun that does not have a clear antecedent.

10. Robert and Stuart are making a Russian folktale into a play, and he read me the first draft of their script.

11. I told Robert that we should work together to revise the draft, and he agreed with my suggestion.

Using *Who* and *Whom*

Write *who* or *whom* to complete each sentence correctly.

12. I made up my own folktale character, _____ is a talkative squirrel named Slim.

13. Slim tells predators _____ plan to eat him long, boring stories.

14. The animals to _____ Slim tells his stories fall asleep, and he gets away.

Subject-Verb Agreement

Circle the correct form of each verb in parentheses.

15. "The Bremen Town Musicians" (is/are) a terrific animal folktale.

16. This story about four old animals (makes/make) me smile every time I read it.

17. An old donkey no longer able to carry heavy loads (goes/go) off to make his fortune.

18. A dog, a cat, and a rooster (joins/join) the donkey along the road to Bremen.

19. Nobody (wants/want) these animals anymore, so they must take care of themselves.

20. Neither the donkey, nor the dog, nor the cat, nor the rooster (sings/sing) very well.

Dangling and Misplaced Modifiers

Underline the verbal phrase in each sentence. If the phrase is a dangling modifier, write *dangling* on the line. If the phrase is a misplaced modifier, write *misplaced* on the line.

21. Traveling to Bremen, a group of robbers is discovered hiding out in a little house. _____

22. The animals drive the robbers out of the house, crowing, barking, and making a terrible racket.

    _____

23. Relaxing and eating the robbers' food, it is a perfect home. _____

Comparative and Superlative Modifiers

Circle the correct form of the adjective or adverb in parentheses.

24. Those animals are the (noisier/noisiest) musicians I have ever heard.

25. The donkey sings even (worse/worst) than the cat.

26. The rooster is the (louder/loudest) singer of all.

Revising Sentences

Rewrite each sentence so it is correct.

27. In the tale "bremen Town musicians," the dog the cat the rooster and the donkey makes an unusual

    entourage. _____

    _____

28. The four of them becomes friends in their quest for a happy life, and allies. _____

    _____

29. A band of robbers are frightened by the terrible sounds of their music and run away. _____

    _____

30. The story of how they outsmart the robbers prove that talent isn't everything. _____

    _____

31. Coyotes, foxes, and wolves is all popular folktale characters. _____

    _____

32. Wolfes in real life is smart, but they usually is the losers in Folktales. _____

    _____

33. Kindness in folktales from most cultures, and cleverness generally wins out over greed. _____

    _____

34. You can gain insights into what qualities a particular culture values if we study its folktales.

    _____

    _____

35. People seeking to learn about a culture's values through its folktales must recognize that we will find different

    values emphasized in different tales. _____

    _____

a. No one **except** Babe the ox could rival Paul Bunyan's size.

b. In Babe, Paul found a friend who could love and **accept** him.

Which sentence has a word that means "approve"? _____

Which sentence has a word that means "other than"? _____

Homophones and Other Commonly Confused Words

Homophones, such as *weather* and *whether,* and words that sound similar, such as *advice* and *advise,* can cause confusion. One way to know which word to use is to consider the context of the sentence.

Words in Context

Write the word that best completes each sentence. Use a dictionary if you need help.

conscience	formally	marshal	conscious	precede
shear	proceed	formerly	martial	sheer

1. Were you _____ of the dangerous storm approaching?

2. The lie Lena told weighed on her _____.

3. Karate is one of the most popular _____ arts.

4. The tour guides _____ crowds through the museum.

5. The _____ curtains let in most of the sunlight.

6. To make wool, you must first _____ the sheep.

7. After a short break, we will _____ with the lesson.

8. The singing of the national anthem will _____ the first inning.

9. We were _____ residents of Los Angeles.

10. You must _____ accept the royal invitation.

Pattern Practice

Replace the underlined word or phrase with a word that means the same thing. Use a dictionary if you need help.

manor	uninterested	burrow	disinterested	manner	borough

11. We need an <u>impartial</u> person to be our judge. _____

12. Paul is <u>not engaged</u> in this game and wants to quit. _____

13. The artist paints in the <u>style</u> of Monet. _____

14. The <u>estate</u> contains a grand house and thousands of acres. _____

15. Kevin lives in a tiny <u>town</u> outside of the capital. _____

16. The prairie dogs <u>dig</u> under the ground for shelter. _____

Read the sentence and circle *True* or *False*. If the sentence is false, replace the word in bold type with a homophone or similar word to make the sentence true. Then rewrite the sentence.

17. True False A ceremony is a way to **formerly** recognize someone.

_____

18. True False A **dessert** is an arid region with little rainfall.

_____

19. True False Someone who is **conscious** is aware of the situation.

_____

20. True False A meteorologist tries to forecast the **weather**.

_____

Use the
Dictionary

Complete each homophone pair. Check your spellings in a print or an online dictionary.

21. overs_____s   Supervises

overs_____s   Abroad

22. b_____ch   A sandy shore

b_____ch   A kind of tree

Diagramming Subject and Object Pronouns

You have learned how to diagram the simple subject and the direct object in a sentence.

Paul Bunyan liked fluffy **pancakes.**

Subject and object pronouns are placed in the same places in a sentence diagram as the nouns they stand for would be placed.

He liked **them.**

He | liked | them

Diagram these sentences. Refer to the models if you need help.

1. I have a book about Paul Bunyan.

2. It contains twelve folktales.

3. My brother and I read them yesterday.

Diagramming Adjective Clauses

You have learned that an adjective clause is a dependent clause that describes a noun or pronoun and begins with a relative pronoun such as *who, that,* or *which.* Notice the way an adjective clause is diagrammed. In this sentence, the relative pronoun *that* is the direct object of the verb *found.*

The huge ox **that Paul Bunyan found** was blue.

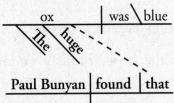

4. What sentence elements does the dashed slanted line connect? _____
   a. the two verbs in the sentence   **b.** the direct object and the relative pronoun *that*
      c. the relative pronoun *that* and the noun to which it refers

In this example, the relative pronoun ***that*** is the subject of the adjective clause.

An ox **that is blue** attracts attention.

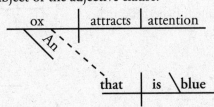

217

Try diagramming these sentences. Be sure to decide whether the relative pronoun is the *subject* of the adjective clause or the *direct object* of its verb.

5. Babe had a body that resembled a blue mountain.

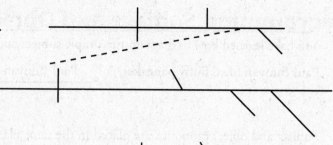

6. The strength that this ox possessed was tremendous.

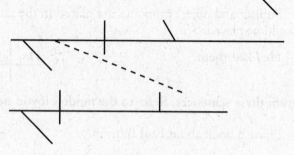

Diagramming Adverb Clauses

You have learned that an adverb clause is a dependent clause that tells about a verb, an adjective, or an adverb and that an adverb clause often begins with a subordinating conjunction such as *although* or *because,* or with a relative adverb such as *when* or *where.*

When Babe bellowed, people listened.

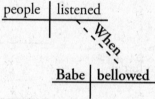

7. Where is the relative adverb *when* placed in this diagram? _____

   a. on a slanted dotted line below the simple subject

   b. on a slanted dotted line connecting the verb in the clause to the word the clause modifies

   c. on a slanted dotted line connecting two subjects

Diagram these sentences. Refer to the model if needed.

8. Although Babe was powerful, he obeyed Paul's commands.

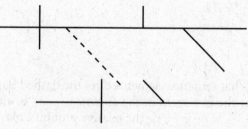

9. Whenever Paul called, Babe appeared.

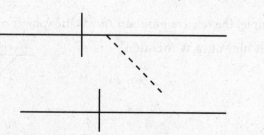

Writing Sentences

These sentences need your help. Rewrite each one so that the subject and verb agree.

1. Nobody are sorry when the wolf falls into the soup pot as he is climbing down the chimney to eat the pigs.

_____

_____

2. Attitudes toward canine characters is more favorable in Native American tales than in European ones.

_____

_____

3. Thoughts of a wonderful new name makes Coyote drift off to sleep, however, and he ends up last of all.

_____

4. "The Three Little Pigs" are a good example of a European folktale with a villainous wolf.

_____

5. When a fox or a wolf appear in a European fairy tale, that animal is usually the villain.

_____

_____

6. "Coyote Gets His Powers" tell how Coyote tries to stay awake all night in order to be first in

line on the day all the animals are to be given names. _____

_____

7. In contrast, Native American folklore portray Coyote as a rascal, not a villain. _____

_____

A piece of writing comparing two characters may be divided into two paragraphs. The first paragraph describes how the characters are alike. The second paragraph might describe the characters' differences. Each paragraph should have a topic sentence stating its main idea. Notice this structure in this model.

At first glance, the character Sleeping Beauty and the character Beauty from "Beauty and the Beast" might seem to be very similar. Both are young and beautiful. Magic spells cause problems for both: Sleeping Beauty is put under a spell that makes her sleep endlessly, while Beauty meets a prince who has had a spell cast on him that makes him appear to be a monster. Also, both characters fall in love.

A closer look shows these characters to be very different, however. Sleeping Beauty is completely helpless. She must wait for someone else to break the spell she is under. In contrast, Beauty herself bravely breaks the spell that traps the Beast. While Sleeping Beauty falls in love at first sight with a handsome prince, Beauty falls in love slowly over time. She recognizes the inner goodness of the ugly Beast. She does not know until after she has fallen in love with him that the Beast is actually a handsome prince. Sleeping Beauty is weak and superficial; Beauty is brave and wise.

Writing a Paragraph

The sentences you repaired on page 219 can be reordered to make one paragraph describing differences between Coyote and Wolf. Decide which sentence is the topic sentence and which sentences are the supporting sentences. Reorder the sentences, and write the paragraph on the lines below.

_____

_____

_____

_____

_____

_____

_____

_____

Write two paragraphs of your own in which you compare two folktale characters. In the first paragraph, tell how the characters are alike. Be sure to use a topic sentence and supporting examples. In the second paragraph, describe differences between the characters. Use the model paragraph on page 219 as a guide. Continue writing on a separate sheet of paper if you need more space.

_____

_____

_____

_____

_____

_____

_____

Read your paragraphs again. Use this checklist to make sure they are complete and correct.

- ❑ My composition has a topic sentence.

- ❑ The subject and verb in each sentence agree.

- ❑ Each paragraph contains a topic sentence and supporting details.

- ❑ My composition has a concluding sentence.

- ❑ I have described both similarities and differences.

Proofreading
Practice

Read this passage about Hans Christian Andersen and find the mistakes. Use the proofreading marks below to show how each mistake should be fixed. Use a dictionary to check and correct spellings.

Proofreading Marks

Mark	Means	Example
℘	delete	Hans Christian Andersen's fairy tales are famous throughout the the world.
∧	add	Hans Christian Andersen's fairy tals are famous throughout the world.
≡	make into an uppercase letter	Hans Christian andersen's fairy tales are famous throughout the world.
˅	add apostrophe	Hans Christian Andersens fairy tales are famous throughout the world.
(sp)	fix spelling	Hans Christian Andersen's phary tales are famous throughout the world.
/	make into a lowercase letter	Hans Christian Andersen's fairy tales are Famous throughout the world.

A Master Storyteller

Before the invenshin of the printing press. Folklore were passed from generation to generation orally. Once the printing press made it possible for storys to be shared and preserved in print, writers began setting these tales down on paper. some writers proved to be most skillful storytellers than others. perhaps the more skillful of all was the Danish writer Hans Christian Andersen, whom took characters and plots from folktales and developed them into long, complecks storys.

Andersens lively tales is full of beautiful images noble characters and inspiring triumphs. It captures some of the best elements of the human spirit. Yet andersen's own life was filled with hardships and sadness. Born too poor parents in Odense, Denmark, Andersen lost his father when he was 11 years old. At the age of 14 he left home and moved to the capital, copenhagen, to try to make a life for him. After finishing school, Andersen began writing Poems, Plays, and Novels. He enjoyed some success, but life remained difficult? Hoping to add to his meager income, stories for children, which he called "trifles," were written. Them proved to be extremly poplar, but for a long time he considered these less importanter than his writings for adults.

Andersen eventually wrote and publish more than 160 tails for children. Many of his storys continues to be popular today. More than a century after his death. In fact, some is now been translated into more than one hundred languages.

221

Proofreading
Checklist

You can use the list below to help you find and fix mistakes in your own writing. Write the titles of your own stories or reports in the blanks at the top of the chart. Then use the questions to check your work. Make a check mark (✔) in each box after you have checked that item.

Proofreading Checklist for Unit 6

	Titles			
Have I used the correct subject and object pronouns?				
Have I made sure that all pronouns are clear and agree with their antecedents in number and gender?				
Have I used *who* and *whom* correctly?				
Does every verb agree with its subject?				
Have I avoided dangling or misplaced modifiers?				
Have I used comparative and superlative modifiers correctly?				

Also Remember…

Does each sentence begin with an uppercase letter?				
Did I use a dictionary to check and correct spellings?				
Have I used commas correctly?				

Your Own List

Use this space to write your own list of things to check in your writing.

Community Connection

In Unit 6 of *Grammar, Usage, and Mechanics,* students learned more about **grammar,** and they used what they learned to improve their own writing. The content of these lessons focuses on the theme **Folktale Characters.** As students completed the exercises, they learned about some traditional folktale characters from different parts of the world. These pages offer a variety of activities that reinforce skills and concepts presented in the unit. They also provide opportunities for students to make connections between the content of the lessons and the community at large.

The Storyteller's Craft

Invite a local storyteller to your class to share some of the stories he or she has collected over time. After the storyteller has finished, identify and evaluate different methods the storyteller used to help bring the stories to life for the listeners.

Sharing Stories

Many people who find it difficult to read for themselves enjoy listening to stories read aloud. Share your storytelling skills by volunteering as a reader at a nearby library, children's hospital, or nursing home. You may want to ask your listeners whether they liked each story you read and why. Use their responses to create a list of appropriate stories for that type of audience.

Community Tales

Talk to several people of different ages and cultural backgrounds about traditional folktales their families tell. Ask each person to tell one story to you. You may wish to record the stories people tell and transcribe them (write them down) later. Use the stories to create a community folktale collection. Make notes that indicate the origin of each story you have collected, the name of the storyteller, and the date the story was recorded. Share the completed collection with your classmates. You may wish to donate your collection to the school library or to a public library in your community.

New Directions

Select one of the folktale characters you read about in Unit 6. Write an original tale in which that character plays the leading role. Adapt the setting so that the story takes place in the modern day in your own community. Make sure you follow all the rules of grammar you learned in Unit 6 when writing the story. Read the completed story aloud to your class or to a group of friends. You may want to submit it to a magazine or local newspaper for publication.

A Storied Event

Plan a storytelling festival for younger children in your school or community. Begin by making these decisions:

- Where and when will the festival be held?
- What stories will be included in the festival?
- Who will tell each story?
- What children will you invite to the festival?
- How will you announce the event?

Use the Storytelling Festival Planner on the following page to help you organize your ideas and plan the event.

Name _____

Storytelling Festival Planner

When the festival will take place:

_____

What stories will be included:

_____

_____

_____

_____

_____

Where it will take place:

_____

Who will tell each story:

_____

_____

_____

_____

_____

Whom to invite to the festival:

_____

_____

_____

How to advertise the event:

_____

_____

_____

_____

Things to bring (props, food, books):

_____

_____

_____

_____

Notes:

_____

_____

_____

_____

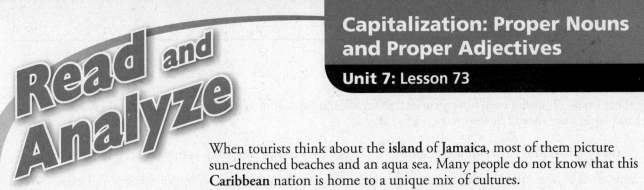

When tourists think about the **island** of **Jamaica**, most of them picture sun-drenched beaches and an aqua sea. Many people do not know that this **Caribbean** nation is home to a unique mix of cultures.

Circle the boldfaced word that names any body of land surrounded by water.
Underline the boldfaced word that names one specific island.
Draw a box around the boldfaced word that is an adjective.

A common noun names a person, place, thing, or idea. A **proper noun** names a specific person, place, thing, or idea. The important words in proper nouns are **capitalized**. **Proper adjectives** are descriptive words formed from proper nouns. They must be capitalized. A **title of respect,** such as *Mr.* or *Judge,* is used before a person's name. This title is also capitalized. The names of the months, the names of the days of the week, and the first word of every sentence are always capitalized.

See Handbook Sections 1, 15

Practice

Draw three lines (☰) under each lowercase letter that should be capitalized. (1–35) Then circle each proper noun and draw a box around each proper adjective.

The caribbean sea is part of the atlantic Ocean. Dozens of islands lie in the Caribbean. Trinidad and tobago are two separate islands that form one country. Haiti and the dominican republic are two countries that share the same island. other caribbean island countries include Jamaica, barbados, antigua, and grenada.

The region's first inhabitants were the Carib, arawak, and warahuns. in october 1492, columbus landed on an island in the Caribbean that he named san salvador. During the decades that followed, spanish explorers established colonies on many of the islands. Most of the native peoples died as a result of diseases brought by the europeans. Many others perished in wars waged against these invading colonial powers.

By 1750, the English, dutch, swedish, and french had settled in parts of the caribbean. Barbados, jamaica, and haiti became sugar plantation colonies. Sugar cane thrived in the fertile volcanic soil. Workers from Africa were forced into labor on the plantations. Laborers from china and india were also brought to the Caribbean. In the 1800s, slavery was abolished in most european countries. During that century, the islands fought for their independence, one by one.

Today's caribbean islanders are the proud descendants of Carib, african, European, east indian, middle Eastern, and chinese cultures. These cultures have combined to create a vibrant mix of traditions found nowhere else.

Name _____

Apply

Draw three lines (≡) under each lowercase letter that should be capitalized. Draw a line (/) through each uppercase letter that should be lowercase. (36–52)

The celebration of Carnival is perhaps the most famous caribbean festival. carnival has its roots in the traditions of african tribal celebrations and european religion. In some areas, Carnival takes place before easter. music, dancing, parades, and costumes are part of the celebration. In other areas, it is held in late Summer.

Paraders wear colorful and elaborate Costumes made of feathers, mirrors, animal horns, shells, and beads. Modern-day costumes might include beach balls, colored light bulbs, and headdresses shaped like satellite dishes. Traditional Characters such as moco jumbie, Midnight Robber, and Pitchy Patchy appear at Carnival festivals throughout the Caribbean. During Carnival, the sound of Steel Drums fills the air as dancers fill the street. The celebration continues nonstop for days and Nights. Carnival celebrations also occur in london, toronto, and New york City.

Reinforce

A character called "archy the cockroach" was created in the 1920s by American humorist Donald Robert Perry Marquis. The character archy was a very talented insect; he typed out wise sayings and poems by hopping from one key to another on Don Marquis's typewriter. With his method of typing, though, archy could not capitalize words because he could not use the shift key. He also could not punctuate sentences.

Read this passage by archy. Then rewrite it with correct capitalization and punctuation. Afterward, discuss with a partner the effect you think the absence of capitalization and punctuation has on the reader.

i have noticed that when chickens quit quarreling over their food they often find that there is enough for all of them i wonder if it might not be the same with the human race

—archys life of mehitabel
random thoughts by archy

53. _____

_____

_____

_____

_____

_____

_____

Why do tourists come to Scotland's **Shetland Islands**? They certainly don't come to bask in the sun—sunny weather is uncommon in Shetland, even in summer. They don't come to see forests or mountain scenery—Shetland's islands have only low hills and are mostly treeless. Most tourists don't come to shop, either, though **Harry's Departmental Store** offers a nice array of gifts, toys, and essential items such as **Yellowstone Headtorches** for seeing at night while camping.

Underline the boldfaced words that are the name of a place. Circle the boldfaced words that are the name of a product. Draw a box around the boldfaced words that are the name of a business.

Proper nouns are the names of particular people, places, or things. Capitalize each important word in geographic names and in the names of people, important events, holidays, periods of time, organizations, companies, and products.

See Handbook Sections 1 and 15

Practice

Circle each word that should begin with an uppercase letter.

1. The shetland islands lie between the orkney islands, also a part of scotland, and the faroe islands, which are administered by denmark.

2. To the west of the shetland islands is the atlantic ocean; to the east is the north sea.

3. Although skies are often gray in shetland from memorial day through the fourth of july, the sky is light much of the time because of the island's northerly location.

4. Shetland's hundred islands do offer dramatic landscapes and seascapes unspoiled by commercial development; tour companies such as wildabout orkney arrange treks for visitors.

5. Scotland has designated shetland as a national scenic area; the islands of foula, muckle roe, fair isle, and herma ness are among the most scenic.

6. Tourists can watch sea mammals such as the common seal and the gray seal all year on the beaches of shetland, and a number of marine mammal species from the arctic also visit these islands.

7. An organization called the shetland sea mammal group publishes an annual report of all seal sightings in the shetland islands.

8. Birdwatchers travel to sumburgh head national nature reserve to see seabirds such as kittiwakes and fulmars.

9. The most prevalent animals on the islands are sheep, and shetland islanders have long been famous for the quality of their wool yarn and the beauty of their sweaters.

10. The brand of yarn called shetland heritage can be purchased at jamieson & smith, 90 north road, lerwick, shetland, and local sweaters are offered at anderson & co. in the shetland warehouse in lewick.

Name _____

Apply

Think of a proper noun to complete each sentence. Write it in the blank. Capitalize each important word.

11. If I could choose an island to visit, it would be _____.

12. A store where I could buy suitable clothes for a visit to that island is _____.

13. This store is located on a roadway named _____.

14. It is located in the community of _____.

15. A perfect holiday on which to visit this island would be _____.

Reinforce

Poets often choose to capitalize words that would not be capitalized in ordinary writing; they may do this to cause readers to notice and think about particular words. Read this verse by one of America's most famous poets:

> I'll tell you how the Sun rose—
> A Ribbon at a time—
> The Steeples swam in Amethyst—
> The news, like Squirrels, ran.
>
> —Emily Dickinson
> *No. 318*

Why do you think the poet chose to capitalize the words she did? _____

_____

_____

_____

_____

_____

Now try your hand at writing a short poem in which you capitalize particular words to grab the readers' attention and make them think about the words.

_____

_____

_____

_____

_____

_____

_____

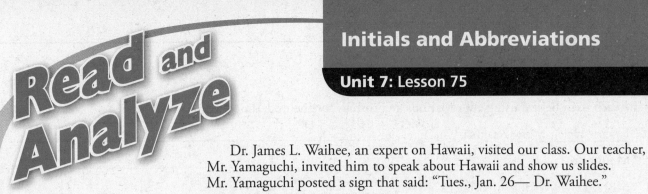

Dr. James L. Waihee, an expert on Hawaii, visited our class. Our teacher, Mr. Yamaguchi, invited him to speak about Hawaii and show us slides. Mr. Yamaguchi posted a sign that said: "Tues., Jan. 26— Dr. Waihee."

Underline a short way to write *Doctor*. Draw a square around a short way to write *Mister*. Circle short ways to write *Tuesday* and *January*. Underline a letter that stands for a name.

An **abbreviation** is a shortened form of a word. Titles of respect are usually abbreviated. So are words in addresses, such as *Street* (*St.*), *Avenue* (*Ave.*), and *Boulevard* (*Blvd.*). The names of days, the names of some months, and certain words in the names of businesses are often abbreviated in informal notes. These abbreviations begin with an uppercase letter and end with a period. An **initial** can replace a person's or a place's name. It is written as an uppercase letter followed by a period.

See Handbook | Section 2

Practice

Draw three lines (≡) under each lowercase letter that should be an uppercase letter. Draw a line (/) through each uppercase letter that should be a lowercase letter. Add periods where they are needed. (1–20)

Dr James l Waihee described the eight main islands of Hawaii. He discussed them in order from east to west. The largest Island is Hawaii, which is often called the *Big Island*.

West of Hawaii is a cluster of four islands. Maui, the largest of these, is called the *Valley Island* because much of its land lies in a fertile valley between two large volcanoes. Nearby is Molokai, called the *Friendly Island* because of the hospitality of its people. South of Molokai is Lanai, the *Pineapple Island*. Castle & Cooke, inc grows and processes pineapples on Lanai. The Company owns 98 percent of the island. Kahoolawe, the smallest of the Main islands, is now dry, windy, and uninhabited. In the early part of the century it was used for raising cattle.

The island of Oahu, which lies to the northwest of the cluster of four islands, is sometimes called the *Gathering Place*. More than 75 percent of the state's people live there. Dr Waihee said that his brother,

Hawaii has eight main islands.

mr Merrill k Waihee, lives on Oahu. He has a house on Ulukani st. in the Town of Kailua.

Because of its many colorful gardens and beautiful greenery, the island of Kauai is called the *Garden Island*. Mt Waialeale, near the center of Kauai, is one of the world's rainiest places, with an average rainfall of 460 inches a year!

Niihau, the westernmost main island, is called the *Forbidden Island*. No one can visit Niihau without the permission of its owners, the Robinson Family. The Robinson family is descended from mrs Elizabeth Sinclair, who bought the island in 1864. Most of Niihau's Residents are native Hawaiian people.

Name _____

Apply

Rewrite each item below, using abbreviations and initials for the underlined words.

21. <u>Doctor</u> Helen Marie Kealoha _____

22. <u>Mount</u> Kaala _____

23. <u>Mister</u> David Glenn Ariyoshi _____

24. <u>Mistress</u> Ellen <u>Claire</u> Takai _____

25. 19 Lahaina <u>Street</u> _____

26. 212 Kalakaua <u>Avenue</u> _____

27. The Koele <u>Company</u>, <u>Incorporated</u> _____

28. <u>Thursday</u>, <u>February</u> 14 _____

29. 2222 Bradley <u>Boulevard</u> _____

30. Haleakala <u>Drive</u> _____

31. <u>Monday</u>, <u>March</u> 22 _____

32. <u>Mistress</u> Ellen Mae Kanata _____

33. Tropic Isles, <u>Incorporated</u> _____

34. <u>Friday</u>, <u>October</u> 30 _____

35. The White Sands <u>Corporation</u> _____

36. <u>Wednesday</u>, <u>January</u> 20 _____

37. <u>Doctor</u> Ralph <u>Peter</u> Shuster _____

Reinforce

Use information from Practice to fill in the puzzle.

Across

1. The Gathering Place
6. The Valley Island
7. The Garden Island
8. The Pineapple Island

Down

2. The Big Island
3. Smallest main island
4. The Friendly Island
5. The Forbidden Island

Read and Analyze

In class we saw a movie titled Hawaii: The 50th State. We also read a poem called "A Hawaiian Memory."

Circle the movie title. Draw a box around the title of the poem. How are they written differently? _____

_____

Underline the **titles** of books, magazines, newspapers, and movies (or videos). These are written in italics in printed text. Use quotation marks around the titles of songs, stories, and poems. Capitalize the first word and the last word in titles. Capitalize all other words except articles, short prepositions, and coordinating conjunctions. Remember to capitalize short verbs, such as *is* and *are*.

See Handbook | Section 3

Practice

Draw three lines (≡) under each lowercase letter that should be an uppercase letter. Underline or add quotation marks to titles.

1. The state song of Hawaii is hawaii ponoi, which means "Hawaii's Own."

2. Last night we watched a movie called the wettest place on Earth.

3. I just finished reading a book titled kings and queens of hawaii.

4. My sister can play a Hawaiian song called the new hawaiian blues.

5. I learned a lot of Hawaiian words from a book titled you can speak hawaiian.

6. After visiting Hawaii, I wrote a poem called aloha hawaii.

7. We watched a short movie in class called lanai: the pineapple island.

8. My mother is reading a book called the mystery of the sleeping volcano.

9. Last night she rented a musical comedy titled honolulu holiday.

10. She bought a travel book called from hawaii to maui in twenty days.

11. Bethany wrote a short story about Hawaii titled the big hurricane.

12. She hopes that a magazine called the voice of hawaii will print her story.

13. She is working on another story titled the sea turtles are gone.

14. I think a great title for a book about Hawaii would be the islands of sunshine and rain.

15. The poem let's save the nene is about Hawaii's state bird.

16. The video Habits of the hawaiian goose shows the nene in its natural environment.

17. Have you seen the movie islands of light?

18. The theme song for the movie is titled rain song.

The nene, or Hawaiian goose, is Hawaii's state bird.

Name _____

Apply

Read the titles of the works on the library shelf and then answer each question by writing a complete sentence. Use correct capitalization and punctuation.

19. Which book probably contains information about Hawaii's natural environment? _____

_____

20. Which book might give historical information about ancient Hawaii? _____

_____

21. Which book would likely be a good place to find traditional tales about Hawaii? _____

_____

22. Which book would probably give information about surfing? _____

_____

23. Which movie might be a humorous mystery? _____

24. Which video would probably give information about Hawaiian history? _____

_____

25. Which video might show viewers how to make mango salsa? _____

_____

26. Which book might inform visitors of the best places to go snorkeling? _____

_____

27. Which video probably describes the process of growing, harvesting, and shipping mangos? _____

_____

Reinforce

A famous Hollywood producer is interested in turning your book about Hawaii into a major motion picture. On another sheet of paper, write a paragraph to convince her to do so. Include the title of the book and create an exciting movie title. Use correct capitalization and punctuation.

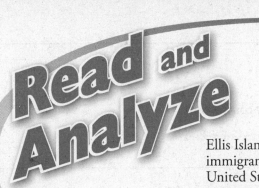

Ellis Island in New York Harbor was the first stop for many of **America's** immigrants between 1892 and 1924. Those immigrants **couldn't** enter the United States until they had passed several inspections there.

Which boldfaced word shows possession or ownership? _____

Which boldfaced word is a combination of two words? _____

To form the possessive of a singular noun, add an **apostrophe** and *s* (*girl's shoe*). For plural nouns that end in *-s*, add an apostrophe (*birds' nests*) to form the possessive. For plural nouns that do not end in *-s*, add an apostrophe and *-s* (*children's boots*). Apostrophes are also used in contractions, two words that have been shortened and combined.

See Handbook Sections 7, 28, 30

Practice

Underline the correct word in parentheses. If the answer is a possessive, write *possessive*. If the answer is a contraction, write the two words from which the contraction was made.

1. In the early nineteenth century, Samuel Ellis was the (island's/islands') owner. _____

2. The United States government bought the island from Mr. Ellis in 1808 but (did'nt/didn't) start using it as an immigrant station until 1892. _____

3. More than 12 million people entered the United States through (Ellis Island's/Ellis Islands') elegant Main Building, which opened in 1900. _____

4. The dining room seated 1,200 people, but pleasing that many (wasn't/was'nt) easy. _____

5. The dietary preferences of various (country's/countries') emigrants differed greatly. _____

6. The (immigrant's/immigrants') journeys by ship took weeks or months. _____

7. Some passengers (weren't/were'nt) in good health when they arrived in America. _____

8. The (stations'/station's) Contagious Disease Hospital had eleven wards. _____

9. They were usually filled with immigrants who had contracted diseases in a (ships'/ship's) damp, crowded quarters. _____

10. Persons with infectious diseases (couldn't/couldnt') enter the United States. _____

11. In addition to undergoing medical exams, newcomers had to answer immigration (inspector's/inspectors') questions. _____

12. Inspectors wanted to make sure applicants (wouldn't/would'nt) be a burden to society.

    _____

13. The restrictions did not spoil (newcomer's/newcomers') dreams: only about two percent of all people processed at Ellis Island were refused admission to the United States. _____

14. Those who (didn't/did'nt) pass inspection were detained, often for weeks. _____

15. Detainees stayed in big dormitories; (mens'/men's) and (women's/womens') areas were separate.

    _____ _____

Name _____

Apply

Rewrite these sentences. Replace boldfaced words with possessives or contractions.

16. In 1924 the **passage of the immigrants** through Ellis Island started to decrease. _____

_____

17. In 1954 the **buildings of the station** were closed completely. _____

_____

18. Sadly, the government **did not** maintain the elegant old buildings. _____

_____

19. The historic structures **could not** withstand the damp, salty air, and they decayed. _____

_____

20. In the 1980s, the National Park Service began major repairs on the **buildings of the island.** _____

_____

21. Today Ellis Island is a museum honoring all **the immigrants of America.** _____

_____

Reinforce

Writers sometimes use apostrophes to change the spellings of certain words to reflect the way the words are actually pronounced in informal speech. This technique is used quite often in representing a *dialect*, or regional speech pattern, in writing.

With a partner, read aloud this stanza of a poem about the famous explorer Sir Francis Drake. Circle the words for which the poet created new spellings, either by changing letters or by replacing letters with apostrophes to make the words mirror the way they would have been spoken. Then, on another sheet of paper, write the words correctly. (22–44)

> Drake he's in his hammock an' a thousand miles away,
>
> (Capten, art tha sleepin' there below?)
>
> Slung atween the round shot in Nombre Dios Bay,
>
> An' dreamin' arl the time o' Plymouth Hoe.
>
> Yarnder lumes the Island, yarnder lie the ships,
>
> Wi' sailor lads a-dancin' heel-an'-toe,
>
> An' the shore-lights flashin', an' the night-tide dashin',
>
> He see et arl so plainly as he saw et long ago.
>
> —Sir Henry Newbolt, from "Drake's Drum"

a. Manhattan Island, the legend goes, was purchased by Dutch settlers in 1626.

b. The settlers paid a group of Native Americans cloth, beads, and small trinkets worth about $24.00.

c. Today Manhattan is the center of the teeming, bustling city known as New York.

Circle the commas in sentence *a*. Circle the commas in sentence *b*.

In which sentence do the commas separate three items in a series? _____

Circle the comma in sentence *c*. What kind of words does it separate?

_____

A **series** is a sequence of three or more words, phrases, or clauses. A **comma** is used to separate items in a series. The last comma in a series goes before the conjunction (*and*, *or*). A comma is also used to separate **coordinate adjectives**—two or more adjectives of a similar kind that are used together to describe a noun. To decide whether to put a comma between adjectives, read the sentence with the word *and* inserted between the adjectives. If the word *and* sounds natural, use a comma.

See Handbook Sections 8, 16

Practice

Add commas where they are needed in these sentences.

1. New York City is a great center of culture finance entertainment and trade.

2. Central Park Times Square and the Empire State Building are world famous.

3. These and other landmarks are on the busy crowded island of Manhattan.

4. Manhattan is the smallest of New York City's five boroughs.

5. The other boroughs are the Bronx Queens Brooklyn and Staten Island.

6. Ferries tunnels and bridges connect Manhattan to the other boroughs.

7. Many thousands of clerks secretaries executives laborers professionals and job seekers commute to Manhattan every day.

8. Some work in sunny spacious offices high in the sky.

9. Others labor in dark windowless rooms.

10. Manhattan is home to the Rockefeller Center the New York Stock Exchange and the United Nations headquarters.

The Empire State Building was once the world's tallest skyscraper.

11. Several of America's largest publishing companies and banks have headquarters there.

12. The Manhattan district of Harlem has been a center of African American business and culture for more than a century.

13. Duke Ellington a suave cosmopolitan bandleader made his home in Harlem.

14. Many musicians actors and dancers come to New York City with high hopes.

15. Some seek experience some want to study and some hope to find work in the theater.

16. Only a few are able to achieve all their goals in this wealthy worldly city.

17. Many others spend years on this glittering island chasing bright elusive dreams.

Apply

Combine each group of sentences to form one sentence. Use *and* or *or* to join the last two items in a series. Add commas where you need them.

18. New York's Greenwich Village is home to poets. Greenwich Village is home to artists. Many dancers live there, too. _____

   _____

19. Greenwich Village is known for its trendy boutiques. It is known for its charming restaurants and art galleries. _____

   _____

20. We could go shopping. We could see a play. We could visit the Museum of Modern Art. _____

   _____

21. Central Park has a large skating pond. The pond is picturesque. _____

   _____

22. Noisy subway trains whisk people from place to place on Manhattan Island. These subway trains are crowded. _____

   _____

Reinforce

Skillful public speakers often use items in a series to emphasize points they wish to make and to stir listeners' emotions. Read each quotation below. Circle the commas that set off items in a series.
Then, with a partner, choose one quotation and explore its meaning.

...government of the people, by the people, for the people, shall not perish from the earth.

—Abraham Lincoln, from his address at Gettysburg

We shall not flag or fail. We shall go on to the end. We shall fight in France, we shall fight on the seas and oceans, we shall fight with growing confidence and growing strength in the air, we shall defend our island, whatever the cost may be, we shall fight on the beaches, we shall fight on the landing grounds, we shall fight in the fields and in the streets, we shall fight in the hills; we shall never surrender.

—Winston Churchill, from Speech on Dunkirk

Let every nation know, whether it wishes us well or ill, that we shall pay any price, bear any burden, meet any hardship, support any friend, oppose any foe to assure the survival and the success of liberty.

—John F. Kennedy, from Inaugural Address

Given what you know about each speaker quoted above, what would you say the three quotes have in common?

23. _____

   _____

   _____

Read and Analyze

"Mariko, will you tell us about Japan?" Mrs. Harris asked.

"Yes, I'd be happy to, but I don't know where to start," she answered.

Circle the name of the person being spoken to in the first sentence. What punctuation mark comes after that name? _____

Draw a line under the word that introduces the comment in the second sentence. What punctuation mark follows this word? _____

Draw a box around the conjunction that joins the two parts of the second sentence. What punctuation mark comes before this conjunction? _____

Commas tell a reader where to pause. A comma is used to separate an **introductory word or element,** a **noun of direct address,** or a **tag question** from the rest of a sentence. A comma is also used to separate the **independent clauses** in a compound sentence.

See Handbook Sections 8, 13

Practice

A comma is missing from each sentence. Add the missing comma. Then tell why the comma is needed: write *I* for *introductory word or element,* *D* for *direct address,* *T* for *tag question,* or *C* for *compound sentence.*

1. "Well Japan is made up of four large islands and thousands of smaller ones," Mariko began. _____

2. "Honshu is the biggest island and most of Japan's people live there." _____

3. "Japan isn't one of the biggest countries in the world but it is one of the most crowded," Raj added. _____

4. "Yes Japan has 11 cities with more than a million people," Mariko replied. _____

5. "Tokyo has about 50 million residents doesn't it?" Raj asked. _____

6. "No Tokyo has about nine million residents," said Mrs. Harris with a smile. _____

7. "Japan's cities are crowded but even big cities have many peaceful gardens," Mariko continued. _____

8. "Raj hold up this picture, would you?" she asked. _____

9. "This traditional garden is hundreds of years old and it's right in the middle of Tokyo," she said. _____

10. "Mrs. Harris is it true that Japan has few natural resources?" Julie asked. _____

11. "Yes Japan must import most of the materials it uses in industry," Mrs. Harris replied. _____

12. "Despite that fact Japan is one of the world's leading industrial nations," Mariko added. _____

13. "Mariko what does Japan export besides autos?" asked Ryan. _____

14. "Well optical equipment and electrical machinery are made in quantity," answered Mariko. _____

15. "Julie, you can name Japan's other three major islands can't you?" asked Mrs. Harris. _____

16. "They are Hokkaido, Kyushu, and Sakhalin aren't they?" Julie said. _____

17. "No Sakhalin is controlled by Russia," said Mrs. Harris. _____

18. "The other main island is Shikoku Julie," said Mariko. _____

Name _____

Apply

Rewrite the sentences, adding the words in parentheses. Be sure to use commas correctly.

19. Is it true that raw fish is popular in Japan? (Mariko) _____

20. Many people like sashimi. (yes) _____

21. I like sea urchin eggs. (but I also like hamburgers) _____

22. Yellowfin tuna is delicious in sushi. (and shrimp is also excellent) _____

23. The green paste in the little bowl is really hot! (wow) _____

24. That paste is called *wasabi*. (Raj) _____

25. It's made from horseradish. (and it's traditionally served with sushi and sashimi) _____

Reinforce

An *interjection* is a word used to express strong or sudden feeling. Interjections are sometimes used as introductory words. (The word *wow*, which you have encountered in this lesson, is an interjection.) If an interjection is said with force or strong feeling, it is followed by an exclamation mark; if a sentence follows it, the first word of the sentence begins with an uppercase letter. If an interjection is not said with force or strong feeling, it is followed by a comma, and the word after the comma is not capitalized.

See Handbook, Section 23

Choose an interjection from the word bank to complete each item. Add appropriate punctuation. Draw three lines (≡) under the first letter of any word that should be capitalized.

Alas	Bravo	Eureka	Hooray	Ahoy	Ugh	Halt	Shh

26. _____ the baby is asleep!

27. _____ this area is closed to the public!

28. _____ this soup tastes terrible.

29. _____ who's in command of this ship?

30. _____ what a magnificent performance!

31. _____ I'm afraid that book is no longer available.

32. _____ we've struck gold!

33. _____ we're all done!

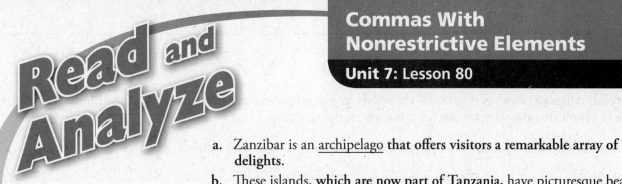

a. Zanzibar is an <u>archipelago</u> **that offers visitors a remarkable array of delights**.

b. These <u>islands</u>, **which are now part of Tanzania**, have picturesque beaches, lush tropical forests, and an alluring port city.

Which sentence contains boldfaced words that are essential for understanding the main idea of that sentence? _____ **Which sentence contains boldfaced words that just give additional information about the underlined noun?** _____ **How are these nonessential words set off from the rest of the sentence?**

_____

A **nonrestrictive element** is a clause or phrase that presents information that is not necessary for understanding the main idea of a sentence. Use commas to set off these words from the rest of the sentence.

See Handbook Section 8

Practice

Look at the boldfaced words in each sentence. If these words are a nonrestrictive clause or phrase, add one or more commas to set off these words from the rest of the sentence.

1. Unguja **also known as Zanzibar Island** is the most populous and most visited island in the Zanzibar archipelago.

2. The 21-mile-wide waterway **separating this fossilized coral island from mainland Africa** is known as the Zanzibar Channel.

3. The place **where most tourists arrive** is Zanzibar Airport; its name in the Kiswahili language means "stadium of birds."

4. Most visitors take taxis or daladalas into Stone Town **which is the capital, main port, and largest city on Unguja.**

5. Much of this city was constructed in the early nineteenth century under the direction of the Arab sultans of Oman **who ruled the island then.**

6. The old section of Stone Town is a maze of narrow, crooked streets and lively bazaars; it is similar to the medinas **found in the oldest parts of cities in North Africa and the Arabian Peninsula.**

7. The food, music, architecture, and traditions **that make Stone Town a delightful place to visit** have come from North Africa, East Africa, Arabia, India, and Europe.

8. The Beit al-Ajaib **called the House of Wonders in English** was built in 1883 by Sultan Barghash.

9. Today this grand building houses the Zanzibar National Museum of History and Culture **which contains many excellent exhibits about the island's colorful past.**

10. **Tantalized by descriptions of coastal beauty** many tourists go on excursions to palm-studded white sandy beaches in northern or eastern Unguja.

11. Jazani Forest, **a large protected tropical forest in the center of the island** is another popular destination for visitors.

12. People **visiting the forest** may catch a glimpse of a troop of Kirk's red colobus monkeys in the treetops.

Apply

Rewrite each sentence below so it includes the words in parentheses as a nonrestrictive clause or phrase. Use commas to set off this clause or phrase from the rest of the sentence.

13. More adventurous tourists take a ferry to Pemba. (Pemba is Zanzibar's other large island.)

_____

_____

14. This island offers excellent fishing and scuba diving, but it is best known for its cloves. (The island lies about 30 miles northeast of Unguja.)

_____

_____

15. Cloves are used in perfumes and in cooking. (Cloves are the dried flower buds of a tall dark-leafed evergreen tree.)

_____

_____

16. More than three million clove trees grow on Pemba. (Those trees scent the air there with a pungent, spicy aroma.)

_____

_____

Reinforce

Poets use commas to separate images and to create rhythms. Read the verse below:

Backward, turn backward, O Time, in your flight,
Make me a child again just for tonight!

—Elizabeth Akers Allen

Rock Me to Sleep

Why do you think this poet used the commas in the first line but did not use any in the second line?

_____

_____

_____

_____

a. The Galápagos Islands are located 600 miles west of Ecuador, they lie along the equator.

b. These isolated islands are home to many unusual creatures: penguins, giant tortoises, and swimming iguanas are just a few of these.

c. Scientists have studied Galápagos wildlife for centuries; they study not only the habits of certain species but also the interactions among them.

In which sentence are two independent clauses separated incorrectly with only a comma and no conjunction? _____

What punctuation marks are used to separate the independent clauses in the other two sentences? _____ _____

A **semicolon (;)** can be used instead of a comma and conjunction to separate the independent clauses in a compound sentence. A **colon (:)** can be used to separate two independent clauses when the second explains the first. It can also be used to introduce a list at the end of a sentence, to separate parts of references in a bibliography, and to separate hours and minutes in an expression of time.

See Handbook Sections 8, 13

Practice

Write a colon or a semicolon to separate the clauses in each sentence. Note: Five sentences require a colon.

1. About five million years ago the Galápagos Islands rose from the sea they are thought to be the result of volcanic explosions deep under the water.

2. These volcanic islands are barren and harsh initially they were lifeless.

3. Scientists have a theory about how wildlife came to the Galápagos creatures from South America rode there on "sea rafts" of vegetation.

4. These creatures were undisturbed for centuries over time they adapted to the environment in unique ways.

5. The marine iguana is quite unusual it swims in the rough surf.

6. Adult marine iguanas can dive forty feet they can stay underwater for thirty minutes.

7. Hundreds of years ago pirates stopped in the Galápagos some hid treasure there.

8. Whalers and seal hunters filled their ships with giant tortoises they used them for food during long voyages.

9. The Spanish name for the tortoises is *galápagos* the islands got their name from this word.

10. The tortoises are huge they can weigh up to 600 pounds.

11. At one time there were 250,000 tortoises in the Galápagos today there are fewer than 15,000.

12. Predators are responsible for much of this decrease they have eaten tortoise eggs and killed adult tortoises.

13. Human beings have caused animal predation we are now trying to protect the remaining tortoises.

14. Humans introduced dogs, pigs, and rats to the islands these animals prey on the tortoises' eggs.

15. Scientists have taken action to save the tortoises from extinction they have built a captive-breeding station.

Name _____

Apply

Draw a line from each sentence on the left to a sentence on the right to make a compound sentence. Then rewrite each pair of sentences as one sentence. Use a semicolon or a colon to separate independent clauses.

Cormorants first flew to the Galápagos many centuries ago.

According to scientists, these birds' bodies changed over time.

Swimming became more important than flying.

Their feet became stronger, and their bodies became more streamlined.

Over time, they lost their flying skills.

They adapted to island life.

16. _____

_____

17. _____

_____

18. _____

_____

Reinforce

The colon has many uses in writing. Think about how the colon is used in these examples. Then draw a line from each example to the rule it matches.

RAMÓN: Look at that iguana!
CARLO: It's coming closer!

The game will begin at 7:15 P.M.

Remember the first rule of the Wildlife Observation Club: "Never touch a wild animal."

O'Dell, Scott. *Cruise of the Arctic Star*. Boston: Houghton Mifflin, 1973.

We saw fourteen iguanas: three adult males, six adult females, and five juveniles.

Use a colon to introduce a list or series at the end of a sentence.

Use a colon after the speaker's name in a play.

Use a colon to separate the place of publication and the name of the publisher in a book reference in a bibliography.

Use a colon to separate hours and minutes in an expression of time.

Use a colon to introduce a quotation.

Now write an example of your own to match each rule.

19. _____
20. _____
21. _____
22. _____
23. _____

a. Gibraltar (pronounced juh BRAHL ter) is not an island, but it is like an island in many ways. Gibraltar is on the southwestern tip of Spain. A barren strip of no-man's-land separates Gibraltar from Spain.

b. Gibraltar-pronounced-juh BRAHL ter is not an island, but it is like an island in many ways. Gibraltar is on the southwestern tip (of Spain). A barren strip of no man's land separates Gibraltar from Spain.

In which paragraph are parentheses ( ) correctly used to enclose information that explains a word in the sentence? _____ In which paragraph are hyphens correctly used to link words that form a compound word? _____

Hyphens, parentheses, and **dashes** are used to make writing clearer.
Use a **hyphen** to
- separate syllables in a word when you must break the word at the end of a line of text.
- link the parts of some compound words, such as *no-man's-land.*
- link some word pairs or groups of words that precede a noun and act as an adjective, such as *best-known attraction*.
- link the parts of numbers (written as words) between twenty-one and ninety-nine.

Use **parentheses** to set off parenthetical elements such as an explanation or an example.

Use **dashes** to set off parenthetical elements such as authorial comments.

See Handbook Section 9

Practice

Write *C* beside each sentence in which hyphens and parentheses are used correctly. Cross out hyphens and parentheses that are used incorrectly. If you are unsure whether a hyphen should be used to link parts of a compound word or adjective phrase, check a dictionary.

1. Gibraltar's inhabitants (who call themselves *Gibraltarians*) are citizens of Great Britain. _____

2. The government of Spain believes that (because Gibraltar is physically attached to Spanish soil), it should be part of Spain. _____

3. In 1967 Gibraltarians were asked whether they wanted to become part of Spain; only forty-four people out of twelve thousand voted in favor of the idea. _____

4. The Rock of Gibraltar is 1,398 feet (426 meters) tall; it rises almost vertically from the sea. _____

5. The Rock is one of the (world's) most recognizable and visually-arresting-natural features. _____

6. The ancient Romans named the rock *ne plus ultra* (go "no more beyond" this point). _____

7. The Moors (people from North Africa) captured Gibraltar from Spain in-the-700s. _____

8. Since then, this two-and-a-half-square-mile outcropping of land has undergone 14 sieges. _____

9. In 1779 the Spanish and the French began a four-year siege. _____

10. This attempt, which was unsuccessful, led to the expression ("safe as the Rock of Gibraltar"). _____

Apply

Add hyphens or parentheses where they belong.

11. Despite its rich and unique history, Gibraltar has a less than certain future.

12. Many residents are Anglophiles people who love Britain and English things who want to continue to live

    under British rule.

13. In 2002, Spain and Great Britain discussed sharing control over this cave filled area.

14. To prevent this plan from becoming law, the people of Gibraltar held a referendum a popular vote on an

    issue in late 2002.

15. In an all but unanimous vote, the residents rejected joint control.

16. Gibraltarians inhabitants of Gibraltar remained under British rule.

Reinforce

A dash is a punctuation mark used to signal a pause. Think about how dashes are used in the sentences in the left-hand column. Draw a line from each sentence to the rule it matches.

I'd like to visit Gibraltar's famous Gorham Cave, but I—	Use a dash to set off and stress a word or phrase at the end of a sentence.
The hike back up the Rock—all the guidebooks warn visitors about this—is exhausting.	Use dashes to set off parenthetical elements, such as nonessential phrases and independent clauses, that interrupt an otherwise complete sentence.
I fear one thing more than anything else—heights.	Use a dash to mark an interrupted or unfinished sentence.

On the lines below, write your own example for each rule about the use of dashes.

17. _____

_____

_____

18. _____

_____

_____

19. _____

_____

_____

Brigid asked, "Is Australia a continent or an island?"
Arthur explained that it is both.

Underline the sentence that shows a speaker's exact words. Circle the marks that begin and end this quotation. Circle the first letter of the quotation.

> A **direct quotation,** also called direct speech, is a speaker's exact words. Use quotation marks at the beginning and end of a direct quotation. Use a comma to separate the speaker's exact words from the rest of the sentence. Begin a direct quotation with an uppercase letter. Add end punctuation (period, question mark, exclamation point, or comma in place of a period) before the last quotation mark. An **indirect quotation,** also called indirect speech, is a retelling of a speaker's words. Do not use quotation marks when the words *that* or *whether* come before a speaker's words.

See Handbook Sections 4, 6

Practice

Write *I* after each indirect quotation and *D* after each direct quotation. Then add quotation marks, commas, and end marks to direct quotations. Draw three lines (≡) under lowercase letters that should be capitalized.

1. Australia is the smallest continent said Arthur. _____

2. Ms. Wetzel added that Australia is the only continent that is also a country. _____

3. look at Australia on the map she said. _____

4. She asked why do you think Australia is called *the land down under*? _____

5. It's in the Southern Hemisphere Ramón replied. _____

6. Ms. Wetzel explained that many unusual creatures live in Australia. _____

7. Wallabies, wombats, and bandicoots are three you may have heard of she said. _____

8. Andre asked what's a wallaby _____

9. Ramón explained that a wallaby is a marsupial similar to a kangaroo. _____

10. He added the wombat is also a marsupial, but you might mistake it for a bear cub. _____

11. A bandicoot looks something like a rat he continued. _____

12. Ms. Wetzel said that the Australian emu is one of the world's largest birds. _____

The platypus has a bill like a duck and fur like a beaver.

13. I read that the platypus is a mammal that lays eggs Randall said. _____

14. This ability makes the platypus unique among mammals Ms. Wetzel replied. _____

15. Randall asked whether any living animals are related to the platypus. _____

16. The platypus is a monotreme, a primitive mammal, said Ms. Wetzel. _____

Apply

Rewrite each indirect quotation as a direct quotation. Rewrite each direct quotation as an indirect quotation. (There is more than one right way to do this.) Be sure to use punctuation marks correctly.

17. Ramón asked whether Australia was once used as a penal colony. _____

_____

18. Ms. Wetzel explained that for almost a century, large numbers of British convicts were sent to Australia to

serve their prison sentences. _____

_____

19. Brigid asked, "Who decided that Australia should be considered a continent?" _____

_____

20. Ms. Wetzel suggested that she do some research to find out. _____

_____

Reinforce

A lengthy passage quoted from a work of literature should be set off from the rest of the text. It can be indented as a block of text without quotation marks. Source information can be given in the preceding sentence or at the end of the quotation.

Read this paragraph from *Questions of Travel* by the Australian author Michelle de Kretser:

> In London the night deepened, and Laura worked on her story for Meera Bryden. She was still exhilarated by the effortlessness of writing on screen—skaters must know that swift sweep and glide. But as her work took shape, her enthusiasm ebbed. The traceless erasure of mistakes, first thoughts, alternatives masked the fallible labour that paper preserved. By the time she had finished writing, she no longer trusted her processed words. Unblemished but unfresh, they put her in mind of supermarket apples.

With a partner, discuss what experience the author is describing and how she makes the description effective. Then, look in a book or story you have read to find a vivid description of a character's experience. On another sheet of paper, write this quotation as a block of text. Be sure to give information about the source of your quote.

Read and Analyze

Coney Island Beach Chalet
Coney Island, NY 11235
August 15, 20___

Dear Carmen,

　　Today my cousins took me to the Boardwalk at Coney Island. Wow! There must have been fifty thousand people there! I rode the roller coaster, which is large and really scary. Aren't you proud of me? This used to be a real island, but the land was filled in to form a peninsula. Now Coney Island is part of Brooklyn, New York. I think it's a really neat place!

Your friend,

　　Rosie

There are five parts of this letter. Two have already been circled.
Circle the other three.

A **friendly letter** has five parts: the heading, the greeting, the body, the closing, and the signature. A friendly letter may include informal language. A **business letter** is a formal letter written to an employer or a business. It has the same parts as a friendly letter, but it also includes the address of the person to whom the letter will be sent. Use a colon after the greeting in a business letter. Omit paragraph indentations and align all letter parts along the left-hand margin. A formal **e-mail** is similar to a letter, but it usually has only four parts: a greeting, a body, a closing, and your name. An e-mail header contains your e-mail address, the e-mail address of the person you are writing to, the date, and a subject line.

See Handbook Sections 2, 34, 35

Practice

Use the appropriate words in the rule box above to label the five parts of this friendly letter.

1. _____ 425 Winters Street
Augusta, GA 30903
August 25, 20___

Dear Rosie, _____ 2.

　　Our camping trip in Minnesota was really fun. We hiked thirty miles in two days. Have you ever hiked that far? I saw a moose and went trout fishing. I have plenty of great pictures to show you.

3. _____

4. _____ Your friend,

5. _____ Carmen

Apply

Rewrite this business letter correctly on the lines below. (Hint: The sender's address and the date go first. The business's, or receiver's, address goes second.)

Brooklyn Gazette 4005 Fifth Avenue New York, NY 10002 Dear Sir or Madam September 18, 20___ Please send me the September issue of your magazine. I am enclosing seven dollars to cover the cost of the issue and the mailing expense. Sincerely Arthur Aiken 6323 Rose Street Detroit, MI 48231

_____

_____

_____

_____

_____

_____

_____

_____

_____

_____

_____

_____

_____

_____

_____

_____

_____

_____

Reinforce

See Handbook Section 37

Think of a place you would like to visit. (This could be an island, but it doesn't have to be.) Find the e-mail address of the chamber of commerce for that place or the e-mail address of a travel agent. On another sheet of paper, write an e-mail to the chamber or the travel agent asking for information about the place you would like to visit. You may want to ask about travel options and costs, places to stay, sights to see, and special events. Be sure to use correct e-mail form.

Review

Capitalization

Draw three lines (≡) under each letter that should be capitalized.

1. great britain is the largest european island.

2. On this island are the countries of england, scotland, and wales.

3. Shoppers from all over the world come to london to shop at elegant stores such as Fortnum & mason.

4. Among the many products this store offers are summer glory preserve, to spread on toast, and the coronation musical biscuit tin, to enliven teatime.

Initials, Abbreviations, and Titles

Draw three lines under each letter that should be capitalized. Add underlines, quotation marks, and periods where they are needed.

5. The most famous golf courses in the world are in st andrews, scotland.

6. I am reading a book titled golf for the enthusiastic beginner.

7. The movie Wuthering Heights takes place on the windy Scottish moors.

8. One of Scotland's best-known artists is wy Macgregor.

Apostrophes

Underline the correct word in each pair. Write *C* if the word is a contraction or *P* if the word is a possessive.

9. (Londons'/London's) most famous museum is the British Museum._____

10. Some of the (worlds'/world's) most valuable artifacts are on display there._____

11. I (didn't/did'nt) know that in Britain, soccer is called *football*._____

Commas, Semicolons, and Colons

Add commas, semicolons, and colons where they are needed. (One item requires a colon.)

12. England Scotland Wales and Northern Ireland are all part of Great Britain.

13. The people of Northern Ireland are industrious and proud some wish for freedom from British rule, but others want to remain part of Great Britain.

14. Yes conflicts continue to occur in Northern Ireland.

15. Despite the violent actions of a few, there is hope for peace large numbers of people on both sides of the issue want the children of Northern Ireland to grow up in a more peaceful world.

16. Betty Williams and Mairead Corrigan two residents of Northern Ireland who risked their lives to stop violence and promote harmony there were awarded the Nobel Peace Prize in 1976.

17. In 1998 George Mitchell an American senator was asked by the governments of Great Britain and Ireland to direct peace.

Hyphens, Dashes, and Parentheses

Add hyphens, dashes, and parentheses where they are needed.

18. The Scottish *lochs* lakes are world famous.

19. Loch Ness is the site of a real life mystery.

20. Dozens of people claim to have seen "Nessie" a dinosaur like creature swimming in the lake.

21. Fans of Nessie I confess that I am one of those fans continue to hope that the monster will someday make an appearance.

Writing Quotations Correctly

Write *D* after each direct quotation and *I* after each indirect quotation. Add quotation marks and other marks where they are needed. Draw three lines (☰) under each letter that should be capitalized.

22. Have you ever visited Great Britain, Mr. Drake? asked Roger. _____

23. Mr. Drake answered yes I toured England and Northern Ireland. _____

24. Roger said that he would like to see the Scottish Highlands. _____

Letters and E-mails

Rewrite this business letter correctly on the blanks.

25. Dear Sir or Madam Island Marvels Travel Company 8835 Bison Avenue Omaha NE 68005 Please send me some travel brochures about Great Britain. Sincerely yours, Lito Gaston 216 Cook Street Grand Island NE 68802 October 14, 20___

_____

_____

_____

_____

_____

_____

_____

_____

_____

_____

_____

We had a spectacular view of the Caribbean waters from our beachfront cottage.

Underline the word with the Latin root *spec*, which means "to look at."
Write a definition for the word. _____

Latin Roots: *spec, volv, ver*

Many words in English contain **Latin roots**. The root *spec*, as in *suspected*, means "to look at." The root *volv*, as in *revolve*, means "to roll." The root *ver*, as in *convert*, means "to turn." Knowing the meanings of common Latin roots will help you figure out the meanings of unfamiliar words you may encounter.

Word Sort

Use the words below to complete the word sort.

respectable	involve	prospect	reversible	inspect	revolution	conversation
spectator	evolve	advertise	controversy	revolve	spectacle	converse

Latin root *spec*	Latin root *volv*	Latin root *ver*

Pattern Practice

controversy	versatile	suspect	revolution	evolve	spectator
anniversary	extrovert	spectacle	revolve	inspect	advertise

Read each definition. Write *spec, volv,* or *ver* to complete each word.

1. an unusual sight or show   _____tacle

2. to develop slowly   e_____e

3. able to do many different things   _____satile

4. a person who is very outgoing   extro_____t

5. to move around a central point   re_____e

6. to look at closely   in_____t

7. to think something is true   su_____t

8. a disagreement or dispute   contro_____sy

Write the word from the word bank above that best completes each sentence.

9. My parents are celebrating their twentieth wedding _____.

10. Tonight's post-game fireworks were quite a(n) _____!

11. Laura will _____ her new business on the Internet.

12. This new waterproof backpack is so _____.

13. Earth makes one _____around the sun every 365 days.

14. Instead of playing football, Josh chose to be a(n) _____.

15. Sami enjoys talking to everyone; she is a(n) _____.

16. The referee's bad call sparked a _____ at the ball game.

Use the Dictionary

Circle the word in each pair that best completes the sentence. Use a print or an online dictionary if you need help.

17. Tamara loved every (prospect/aspect) of this movie.

18. We didn't want to (revolve/involve) you in our argument.

19. Mike is an (introvert/extrovert) who prefers to be alone.

(you) | Diagram | sentences

See Handbook · Section 40

Look at each model sentence diagram below. Then diagram the numbered sentences on another sheet of paper. Look back at the lessons on diagramming sentences if you need help.

Diagramming Subjects, Verbs, Adjectives, Articles, and Direct Objects

A distant rumble filled the air.

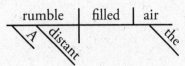

1. The mountain belched black smoke.
2. Frightened residents left the area.
3. The eruption surprised scientists.

Diagramming Compound Subjects, Compound Predicates, and Compound Sentences

Goats and sheep pawed the ground and bleated.

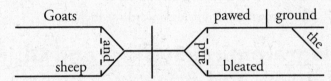

4. The mountain trembled and made loud noises.
5. An explosion rocked the village, and a strong odor filled the air.
6. Sulfur and other gases were released.

Diagramming Understood *You*, Possessive Pronouns, Demonstrative Pronouns, and Indefinite Pronouns

Cover your eyes!

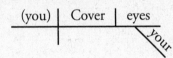

7. The villagers gathered their belongings.
8. Someone grabbed a flashlight.
9. That was a good idea!
10. Leave the village!

Diagramming Linking Verbs, Predicate Nouns, Predicate Adjectives, and Adverbs

Molten lava moves slowly.

The villagers were very courageous.

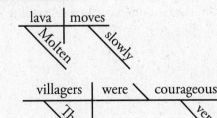

11. One woman quickly gathered the children.
12. The children were frightened, but most were quite brave.
13. A volcanic eruption is an awesome sight.

Diagramming Prepositional Phrases, Indirect Objects, and *There*

There was one man with a small infant.

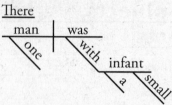

A woman handed her older son a camera.

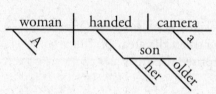

14. The boy put the camera in his pocket.
15. There was a family in a small truck.
16. They offered their neighbors a ride.
17. The driver drove quickly toward the highway.

Diagramming Subject and Object Pronouns, Adjective Clauses, and Adverb Clauses

Although some villagers feared the worst, everyone reached the safety of the distant hills.

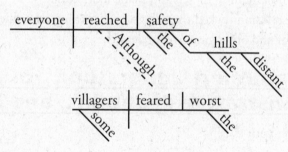

The emergency procedures that they practiced worked perfectly.

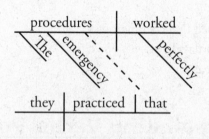

18. Because a sudden rainstorm drenched the area, fires from the lava were quickly extinguished.
19. Ash that spewed from the mountain covered everything.
20. It blanketed trees and houses.

Writing Sentences

Rewrite each sentence so it makes sense. Make each one easier to understand by using correct punctuation and capitalization.

1. Nantucket is an island off the coast of Massachusetts: with an area of fifty seven square miles. _____
   _____
   _____

2. She told me that "it's a Native American word meaning "faraway island." _____
   _____

3. Now I'm reading a book called nightbirds on Nantucket, by J R Aiken; I'll lend it to you as soon as I get home.
   _____
   _____

4. Visiting my aunt my uncle (and my cousins) in Nantucket, and I'm having a great time. _____
   _____
   _____

5. I thought the island's name sounded interesting, I asked my aunt what does Nantucket mean? _____
   _____
   _____

A friendly letter has a heading, greeting, body, closing, and signature. A well-written letter has a friendly tone, includes specific information, uses description to create pictures in the mind of its reader, and asks the reader questions to give him or her ideas for writing a letter in return. As you read the model letter below, notice the use of specific details and questions to the reader.

> 24 Coral Drive
> Key Largo, FL 33037
> July 7, 20____

Dear Lin,

    I can't believe it's already been a whole month since school let out! I've been having a good summer. For a few weeks I babysat the neighbors' three kids. It was hard work! I had fun taking them to the swimming pool, though. I even helped the youngest one learn how to swim.

    Now I'm visiting my grandparents in Key Largo. It's one of the Florida Keys, a chain of little islands off the southern tip of Florida. Key Largo is famous because an old Humphrey Bogart movie called Key Largo was filmed there.

    The best part of my vacation so far has been the glass-bottom boat ride we took over John Pennekamp Coral Reef State Park. Through the bottom of the boat we could see beautiful tropical fish and lots of scuba divers. I can see why Key Largo is called the Diving Capital of the World! I really want to take some scuba lessons while I'm here.

    I hope your summer is going well. How do you like your job as a camp counselor? Please write back and tell me all about it!

> Your friend,
> Lakeesha

Writing a Paragraph

The sentences you revised on page 255 can be used as the body of a friendly letter. Decide what order the sentences should be in. Write them on the lines below. Then add a heading, greeting, closing, and signature.

_____

_____

_____

_____

_____

_____

_____

_____

_____

_____

_____

Imagine that you have just spent five days on an island you've always wanted to visit. Write an e-mail to a friend back home. Include facts, descriptions, and questions. Make up e-mail addresses for you and your friend.

From: <your e-mail address> _____

To: <your friend's e-mail address> _____

Date: _____

Subject: _____

_____

_____

_____

_____

Reread your e-mail. Use this checklist to make sure your letter is complete and follows the correct form.

❑ Does my e-mail have all four parts?

❑ Have I punctuated the sentences correctly?

❑ Have I included specific information?

❑ Have I used abbreviations correctly?

❑ Have I capitalized proper nouns?

❑ Have I asked questions my reader will want to answer in a return e-mail?

❑ Have I used commas and semicolons correctly?

Proofreading
Practice

Read this passage about the island of Tahiti. Use the proofreading marks below to show how each mistake should be fixed. Use a dictionary to check and correct spellings.

Proofreading Marks

Mark	Means	Example
✄	delete	Papayas, coconuts, and and bananas grow on Tahiti.
∧	add	Papayas, coconuts, and bananas grow on Tahiti.
≡	make into an uppercase letter	papayas, coconuts, and bananas grow on Tahiti.
⊙	add a period	Papayas, coconuts, and bananas grow on Tahiti
∧	add a comma	Papayas, coconuts, and bananas grow on Tahiti.
sp	fix spelling	Papayas, cocconuts, and bananas grow on Tahiti.
/	make into a lowercase letter	Papayas, Coconuts, and bananas grow on Tahiti.

A Paradise Island

For 200 years, the lush tropical, island of Tahiti has been a dream destination for those who wish to return to a simpler life. Tahiti was first settled by polynesians who arrived by see from Asia. In 1767, a british explorer named samuel wallis visited the Island and claimed it for Great britain. Wallis was'nt the only european explorer to take notice of this South Pacific jewel. The following year a french navagator, Louis Antoine Bougainville, claimed the island for france. Today Tahiti is a French overseas territorie.

tahiti gained fame as a tropicle paradise in the late 1800s. The french painter paul gaugin made the island his home in 1891 he lived there for most of his later life. Gaugins' powerfull paintings illustrate the lush beauty of the island. Gaugin wrote about his life in Tahiti in the book Noa Noa which was published in 1897. At least three notable writers have also spent time in Tahiti James Michener herman melville and Robert louis Stevenson.

Tahiti is 402 square miles 1,041 square kilometers in size. The interior of the island is steep, rugged terrain covered by thick vegetation. Most of tahitis residents live in villages near the coast or in papeete pah pee AY tee, its largest city. Not surprisingly the islands'cheif industry is Tourism.

Proofreading
Checklist

You can use the list below to help you find and fix mistakes in your own writing. Write the titles of your own stories or reports in the blanks at the top of the chart. Then use the questions to check your work. Make a check mark (✓) in each box after you have checked that item.

Proofreading Checklist for Unit 7

	Titles			
Have I capitalized proper nouns and proper adjectives?				
Have I used commas correctly to punctuate items in a series and after introductory words?				
Have I used apostrophes correctly in possessives and contractions?				
Have I used colons and semicolons correctly?				
Have I used hyphens, dashes, and parentheses correctly?				
Have I written quotations correctly?				

Also Remember…

Does each sentence begin with an uppercase letter?				
Did I use a dictionary to check and correct spellings?				
Have I used the correct end marks at the end of sentences?				

Your Own List
Use this space to write your own list of things to check in your writing.

Community Connection

In Unit 7 of *Grammar, Usage, and Mechanics,* students learned about **capitalization, punctuation, and other aspects of writing mechanics** and used what they learned to improve their writing. The content of these lessons focuses on the theme **Islands and Near-Islands.** As students completed the exercises, they learned about islands around the world and what makes each one distinctive. These pages offer a variety of activities that reinforce skills and concepts presented in the unit. They also provide opportunities for the student to make connections between the materials in the lessons and the community at large.

Friendly Skies

Have you ever wondered what it's like to work 30,000 feet above the ground? Invite a flight attendant who lives in your community to visit your class and describe his or her job. Before the visit, compile a list of questions to ask during the interview. You might want to find out about the training required to become a flight attendant, what responsibilities the job entails, or learn more about emergency procedures designed to keep airline passengers safe.

Passports

The United States requires its citizens to carry a passport when they are traveling to most international destinations. Find out about the process of obtaining a passport, the requirements for receiving a passport, the differences among the three kinds of passports issued in the United States, and the reasons why passports are required for international travel. Also find out which nations require American visitors to apply for a visa. Use what you learn to create a passport guide for potential travelers.

Careers on the Go

Find out more about careers related to travel and the tourist industry. You may want to explore one of these careers:

- travel agent
- cruise ship captain or navigator
- airline pilot
- wilderness guide
- hotel manager
- air tower control operator

Try to arrange an interview with a person in your community who is in the profession that interests you. Find out what the job is like and about the qualifications and training required. If possible, arrange to accompany that person on a tour of his or her workplace.

Hometown Attractions

Think about and list the things you think make your community an enjoyable place to visit. Then produce a brochure that advertises your community to potential visitors and helps them get the most out of a trip to your area. If you need any additional information to complete your brochure, contact the local tourist information center or the chamber of commerce.

Name _____

Big Plans

Create an itinerary for a trip to any island in the world. You can obtain travel information about the island in travel books, at an embassy or consulate, at a travel agency, or on the Internet. When making your travel plans, consider these issues:

- when you will go on the trip and what the weather will be like during that season
- how you will get to your destination and the cost of the airfare or boat ticket
- where you will stay and the cost of lodging
- how much money you will need for expenses and in what form you will bring it
- what travel documents (such as a passport or visa) you will need
- what inoculations (if any) you will need to remain healthy in this part of the world
- what you will pack

Use the planner below to help you organize the information you find.

Island Trip Planner

Destination: _____

Numbers to call for information:

_____

_____

Travel documents needed:

_____

_____

Transportation/travel dates:

Departure _____

Arrival _____

Departure _____

Arrival _____

Cost of transportation:

_____

_____

Additional costs:

_____

What to pack:

_____   _____   _____   _____

_____   _____   _____   _____

Inoculations needed:

_____

_____

Expected weather:

_____

_____

Lodging/dates needed:

_____

_____

_____

_____

Cost of lodging:

_____

_____

Appendix Table of Contents

 **TEST TIP:** Read each question carefully. Then quietly tell yourself what you need to do. For example, after you read item 1, you might say, "I need to find the answer choice that is the complete predicate."

Read each item carefully. Fill in the circle next to the best answer.

1. Read this sentence.

> The ruins of the ancient city of Machu Picchu attract many visitors to Peru each year.

What is the complete predicate of the sentence?

- Ⓐ the ruins of the ancient city of Machu Picchu
- Ⓑ the ancient city of Machu Picchu
- Ⓒ attract many visitors
- Ⓓ attract many visitors to Peru each year

2. Read this sentence.

> A wall of stones surrounds this city in the clouds.

What are the simple subject and the simple predicate of the sentence?

- Ⓐ wall; stones
- Ⓑ wall; surrounds
- Ⓒ stones; surrounds
- Ⓓ surrounds; city

3. Which of the following sentences has a compound subject?

- Ⓐ People of the Inca empire began the construction of Machu Picchu about 600 years ago.
- Ⓑ They built palaces for royal family members and houses for workers and servants.
- Ⓒ Farmers and weavers produced goods for the royalty.
- Ⓓ The combination of steep cliffs and remote location protected the city from invaders.

4. Read this sentence.

> The high altitude of Machu Picchu can give visitors headaches for days.

What is the indirect object of this sentence?

- Ⓐ Machu Picchu
- Ⓑ visitors
- Ⓒ headaches
- Ⓓ days

5. Read this sentence.

> The ancient Inca built roads through the mountains and bridges across rivers.

Which nouns are the direct objects in this sentence?

- Ⓐ roads, mountains
- Ⓑ mountains, bridges
- Ⓒ roads, bridges
- Ⓓ bridges, rivers

6. Read the sentences.

> The Inca empire was large and powerful at its height. Its fine system of roads was a key to the control of other Andes peoples.

Which statement tells about the sentences?

- Ⓐ Both sentences contain predicate nouns. The first sentence contains a compound predicate noun.
- Ⓑ Both sentences contain predicate adjectives. The first sentence contains a compound predicate adjective.
- Ⓒ The first sentence contains a compound predicate noun. The second contains a predicate adjective.
- Ⓓ The first sentence contains a compound predicate adjective. The second contains a predicate noun.

7. Which sentence has a prepositional phrase underlined?

- Ⓐ The Inca <u>did not use</u> wheeled vehicles.
- Ⓑ They did not <u>write and solve</u> mathematical problems.
- Ⓒ They did not <u>develop a written language</u>.
- Ⓓ Nevertheless, the Inca ruled the largest empire <u>in the pre-Columbian Americas</u>.

Read each item carefully. Fill in the circle next to the best answer.

8. Read this sentence.

> Inca buildings of carved stone have withstood earthquakes for five centuries and remain intact today.

Which group of words is an adjectival prepositional phrase?

(A) of carved stone
(B) have withstood earthquakes
(C) for five centuries
(D) remain intact today

9. Read this sentence.

> Teams of stone haulers moved blocks of tremendous weight to construction sites.

Which group of words is an adverbial prepositional phrase?

(A) of stone haulers
(B) moved blocks
(C) of tremendous weight
(D) to construction sites

10. Which sentence has an appositive underlined?

(A) Teams of stone haulers may have included 250 people or more.
(B) A cobblestone road, a path with a surface of small rocks, made movement easier.
(C) A carved rock of 15 tons could have been moved along a cobblestone path by a large team.
(D) Carefully, in a short period of time, the Inca built hundreds of structures with huge stone blocks.

11. Read each sentence. Which sentence provides the most useful information?

(A) Dictionaries give information about words.
(B) Dictionaries help people agree on what particular words mean.
(C) In about 600 B.C. both Akkadian and Greek linguists began compiling dictionaries to help speakers and writers of the language use words in consistent ways.
(D) Languages change, so dictionaries have to be revised.

12. Read this sentence.

> How helpful bilingual dictionaries are to travelers!

What type of sentence is this?

(A) declarative
(B) interrogative
(C) imperative
(D) exclamatory

13. Read this sentence.

> Were bilingual dictionaries commonly used in Europe during the Middle Ages?

What type of sentence is this?

(A) declarative
(B) interrogative
(C) imperative
(D) exclamatory

Read each item carefully. Fill in the circle next to the best answer.

14. Read this sentence.

> Ancient settlements of the Anasazi peoples fascinate both researchers and tourists.

What is the complete predicate of the sentence?

Ⓐ Ancient settlements of the Anasazi peoples
Ⓑ of the Anasazi peoples fascinate both researchers and tourists
Ⓒ fascinate both researchers and tourists
Ⓓ both researchers and tourists

15. Read this sentence.

> Visitors to Mesa Verde National Park see remarkable cliff dwellings.

What are the simple subject and the simple predicate of the sentence?

Ⓐ Visitors; see
Ⓑ Mesa Verde National Park; see
Ⓒ see; remarkable
Ⓓ Mesa Verde National Park; dwellings

16. Which of the following sentences has a compound subject?

Ⓐ Tall mesas are separated by narrow canyons in Mesa Verde.
Ⓑ The first group of settlers established homes and farms on these flat-topped hills about A.D. 600.
Ⓒ These first residents built underground homes and raised beans and grain.
Ⓓ Roots, nuts, berries, and wild game were also important foods.

17. Read this sentence.

> The settlers on the mesas built dams and reservoirs for water collection and storage.

Which nouns are the direct objects in this sentence?

Ⓐ settlers, mesas
Ⓑ dams, reservoirs
Ⓒ reservoirs, water
Ⓓ collection, storage

18. Read this sentence.

> Late summer rainstorms brought Anasazi farmers water every year.

What is the indirect object of this sentence?

Ⓐ summer
Ⓑ farmers
Ⓒ water
Ⓓ year

19. Read these sentences.

> By A.D. 800 the Anasazi villages looked impressive and quite different from the first settlements. Houses were small aboveground structures.

Which statement tells about the sentences?

Ⓐ Both sentences contain predicate nouns. The first sentence contains a compound predicate noun.
Ⓑ Both sentences contain predicate adjectives. The first sentence contains a compound predicate adjective.
Ⓒ The first sentence contains a compound predicate noun. The second contains a predicate adjective.
Ⓓ The first sentence contains a compound predicate adjective. The second contains a predicate noun.

Read each item carefully. Select the best answer and fill in the circle on the answer sheet below.

20. Which sentence has a prepositional phrase underlined?

 (A) The bow and arrow had <u>replaced the spear</u> as a hunting device.
 (B) Farmers now planted <u>squash, corn, and melons</u>.
 (C) Farmers kept dogs <u>as lookouts</u>.
 (D) Dogs typically bark furiously when they sense human <u>or animal intruders</u>.

21. Read this sentence.

> In time, the Anasazi homes atop the mesas became taller and grander.

Which group of words is an adjectival prepositional phrase?

 (A) in time
 (B) the Anasazi homes
 (C) atop the mesas
 (D) became taller and grander

22. Read this sentence.

> At a later time, some kind of grave difficulty caused dramatic changes in these Anasazi communities.

Which group of words is an adverbial prepositional phrase?

 (A) At a later time
 (B) of grave difficulty
 (C) caused dramatic changes
 (D) in these Anasazi communities

23. Which sentence has an appositive underlined?

 (A) The villagers deserted the mesas and built new homes <u>on the steep canyon walls</u>.
 (B) Perhaps winter weather atop the mesas <u>had become too cold</u>.
 (C) Perhaps drought, <u>a lack of rainfall</u>, had made farming atop the mesas difficult.
 (D) Most likely, <u>enemies had threatened</u>, and the Anasazi built the cliff dwellings as a refuge.

24. Read each sentence. Which sentence provides the most useful information?

 (A) Native peoples in the Americas grew pineapples.
 (B) Europeans first encountered this tasty fruit in 1493; in that year Spanish explorers visited the island of Guadeloupe and found the residents cultivating it.
 (C) The people of Guadeloupe made decorations out of pineapple plants.
 (D) A European called the pineapple "one of the best fruits in the world."

25. Read this sentence.

> Be careful of the prickly knobs as you peel that pineapple.

What type of sentence is this?

 (A) declarative
 (B) interrogative
 (C) imperative
 (D) exclamatory

 **TEST TIP:** Don't spend too much time on one test item.

Read each item carefully. Fill in the circle next to the best answer.

1. **Which of the following sentences is a compound sentence?**

   (A) Sea dragons live in the ocean near Australia; they are a type of sea horse.

   (B) The leafy sea dragon has greenish flaps of flesh that grow out from its body.

   (C) If you saw a leafy sea dragon, you might think it was dragging along pieces of seaweed.

   (D) These creatures hide in clumps of seaweed and use their disguise to sneak up on prey.

2. **Read this sentence.**

   > Individual humpback whales are easy to identify because each one has distinctive body marks and pigmentation.

   What types of clauses are in this sentence?

   (A) The first is an independent clause; the second is dependent.

   (B) The first is a dependent clause; the second is independent.

   (C) Both are dependent clauses.

   (D) Both are independent clauses.

3. **Which of the following is a complex sentence?**

   (A) Have you had a chance to visit the National Aquarium in Baltimore?

   (B) When you visit, you should spend time in the center of the Atlantic reef ring tank.

   (C) You will be surrounded by fish, and you can watch them swim.

   (D) Another interesting sight is the 63-foot-long skeleton of a humpback whale.

4. **Which sentence has an adjective clause underlined?**

   (A) The orca is a large marine mammal <u>with a huge appetite</u>.

   (B) Another name <u>for this creature</u> is the killer whale.

   (C) An adult orca may be 25 feet long <u>and weigh seven tons</u>.

   (D) One orca <u>that is in captivity</u> eats more than 200 pounds of fish a day.

5. **Which sentence has an adverb clause underlined?**

   (A) Orcas perform <u>at some wildlife theme parks</u>.

   (B) Trainers teach them <u>to perform stunts in a sequence</u>.

   (C) <u>When an orca performs its stunts well</u>, the trainer gives it food.

   (D) Many people <u>who work with orcas</u> consider them very intelligent.

6. **Which of the following sentences has a restrictive clause underlined?**

   (A) Orcas, <u>which are the largest of the dolphins</u>, are among the world's most powerful predators.

   (B) Orcas hunt in pods, <u>which are groups of up to 40 related individuals</u>.

   (C) Orcas have teeth <u>that can be four inches long</u>.

   (D) Orcas hunt seals, <u>which they sometimes grab right off the ice</u>.

7. **Read this sentence.**

   > Orca pods use cooperative hunting techniques <u>that are quite effective</u>.

   What type of phrase or clause is underlined in this sentence?

   (A) adjective phrase

   (B) adverb phrase

   (C) adjective clause

   (D) adverb clause

Read each item carefully. Fill in the circle next to the best answer.

8. Which sentence has an infinitive phrase underlined?

   (A) Many orcas in captivity appear <u>to enjoy contact with humans</u>.
   (B) An orca may give a trainer <u>a ride on its back</u>.
   (C) One orca plays hide-and-seek with its trainer, <u>who looks through windows in the tank</u>.
   (D) Orcas respond <u>to eye contact with humans</u>.

9. Read this sentence.

   > The creature staring at us from the tank is a giant Pacific octopus.

   Which of these phrases is a participial phrase in the sentence?

   (A) the creature
   (B) from the tank
   (C) staring at us
   (D) a giant Pacific octopus

10. Which of these sentences has a gerund phrase underlined?

    (A) Octopuses are invertebrates, <u>but they have eyes like vertebrates</u>.
    (B) The red Pacific octopus is <u>the largest</u> of all octopuses.
    (C) <u>Seeing its 15-foot-long arms</u> can be frightening.
    (D) An octopus <u>encountering an enemy</u> may eject an inky fluid to help itself escape.

11. Which of the following sentences is written correctly?

    (A) Deep sea fishing, the most exciting type of fishing.
    (B) For me, the beach is the best place to have fun.
    (C) I dig for clams, I also collect mussels in rocky areas.
    (D) My uncle catches crabs in the winter months, and sometimes he takes me with him, and I help him set the traps and also haul them in, and I know how to be careful on the boat so I don't slip and go overboard.

12. Which of the following sentences shows the relationship between ideas most effectively?

    (A) Many sport fishing enthusiasts try to catch swordfish; conservationists do not worry about this, though, because swordfish remain plentiful in the seas.
    (B) Swordfish are a popular type of sport fish.
    (C) Conservationists do not worry about the popularity of swordfish with sport fishing enthusiasts.
    (D) Swordfish remain plentiful in the seas, so conservationists don't worry about the popularity of this fish with sport fishing enthusiasts.

13. Which of the following sentences is a compound sentence?

    (A) If you saw a thornback ray from the bottom, you might think you were in a science fiction movie.
    (B) This flat, broad fish is an eerie silver color, with shades of rose and blue.
    (C) You would see a yellow mouth and two dark, scary eyes.
    (D) Those "eyes" are actually nostrils; the thornback ray's real eyes are on its top side.

14. Read this sentence.

    > When fiddler crabs tear leaves into tiny bits, they create an important element in the web of life in a red mangrove swamp.

    What types of clauses are in this sentence?

    (A) The first is an independent clause; the second is dependent.
    (B) The first is a dependent clause; the second is independent.
    (C) Both are dependent clauses.
    (D) Both are independent clauses.

Read each item carefully. Fill in the circle next to the best answer.

15. **Which of the following is a complex sentence?**

    (A) My friend Ricardo did not like aquariums until he visited one.

    (B) He loved the tidepool exhibits, and the shark tank left him speechless.

    (C) Watching the otters crack open shellfish delighted him.

    (D) He was wise to visit on a weekday; the aquarium was not too crowded.

16. **Which sentence has an adjective clause underlined?**

    (A) Humpback whales live in oceans <u>throughout the world</u>.

    (B) In summer they swim in deep, cold waters <u>that teem with small fish and crustaceans</u>.

    (C) In winter they live in warm tropical waters, <u>and they breed there</u>.

    (D) An adult humpback whale can be fifty feet long <u>and weigh fifty tons</u>.

17. **Which sentence has an adverb clause underlined?**

    (A) Humpback whales produce <u>lengthy, varied songs</u>.

    (B) The high notes sound like whistles, <u>and the low notes sound like rumbles</u>.

    (C) <u>Although the songs are sung throughout the year</u>, they are sung most frequently in mating season.

    (D) Whales <u>that are alone</u> sing these songs the most.

18. **Which of the following sentences has a nonrestrictive clause underlined?**

    (A) The lionfish, <u>whose scientific name is Pterois</u>, is a venomous marine creature.

    (B) The lionfish has colorful markings <u>that warn other creatures of its deadly nature</u>.

    (C) Divers must take great care in areas <u>where lionfish populations are large</u>.

    (D) A diver <u>who comes in contact with a lionfish's fin rays</u> can experience severe pain, nausea, and dizziness.

19. **Read this sentence.**

    > More than 1,500 species <u>of starfish</u> inhabit seabeds around the world.

    What type of phrase or clause is underlined in this sentence?

    (A) adjective phrase

    (B) adverb phrase

    (C) adjective clause

    (D) adverb clause

20. **Read this sentence.**

    > <u>If you visit tide pools on the Pacific Coast</u>, you may see a number of brightly colored starfish.

    What type of phrase or clause is underlined in this sentence?

    (A) adjective phrase

    (B) adverb phrase

    (C) adjective clause

    (D) adverb clause

Read each item carefully. Fill in the circle next to the best answer.

21. **Which sentence has an infinitive phrase underlined?**

    Ⓐ Most humpbacks in the North Pacific swim to Hawaii in late fall.

    Ⓑ Swimming in the warm water there, they breed and care for their young.

    Ⓒ These huge creatures eat little or nothing while in this region.

    Ⓓ In late spring they return to cold ocean waters to feed.

22. **Read this sentence.**

    > Some tourists cruising through southeast Alaska are thrilled to see Steller sea lions on rocky outcrops.

    Which of these phrases is a participial phrase in the sentence?

    Ⓐ cruising through southeast Alaska

    Ⓑ are thrilled

    Ⓒ to see Steller's sea lions

    Ⓓ on rocky outcrops

23. **Which of these sentences has a gerund phrase underlined?**

    Ⓐ Unlike some other sea lions, Steller sea lions avoid human beings.

    Ⓑ Some Steller sea lions are permanent residents of protected waters.

    Ⓒ Many others move between these waters and the open ocean.

    Ⓓ Photographing these marine mammals may be easiest in late September.

24. **Which of the following sentences shows the relationship among ideas most effectively?**

    Ⓐ A new species of sea snake was discovered.

    Ⓑ The discovery in Australia of an unusual new species of sea snake was announced on February 21, 2012; the species, which has been named *Hydrophis donaldi,* is the only sea snake that has spiny scales all over its body.

    Ⓒ *Hydrophis donaldi,* a newly discovered species of sea snake, has spiny scales all over its body.

    Ⓓ A big discovery was announced on February 21, 2012; the creature discovered is a new species of sea snake, and it was found off the coast of Australia.

25. **Which of the following sentences is written correctly?**

    Ⓐ I am fascinated by sea creatures of all kinds, and I love to swim, and I have never gotten seasick, and my friends are scared of things like giant clams, but I'm not, and I hope to study them someday.

    Ⓑ My goal is to become a scuba diver.

    Ⓒ I have taken lessons in a pool, soon I will make my first ocean dive.

    Ⓓ If I ever get a chance to swim with a sea turtle!

 **TEST TIP:** Eliminate answer choices that you know are incorrect.

Read each item carefully. Fill in the circle next to the best answer.

1. Read this sentence.

> Charles Steinmetz helped the young General Electric Company become a success.

Which of these choices is a common noun in this sentence?

(A) Charles Steinmetz
(B) young
(C) General Electric Company
(D) success

2. Read this sentence.

> Charles Steinmetz had great <u>difficulty</u> with mathematics in elementary school, but he later became a top student.

What kind of noun is underlined?

(A) abstract noun
(B) concrete noun
(C) collective noun
(D) possessive noun

3. Read this sentence.

> Steinmetz, a brilliant engineer, solved many problems having to do with electrical circuits.

Which of these words is a singular noun in this sentence?

(A) engineer
(B) problems
(C) electrical
(D) circuits

4. Read this sentence.

> This _____ spine was abnormally curved, but he did not let this disability affect his career.

Which of these words would properly complete the sentence?

(A) genius'
(B) genius's
(C) geniuses'
(D) geniuses's

5. Read this sentence.

> Helen Keller was born with sight and hearing, but <u>she</u> lost the ability to see and hear as the result of a childhood illness.

What kind of personal pronoun is underlined?

(A) first person
(B) second person
(C) third person singular
(D) third person plural

6. Read this sentence.

> Helen Keller's teacher was a woman named Anne Sullivan; she herself had limited vision.

What word from the sentence is an intensive pronoun?

(A) teacher
(B) woman
(C) she
(D) herself

7. Read this sentence.

> Anne Sullivan taught young Helen signs for words, and Helen quickly began developing _____ language skills.

Which of these is the correct pronoun form to use to complete this sentence?

(A) she
(B) her
(C) their
(D) hers

Read each item carefully. Fill in the circle next to the best answer.

8. Read each sentence. Look at the underlined word in it. Which sentence is written *incorrectly*?

Ⓐ White water rafting is a sport <u>that</u> requires arm strength, cooperation, and good judgment.

Ⓑ People <u>who</u> cannot use their legs can become expert white water rafters.

Ⓒ People <u>what</u> have other disabilities can also enjoy this sport.

Ⓓ Environmental Traveling Companions, <u>which</u> is based in San Francisco, California, runs many river trips for disabled people.

9. Read this sentence.

> Almost all of the players in the National Basketball Association are taller than average height.

Which word from the sentence is an indefinite pronoun?

Ⓐ almost
Ⓑ all
Ⓒ taller
Ⓓ average

10. Read this sentence. Look at the underlined word in it.

> Tyrone "Muggsy" Bogues became <u>an</u> NBA star even though he was only 5 feet 3 inches tall.

What kind of adjective is the underlined word?

Ⓐ an adjective that tells what kind
Ⓑ an adjective that tells how many
Ⓒ an article
Ⓓ None of the above

11. Read this sentence.

> These players are stronger, but _____ players are quicker.

Which of these words would correctly complete this sentence?

Ⓐ this
Ⓑ that
Ⓒ these
Ⓓ those

12. Read this sentence.

> All serious athletes should eat healthful nutritious foods.

How should this sentence be rewritten?

Ⓐ All, serious athletes should eat healthful nutritious foods.
Ⓑ Serious all athletes should eat healthful nutritious foods.
Ⓒ All serious athletes should eat healthful, nutritious foods.
Ⓓ All serious athletes should eat nutritious healthful foods.

13. Read this sentence.

> Daniel Inouye, who was a resident of Hawaii, fought bravely for the United States in World War II.

Which of these choices is a common noun in this sentence?

Ⓐ Daniel Inouye
Ⓑ resident
Ⓒ the United States
Ⓓ World War II

Read each item carefully. Fill in the circle next to the best answer.

14. Read this sentence.

> Inouye was studying medicine at the University of Hawaii when Japanese planes bombed Pearl Harbor in a surprise attack.

What kind of noun is underlined?

- (A) abstract noun
- (B) concrete noun
- (C) collective noun
- (D) possessive noun

15. Read this sentence.

> Daniel Inouye enlisted in the U.S. Army and joined the 442nd Regimental Combat Team, a unit made up primarily of Japanese Americans.

What kind of noun is underlined?

- (A) abstract noun
- (B) concrete noun
- (C) collective noun
- (D) possessive noun

16. Read this sentence.

> Many soldiers in Inouye's unit suffered terrible injuries; Inouye himself lost an arm.

Which of these words is a singular noun in this sentence?

- (A) soldiers
- (B) unit
- (C) injuries
- (D) himself

17. Read this sentence.

> This brave _____ injury did not prevent him from becoming a very successful politician.

Which of these words would correctly complete the sentence?

- (A) man's
- (B) mans'
- (C) men's
- (D) mens'

18. Read this sentence.

> After serving as a representative and a senator in Hawaii, he was elected to the U.S. House of Representatives and then to the Senate.

What kind of personal pronoun is underlined?

- (A) first person
- (B) second person
- (C) third person singular
- (D) third person plural

19. Read this sentence.

> Like most outstanding distance runners, Marla Runyan constantly pushes herself.

Which word from the sentence is a reflexive pronoun?

- (A) most
- (B) outstanding
- (C) runners
- (D) herself

Read each item carefully. Fill in the circle next to the best answer.

20. Read this sentence.

> Although _____ vision is very poor, she made herself into an Olympic athlete.

Which of these is the proper pronoun form to use to complete this sentence?

Ⓐ her
Ⓑ their
Ⓒ its
Ⓓ hers

21. **Read each sentence. Look at the underlined word in it. Which sentence is written *incorrectly*?**

Ⓐ Neil Parry is an athlete <u>who</u> has overcome incredible adversity.
Ⓑ A football wound <u>that</u> severed an artery caused him to have part of a leg amputated.
Ⓒ Parry, <u>who</u> was a San José State University varsity player, was fitted with an artificial leg.
Ⓓ Two years after his injury, Neil Parry took the field again and became the first major college position player <u>which</u> competed with an artificial leg.

22. Read this sentence.

> Anyone who follows San José State football is likely to have heard Neil Parry on the radio; he became a broadcaster in 2005.

Which word from the sentence is an indefinite pronoun?

Ⓐ Anyone
Ⓑ who
Ⓒ likely
Ⓓ he

23. **Read this sentence. Look at the underlined word in it.**

> Ralf Hotchkiss gained <u>international</u> fame as the designer of lightweight wheelchairs.

What kind of adjective is the underlined word?

Ⓐ an adjective that tells what kind
Ⓑ an adjective that tells how many
Ⓒ an article
Ⓓ None of the above

24. Read this sentence.

> _____ wheelchairs across the street were designed by him.

Which of these words would correctly complete this sentence?

Ⓐ This
Ⓑ That
Ⓒ These
Ⓓ Those

25. Read this sentence.

> Wheelchairs used in most athletic competitions must have strong, durable frames.

How should this sentence be rewritten?

Ⓐ Wheelchairs used in most, athletic competitions must have strong durable frames.
Ⓑ Wheelchairs used in most athletic competitions must have strong durable frames.
Ⓒ Wheelchairs used in most athletic competitions must have durable strong, frames.
Ⓓ It should not be rewritten; it is correct as written.

 **TEST TIP:** Read every choice before deciding on an answer.

Read each item carefully. Fill in the circle next to the best answer.

1. **Read these sentences.**

   > The summer sun bakes inland valleys in the Far West. However, the coastal lands remain cool.

   What kinds of verbs are in these sentences?

   Ⓐ first sentence—action verb; second sentence—linking verb
   Ⓑ first sentence—linking verb; second sentence—action verb
   Ⓒ both sentences—action verbs
   Ⓓ both sentences—linking verbs

2. **Read each sentence. Which sentence has an intransitive verb?**

   Ⓐ The valley heat pulls ocean air inland.
   Ⓑ Coastal mountains keep the cool, moist air out of the valleys.
   Ⓒ Temperatures in the valleys soar above 100°F.
   Ⓓ Fog blankets the lands along the coast day after day.

3. **Which sentence has a verb in the passive voice?**

   Ⓐ Silkworms spin cocoons of fine thread.
   Ⓑ People in China have raised silkworms for many centuries.
   Ⓒ Fine silk thread was produced from the cocoons by skilled workers.
   Ⓓ China's emperors kept the process a secret from foreigners.

4. **Read this sentence.**

   > The metamorphosis of that insect yielded a product more valuable than gold.

   In what tense is the underlined verb?

   Ⓐ past
   Ⓑ present
   Ⓒ future
   Ⓓ None of the above

5. **Read this sentence.**

   > Max has been studying tarantulas for several months.

   Which of these words is the main verb in the sentence?

   Ⓐ has
   Ⓑ been
   Ⓒ studying
   Ⓓ several

6. **Read the sentence.**

   > That tarantula has shed its old skin.

   In what tense is the underlined verb?

   Ⓐ past perfect
   Ⓑ present perfect
   Ⓒ future perfect
   Ⓓ None of the above

7. **Read the sentence.**

   > A bird of prey is eyeing the tarantula hungrily.

   In what form is the underlined verb?

   Ⓐ past progressive
   Ⓑ present progressive
   Ⓒ future progressive
   Ⓓ None of the above

Read each item carefully. Fill in the circle next to the best answer.

8. Read this sentence.

> Max did not interfere with the bird's hunting, even though he feels sorry for the tarantula.

How should this sentence be changed to make it correct?

(A) The phrase *did not interfere* should be changed to *had not interfered*.

(B) The phrase *did not interfere* should be changed to *was not interfering*.

(C) The verb *feels* should be changed to *felt*.

(D) It should not be changed. It is correct as written.

9. Read this sentence.

> Until the tarantula's new skin hardens, the tarantula cannot effectively avoid predators.

Which of these words is an adverb in the sentence?

(A) until

(B) new

(C) hardens

(D) effectively

10. Read the sentence.

> Each of the moon's phases has its own name.

Which of these words is a preposition in the sentence?

(A) each

(B) of

(C) its

(D) own

11. Read this sentence.

> The waxing crescent moon appears after the new moon, and the waning crescent moon appears before the new moon.

Which of these words is a coordinating conjunction in the sentence?

(A) appears

(B) after

(C) and

(D) before

12. Read each sentence. Which sentence has a pair of correlative conjunctions?

(A) When you see the right half of the moon, you are seeing the first quarter moon.

(B) When you see the left half, you are seeing the last quarter moon.

(C) Neither the waxing gibbous moon nor the waning gibbous moon has the beauty of the full moon.

(D) As you may have guessed, *waxing* means "increasing," and *waning* means the opposite.

13. Read these sentences.

> Maple trees lose their leaves in the fall. They are deciduous.

What kinds of verbs are in these sentences?

(A) first sentence—action verb; second sentence—linking verb

(B) first sentence—linking verb; second sentence—action verb

(C) both sentences—action verbs

(D) both sentences—linking verbs

Read each item carefully. Fill in the circle next to the best answer.

14. Read each sentence. Which sentence has an intransitive verb?

    Ⓐ Many people visit New England each fall.
    Ⓑ They love the splendor of the fall colors there.
    Ⓒ Deciduous trees sense the diminishing length of days.
    Ⓓ The color of their leaves changes from green to yellow or red.

15. Which sentence has a verb in the passive voice?

    Ⓐ The trees in the north change color first.
    Ⓑ Visitors follow the changing colors south.
    Ⓒ Hikers dress warmly because of the chilly temperatures.
    Ⓓ Pictures are taken by many of the visitors.

16. Read this sentence.

    Trees change color less spectacularly in other parts of the United States.

    In what tense is the underlined verb?

    Ⓐ past
    Ⓑ present
    Ⓒ future
    Ⓓ none of the above

17. Read this sentence.

    A beekeeper recently has spoken to our group about the life cycle of the honeybee.

    Which of these words is an auxiliary verb?

    Ⓐ recently
    Ⓑ has
    Ⓒ spoken
    Ⓓ life

18. Read this sentence.

    Each year a honeybee hive will produce a new queen.

    Which of these words is a main verb?

    Ⓐ year
    Ⓑ hive
    Ⓒ will
    Ⓓ produce

19. Read the sentence.

    Before the new queen has begun laying eggs, the old queen will have left the hive with a swarm of worker bees.

    In what tense is the underlined verb?

    Ⓐ past perfect
    Ⓑ present perfect
    Ⓒ future perfect
    Ⓓ None of the above

Read each item carefully. Fill in the circle next to the best answer.

20. Read the sentence.

> Yesterday a swarm of bees <u>was hanging</u> from a branch in our yard.

In what form is the underlined verb?

- (A) past progressive
- (B) present progressive
- (C) future progressive
- (D) None of the above

21. Read this sentence.

> My sister Mimi discovered the bees, and she alerts the neighbors to their presence.

How should this sentence be changed to make it correct?

- (A) The verb *alerts* should be changed to *alerted*.
- (B) The verb *alerts* should be changed to *had alerted*.
- (C) The verb *alerts* should be changed to *will have alerted*.
- (D) It should not be changed. It is correct as written.

22. Read this sentence.

> The swarm eventually will find a suitable location for a new hive.

Which of these words is an adverb in the sentence?

- (A) eventually
- (B) will
- (C) suitable
- (D) new

23. Read the sentence.

> A snake sheds its outer skin when that layer becomes worn from its activity.

Which of these words is a preposition in the sentence?

- (A) its
- (B) outer
- (C) when
- (D) from

24. Read this sentence.

> A molting snake loosens the skin around its head and then crawls out of the old skin.

Which of these words is a coordinating conjunction in the sentence?

- (A) around
- (B) and
- (C) then
- (D) out

25. Read each sentence. Which sentence has a pair of correlative conjunctions?

- (A) Snakes in the tropics shed their skin more frequently than do snakes in other areas.
- (B) Some snakes molt six times a year, but others only shed their skin twice annually.
- (C) Young, active snakes shed their skin often.
- (D) Neither my sister nor I have ever seen a snake shed its skin.

 **TEST TIP:** Mark your answers neatly. If you erase, erase completely and clearly without smudging.

Read each item carefully. Fill in the circle next to the best answer.

1. **Which of the following sentences has _your_ or _you're_ used _incorrectly_?**

   Ⓐ You're going to enjoy your trip to Tuscany.
   Ⓑ The great museums of Florence should be on you're itinerary.
   Ⓒ Did any of your ancestors come to the United States from this part of Italy?
   Ⓓ When you reach Lucca, you're certain to appreciate its peacefulness.

2. **Read this sentence.**

   > People expect to find good food in Italy, and _____ seldom disappointed.

   Which word would complete the sentence correctly?

   Ⓐ their
   Ⓑ there
   Ⓒ they're
   Ⓓ theyre

3. **Which of the following sentences has _its_ or _it's_ used _incorrectly_?**

   Ⓐ The Cyrillic alphabet is used in Bulgaria; it's also used in Russia and Serbia.
   Ⓑ Its name comes from Cyril, the name of one of the brothers who developed it.
   Ⓒ Bulgaria celebrates it's alphabet and culture with a holiday.
   Ⓓ It's called Slavic Script and Bulgarian Culture Day.

4. **Read each sentence. Look at the underlined word in it. Which sentence is written _incorrectly_?**

   Ⓐ <u>Who's</u> visited Sofia, Bulgaria, on Slavic Script and Bulgarian Culture Day?
   Ⓑ Laura is one of the few Americans <u>who's</u> been in Sofia on May 24.
   Ⓒ <u>Who's</u> passport is this?
   Ⓓ A person <u>whose</u> passport is missing should contact his or her embassy.

5. **Read each sentence. Look at the underlined word in it. Which sentence is written _incorrectly_?**

   Ⓐ A visitor <u>to</u> Malaysia should visit the state of Sarawak, on the Island of Borneo.
   Ⓑ Sarawak has outstanding cultural museums and beautiful natural areas, <u>too</u>.
   Ⓒ A bus leaves the city of Kuching for Kubah National Park every <u>two</u> hours.
   Ⓓ The park features beautiful waterfalls, many varieties of palms, and wild orchids, <u>to</u>.

6. **Read each sentence. Look at the underlined word in it. Which sentence is written _incorrectly_?**

   Ⓐ Many visitors are more interested in Sarawak's indigenous peoples <u>than</u> in its natural wonders.
   Ⓑ If you are interested in unusual dwellings, <u>then</u> you should visit one of Sarawak's longhouses.
   Ⓒ These traditional dwellings of the Dayaks and the Orang Ulu are less common <u>then</u> in the past, but many are still in use.
   Ⓓ Some longhouses are more <u>than</u> one-half mile long.

7. **Read each sentence. Which sentence is written _incorrectly_?**

   Ⓐ The Hopi Indians would not be able to raise crops without rain.
   Ⓑ No large rivers or lakes furnish water to their desert homeland.
   Ⓒ It shouldn't surprise nobody that many Hopi celebrations focus on rain and fertility.
   Ⓓ The celebrations can require stamina: it isn't easy to dance and sing for hours without stopping.

Read each item carefully. Fill in the circle next to the best answer.

8. Read each sentence. Look at the underlined word in it. Which sentence is written *incorrectly*?

  Ⓐ Tai's family <u>likes</u> attending Native American festivals.

  Ⓑ They <u>went</u> on a long trip to Arizona and New Mexico last year.

  Ⓒ The Hopi, Zuni, and Navajo peoples have reservations there; Tai's family visited reservations of <u>all</u> three peoples.

  Ⓓ On the way home, Tai <u>went</u>, "I'll probably never have a more interesting vacation!"

9. Read each sentence. Look at the underlined word in it. Which sentence is written *incorrectly*?

  Ⓐ You have <u>lain</u> in bed all morning; we shouldn't waste the time we have in Cornwall.

  Ⓑ Come with me and <u>lay</u> flowers by the paths in the village of Padstow.

  Ⓒ May Day will be here soon, and we should not <u>set</u> in our room and miss the festivities.

  Ⓓ I have <u>set</u> a brochure about the Padstow 'Obby 'Oss celebration on the table.

10. Read each sentence. Look at the underlined word in it. Which sentence is written *incorrectly*?

  Ⓐ My sister has <u>taken</u> a course in cultural anthropology.

  Ⓑ She has <u>saw</u> films about indigenous people in many regions.

  Ⓒ She <u>ate</u> foods from Kenya, Ethiopia, and Egypt last week.

  Ⓓ She has <u>written</u> papers on the customs of several peoples of Africa.

11. Read each sentence. Look at the underlined word in it. Which sentence is written *incorrectly*?

  Ⓐ Many people in East Africa now raise crops that were not <u>growed</u> there in the past.

  Ⓑ Corn and avocados have been <u>brought</u> to Kenya and Tanzania from North America.

  Ⓒ In recent years cooks have <u>prepared</u> dishes from India more frequently.

  Ⓓ Traders <u>took</u> spices from India to cities and settlements in eastern Africa, and residents learned to love curries.

12. Read each sentence. Look at the underlined word in it. Which sentence is written *incorrectly*?

  Ⓐ The Algarve is the southernmost part of Portugal; <u>it</u> is very popular with tourists.

  Ⓑ In summer <u>its</u> sunny beaches are filled with vacationers.

  Ⓒ People <u>who</u> prefer less crowded spots can find many in this region.

  Ⓓ The town of Tavira <u>it</u> is one of many pleasant places in the Algarve where tourists can find peace and beauty.

13. Read the sentence.

> About 3,000 years ago the Phoenicians, a great seafaring people, established trading posts along the coast of the Algarve, so their ships could dock and exchange goods with local people.

Which words in this sentence are unnecessary and should be eliminated?

  Ⓐ about 3,000 years ago
  Ⓑ a great seafaring people
  Ⓒ along the coast of the Algarve
  Ⓓ so their ships could dock and exchange goods with local people

Read each item carefully. Fill in the circle next to the best answer.

14. Which of the following sentences has *your* or *you're* used *incorrectly*?

Ⓐ You're fond of traveling, aren't you?

Ⓑ If you save your money, you can take a trip to Asia.

Ⓒ You're going to be surprised at how affordable a trip with a group can be!

Ⓓ Make sure to select a trip that will attract people with you're high energy level!

15. Read this sentence.

The people of Japan welcome visitors to _____ colorful festivals.

Which word would complete the sentence correctly?

Ⓐ their

Ⓑ there

Ⓒ they're

Ⓓ theyre

16. Which of the following sentences has *its* or *it's* used *incorrectly*?

Ⓐ Kyoto is famous for its Gion Matsuri festival.

Ⓑ This festival had it's beginnings more than 1,100 years ago.

Ⓒ It's an early summer event that features a parade.

Ⓓ Look at that float: its wheels are almost ten feet tall!

17. Read each sentence. Look at the underlined word in it. Which sentence is written *incorrectly*?

Ⓐ Who's visited the European nation of Belgium?

Ⓑ Belgium, whose residents speak French or Flemish, is famous for its chocolate.

Ⓒ Bruges is a city who's canals make it picturesque.

Ⓓ Tourists whose interests include Renaissance art will particularly enjoy Bruges.

18. Read each sentence. Look at the underlined word in it. Which sentence is written *incorrectly*?

Ⓐ New Zealand comprises two large islands.

Ⓑ Travelers to this nation can learn about Maori culture.

Ⓒ The Maoris lived in New Zealand long before the first Europeans came to settle.

Ⓓ In traditional Maori culture, when to people meet, they press their noses together.

19. Read each sentence. Look at the underlined word in it. Which sentence is written *incorrectly*?

Ⓐ In older times Maoris were hunters and fishers; then some became farmers.

Ⓑ Maori woodcarvers were more skillful than carvers on many other islands.

Ⓒ World War II created both hardships and opportunities, and many Maoris moved to cities then.

Ⓓ Maoris have their own language; they speak it far more then English at Maori gatherings.

Read each item carefully. Fill in the circle next to the best answer.

20. Read each sentence. Which sentence is written *incorrectly*?

    Ⓐ I haven't never heard anyone blow a wooden horn.

    Ⓑ Wooden horns aren't used in the Netherlands as musical instruments.

    Ⓒ Ancient people there didn't want evil winter spirits to bother them.

    Ⓓ Wouldn't the noise from that wooden horn frighten just about anything?

21. Read each sentence. Look at the underlined word in it. Which sentence is written *incorrectly*?

    Ⓐ My grandparents <u>go</u> to Cape Breton Island every year.

    Ⓑ They both <u>like</u> the traditional fiddle music played there.

    Ⓒ This spring they were <u>all</u>, "Why don't you come with us this summer?"

    Ⓓ I told them yes, because of <u>all</u> instruments, the fiddle is my favorite.

22. Read each sentence. Look at the underlined word in it. Which sentence is written *incorrectly*?

    Ⓐ When I was in Bangkok, I <u>set</u> on a bench and painted a picture of a temple.

    Ⓑ When I got back to my hotel, I <u>set</u> the painting on my bedside table.

    Ⓒ I <u>laid</u> my paintbrush down on the table and admired my painting.

    Ⓓ That night I <u>lay</u> on my bed and thought about what a great day it had been.

23. Read each sentence. Look at the underlined word in it. Which sentence is written *incorrectly*?

    Ⓐ Many cultures have <u>held</u> festivals in the middle of winter.

    Ⓑ The ancient Druids of Britain <u>built</u> a bonfire on the shortest day of the year.

    Ⓒ They <u>singed</u> and danced around the fire.

    Ⓓ They <u>thought</u> that this ceremony ensured the return of spring.

24. Read each sentence. Look at the underlined word in it. Which sentence is written incorrectly?

    Ⓐ The 5,000-mile-long Trans-Siberian Railway is <u>one</u> of the world's most famous rail lines.

    Ⓑ <u>Its</u> route stretches eastward from Yekaterinburg all the way to Vladivostok, on the Pacific Coast.

    Ⓒ This railroad, <u>it</u> was the first built across the vast region of Siberia.

    Ⓓ Travelers today typically board the train in Moscow, and <u>they</u> arrive on the Pacific shore seven days later.

25. Read the sentence.

> Another rail line across Siberia was completed in 1991, only a few decades ago; known as the BAM train, this rail line carries travelers across 2,500 miles of mostly unpopulated land.

Which words in this sentence are unnecessary and should be eliminated?

Ⓐ across Siberia

Ⓑ only a few decades ago

Ⓒ known as the BAM train

Ⓓ of mostly unpopulated land

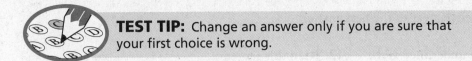

TEST TIP: Change an answer only if you are sure that your first choice is wrong.

Read each item carefully. Fill in the circle next to the best answer.

1. Read this sentence.

> Throughout Africa, people tell talking animal tales; they tell them to convey traditional values.

Which word in the sentence is an object pronoun?

Ⓐ throughout Ⓒ they
Ⓑ people Ⓓ them

2. Read each sentence. **Which sentence is written** *incorrectly*?

Ⓐ Grandma told a tale about a lizard and a python to my sister and I.
Ⓑ My sister and I heard how Lizard stole a special drum from his friend Python.
Ⓒ Grandma described to my sister and me how Lizard then taunted Python.
Ⓓ Although she and we thought Python should punish Lizard, the snake saved Lizard's life.

3. Read this sentence.

> Animal stories such as this tale teach lessons, and they entertain listeners.

Which is the antecedent for the underlined pronoun?

Ⓐ stories Ⓒ lessons
Ⓑ tale Ⓓ listeners

4. Read these sentences from a paragraph. Look at the underlined word in each one. **Which sentence is written** *incorrectly*?

Ⓐ Would you like to study animal stories from several different cultures?
Ⓑ You may be surprised at how many cultures have traditional tales with animal characters.
Ⓒ As you might guess, animals judged to be clever in real life are the main characters in many of these tales.
Ⓓ We might begin by reading traditional tales of some Native American peoples.

5. Read each sentence. Look at the underlined word. **Which sentence has a pronoun that does not have a clear antecedent?**

Ⓐ Hannah and Kathy told folktales about turtles from several countries; other students praised them.
Ⓑ Ryan and Jim collected tales about mice, and they told several of them to the class.
Ⓒ Martha hoped to find traditional tales about poodles, but she was not able to locate any.
Ⓓ "This has a tale about a dog with curly hair," Lucia said, and she gave Martha a book of Albanian folktales.

6. Read each sentence. Look at the underlined word. **Which sentence is** *not* **correct?**

Ⓐ Anyone who likes folktales is likely to enjoy "The Magic Pot."
Ⓑ A woodcutter whom fortune has treated poorly finds a brass pot.
Ⓒ He brings it home to his wife, whom is very happy with it.
Ⓓ She is the one who notices that the axe her husband put into it has turned into two axes.

7. Read each sentence. Look at the underlined verb. **Which sentence is** *not* **correct?**

Ⓐ A pot with such magical powers create opportunities.
Ⓑ Any object dropped into the pot becomes two.
Ⓒ In folktales, of course, magic inevitably causes problems.
Ⓓ A wife who falls into a pot of this kind suddenly becomes two identical wives!

Read each item carefully. Fill in the circle next to the best answer.

8. Read each sentence. Look at the underlined verb. Which sentence is *not* correct?

   Ⓐ Twilight or midnight <u>is</u> a good time to tell a scary story.

   Ⓑ A big crocodile or a giant bear <u>is</u> certainly a scary character!

   Ⓒ The smell or the noises of such an animal, when described vividly, <u>adds</u> to the fear.

   Ⓓ Neither young storytellers nor an elderly tale teller <u>wants</u> listeners to become too frightened.

9. Read each sentence. Look at the underlined verb. Which sentence is *not* correct?

   Ⓐ "Goldilocks and the Three Bears" <u>has</u> many lessons to teach.

   Ⓑ Almost everyone here <u>have heard</u> this very old tale.

   Ⓒ A bear family <u>goes</u> for a walk before mealtime.

   Ⓓ While the family <u>is</u> away from their home, someone enters it without permission.

10. Read each sentence. Which sentence is *not* correct because it contains a dangling modifier?

    Ⓐ Showing very bad manners, the bears' breakfast is tasted by the intruder.

    Ⓑ Sampling Papa Bear's porridge, the intruder pronounces it too hot.

    Ⓒ Discussing the intruder's behavior, our family decided that she deserved punishment.

    Ⓓ Knowing how the story ends, we wondered if being badly frightened by bears is enough of a punishment.

11. Read each sentence. Which sentence is *not* correct because it contains a misplaced modifier?

    Ⓐ Anyone behaving like Goldilocks deserves a reprimand.

    Ⓑ A person entering a home without permission is breaking the law.

    Ⓒ Intended for someone else, most people would not eat any food.

    Ⓓ The bears must have felt sad when they saw the chair broken by Goldilocks.

12. Read this sentence.

    In "Goldilocks and the Three Bears," the animals behave _____ than the human does.

    Which choice would complete the sentence correctly?

    Ⓐ gooder

    Ⓑ more good

    Ⓒ better

    Ⓓ more better

13. Read this sentence.

    The Little Mermaid is the main character in one of Hans Christian Andersen's fairy tales; you can see a statue of her in Copenhagen, Denmark.

    Which word in the sentence is an object pronoun?

    Ⓐ character

    Ⓑ you

    Ⓒ statue

    Ⓓ her

Read each item carefully. Fill in the circle next to the best answer.

14. Read each sentence. Which sentence is written *incorrectly*?

Ⓐ My brother and I perform puppet shows for our friends.

Ⓑ Our cousin Gretchen asked him and I to create a new show.

Ⓒ She told him and me to perform Hans Christian Andersen's "Ugly Duckling."

Ⓓ I showed my brother and her how to make duck puppets.

15. Read this sentence.

Hans Christian Andersen wrote stories for adults, too, but nowadays very few people read them.

Which is the antecedent for the underlined pronoun?

Ⓐ stories

Ⓑ adults

Ⓒ nowadays

Ⓓ people

16. Read this sentence.

The Hans Christian Andersen Museum is located in Odense, the town in which he was born; it opened in 1908.

What is the antecedent for the underlined pronoun?

Ⓐ the Hans Christian Andersen Museum

Ⓑ Odense

Ⓒ town

Ⓓ 1908

17. Read these sentences from a paragraph. Look at the underlined word in each one. Which sentence is written *incorrectly*?

Ⓐ Library visitors should keep their voices low.

Ⓑ They should not talk more than is necessary.

Ⓒ When they finish using a book, they should return it to its place on the shelf.

Ⓓ Librarians want to assist patrons, not discipline us.

18. Read each sentence. Look at the underlined word. Which sentence has a pronoun that does not have a clear antecedent?

Ⓐ Our group is looking for folktales from China, and a librarian is helping us.

Ⓑ Sampson and Dustin are working on it together.

Ⓒ Wendy told Sheila about a tale she really liked, and Sheila read it and liked it, too.

Ⓓ Ronnie and I asked Sheila to lend us the book with that folktale in it, and she gave it to us.

19. Read each sentence. Look at the underlined word. Which sentence is *not* correct?

Ⓐ Whom among your friends is the best storyteller?

Ⓑ A person who can keep an audience fascinated just with words is a powerful person indeed.

Ⓒ My cousin is a person to whom storytelling comes naturally.

Ⓓ A 12-year-old who tells ancient tales is a rarity.

Read each item carefully. Fill in the circle next to the best answer.

20. **Read each sentence. Look at the underlined verb. Which sentence is *not* correct?**

    Ⓐ Either Homer or Aesop <u>was</u> the greatest ancient storyteller in my opinion.
    Ⓑ Homer's *Iliad,* a tale of the Trojan War, <u>thrills</u> people today.
    Ⓒ The fables of Aesop <u>contain</u> more useful wisdom than Homer's epics do.
    Ⓓ Which one of his fables do you think <u>teach</u> the most important lesson?

21. **Read each sentence. Look at the underlined verb. Which sentence is *not* correct?**

    Ⓐ My mother and my brother <u>believe</u> that "The Tortoise and the Hare" conveys great wisdom.
    Ⓑ Neither she nor he ever <u>quits</u> before the end of a project.
    Ⓒ My grandfather and I <u>value</u> the message of "The Boy and the Wolf" a lot.
    Ⓓ One false cry or two false cries <u>ruins</u> a person's credibility.

22. **Read each sentence. Look at the underlined verb. Which sentence is *not* correct?**

    Ⓐ "The Town Mouse and the Country Mouse" <u>remind</u> us that we feel comfortable in familiar places.
    Ⓑ This collection of fables <u>includes</u> "The Goose and the Golden Eggs."
    Ⓒ Anyone who gives in to greed and impatience <u>risks</u> suffering the fate of the man in this fable.
    Ⓓ An output of one golden egg a day <u>sounds</u> fine to me.

23. **Read each sentence. Which sentence is *not* correct because it contains a dangling modifier?**

    Ⓐ Laying one golden egg a day, the man's goose made him rich.
    Ⓑ Wanting more wealth faster, the man decided on a plan.
    Ⓒ Believing that he could get many golden eggs at once, the goose was slain by the man.
    Ⓓ Looking inside the poor goose, the man found no golden eggs.

24. **Read each sentence. Which sentence is *not* correct because it contains a misplaced modifier?**

    Ⓐ Rewards are given to characters showing compassion toward the poor or the weak.
    Ⓑ Clever characters are generally rewarded, but characters are almost always punished, using trickery to gain wealth or power.
    Ⓒ A character favored by the storyteller is called clever when she uses deception.
    Ⓓ An unsympathetic character employing the same kind of deception is usually labeled as deceitful.

25. **Read this sentence.**

    In real life as in folktales, coyotes may be the _____ animals of all.

    Which choice would complete the sentence correctly?

    Ⓐ shrewder
    Ⓑ more shrewd
    Ⓒ shrewdest
    Ⓓ most shrewd

TEST TIP: Review your work. If you finish a test before time is up, go back and check your work.

Read each item carefully. Fill in the circle next to the best answer.

1. Read this sentence.

> Trinidad is a large island in the Caribbean Sea near the Nation of Venezuela.

Which term should not be capitalized?

Ⓐ Trinidad
Ⓑ Caribbean Sea
Ⓒ Nation
Ⓓ Venezuela

2. Read this sentence.

> The trinidad and tobago manufacturers' association represents such island companies as unicom limited.

Which words should be capitalized?

Ⓐ trinidad, tobago, manufacturers', association, unicom, limited
Ⓑ trinidad, tobago, manufacturers', association, island, companies
Ⓒ island, companies, unicom, limited
Ⓓ unicom, limited

3. Read this sentence.

> **Mister George Maxwell Richards** became president of Trinidad and Tobago in 2003.

How should the boldfaced name be written with initials and abbreviations?

Ⓐ Mr. G.M. Richards
Ⓑ Mr. GM. Richards
Ⓒ Mr G M Richards
Ⓓ Mr. GM Richards

4. Read each sentence. In which sentence is the title written correctly?

Ⓐ My sister is reading a book titled "The Modern History of the Caribbean Islands."
Ⓑ The author also wrote a story titled Mystery in the Caribbean.
Ⓒ My sister has written a poem titled "My First Free Breath."
Ⓓ She dedicated it to our grandmother, who grew up in Jamaica and once wrote a song titled Dreams for My Grandchildren.

5. Read each sentence. Look at the underlined word. Which sentence is written *incorrectly*?

Ⓐ Those musician's instruments were made from oil drums.
Ⓑ These instruments' tones are bright and resonant.
Ⓒ Steel drum music is an invention of Trinidad's people.
Ⓓ This island's Carnival celebrations feature the Calypso music of steel drum orchestras.

6. Read each sentence. Look at the commas. Which sentence is written correctly?

Ⓐ Do you know which country comprises the islands of Hokkaido, Honshu, Shikoku, and, Kyushu?
Ⓑ Luzon, Mindanao, and Palawan, are major islands in what nation?
Ⓒ Which country in Southeast Asia includes the islands of, Java, Sumatra, and Sulawesi?
Ⓓ If you answered Japan, the Philippines, and Indonesia, you are correct!

7. Read this sentence.

> Yes Haiti was the first Caribbean country to gain its independence.

Where should a comma be placed in this sentence?

Ⓐ After *yes*   Ⓒ After *country*
Ⓑ After *first*   Ⓓ After *gain*

Read each item carefully. Fill in the circle next to the best answer.

8. Read this sentence.

> "Haiti shares an island with the Dominican Republic doesn't it?" asked Sal.

Where should a comma be placed in this sentence?

Ⓐ After *Haiti*
Ⓑ After *island*
Ⓒ After *Republic*
Ⓓ After the question mark

9. Read this sentence.

> The largest of the Shetland Islands which is known simply as Mainland is the fifth largest of the British Isles.

Where should commas be placed in this sentence?

Ⓐ After *largest* and *Islands*
Ⓑ After *Islands* and *Mainland*
Ⓒ After *Mainland* and *largest*
Ⓓ No commas are needed in this sentence.

10. Read this sentence.

> The Shetland Islands are famous for two distinctive items their woolen sweaters and their ponies.

Where should a colon be placed in this sentence?

Ⓐ After *Islands*
Ⓑ After *famous*
Ⓒ After *items*
Ⓓ After *sweaters*

11. Read each sentence. Which sentence is *not* punctuated correctly?

Ⓐ Rising sea levels—a result of global warming—threaten low-lying islands.
Ⓑ Island nations in the southwest Pacific (Vanuatu is one) are losing land to sea.
Ⓒ Many of these nations' islands are very small to-begin-with.
Ⓓ If sea levels rise even another foot (a likely possibility, according to some scientists), some well-populated islands will become uninhabitable.

12. Read each sentence. Which sentence is *not* punctuated correctly?

Ⓐ Karl asked, "What country is building artificial islands?"
Ⓑ Diana said that she thought the city of Dubai in the United Arab Emirates was doing this.
Ⓒ "Do the islands float, or are they built up from the sea floor?" Karl asked.
Ⓓ I'm not sure; I'll need to do some research, said Diana.

13. Read this friendly letter.

1168 West Wind Ct.
Honolulu, HI 96820
April 3, 20__

Bradley, I can't wait to visit you, Melanie, Uncle Paul, and Aunt Iris! The Hawaiian Islands are great, but I'm ready for some time in the desert with you. Keep things nice and warm until I get there!

Your cousin,
Walter

Which part of the letter is missing?

Ⓐ heading
Ⓑ greeting
Ⓒ closing
Ⓓ signature

Read each item carefully. Fill in the circle next to the best answer.

14. Read this sentence.

> Reindeer Island is an island in Lake Winnipeg in Manitoba, a Province of Canada.

Which term should not be capitalized?

(A) Reindeer Island
(B) Manitoba
(C) Province
(D) Canada

15. Read this sentence.

> Fish from lake winnipeg are marketed by the freshwater fish marketing corporation.

Which words should be capitalized in this sentence?

(A) lake, winnipeg
(B) freshwater, fish, marketing, corporation
(C) marketing, corporation
(D) lake, winnipeg, freshwater, fish, marketing, corporation

16. Read this sentence.

> Our neighbor, **General David Julio Estaris,** is obsessed with that island.

How should the boldfaced name be written with initials and abbreviations?

(A) Gen. DJ Estaris
(B) Gen. D.J. Estaris
(C) Gen D J Estaris
(D) Gen D. J. Estaris

17. Read each sentence. In which sentence is the title written correctly?

(A) He wants to film a movie called <u>Escape to Reindeer Island</u>.
(B) He has written a song called <u>Rudy, the Mayor of Reindeer Island</u>.
(C) Would you believe that he's written a poem titled You Won't Freeze If You Say Please?
(D) According to this book titled "Inland Islands in the Prairie Provinces," General Estaris may be a bit disappointed if he does visit Reindeer Island.

18. Read each sentence. Look at the underlined word. Which sentence is written *incorrectly*?

(A) <u>Norway's</u> hikers flock to the Lofoten Islands in summer.
(B) These rocky <u>islands'</u> trails are challenging, but views from the trails are breathtaking.
(C) Several <u>postcard's</u> photos show hikers hopping from rock to rock.
(D) A <u>hiker's</u> boots must provide traction on the rugged rocks.

19. Read each sentence. Look at the commas. Which sentence is written properly?

(A) Lahaina, Kahului, and Makawao, are towns on the island of Maui.
(B) On the island of Kauai are the towns of Kalaheo, Lihue, and Kapaa.
(C) The big island of Hawaii has Honokaa, Hilo, and, Mountain View.
(D) Honolulu, located on the island of Oahu, is Hawaii's largest city; other communities on that island include, Waipahu, Pearl City, and Kaneohe.

Read each item carefully. Fill in the circle next to the best answer.

20. Read this sentence.

> Yes the Republic of Singapore is an island nation at the tip of the Malay Peninsula.

Where should a comma be placed in this sentence?

Ⓐ After *yes*
Ⓑ After *Singapore*
Ⓒ After *island*
Ⓓ After *tip*

21. Read this sentence.

> Singapore Airport also known as Changi Airport is considered by many travelers to be the best airport in the world.

Where should commas be placed in this sentence?

Ⓐ After *Singapore Airport* and after *Changi Airport*
Ⓑ After *Singapore Airport* and after *travelers*
Ⓒ After *travelers* and after *airport*
Ⓓ No commas are needed in this sentence.

22. Read this sentence.

> The population density of Singapore is one of the highest of any nation more than 16,000 people per square mile.

Where should a colon be placed in this sentence?

Ⓐ After *Singapore*
Ⓑ After *highest*
Ⓒ After *nation*
Ⓓ After *16,000*

23. Read each sentence. Which sentence is *not* punctuated correctly?

Ⓐ Singapore—a separate nation since 1965—is very prosperous.
Ⓑ Its only natural resource is fish (a resource that every nation with a coastline has).
Ⓒ Its land area is only 267 square miles (693 sq km).
Ⓓ It has gained prosperity (primarily because of the skills, talents, and education of its residents).

24. Read each sentence. Which sentence is *not* punctuated correctly?

Ⓐ "Many financial institutions have offices in Singapore," said Hiro.
Ⓑ Karishma said that chemicals are manufactured there.
Ⓒ Tam said that "his uncle manages an electronics plant in Singapore."
Ⓓ "I hope he gives you free cell phones," said Karishma, smiling.

25. Read this friendly letter.

Dear Valerie,

I am trying to memorize the names of 1,000 islands this summer. Since I managed to memorize the names of 1,000 rivers last summer, I don't think it will be that big of a challenge. What are your summer plans?

Your pal,
Edie

Which part of the letter is missing?

Ⓐ heading
Ⓑ greeting
Ⓒ closing
Ⓓ signature

Lesson 1 Circle the complete subject in each sentence. Underline the complete predicate.

1. I am taking guitar lessons.

2. My lessons are on Thursdays.

3. Some of the exercises are difficult.

4. I practice really hard.

5. My teacher doesn't know any new songs.

6. His favorite songs are from the 1980s.

7. Alternative music is my favorite.

8. I took my teacher a tape of my favorite song.

9. He figured out the chords.

10. Most of the chords were actually very simple.

11. I learned them with no trouble.

12. My love for the song made practicing fun.

13. We played it together last week.

14. My teacher liked the song a lot.

15. Our lessons are teaching him about today's music.

Lesson 2 Circle the simple subject in each sentence. If the subject is understood *you*, write *you* on the line. Underline the simple predicate.

1. Hummus is a Middle Eastern dish. _____

2. My sister gave me the recipe. _____

3. Pour a can of garbanzo beans into a blender. _____

4. Some people call garbanzo beans chickpeas. _____

5. Squeeze one whole lemon over the beans. _____

6. I use even more lemon sometimes. _____

7. Add crushed garlic, olive oil, salt, and tahini. _____

8. Tahini is sesame seed paste. _____

9. The action of the blender squashes the beans. _____

10. Hummus on pita bread makes a great sandwich. _____

11. Slice the bread into two half-circles. _____

12. Open the pita pocket carefully with your hand. _____

13. This bread breaks sometimes. _____

14. Put hummus, lettuce, tomato, and anything else into the pocket. _____

15. Many people simply dip the pita into the hummus. _____

Lesson 3 Each sentence has a compound subject or a compound predicate. Circle the two or three simple nouns or pronouns that make up each compound subject. Underline the two verbs that make up each compound predicate.

1. Marisa and Rachel play on a soccer team together.

2. Kelly, Raph, and I watched one of their games.

3. Rachel ran down the field and trapped the ball.

4. The goalie and a defensive player ran toward her.

5. Rachel saw Marisa and kicked the ball to her.

6. Marisa took a shot and scored a goal.

7. Raph and Kelly cheered.

8. I put two fingers in my mouth and whistled.

9. We shouted and clapped for a long time.

10. Marisa, Rachel, and I went out for pizza after the game.

11. Rachel and I wanted pizza with mushrooms and pepperoni.

12. Marisa dislikes mushrooms and suggested olives instead.

13. I went to the counter and ordered a large pizza.

14. Mushrooms and pepperoni were on one half of the pizza.

15. The other half was for Marisa and had olives on it.

Lesson 4 Circle each direct object in the sentences below.

1. An artist painted a mural in my neighborhood.

2. I watched her every afternoon.

3. First she sketched a plan.

4. She drew dancers at a carnival.

5. The artist chose bright colors at the paint store.

6. Then she mixed the colors together into new shades.

7. She built a scaffold next to the wall.

8. The scaffold raised her to the level of the mural.

9. The artist painted masks and feathers on the dancers.

10. One dancer in the mural carries a huge, colorful umbrella.

11. Another juggles flaming torches.

12. Some of the dancers resemble people in my neighborhood.

13. I recognized the face of my math teacher on the juggler.

14. One acrobat actually resembles me!

15. Everyone likes the new mural.

Extra Practice

Lesson 5 Circle the indirect object in each sentence below.

1. Charlie's uncle gave Charlie a ticket to a comic book convention.
2. Charlie's aunt gave them a ride to the convention center.
3. Inside, dealers offered collectors rare comic books.
4. Some collectors were paying dealers large sums for the best comics.
5. Charlie showed a dealer his prized old comic.
6. On the cover, a villain was giving a superhero a blast of supersonic cold rays.
7. The dealer offered Charlie a trade for another rare comic.
8. Charlie and his uncle gave the trade careful consideration.
9. They made the dealer an offer for two comics.
10. On the convention stage, a famous illustrator told the audience stories about his career.
11. The illustrator's friends had often given him ideas for comic book heroes.
12. An archaeologist friend had given him the inspiration for Dino-Woman.
13. She had told the illustrator many fascinating tales about dinosaurs.
14. The illustrator's talents had won him many awards.
15. Afterward, the illustrator drew Charlie a picture and then signed it.

Lesson 6 Write *PN* if the boldfaced term is a predicate noun. Write *PA* if the boldfaced term is a predicate adjective. Circle the linking verb in each sentence.

1. The rafflesia is a **flower**. _____
2. Its home is the **rain forest**. _____
3. These blossoms are **huge**. _____
4. Some blossoms are three feet **wide**. _____
5. They look **beautiful**. _____
6. The thick, heavy petals are dark **red**. _____
7. Rafflesias smell **terrible**, however. _____
8. The flower's scent is the **smell** of rotten meat. _____
9. But this scent smells **wonderful** to flies. _____
10. Flies are the main **pollinators** of this rare plant. _____
11. Rafflesias have become **endangered**. _____
12. Rain forest logging and slash-and-burn agriculture are the main **threats** to the flower's survival. _____
13. The rafflesia is still so little **understood**. _____
14. Scientists are **hopeful** about future studies of this plant. _____
15. The extinction of this plant would be a **tragedy**. _____

Lesson 7 Underline each prepositional phrase. Circle the preposition that begins each phrase. Draw a box around the object of the preposition. There may be more than one prepositional phrase in each sentence.

1. In July my camp went on a rafting trip.

2. Our bus drove through the woods and stopped at a river.

3. We carried rubber rafts from the bus to the water.

4. Soon we were floating down the river.

5. Our paddles dipped into the water.

6. Across the river a bird fished with its beak.

7. After a calm stretch, we paddled through some rapids.

8. Foamy waves splashed over us.

9. We held tightly to the raft.

10. My friend Peg was swept into the water.

11. For a minute, we could only see her hat bobbing on the waves.

12. Then we saw Peg drifting down the rapids.

13. She floated on her back and kept her feet above the water.

14. We did exactly what we'd learned in safety class, and soon Peg was in the boat again.

15. Before nightfall, we climbed onto the bus and returned to camp.

Lesson 8 Underline each adjectival prepositional phrase. Circle the noun it tells about. Some sentences have more than one adjectival prepositional phrase.

1. Noel's summer job earns her money for CDs.

2. She washes the windows of her neighbors' houses.

3. First she gets a bucket of warm water.

4. Then she carefully adds one capful of ammonia.

5. The fumes from the ammonia sometimes make Noel's eyes water.

6. Noel next uses a wet cloth from the bucket.

7. Then a quick wipe with a squeegee removes the streaks.

8. The sound of the squeegee makes Noel giggle.

9. A window without streaks is a beautiful sight.

10. The windows in Noel's neighborhood sparkle.

11. Noel's job gave me an idea for my own summer job.

12. I have started mowing the lawns in front of my neighbor's houses.

13. The smell of the grass is wonderful.

14. A cap with a big brim keeps away the glare of the sun.

15. My weekdays in the mowing business leave my Saturdays free.

Extra Practice

Lesson 9 Underline each adverbial prepositional phrase. Circle the verb or verb phrase it modifies. There may be more than one prepositional phrase in a sentence.

1. I make origami figures in my spare time.

2. This craft originated in Japan.

3. Origami paper is folded into elaborate shapes.

4. On Tuesday I made an origami frog.

5. I folded some green paper in half.

6. Then I folded the right side over the left.

7. For twenty minutes I carefully made more and more folds.

8. In the end, I had a little green paper frog.

9. If you push on its back, the frog hops across the table.

10. I have placed many origami figures around my room.

11. A boat, a giraffe, a spider, and three fish sit on my shelf.

12. With a hanger and ten origami cranes, I made a mobile.

13. It hangs over my desk.

14. My friends received origami stars for the Fourth of July.

15. In my opinion, origami is a terrific hobby.

Lesson 10 Underline the appositive phrase in each sentence.

1. Miacis, a prehistoric weasel-like animal, was the ancestor of cats.

2. Ancient Egyptians, the first people to domesticate cats, considered the animal sacred.

3. Cats, excellent hunters of mice and rats, kept houses free of vermin.

4. In Medieval Europe, cats, supposedly "evil" animals, were killed in large numbers.

5. The resulting increase in rat populations helped spread the Black Death, a plague carried by the rats' fleas.

6. The Egyptian Mau, an ancient cat breed, has a striped and spotted coat and green eyes.

7. The Manx, a breed that originated on the Isle of Man in the Irish Sea, usually has no tail.

8. The Japanese bobtail, another breed with an unusually short tail, is considered good luck in Japan.

9. The Siamese is a breed with a colorpoint coat, a coat with contrasting patches of color on the face, ears, tail, and feet.

10. A tabby coat, one with patterns of dark stripes, is often found on American shorthair cats.

11. The Scottish fold, a breed with ears that fold down, originated in Scotland.

12. The largest breed, the Maine coon cat, resembles a raccoon.

13. Crossbreds, cats with characteristics from more than one breed, are often healthier than purebred cats.

14. Animal shelters, facilities found in most communities, are excellent places to find a cat.

15. The cats at a shelter, crossbreds as well as cats of different breeds, need a good home.

Lesson 11 Combine the information in each group of sentences to write one sentence.

1. Sea turtles are found in most of the world's oceans. Only the Arctic Ocean does not have sea turtles. _____
_____

2. The leatherback is the largest sea turtle. It is six to seven feet long. It can weigh up to 1,300 pounds. _____
_____

3. Sea turtles are omnivores. Omnivores eat plants. They also eat animals. _____
_____

4. Animals that sea turtles eat include jellyfish and sea sponges. They might also eat shrimp and fish. Plants consumed by sea turtles include algae, seaweed, and seagrass. _____
_____

5. Sea turtles spend most of their time in the water. However, the females do come ashore. They come to lay their eggs on sandy beaches. _____
_____

6. It is illegal to hunt sea turtles in most places. People still catch them though. They are mostly used for food.
_____
_____

Lesson 12 Add the correct punctuation mark to each sentence. Then label each sentence *declarative, interrogative, imperative,* or *exclamatory.*

1. Wow, we're going to the natural history museum _____

2. What time do the doors open _____

3. Will there be bones from a *Tyrannosaurus rex* _____

4. That would be so cool _____

5. Make sure you get a map at the information desk _____

6. If we have a map, we won't miss anything _____

7. Which exhibit would you most like to see _____

8. Would you rather see dinosaurs or plant fossils _____

9. We might have to split up this morning _____

10. Meet me at the cafeteria at noon _____

11. We can have lunch before seeing the gemstone exhibit _____

12. I've heard that the museum has a 35-carat diamond _____

13. That is one huge diamond _____

14. Bring your watch so we can keep track of the time _____

15. We will need to leave by four o'clock _____

Extra Practice

Lesson 13 Write *S* next to each simple sentence and *CD* next to each compound sentence. Circle the comma and conjunction or the semicolon in each compound sentence.

1. Some people avoid packaged prepared food, but I like it. _____

2. Those salty peanuts always taste delicious. _____

3. I enjoy opening little packets of cheese and crackers. _____

4. You can have lasagna, or you can try a rice bowl. _____

5. Washed and peeled baby carrots are the most perfect snack in the world. _____

6. This salad comes with dressing on the side; it also comes with a fork. _____

7. The enchiladas sit invitingly in neat compartments. _____

8. I love cooking, but I often don't have time. _____

9. Some companies offer tasty vegetarian meals. _____

10. I've heard about those meals, but I have never tried them myself. _____

11. Some prepared foods contain large amounts of salt. _____

12. Salt can make foods tastier, but too much salt can cause health problems. _____

13. Green, leafy vegetables are recommended for health. _____

14. A serving of spinach can make any meal healthier, and a portion of broccoli can do the same. _____

15. A quick but healthy meal is a good thing! _____

Lesson 14 Draw one line under each independent clause and two lines under each dependent clause. Circle the subordinating conjunction that begins each dependent clause.

1. Because Tim enjoys acting, he auditioned for the school play.

2. Although he wanted the part of the hero, he was cast as the bandit.

3. If he hadn't had a cold for his audition, he would have gotten a bigger part.

4. He had trouble with his lines at the audition because his nose was stuffed up.

5. He was still happy with this part because the bandit is a colorful character.

6. As the curtain rose, the bandit was pacing back and forth on the stage.

7. He was planning revenge because the hero had laughed at his science experiments.

8. Although the hero called him crazy, he was making fantastic discoveries about time travel.

9. He would have the last laugh when he committed the perfect crime!

10. The audience booed when he announced his evil scheme.

11. While the hero innocently ate dinner, Tim tied knots in his shoelaces.

12. The hero was saved because his sister warned him.

13. Although they were all nervous, the cast performed well on opening night.

14. When they took their bows, the audience gave them a standing ovation.

15. Tim will be a professional actor someday, if everything goes according to his plan.

Lesson 15 Write *CD* next to each compound sentence and *CX* next to each complex sentence. Write *CCX* next to each compound-complex sentence.

1. Although diatoms are invisible to the naked eye, they may be the most important sea creatures. _____

2. Diatoms are microscopic one-celled plants; most drift in the top layer of the ocean. _____

3. Diatoms live in the top layer because sunlight penetrates the water there. _____

4. Although most diatoms drift with the currents, some can move independently. _____

5. Diatoms have glasslike silicon shells; though they all consist of two halves, they come in different shapes resembling saucers, flowers, propellers, buttons, and beads. _____

6. Because the shapes are so beautiful, hobbyists have collected diatom shells since the 1700s. _____

7. Collectors must use one tiny hair for a tool as they place diatoms on microscope slides. _____

8. Diatoms may be small, but their huge populations feed countless marine animals. _____

9. Diatoms have been called the "grass of the sea" because they are food for huge schools of krill. _____

10. These schools of krill feed small fish; they are the base of the marine food chain. _____

11. Krill aren't eaten by small fish only; even though they are tiny, they are also eaten by giant sea creatures. _____

12. As a baleen whale swims through a school of krill, it filters them out of the water. _____

13. The whale shark is the largest fish in the world, but it uses a similar method for eating krill. _____

14. If diatoms died out, other sea life would die, or it would be seriously endangered. _____

15. Because diatoms produce much of our oxygen, we also depend on them; keeping them alive is critical. _____

Lesson 16 Underline the adjective clause in each sentence. Circle the noun it describes. Draw a box around the relative pronoun or the relative adverb that begins the clause.

1. Last week I tried sea kayaking on a day when school was out.

2. Sea kayaks are large, stable boats that are hard to tip over.

3. There's a reason why the kayak paddle has two blades: it allows kayakers to steer through the water.

4. Our instructor, who is an expert kayaker, showed us the best paddling methods.

5. We sat in our kayaks on the beach where a wave would pull us out into the bay.

6. My friend Matt, who came along with me, paddled fast.

7. We encountered marine animals that we had never seen up close before.

8. We passed an otter whose stomach was draped in kelp.

9. Matt saw a whiskered, large-eyed seal at a moment when he least expected it.

10. Kayakers often encounter seals in places where the curious creatures are abundant.

11. There's no reason why the seals aren't as interested in us as we are in them.

12. Certain laws protect marine mammals in states where these animals must interact with humans.

13. The instructor who led our trip kept a wide space between our kayaks and the seals and otters.

14. People who get too close to seals or otters may face fines and other penalties.

15. I would like to try sea kayaking again at a time when I am less busy.

Lesson 17 Underline the adverb clause in each sentence. Draw a box around the subordinating conjunction that begins the clause.

1. Because oceans are so broad and so deep, they have always been mysterious.

2. People imagined gigantic sea monsters before they were able to explore the ocean's depths.

3. Scylla and Charybdis, two sea monsters of Greek myth, supposedly lived where the sea passed through a narrow channel.

4. Whenever Charybdis sucked water into her huge mouth, a perilous whirlpool formed.

5. Although Charybdis was dangerous, sailors feared Scylla even more.

6. As a boat passed between the two monsters, Scylla used her twelve tentacles to grab a meal of sailors.

7. One of the exciting parts of Homer's *Odyssey* comes when Ulysses encounters Scylla and Charybdis.

8. Ulysses steers his ship through the middle of the passage because he knows the dangers on both sides.

9. Although Ulysses tries his best, Scylla drags his boat toward her with her tentacles.

10. As everyone shrieks in horror, Scylla devours six sailors.

11. Ulysses somehow steers the boat past the monsters before any more of his crew are lost.

12. Wherever sailors took to the sea, people told tales of monsters.

13. When a Scottish sea serpent died, its coiled body became the island of Iceland, according to a legend.

14. After oceanographers were able to study deep-sea life, they discovered truths behind some legends.

15. Some real "sea monsters" like the giant squid are even stranger than the imaginary creatures were.

Lesson 18 Read each sentence. Draw a line under the dependent clause and circle the noun it modifies. Write *RC* if it is a restrictive clause and *NC* if it is a nonrestrictive clause.

1. This arboretum has a number of trees that were planted a hundred years ago. _____

2. That giant oak, which has become a home for squirrels, is fifty feet tall. _____

3. The maple trees, which are a flaming red in autumn, were imported from Japan. _____

4. The flowers that bloom on the magnolia trees are as big as dinner plates. _____

5. The birch trees, whose bark looks like shredded paper, form a circle around the pond. _____

6. All the trees that never lose their leaves are called evergreens. _____

7. These trees, which are common in northern climates, have needles and produce cones. _____

8. The deciduous trees, which lose their leaves, look like skeletons in the winter. _____

9. Then in spring, which is my favorite season, little buds will appear on their branches. _____

10. The willow tree that droops lazily over the fence is my favorite tree. _____

11. I also like the redbud, which has unusual heart-shaped leaves. _____

12. The arboretum is also a place where many species of birds and mammals live. _____

13. In addition to the trees, there are colorful flowerbeds, which are tended by several gardeners. _____

14. The arboretum is like a beautiful park where peace and quiet can always be found. _____

15. My grandmother, who has grown flowers all her life, would love this place, too. _____

Lesson 19 Look at the boldfaced group of words in each sentence. Underline the word or words it modifies. Then write *PH* if it is a phrase or *CL* if it is a clause.

1. Mr. Chin's class presents a talent show **every year**. _____

2. The show is held in the auditorium, **where there is a big stage**. _____

3. Friends and relatives **of the students** love to come and watch. _____

4. This year, Tiffany, **who is in the school orchestra**, will play the flute. _____

5. Terrence will sing a solo that he has been practicing **for weeks**. _____

6. The Cabrera twins will play a trumpet duet **that they wrote themselves**. _____

7. Not all of the performances **in the show** will be musical, however. _____

8. Jonathan will juggle five oranges **while he stands on one foot**. _____

9. Kate and Isla have prepared a gymnastics routine **with jumps and tumbles**. _____

10. Ian is polishing his tap shoes **because he is going to dance for everyone**. _____

11. Nathan, **who is definitely the class clown**, has prepared jokes to tell. _____

12. Vivian will march **around the stage** twirling her baton. _____

13. Jake will make several objects disappear **before our eyes**! _____

14. It seems that every student **in Mr. Chin's class** has some unique ability. _____

15. He will congratulate all the performers **after the curtain falls**. _____

Lesson 20 Underline the infinitive phrase in each sentence.

1. In art class I learned how to make a clay pot.

2. The clay must be soft enough to mold easily.

3. To make the clay soft, potters knead it with their hands.

4. This also helps to remove any air bubbles from the clay.

5. Now the potter is ready to shape the pot.

6. Some potters use their fingers to pinch the pot into shape.

7. Others coil strips of clay to form the pot's sides.

8. The coil method is an ancient way to make pottery.

9. Potters use slip, a mixture of clay and water, to join the coils together.

10. To smooth the surface of a coil pot, the potter rubs it gently.

11. My favorite way to make a pot is the potter's wheel.

12. As the lump of clay spins on the wheel, the potter uses his or her hands to press it into shape.

13. Potters are able to create a wide range of shapes and sizes on the wheel.

14. The heat of a kiln helps to harden the finished pot.

15. Many potters use brilliant glazes to color their pots.

Lesson 21 Underline the participial phrase in each sentence. Circle the participle.

1. Wrestling with each other, lion cubs learn important skills.

2. These skills, acquired in play, will make the lions effective hunters as adults.

3. My kitten moves forward silently, stalking a ball of string.

4. Pretending the ball of string is a mouse, she bats it with her paw and then pounces on it.

5. I often play with my kitten, swinging a toy on a string.

6. Attracted by the sudden movements, she attacks the toy.

7. Other kinds of young animals also play games, developing different types of skills.

8. Fetching balls or sticks, dogs play happily with humans.

9. Growling at each other, puppies learn protective skills.

10. Young goats play in the mountains, jumping from rock to rock.

11. Dolphins play together in the water, leaping in pairs through the foamy wake.

12. Young chimpanzees, known for their high intelligence, chase one another for fun.

13. Playing just for the fun of it, children and young animals prepare for adulthood.

14. Human children also learn through play, imitating older children and adults.

15. Social skills learned in play stay with a person throughout life.

Lesson 22 Underline the gerund phrase in each sentence. Draw a box around the gerund.

1. Becoming a triathlete is my dream.

2. A triathlon involves competing in three different events.

3. Triathletes compete without even taking a rest between events!

4. Swimming almost a mile is the first event of most triathlons.

5. Bicycling 25 miles comes next.

6. The hardest part, though, may be running six miles at the end.

7. Finishing a triathlon successfully is considered the ultimate athletic challenge.

8. Each week I spend some time on training for the triathlon.

9. I really enjoy riding my bike to and from school.

10. Running long distance is my best event in track.

11. I am not as good at swimming laps, however.

12. I plan to work on swimming long distances at the pool this summer.

13. A friend will help me by timing my laps.

14. The real trick will be putting all three events together.

15. Training for nine to twelve months should prepare me for the competition.

Name _____

Lesson 23 Read each pair of sentences. Mark a star beside the one that more effectively expresses the idea and shows relationships. Then label the sentences *S* for simple, *CD* for compound, *CX* for complex, or *CCX* for compound-complex.

1. Mariachi music began long ago in an area of Mexico. _____

   Mariachi music began in the state of Jalisco, Mexico, when groups of nineteenth-century musicians traveled from town to town playing stringed instruments. _____

2. Although much music of that time had a simple, straightforward beat, mariachi music was syncopated; the musical term *syncopated* is a common one that means that some notes fall in between the beat.
   _____

   Much music of that time had a simple, straightforward beat, but mariachi was syncopated with notes falling in between the beats. _____

3. Because the syncopated mariachi music had a new, unique quality, it really had an effect on people.
   _____

   The syncopation gave the mariachi music a new, unique quality, and the music really had an effect on people as a result of this. _____

4. A mariachi performance could include instruments only, or it could feature both instruments and singers. _____

   There were two ways that mariachi music was performed; though a performance could include instruments only, it could also include singers and instruments. _____

5. People did special dances to mariachi music, such as the *zapateado* and the Mexican hat dance. _____
   Mariachi music was often accompanied by special dances: the *zapateado* called for dancers to stomp their boots to the beat, and for the Mexican hat dance, dancers moved around a hat called a sombrero. _____

Lesson 24 Label each item *F* (fragment), *RO* (run-on), *CS* (comma splice), or *RA* (ramble-on).

1. The saguaro is often called the giant cactus it grows up to sixty feet tall. _____

2. Up to ten tons in weight. _____

3. The saguaro's trunk is shaped like a thick column, a few branches point upward. _____

4. When I saw a saguaro cactus I thought that in my opinion the branches looked like the arms of a human person who was waving hello to somebody the person knew. _____

5. Found in Arizona, southern California, and parts of Mexico. _____

6. Because the region receives very little rain. _____

7. The saguaro soaks up rain, grooves in its trunk expand to hold the water. _____

8. When the rainstorms finally come. _____

9. The saguaro's grooves expand and contract like an accordion, which is a musical instrument that has grooves that expand and contract in much the same way. _____

10. The saguaro has white, funnel-shaped flowers they bloom on summer nights. _____

Lesson 25 Underline each proper noun. Circle each common noun.

1. Liechtenstein is a very small country.

2. It is about the size of Washington, D.C.

3. This country lies in the Alps, which are among the highest mountains in Europe.

4. Trains pass through Liechtenstein as they travel between Austria and Switzerland.

5. German is the official language of Liechtenstein.

6. This tiny country is ruled by a prince.

7. Vaduz is the capital of Liechtenstein, and it is also the location of the royal castle.

8. Surrounded by forested mountains, Liechtenstein lies on the banks of the Rhine River.

9. The region was once controlled by Charlemagne, king of the Franks.

10. It later became a part of the Holy Roman Empire.

11. In 1712 Johann-Adam Liechtenstein became ruler of what would become Liechtenstein.

12. Liechtenstein has been independent since 1719, except for a short time when Napoleon conquered it.

13. Tourists from around the world visit this picturesque country.

14. Collectors prize stamps from Liechtenstein.

15. The stamps are decorated with paintings by famous artists such as Rembrandt and Rubens.

Lesson 26 Read each sentence. Circle the boldfaced word that is the type of noun listed in parentheses.

1. Shelly belongs to a youth **group** that volunteers around **town**. (collective)

2. She and her **friends** think it is important to show **kindness** to others. (abstract)

3. Last week, she got an **education** by helping build a new **house** for a family of six. (concrete)

4. She now knows the proper **technique** for hammering a **nail**! (abstract)

5. Next she and her friends will ride in a **caravan** of **cars** to deliver flowers to senior

   citizens. (collective)

6. In a month's **time**, the youth group is scheduled to pick up trash in the city **park** twice. (concrete)

7. There are always lots of napkins and plastic **bottles** under the **stand** of trees by the entrance. (collective)

8. Shelly can't believe the lack of **care people** show when they litter. (abstract)

9. Shelly's group doesn't just help humans; they also have the **joy** of working with stray **dogs**. (concrete)

10. At the city animal shelter, they feed and exercise a **pack** of grateful **canines**. (collective)

11. The **group** also cleans the **cages** and sweeps the concrete floors. (concrete)

12. Shelly feels much **sympathy** for the **dogs** and wants to take them all home! (abstract)

Name _____

Lesson 27 Write each noun in parentheses in its correct plural form.

1. Two (day) ago my (parent), my brother, and I moved to a new town. _____

2. I heard the (echo) of the movers' (voice) in our empty new house. _____

3. Everything was packed in (box) and (crate). _____

4. My brother and I sat on the (step) and talked about our new (school). _____

5. My brother was scared to meet the (child) in his new second-grade class. _____

6. I wasn't looking forward to starting (class), either. _____

7. Mom said, "Don't dwell on your (worry). Set up your new (room)." _____

8. I unpacked my (book) and placed them on (shelf) in my room. _____

9. As I was changing my (shoe), I heard (noise) in the hall. _____

10. I opened my door and saw two (puppy) wagging their (tail). _____

11. I decided that not all the (surprise) in this new town would be bad. _____

12. One puppy was black with white (patch) on his paws, and the other was brown with black (fleck).

    _____

13. We ran out into the garden, where the little dogs leaped like (fox) and howled like (wolf).

    _____

14. Then they ran off to chase (butterfly) and hide under (bush). _____

15. My brother and I wrote about our new (pet) in our (diary). _____

Lesson 28 Write the possessive form of each noun in parentheses. Circle each plural possessive noun you write.

1. My (day) work begins with a ride on the bus. _____

2. The bus hurries through the (city) traffic. _____

3. The (wheels) rumbling is a relaxing sound. _____

4. (Passengers) minds wander as they ride. _____

5. Some find entertainment in a (book) pages. _____

6. I wonder if it is any (author) dream to be read on all the buses in the country. _____

7. You can learn a lot from (riders) conversations. _____

8. The sound of (children) giggling often fills the bus. _____

9. I enjoy looking out the (bus) windows. _____

10. That's the best way to get a feel for a (city) character. _____

11. (Shops) windows filled with interesting things can be seen all along the route. _____

12. You can watch different (pedestrians) walking rhythms. _____

13. The (leaves) shadows flicker on the sidewalk. _____

14. The (bus) engine wheezes as it climbs steep hills. _____

15. At the (ride) end, the doors swing open in a new neighborhood. _____

Lesson 29 Circle each personal pronoun. Write *1* if it is a first person pronoun, *2* if it is second person, or *3* if it is third person.

1. I played handball with Marc yesterday. _____

2. Is he a good player? _____

3. You are just as good. _____

4. Juan beat him in three games last week. _____

5. They played at the park. _____

6. Marc beat me, though. _____

7. We played twice yesterday. _____

8. Did you play a good game? _____

9. I was moving fast. _____

10. You should play Marc. _____

11. Have you played against Maria? _____

12. She is surprisingly quick. _____

13. Juan lost to her in an intense game. _____

14. Marc said the two of them are the best players in the neighborhood. _____

15. Maybe Juan and Maria will play doubles against us sometime. _____

Lesson 30 Read each sentence. Underline each compound personal pronoun that is a reflexive pronoun. Circle each compound personal pronoun that is an intensive pronoun.

1. You should sign yourself up for tennis lessons at the community center.

2. I myself have been playing tennis for about a year.

3. At first, serving the ball was difficult, and I was frustrated with myself.

4. But my instructor, Tara, made herself available most afternoons.

5. She herself was once a professional player.

6. After many hours with Tara, I finally had something to show for myself.

7. I could manage a serve that Tara herself couldn't return!

8. After perfecting my serve, I told myself I would work on my footwork.

9. When my older brother Ty played tennis, he put himself through many drills to improve his footwork.

10. He always says that the way to make yourself a better player is to move your feet!

11. Like Tara, Ty himself has had some success on the tennis courts.

12. Both Ty and Tara forced themselves to practice six days a week.

13. They are proud of themselves and all their accomplishments.

14. Ty and I sometimes play by ourselves after everyone has gone home.

15. I count myself lucky to have such a great older brother!

Extra Practice

Lesson 31 Circle each possessive pronoun.

1. My dog is bigger than Lia's dog.

2. Hers is a tiny, yappy dog.

3. I don't like it as much as I like yours.

4. Mine is huge.

5. Most other dogs are afraid of my dog.

6. But he just wants to be their friend.

7. His tail thumps on the ground.

8. Soon the other dogs are wagging theirs.

9. Our neighborhood has lots of dogs in it.

10. Your dog is the nicest.

11. Lia's dog may be small, but have you seen her cat?

12. "Kitty" is bigger than both of my cats put together.

13. His fur puffs out in all directions.

14. That cat's enormous tail has stripes all down its length.

15. Some cats' meows sound strangely human, but his sound more like a lion's roar.

Lesson 32 Circle each relative pronoun and underline the noun it refers to. Draw a box around each interrogative pronoun.

1. What is a bobcat?

2. It is a wildcat that lives in North America.

3. The bobcat gets its name from its tail, which is short, or "bobbed."

4. You can also recognize bobcats by the long hairs on the sides of the face, which resemble sideburns.

5. Who has seen a bobcat?

6. These animals, which are shy and active mainly at night, are hard to observe.

7. What is a bobcat's habitat?

8. Bobcats live in areas that are wooded, swampy, or mountainous.

9. Mountain climbers who venture into the back country occasionally encounter bobcats.

10. For their dens, bobcats prefer small caves and hollow trees, which provide shelter and security.

11. Practically any animal that is not a predator can become a meal for a bobcat.

12. Which do bobcats hunt in the wild?

13. Rabbits, birds, mice, rats, and squirrels are some of the animals that make up a bobcat's diet.

14. Who must keep an eye out for bobcats on the prowl?

15. Farmers who keep chickens must protect their flocks from bobcats.

Lesson 33 Circle each indefinite pronoun.

1. Everyone in our family thinks that spaghetti is the best food on earth.

2. My dad knows everything there is to know about cooking spaghetti.

3. Nothing could taste better.

4. Most of us prefer spaghetti with marinara sauce.

5. My sister is the only one who likes carbonara sauce better.

6. Both are really delicious.

7. Would you prefer a spaghetti dish with meatballs or one with sun-dried tomatoes?

8. Either would make me happy.

9. Few enjoy spaghetti as much as I do.

10. No one could possibly be any hungrier than I am right now.

11. Won't someone bring me a plateful of spaghetti?

12. Everybody come to the table; it's dinnertime!

13. I can't think of anything I'd rather do.

14. Somebody pass the Parmesan cheese, please.

15. There's none left, so you'll have to eat your spaghetti plain.

Lesson 34 Circle each adjective that describes or tells what kind. Underline each adjective that tells how many. Draw a box around each article (*a, an, the*).

1. An ancient oak leans over the bank of the lake.

2. Its numerous roots dip into the placid water.

3. A rope is tied to a high branch.

4. I have swung on it on many warm afternoons.

5. You should stand on the grassy bank and grab the thick rope.

6. Swing out over the deep, clear water.

7. Then let go and plunge in with a thunderous splash.

8. You may descend to a depth of ten feet.

9. Everything looks green under the glassy surface.

10. The cold water may make you feel breathless.

11. A few seconds of vigorous swimming will make you warm.

12. If you swim to shallow water, you can do impressive handstands.

13. You might even see a white egret fishing with its long beak in the slender reeds.

14. Then you can swim to shore and scramble up the slippery bank.

15. After a brief rest, you can catch the rope and swing again.

Lesson 35 Circle each demonstrative adjective. Underline each demonstrative pronoun.

1. This store sells loose beads for making jewelry.

2. I made this the last time I came here.

3. That is an interesting bracelet; how did you make it?

4. I strung these beads on wire and made loops to form flower petals.

5. What are those beads in the center of each flower?

6. Those are seeds with holes drilled through them.

7. These beads in the big jar are made out of old buttons.

8. Those beads over there are made of plastic.

9. This is a cowry shell.

10. People once used these shells as money.

11. Look at those colorful beads in the basket.

12. Craftspeople molded those out of multicolored glass.

13. That is my favorite one.

14. This wooden bead is carved in the shape of a turtle.

15. These would make a beautiful bead necklace.

Lesson 36 Underline the adjectives in parentheses that are written correctly.

1. Shane has (beautiful many/many beautiful) rocks and minerals in his collection.

2. This is a piece of (smooth glassy/smooth, glassy) rose quartz.

3. Its light pink color reminds me of the (new three/three new) rosebushes in my garden.

4. Shane's piece of granite has (tiny multicolored/multicolored tiny) specks.

5. This rock is made up of (different three/three different) minerals.

6. The (old memorial/memorial old) statue in the town square is made of granite.

7. Shane's talc specimen has a (soft, powdery/soft powdery) texture.

8. His (shiny, metallic/shiny metallic) piece of pyrite looks remarkably like gold.

9. Shane says this mineral has fooled (most new/new most) rock collectors.

10. Shane's (large crystal-filled/crystal-filled large) geode is his favorite rock.

11. A geode is a hollow rock with (sparkling many/many sparkling) crystals growing inside.

12. Some of Shane's rocks contain (impressive, desirable/impressive desirable) fossils.

13. Several of these fossils were collected in a (Mexican faraway/faraway Mexican) riverbed.

14. Shane also has a piece of flint with (ancient Mayan/Mayan ancient) writing on it.

15. He found it in a (dusty, molding/dusty molding) shop downtown.

Extra Practice

Lesson 37 Underline each action verb. Circle each linking verb.

1. Plants make sugar with the sun's energy.

2. A water molecule is a combination of hydrogen and oxygen.

3. Plants obtain water from the soil.

4. Their leaves absorb carbon dioxide from the air.

5. Plants appear green because of the substance chlorophyll.

6. With energy from sunlight, a plant's chlorophyll splits water molecules into hydrogen and oxygen.

7. A combination of this hydrogen and carbon dioxide forms sugar.

8. Fruit tastes sweet because of this sugar.

9. *Photosynthesis* is the name of this process.

10. Oxygen is a waste product of photosynthesis.

11. Animals breathe this oxygen.

12. Plants are an important food source for animals.

13. Inside animals, plant sugars and oxygen become energy.

14. Animals exhale carbon dioxide for the plants.

15. Plants and animals depend on each other for survival.

Lesson 38 Underline each transitive verb and draw a box around its direct object. Draw a circle around each intransitive verb.

1. Like all the planets in our solar system, Earth orbits the sun.

2. It completes one rotation each year.

3. Earth's position in relation to the sun causes the seasons.

4. Earth's axis tilts during its orbit.

5. In North America's winter, the North Pole points away from the sun.

6. Rain and snow fall frequently in the Northern Hemisphere.

7. The winter solstice marks the shortest day of the year in the Northern Hemisphere.

8. It occurs on December 21 or 22.

9. This day marks the first day of summer in the Southern Hemisphere.

10. For the next three months, the Southern Hemisphere experiences its summer season.

11. The equator divides Earth's Northern and Southern hemispheres.

12. The vernal equinox, the start of spring, occurs in March.

13. The autumnal equinox happens in September.

14. During the equinoxes, the sun shines directly on the equator.

15. At these times, the length of the day equals the length of the night.

Name _____

Lesson 39 Write *A* if the verb in the sentence is in the active voice. Write *P* if the verb in the sentence is in the passive voice.

1. Seafood is eaten by people all over the world. _____
2. Squid is called *calamari* by Italian chefs. _____
3. They often fry calamari in batter. _____
4. *Sashimi,* sliced raw fish, is offered as an appetizer in Japanese restaurants. _____
5. In the Japanese dish *sushi,* rice and raw fish are carefully wrapped in seaweed by master chefs. _____
6. Japanese chefs broil eels for another popular seafood dish. _____
7. Many people enjoy raw oysters on the half shell. _____
8. Sturgeon are caught by fishers in the Caspian Sea. _____
9. Restaurants serve the eggs of these large fish as caviar. _____
10. Chicken, sausage, rice, and several kinds of seafood are mixed together by skillful chefs in the Spanish dish *paella.* _____
11. Soft-shell crabs have shed their hard exoskeletons. _____
12. In Maryland these crabs are eaten whole by hungry diners. _____
13. Lobsters from Maine are considered a delicacy by gourmets. _____
14. These crustaceans have tender, sweet, pinkish meat inside their tough red shells. _____
15. Lobster bibs are often worn by diners for this messy treat. _____

Lesson 40 Circle each present tense verb. Underline each past tense verb. Draw a box around each future tense verb.

1. The monsoon cycle controls rainfall in parts of Asia, Africa, and Australia.
2. Temperature differences between sea air and inland air cause the monsoon.
3. Dry winds blow from the northeast in winter.
4. By midsummer, southwest winds will bring torrential rain to the parched land.
5. In July 2005, 37 inches of monsoon rain fell on Mumbai, India, in a single day.
6. With so much rain, the city streets became severely flooded.
7. A violent cyclone devastated Bangladesh during the 1991 monsoon season.
8. More than 138,000 people died in that storm.
9. The rains bring new life along with destruction, however.
10. Heavy monsoon rains are essential for healthy crops.
11. Every summer, people watch the weather reports anxiously for news of the monsoon.
12. Right now, no one accurately predicts the time or strength of the monsoon very far in advance.
13. Accurate predictions will come eventually, though.
14. In 1978 scientists began MONEX, a wide survey of the monsoon.
15. With more intensive study, we will understand this cycle better.

Lesson 41 In each sentence, circle the main verb and underline the auxiliary verb or verbs.

1. Will you travel to Washington, D.C., during spring break?

2. The cherry trees should be blooming at that time.

3. Their pink and white blossoms have made the city even more beautiful.

4. You must visit the Lincoln Memorial on the National Mall.

5. This stately monument was designed in the style of a Greek temple.

6. Its large sculpture of Abraham Lincoln has been staring down at people since the 1920s.

7. The Jefferson Memorial is also considered a must-see attraction in Washington, D.C.

8. It has stood on the bank of the Potomac River for over seventy years.

9. The Vietnam Veterans Memorial was conceived by young architect Maya Lin as a class project.

10. The names of almost 60,000 soldiers have been carved into its walls.

11. A stroll through the National Portrait Gallery will offer a look at famous paintings of the Founding Fathers.

12. And, of course, you should schedule a tour of the White House.

13. Have you studied the history of this national landmark in school?

14. It has been the official residence of the president since 1800.

15. I could talk forever about the sights and sounds of Washington, D.C.

Lesson 42 Circle the boldfaced verbs in present perfect tense. Underline the boldfaced verbs in past perfect tense. Draw a box around the boldfaced verbs in future perfect tense.

1. I **had liked** rubber bands since I was in kindergarten, but I had never collected them before last year.

2. My interest **has grown** even greater since then.

3. Every day, once I **have finished** my homework, I look for rubber bands to add to my collection.

4. As soon as I **had collected** twenty rubber bands, I began forming a rubber band ball.

5. The ball **has grown** much larger since then.

6. I **have added** rubber bands of all sizes and colors.

7. Once I had to knock my rubber band ball out of a tree; it **had bounced** up after I threw it at the sidewalk.

8. I began my collection several months ago; by March I **will have kept** it for one year.

9. The biggest rubber band ball weighs more than 4,000 pounds; I **had seen** a picture of it in a book.

10. By the time I graduate from high school, my rubber band ball **will have grown** even larger than that one.

11. I **have researched** some other rubber band records recently.

12. Surely you **have heard** about the longest rubber band in the world.

13. Students who **had tied** thousands of rubber bands together found that the chain measured more than 19 miles in length.

14. I **have thought** about starting a rubber band chain myself.

15. I will not rest until I **have broken** a rubber band record!

Lesson 43 Circle each boldfaced verb in a progressive form. Underline each boldfaced verb that is not in a progressive form.

1. I **am having** a bad day.

2. It **was raining** when I woke up.

3. My sister **had eaten** the last of my favorite cereal.

4. I still **have** not **forgiven** her for it.

5. Outside, a big gust of wind blew just as I **was opening** my umbrella.

6. Soon it **had turned** inside out; it was ruined.

7. I guess this weekend I **will be buying** a new umbrella.

8. As I got to the bus stop, the bus **was driving** away.

9. Since I **had missed** the bus, I had to walk to school.

10. I got very wet while I **was walking**.

11. I **have been** on time every day this semester, but today I was late.

12. Just as I walked in, my teacher **was distributing** a pop quiz.

13. Now, however, my day **is getting** a little better.

14. My teacher announced that next week we **will be going** to the aquarium.

15. I **have decided** to put this terrible morning behind me.

Lesson 44 Read each sentence. If a verb in the sentence creates a time shift that doesn't make sense, mark an *X* through the verb. Write the correct tense of the verb on the line.

1. Bryan had never been comfortable in water, so he was hesitant to try waterskiing. _____

2. "You'll be fine, Bryan," said Uncle Ron, as he starts up the boat. _____

3. Bryan shook a little as he is putting on his life jacket. _____

4. Uncle Ron sped around the lake a few times to show Bryan how fast the boat would go. _____

5. "There's a reason why they call it a speedboat," Bryan thinks to himself. _____

6. Then Bryan's cousin Nelson, the waterskiing star, jumped in the water to show Bryan how it was done.

    _____

7. With little effort, Nelson kept his balance on the skis as he will fly across the lake. _____

8. He even did a few tricks; he is really enjoying showing off his skills. _____

9. Bryan couldn't put it off any longer; it was now his turn to put on the skis. _____

10. "Hold on to the rope tightly and let the boat pull you up," Uncle Ron is shouting. _____

11. As the boat rolled forward, Bryan shoots out of the water and then promptly fell back in. _____

12. Bryan was surprised at how difficult it was to stay vertical on the skis. _____

13. He tried to stand up again, but he will tumble back into the water. _____

14. Just as he was about to give up, he stays upright for several seconds. _____

15. "This is exactly like flying!" he shouted with a look of pure joy on his face. _____

Lesson 45 Circle each adverb. Then tell whether the adverb explains *how, when, where,* or *to what extent.*

1. The dancers leaped high into the air. _____

2. They moved gracefully. _____

3. They balanced daintily on their toes to delicate music. _____

4. Then the music changed to a loud, dramatic piece. _____

5. The company stomped thunderously with their heels. _____

6. They seemed to dance effortlessly. _____

7. It must be extremely difficult to learn and practice complicated dance steps. _____

8. One dancer performed a solo beautifully. _____

9. Another dancer tripped on some scenery there. _____

10. He fell clumsily to the floor. _____

11. He had twisted his ankle severely. _____

12. He was helped off the stage and his ankle was immediately examined. _____

13. The ankle was only sprained. _____

14. Afterward, the dancer appeared for a curtain call. _____

15. Everyone clapped loudly for the dedicated dancer. _____

Lesson 46 Underline each prepositional phrase. Circle the preposition and draw a box around its object. There may be more than one prepositional phrase in a sentence.

1. The strangler fig grows in the rain forest.

2. Birds and bats drop its seeds over tall trees.

3. In the leafy canopy, a fig seed sprouts.

4. Long vines grow from that seed.

5. These strong vines encircle the trunk of a host tree.

6. The fig plant then drops roots to the forest floor.

7. After a while, the host tree dies and rots away.

8. The strong lacework of vines stands on its own.

9. You can climb inside the hollow strangler fig.

10. The interior of the hollow trunk towers above your head.

11. You could imagine you are in a deep well.

12. Then you grab onto the sturdy vines and climb through the hollow center.

13. The spaces between the vines resemble small windows.

14. You can see amazing sights from that vantage point.

15. The rain forest floor lies beneath you.

Name _____

Lesson 47 Underline each coordinating conjunction. Circle each subordinating conjunction.

1. Before my brother started playing the bagpipe, I had never heard the instrument.

2. The bagpipe is an ancient instrument, but no one knows its origins.

3. Scottish bagpipes are made of a leather bag and five pipes.

4. When a musician blows into the *blowpipe,* the bag inflates.

5. The musician presses the bag, and air flows out of the pipes.

6. Each of the three *drone* pipes makes one continuous note, but the musician plays tunes by covering holes on the *chanter* pipe.

7. Although Scottish bagpipes can only produce nine notes, many bagpipe tunes are challenging.

8. Since my brother started playing, he has learned ten tunes.

9. Because bagpipes are expensive, my brother started with a practice instrument called a chanter.

10. The chanter is basically a blowpipe and a chanter pipe combined.

11. When my brother had learned to play the chanter well, he bought a real bagpipe.

12. If you've ever heard a bagpipe, you know it sounds very different from most other instruments.

13. Its sounds make me think of a person humming, the ocean roaring, or a duck quacking.

14. I like my brother's music, but I wish his bagpipes weren't so loud.

15. He practices outside, because he would drive everyone in the house crazy otherwise.

Lesson 48 Circle each conjunction. If a sentence contains correlative conjunctions, write *CC* on the line.

1. My sister and I are identical twins. _____

2. We not only look alike but also sound alike. _____

3. Both our friends and our parents can tell us apart, however. _____

4. Neither my sister nor I like to wear identical clothes. _____

5. We may look alike, but our personalities are different. _____

6. After school, my sister is usually either playing sports or practicing ballet. _____

7. I prefer reading and acting in plays. _____

8. Still, my twin is not only my sister but also a good friend. _____

9. Both she and I enjoy hiking in the wilderness. _____

10. We often take hikes or just short walks together. _____

11. We joke around and talk about whatever is on our minds. _____

12. We share a sense of humor; often either she is playing a practical joke or I am telling a funny story. _____

13. Once we switched clothes and pretended to be each other. _____

14. Some of our friends were fooled at first, but after a while they figured out the trick. _____

15. Neither our teachers nor our parents were fooled. _____

Lesson 49 Fill in the blanks with *your* or *you're*. Remember to capitalize a word that begins a sentence.

1. What is _____ favorite sport?

2. Lucia told me that _____ a fan of gymnastics.

3. Is becoming an Olympic gymnast _____ dream?

4. If _____ planning to become a gymnast, be prepared to work very hard.

5. You will have to spend part of every day at _____ gym.

6. _____ coach will teach you many new skills.

7. She will also help you build _____ strength.

8. _____ going to need to eat lots of healthful foods to build up muscles.

9. Soon _____ going to be doing flips and handstands.

10. _____ safety is extremely important; a "spotter" will make sure you don't hurt yourself on difficult moves.

11. When _____ ready, you can enter competitions.

12. You'll need to put together all _____ new skills into a smooth routine.

13. _____ probably going to be nervous.

14. Still, try to keep _____ mind on the routine.

15. If you always do _____ best, you will be satisfied with whatever you accomplish.

Lesson 50 Fill in the blanks with *their, they're,* or *there*. Remember to capitalize a word that begins a sentence.

1. _____ are many European legends about elves.

2. _____ imaginary creatures who are said to have magic powers.

3. Elves are said to tell people where _____ are rich veins of gold.

4. In some stories elves use _____ powers to help people.

5. For example, elves might help lost travelers find _____ way.

6. In other stories, though, _____ mean and unpleasant.

7. Some stories tell about elves who kidnap humans and take them to _____ secret land.

8. When the humans return, _____ old and gray.

9. A storyteller may point out a round hill and say, "Elves live under _____!"

10. _____ also said to live on magical islands.

11. Time passes very slowly _____, so elves seem never to reach old age.

12. When elves ask humans for _____ help and the humans provide that help, the elves usually repay the humans handsomely.

13. Many authors have included elves in _____ stories.

14. You may have heard of Legolas, Elrond, or Galadriel; _____ all elves in books by J.R.R. Tolkien.

15. You can read more about elves in the book over _____ by the clock.

Lesson 51 Circle the correct word in parentheses.

1. (It's/Its) amazing how many different kinds of fish there are.

2. What is the largest fish in the world? (It's/Its) the whale shark, which can weigh more than 15 tons.

3. (It's/Its) diet is primarily made up of tiny aquatic organisms.

4. I was relieved to learn that (it's/its) harmless to people.

5. The black swallower can eat fish twice (it's/its) size.

6. It does this by unhinging (it's/its) jaw in the same way a boa constrictor does.

7. The flying hatchet fish can use (it's/its) pectoral fins as wings.

8. (It's/Its) actually able to take off from the water's surface and fly for up to ten feet.

9. The porcupine fish uses (it's/its) prickly spines for protection.

10. (It's/Its) also able to fill itself with water to appear larger than it actually is.

11. If someone asks you what fish has four eyes, tell her (it's/its) the anableps.

12. (It's/Its) eyes are divided in two, so it can swim just below the surface and see above and below the water.

13. A cave fish is adapted to life in total darkness; (it's/its) eyes may be small and sightless, or nonexistent.

14. An archerfish catches (it's/its) prey by spitting water through the air.

15. (It's/Its) an expert at catching small insects it knocks into the water.

Lesson 52 Circle the correct word in parentheses.

1. (Whose/Who's) interested in puppets?

2. I first became interested through a friend (whose/who's) mother is a puppeteer.

3. I know another puppeteer (whose/who's) going to teach me his craft.

4. He says that anyone (whose/who's) as interested as I am is sure to do well.

5. I made a puppet (whose/who's) head is a sock.

6. The puppet looks like the Cheshire Cat, (whose/who's) my favorite character.

7. I have a friend (whose/who's) working on a puppet of her own.

8. It's a paper bag puppet (whose/who's) hair is made of shredded newspaper.

9. We can't decide (whose/who's) puppet is funnier.

10. My hero is Mario Lamo Jiménez, (whose/who's) the author of the puppet play *Andar nas Nuvens*.

11. I've been reading about different kinds of puppets in a book (whose/who's) author is a famous puppeteer.

12. Marionettes are puppets (whose/who's) movements are controlled by strings or wires.

13. (Whose/Who's) familiar with the Japanese form of puppetry known as Bunraku?

14. A friend of mine (whose/who's) seen Bunraku told me that the puppeteers dress all in black but don't hide out of sight.

15. Some of the most popular entertainers in Indonesia are puppets (whose/who's) shadows are projected onto screens.

Lesson 53 Fill in each blank with *to, too,* or *two* to complete each sentence correctly.

1. Yesterday I went _____ the African art museum.

2. I took the special tour on battles, which began at _____ o'clock.

3. The tour took _____ hours, but the time passed very quickly.

4. I learned about historic African weapons and armor and battle customs, _____.

5. Many Central African throwing knives had _____ points, one on each side.

6. The throwing method was similar _____ that of throwing a boomerang.

7. Although some knives were only used in battle, others had ceremonial functions, _____.

8. Some African cavalrymen rode _____ battle wearing quilted cloth armor.

9. Their horses wore this kind of armor, _____.

10. Fulani cavalrymen wore quilted battle coats, but they also protected their bodies from shoulder _____ waist with heavy iron armor.

11. A warrior who fell off his horse in battle could not remount because the armor was _____ heavy.

12. Often a soldier carried a sword and _____ spears into battle.

13. Most of the soldiers used shields, _____.

14. Beautiful silverwork often attached a lion's mane or tail _____ an Ethiopian warrior's shield.

15. The Maasai and the Kikuyu peoples often held a duel between their _____ best warriors before a battle.

Lesson 54 Fill in each blank with *than* or *then* to complete each sentence correctly.

1. Earthquakes happen almost every day in some part of California; now and _____ one of them is strong enough for people to feel.

2. I think small earthquakes are more exciting _____ frightening.

3. Some earthquakes begin more _____ 400 miles below ground.

4. First, Earth's crust starts moving deep below the surface; _____ energy waves go through the ground.

5. Compressional, or primary, waves travel faster _____ shear, or secondary, waves.

6. This is why compressional waves arrive first, and _____ shear waves arrive.

7. Both of these waves travel faster deep inside Earth's crust _____ they do near the surface.

8. If the ground continues to shake for a long time, buildings may shake apart and _____ collapse.

9. If you're inside and feel an earthquake begin, take shelter right _____ under a desk or table.

10. Wait until you are sure the quake is over; only _____ should you come out.

11. When it comes to earthquakes, nothing is more important _____ being prepared.

12. Schools and businesses practice emergency procedures; _____ everyone knows what to do in a disaster.

13. Often more damage is caused by the by-products of earthquakes _____ by the earthquakes themselves.

14. An undersea earthquake may cause a tsunami, which may _____ roll toward land.

15. Sometimes, fires started by ruptured gas lines cause more damage _____ the earthquake.

Lesson 55 Write *X* after each sentence that uses negatives incorrectly. Write *C* after each sentence that is written correctly.

1. I haven't never had a pet before, but my father says I can get one for my birthday. _____

2. I can't decide what kind of pet I want. _____

3. My dad doesn't want no cat in the house because he's allergic to them. _____

4. Tropical fish are beautiful, but they don't do nothing but swim. _____

5. You can't take them nowhere, neither. _____

6. A friend of mine has a gerbil, and it never stops running on its exercise wheel. _____

7. My dad doesn't like the idea of having a rat in the house. _____

8. Snakes are cool, but I wouldn't want to feed them no live mice. _____

9. Insects aren't really pets, in my opinion. _____

10. An ant farm doesn't count, and neither does a beehive. _____

11. Parrots are pretty, but my dad wouldn't never let me have such a noisy pet. _____

12. Besides, birds aren't very cuddly, and you can't really play with them. _____

13. I can't think of nothing wrong with dogs. _____

14. My dad doesn't have any problems with dogs either. _____

15. It won't be long before we have a new puppy in the family. _____

Lesson 56 Cross out each incorrect usage of *go, went, like,* and *all.* (If the word *was* is part of the incorrect expression, cross that out also.) Write correct words to replace the crossed out words if a replacement is needed.

1. Jamal was all, "My friend Tatiana is going to enter a math competition." _____

2. Then he goes, "She is one of the smartest people I know." _____

3. He was, like, so insistent that she would win, like, no matter who else entered the contest. _____

4. Marjorie was like, "What will happen if she does win?" _____

5. Jamal said if she, like, *did* win locally, she'd go against students from, like, all over the state. _____

6. Then he went, "All the winners of the state contest will compete in the national competition."
_____

7. So Marjorie goes, "Do you think she'll get that far?" _____

8. Jamal was like, "She was on the winning team last year, and I think she'll do it again." _____

9. Marjorie was all, "Tatiana sounds like a very smart person. I'd like to meet her." _____

10. Jamal said that he would, like, introduce us after school. _____

11. Then we, like, ran into Tatiana. _____

12. She went, "Oh, hi, how are you?" _____

13. At first I thought she was kind of, like, shy. _____

14. Then she goes, "I heard you guys are really good in math." _____

15. She, like, asked us to join her team for the competition! _____

Extra Practice

Lesson 57 Circle the correct word in parentheses.

1. From where we (sit/set), we can see the pyramids of ancient Egypt on the west bank of the Nile River.

2. The mummified bodies of pharaohs once (lay/laid) in them.

3. Realistic statues showing a pharaoh (sitting/setting) on his throne were believed to help the pharaoh's spirit recognize the pyramid as its home.

4. Statues' eyes were often (sit/set) with quartz crystal to make them as lifelike as possible.

5. Some experts believe that the pyramids were built by farm laborers during the part of each year when Nile floodwaters (lay/laid) on the fields.

6. A major step in building the pyramids was to build ramps and (lie/lay) planks on them to reduce friction.

7. Then workers slid enormous blocks of limestone up the ramps and (sat/set) them in layers.

8. Archaeologists have calculated that the workers had to (sit/set) one block every two and a half minutes.

9. Finally, workers (lay/laid) a smooth coating of smaller stones over the top.

10. Once these smaller stones were (sat/set) in place, the pyramid looked like solid stone from a distance.

11. Archaeologists have made interesting discoveries about the lives of the workers who (lay/laid) the stones.

12. The remains of a bakery and of a workers' graveyard still (lie/lay) near the pyramids.

13. Some workers were (lay/laid) to rest under miniature pyramids made of mud bricks.

14. Ancient robbers looted the pharaohs' pyramids for the treasures that (lay/laid) inside them.

15. After about 1700 B.C., Egyptians (lay/laid) their pharaohs in secret tombs to hide them from robbers.

Lesson 58 Circle the correct word in parentheses.

1. I (thought/thinked) I saw a dog in the alley.

2. It turned and (shaked/shook) its tail at me.

3. I (threw/throwed) a rubber ball to it.

4. The next day I (bringed/brought) it some food.

5. Someone had (built/builded) a small shelter for it.

6. Unfortunately, the wind had (blew/blown) some of the boards apart.

7. I was glad I had (wore/worn) a scarf.

8. The alley was (lit/litten) by a rosy sunset.

9. As it (grew/grown) darker, I worried that I wouldn't see the dog again.

10. My heart (sang/singed) when I saw the dog come around the corner.

11. It (ate/eated) the food eagerly.

12. Then I (gone/went) home slowly.

13. At my door I turned and saw that the dog had (ran/run) after me, wagging its tail.

14. My parents (said/sayed) we could keep the dog if no one reported it as missing.

15. We (drived/drove) to the vet to make sure the dog was healthy and to get it its shots.

Lesson 59 Read each sentence. If the sentence has an unnecessary pronoun, draw a line through it.

1. Galileo he was an Italian astronomer and philosopher born in 1564.

2. This great scientist he has been called the "Father of Modern Science."

3. Galileo is perhaps best known for his improvements to the telescope.

4. He made many observations about the sun, moon, and planets.

5. Most people of the time they believed that the bodies of the solar system revolved around Earth.

6. This theory is known as geocentrism.

7. But Galileo he saw evidence that Earth and the other planets revolve around the sun.

8. His idea it was controversial because it meant that Earth's humans were not the center of the universe.

9. Pope Urban, an important world leader, he was angered by Galileo's views.

10. Galileo was tried and forced to spend the rest of his life under house arrest.

11. He continued to write about his observations after his arrest.

12. Galileo also discovered Jupiter's four largest moons.

13. These satellites they are called the Galilean moons, after Galileo.

14. Galileo also observed sunspots, discovered the phases of Venus, and invented many scientific instruments.

15. His ideas and innovations they were endless!

Lesson 60 Draw a line through unnecessary words in each sentence.

1. Before it was a part of the United States, Texas was ruled by the sunny Mediterranean country of Spain.

2. In 1820, Spain began to allow settlers of all backgrounds to start colonies in this territory, which was a pretty interesting development.

3. Moses Austin was given permission to leave everything behind and start a colony.

4. He became the first *empresario,* which was the name from the language of Spain given to those who agreed to colonize Texas.

5. Unfortunately, especially for his family, Austin died before he could bring colonists to the area.

6. In 1821, only a year later, Mexico won its independence from Spain.

7. The land we now, in this day and age, call Texas was controlled by the new country of Mexico.

8. The Mexican government, which made its laws, continued to allow empresarios to settle in Texas.

9. Austin's son Stephen made a command decision and took over his father's contract to colonize Texas.

10. The first group of settlers Stephen Austin brought to Texas was called the Old Three Hundred, probably because there were almost 300 of them.

11. They bought land and set up households along the Brazos River, the longest river in Texas.

12. Soon many Americans wanted to become colonists and live and work in Texas.

Extra Practice

Lesson 61 Circle each boldfaced word that is a subject pronoun. Underline each boldfaced word that is an object pronoun.

1. **You** won't believe what **we** got from Mildred.
2. **She** gave **us** a fruitcake.
3. **We** thanked **her** politely.
4. **It** was as hard as a rock.
5. Floyd told **me** that **he** likes fruitcake.
6. **I** sent the cake to **him**.
7. **He** could not eat **it**.
8. His cousins like sweets; **he** gave it to **them**.
9. **They** don't want **it** either.
10. Maybe **they** will send it to **you**.
11. **I** have thought of a gift that **we** all want.
12. **It** is useful to all of **us**.
13. **I** will give **you** a hint.
14. **You** write your thoughts in **it**.
15. **You** guessed **it**: a pocket notebook.

Lesson 62 Circle the correct pronoun in each pair. Write *S* if you chose a subject pronoun and *O* if you chose an object pronoun.

1. Brock and (I/me) met MacDougal at the scene of the crime. _____
2. (He/Him) and Findley were dusting for fingerprints. _____
3. I asked them to give Brock and (I/me) the lowdown. _____
4. They said Lizzie had given the Tenth Precinct and (we/us) the slip. _____
5. As Brock and (I/me) interviewed Mrs. Patel, the owner of the jewelry store, her son Billy came in. _____
6. (He/Him) and Mrs. Patel got into an argument about whether Mrs. Patel had locked the door. _____
7. (She/Her) and Billy were the last to leave the store before the robbery. _____
8. They told Brock and (I/me) that everything had seemed normal that night. _____
9. I told Brock and (they/them) that Lizzie and her accomplices always strike when you least expect it. _____
10. I knew it would be hard to catch Lizzie and (they/them). _____
11. Brock and (I/me) were determined to give it our best shot. _____
12. There's an old score to settle between Lizzie and (I/me). _____
13. (She and I/Her and me) worked together once, before she turned to the wrong side of the law. _____
14. I knew Lizzie couldn't resist the lasagna served at the restaurant where (she and I/her and me) used to get lunch on our break. _____
15. We staked out the restaurant, and, sure enough, the lasagna and (I/me) captured the thief. _____

Lesson 63 Circle the antecedent or antecedents of each boldfaced pronoun.

1. Rachelle and her mother and brother drove across the United States when **they** moved from Philadelphia to Los Angeles.

2. Rachelle kept a diary of everything **she** saw along the way.

3. In her diary, Rachelle wrote about the Willis Tower in Chicago; **it** is a very tall building.

4. Rachelle's mother pointed out the Mississippi River to **her**, and Rachelle wrote about that, too.

5. When the trip got boring, Rachelle played the license plate game to pass the time; **she** kept track of each new state's license plate she saw.

6. The car broke down somewhere near Denver, but a mechanic fixed **it**.

7. The mechanic was friendly, and Rachelle wrote about **him** in her diary.

8. Rachelle wrote about the Rocky Mountains when her mother drove through **them**.

9. In Utah, Rachelle's brother asked to visit Zion National Park; **he** had read that the park is beautiful.

10. Rachelle, her mother, and her brother parked the car so **they** could go hiking in the colorful canyons.

11. In some places, the canyon walls were so close together Rachelle could touch **them** both at the same time.

12. Back in the car, Rachelle wrote about Zion; she said **it** was the most amazing place she had ever visited.

13. As Rachelle's mother navigated the streets of Las Vegas, **she** pointed out all the flashing signs.

14. Rachelle wrote in her diary that the lights looked like stars to **her**.

15. Finally, the family arrived at the Pacific Ocean, and **they** went for a swim.

Lesson 64 Circle the pronoun that agrees with the antecedent in each pair of sentences.

1. Everyone in our class has to complete a creative writing project. (They/It) must be at least three pages.

2. This assignment is quite unlike the research reports we finished last week. (It/They) gives us much more freedom.

3. Josie and I enjoy reading poetry. (We/It) will try to write sonnets.

4. Josie has been making a list of rhyming words. I've never seen (them/her) so excited about homework.

5. We've decided that our sonnets will be about nature. Of course, (it/they) will be fourteen lines long.

6. Nguyen will probably write one of her great short stories. (We/They) are always so fun to read!

7. Mr. Diaz thinks Nguyen could be a professional writer someday. Three of (his/her) stories have been published.

8. Because Nguyen is so shy, she really relies on writing. (It/They) helps her communicate with others.

9. Jackson is planning to write a science fiction story. (He/It) says it will be set in the year 2225.

10. Jackson will include illustrations with the text. I'm sure (he/they) will help him establish the setting.

11. Jackson has shown me some of his drawings. (He/They) depict a colony of humans on the moon's surface.

12. Grant is always telling jokes. Josie thinks (she/he) will write a humorous piece.

13. Beth is inventing a folktale with animal characters. I wonder whether (it/they) will have a moral.

14. Mr. Diaz has advised Shawna to write a personal narrative. (He/She) thinks her trip to Europe would be an interesting subject.

15. Shawna agrees, but she would rather write fiction. (It/She) wants to use her imagination.

Extra Practice

Lesson 65 Read each boldfaced pronoun. If the pronoun does not have a clear antecedent, mark an *X* through it.

1. We spent a day in Seattle before our cruise to Alaska. **It** was so much fun!

2. At the famous Pike Place Market, we tasted local berries and fresh croissants and decided **they** were the best we had ever had.

3. We also watched the fishmongers as **they** tossed salmon and trout to each other.

4. There were many people outside selling flowers and jewelry. **They** made the market such a colorful place.

5. Later we packed a picnic basket and took **it** to a scenic beach.

6. My little brothers saw a family of seals as **they** played near the water.

7. Suddenly, dark clouds gathered and raindrops began to fall. **It** was ruined!

8. We took refuge in the Seattle Art Museum after a sprint through the rain. **It** took our breath away!

9. We saw a work by my father's favorite artist. **He** studied painting in New York City.

10. "How about some dinner?" Dad asked as **he** led us out of the museum.

11. We could see that the sky had cleared. In fact, **it** was the brightest blue I have ever seen.

12. "We should check out that view from the Space Needle first," said Mom. "**It** is supposed to be spectacular."

13. I followed **them** down the street toward the observation tower that looked like a spaceship.

14. We could see for miles and miles from the top of the Space Needle. I'd never seen anything like **it**.

15. We all agreed that we should visit Seattle again someday. **It** is truly a great city.

Lesson 66 Circle the pronoun in parentheses to complete each sentence correctly.

1. (Who/Whom) is playing first base?

2. The player (who/whom) the league named MVP for last year is the first baseman.

3. (Who/Whom) or what is an "MVP"?

4. MVP stands for Most Valuable Player, a player without (who/whom) the team would be lost.

5. I have a cousin (who/whom) admires that player very much.

6. (Who/Whom) is that over there?

7. To (who/whom) are you referring?

8. I am referring to the person (who/whom) is sitting in the front row of the bleachers.

9. I still can't tell to (who/whom) you are pointing.

10. I mean that woman (who/whom) is eating a hot dog.

11. Oh, she is someone of (who/whom) you may have heard.

12. She's the one (who/whom) starred in that movie.

13. Do you mean the movie with the director (who/whom) won an Academy Award?

14. That's a person (who/whom) I would like to meet!

15. Let's find someone (who/whom) will introduce us.

Extra Practice

Lesson 67 Circle the simple subject in each sentence. Then underline the correct form of each verb in parentheses.

1. A new set of watercolors (is/are) what I want for my birthday.

2. Tubes of paint (works/work) best for my style of painting.

3. Mineral-based pigments (gives/give) the paints their colors.

4. Paints made with the pigment cadmium (looks/look) red.

5. Cobalt, another pigment, (turns/turn) paints blue.

6. Compounds of chrome and lead (produces/produce) brilliant pigments.

7. The many colors of chrome (includes/include) red, yellow, orange, and bright green.

8. The health risks of lead (necessitates/necessitate) handling these pigments with great care.

9. A mixture of iron oxide, clay, and sand (creates/create) ocher, a yellowish-brown pigment.

10. A material called gum arabic (holds/hold) watercolors together.

11. Blobs of paint (dot/dots) my mixing palette.

12. A skillful artist always (mixes/mix) shades carefully.

13. Drops of water (lightens/lighten) a color; I add the drops slowly.

14. Long, quick strokes with a big brush (creates/create) a thin wash of color.

15. Layers of transparent color (overlaps/overlap) to make a new shade.

Lesson 68 Look at the compound subject in each sentence. Circle the conjunction. Then underline the correct verb.

1. My friends and my brother (likes/like) eating in the cafeteria.

2. Either Mr. Novak or Mrs. MacGee usually (serves/serve) us the entree.

3. The window table or the corner table (is/are) a good place to sit.

4. Fresh-baked bread or muffins often (appears/appear) on Mondays.

5. Jaia and Piper (likes/like) muffins a lot.

6. A vegetarian entree and a sugar-free dessert (is/are) always available.

7. On Tuesdays, hamburgers or vegetable lasagna (is/are) the featured entree.

8. Gerome and Garth always (chooses/choose) hamburgers.

9. Sometimes Gerome or Garth (lets/let) me have a few french fries.

10. Either baked ziti or fried chicken (is/are) served on Wednesdays.

11. Thursdays are my favorite because fajitas and black bean chili (is/are) on the menu that day.

12. Neither the fried chicken nor the hamburgers (tastes/taste) as good as the black bean chili.

13. Neither cake nor pie (is/are) ever served for dessert on Fridays.

14. Jaia and I usually (orders/order) bread pudding that day.

15. Today, a baked potato and a salad from the salad bar (sounds/sound) good to me.

Lesson 69 Circle the simple subject in each clause. Then underline the correct form of each verb in parentheses.

1. "Megatoaster" (is/are) the name of our band.

2. Dimitri and Damon (is/are) in the group with me.

3. The group (sounds/sound) really good now.

4. We always (plays/play) our own original music.

5. "Walls and Windows" (is/are) a new song I've just written.

6. The band (plays/play) at teen clubs and picnics.

7. Everyone (dances/dance) when we play.

8. "I Froze My Toes" (is/are) our most popular song.

9. The whole crowd (cheers/cheer) when we start playing it.

10. At that moment, everything (seems/seem) great.

11. My family (does/do) not come to hear us very often.

12. No one (says/say) the music is too loud, but all of them cover their ears when we play.

13. Earplugs (helps/help) protect our eardrums from the noise.

14. Nothing (stops/stop) us in the middle of a song.

15. Our sound equipment sometimes (blows/blow) fuses, but we keep playing.

Lesson 70 Underline the verbal phrase that begins each sentence. If the phrase is a dangling modifier, write *dangling* on the line. If the phrase is used correctly, circle the word it modifies and write *C* on the line.

1. Learning to knit, sweaters can be made. _____

2. Wanting to try a new hobby, Maxine learned to knit. _____

3. Never having knitted before, a simple pattern was chosen. _____

4. Looping yarn around long needles, the project seemed easy. _____

5. Glancing briefly at the instructions, Maxine began knitting very quickly. _____

6. Knitting the front of the sweater, mistakes were made. _____

7. Covered with holes and lumps in the stitches, the sweater was not wearable. _____

8. Unraveling it stitch by stitch, disappointment was inevitable. _____

9. Determined to learn, it was time to make a new start. _____

10. Studying the instructions carefully, Maxine realized where she had gone wrong. _____

11. Knitting carefully this time, the sweater slowly took shape. _____

12. Spaced evenly and neatly, the rows of stitches looked better. _____

13. Taking her time, Maxine created a beautiful sweater. _____

14. Made with her own two hands, she was very content. _____

15. Having knit one sweater successfully, she is ready to begin another. _____

Lesson 71 Read each boldfaced verbal phrase. If the phrase is misplaced, draw an arrow from the phrase to the place in the sentence where it should be placed.

1. **Covering the ground,** we gazed with delight at the deep snow.

2. **Listening to the weather report,** we were shocked that we had gotten eight inches!

3. It was the perfect day to spend **sledding at the park.**

4. Ronan looked like a bear **bundled up in his brown snowsuit.**

5. We were out the door in minutes **dressed for the cold from head to toe.**

6. **Excited about our icy adventure,** Ronan raced ahead of me toward the park.

7. I was left on the treacherous sidewalk **dragging both our sleds.**

8. We could see that everyone in the neighborhood had had the same idea **arriving at the sledding hill.**

9. **Teeming with dozens of sledders,** the snowy slope looked like an ant hill.

10. We trudged up to the top of the hill **looking forward to our first slide.**

11. **Twinkling below us,** we could see the lights of our quaint town.

12. Ronan, **tired of waiting for me,** suddenly jumped on his sled and started down the hill.

13. He flew across the slippery ground **shrieking with joy.**

14. **Gripping my sled tightly,** I slid down the hill after him.

15. The cold wind **whipping across my face** felt exhilarating.

Lesson 72 Think about how many things are being compared in each sentence. Then underline the correct form of the adjective or adverb in parentheses.

1. Jamal runs (faster/fastest) than I do.

2. But Aya is the (faster/fastest) runner on the track team.

3. She runs even (better/best) than our coach.

4. Last month I started practicing (harder/hardest) than I ever had before.

5. I ate the (healthier/healthiest) foods I could find.

6. I spent (longer/longest) than usual warming up each day before races.

7. Yesterday was the (bigger/biggest) race of the season.

8. It was scheduled (earlier/earliest) than I had expected.

9. Still, I felt (more ready/most ready) than I feel before most races.

10. I also felt the (more nervous/most nervous) I had ever felt in my life.

11. I pushed myself (more determinedly/most determinedly) than anyone else in the race.

12. I almost ended up with a (better/best) time than Aya.

13. Even though I didn't win, I was the (prouder/proudest) one there.

14. She's still the (swifter/swiftest) runner of all.

15. But now no one will think of me as the (slower/slowest) on the team.

Lesson 73 Draw three lines (≡) under each lowercase letter that should be capitalized. Draw a line (/) through each uppercase letter that should be lowercase.

1. The country of fiji is in the South pacific.

2. more than 300 Islands and 500 reefs make up this tropical Nation.

3. viti levu, or Big Fiji, is the Largest island.

4. Smaller islands include Kandavu and vanua levu.

5. thousands of years ago, people migrated to fiji from indonesia.

6. Nearly 2,000 years ago, a group of polynesians settled there.

7. A dutch navigator named abel tasman was the first european explorer to visit the islands.

8. In 1774 captain james cook visited a southern Island called vatoa.

9. In the decades that followed, many european traders and Missionaries settled in Fiji.

10. Thousands of workers from india were brought to fiji to work on sugar plantations.

11. A few escaped convicts from australia also made fiji their home.

12. Many of today's Fijians are of indian, polynesian, Chinese, micronesian, and european descent.

13. Fiji has been an independent Nation since 1970.

14. The official language of fiji is english, but many island residents speak fijian or hindi.

15. Fiji's capital and largest City is suva, which lies along the southern coast of viti levu.

Lesson 74 Circle each word that should begin with an uppercase letter.

1. "Marta's birthday falls during the weekend of memorial day," said Chad.

2. Chad and Lisa were waiting outside of thomas jefferson middle school for their friend Marta.

3. "We should throw her a surprise party!" Lisa said. "We could have it at riverside park."

4. "Is that the park in adams falls at the corner of center street and hoffman boulevard?" asked Chad.

5. "Yes, it's across from stephen t. shetler memorial library," Lisa replied.

6. "I think I went to a fourth of july celebration there once," Chad recalled.

7. "We can go to patty's party supplies and buy balloons and streamers," suggested Lisa.

8. "And lawson's fine foods will have her favorite snack food, cheesy crisps," Chad added.

9. "My aunt works at something sweet in downtown evansville," Lisa said. "She can make the cake."

10. "This is going to be the best party since the adams falls sweet corn festival!" exclaimed Chad.

11. "I know exactly how to get her to the park," said Lisa. "I'll tell her we're volunteering for the adams falls beautification society."

12. "And I'll say I'm visiting family in indianapolis so she won't suspect anything," said Chad.

13. "Good idea!" Lisa replied. "We'll ask our friends at selby recreation center to help, too."

14. "Let's start planning," said Chad. "It's friday, april 25th, so we have only a month."

15. Just then, Marta came jogging down third street. Chad and Lisa hid their smiles.

Name _____

Lesson 75 Rewrite each item below. Use initials and abbreviations where you can.

1. Doctor Martha Jane Brown _____
2. Mister Miguel Garcia _____
3. Stanyan Street _____
4. Mount Shasta _____
5. Riverland Avenue _____
6. Mistress Madeline Trimble _____
7. Castle Corporation _____
8. General Robert Edward Lee _____
9. Monterey Boulevard _____
10. Mister Gino Raffetto _____
11. Bonnview Road _____
12. Doctor Peter Murray _____
13. Cellular Network, Incorporated _____
14. Cassock Drive _____
15. Mister Robert Elwood Jones _____

Lesson 76 Draw three lines (≡) under the letters that should be capitalized. Underline or add quotation marks where they are needed in titles.

1. My family rented the movie south pacific, and we found it very entertaining.
2. Now I am writing an adventure story titled lost in the south Pacific.
3. I found information about the region in the book journeys in paradise.
4. I also found information in a DVD titled island escapes.
5. I read a book called in search of the coral reef.
6. My favorite short story in the book was shark escape.
7. I also enjoyed the story marlin adventure.
8. My sister wrote a beautiful poem called Reef dream.
9. She also wrote a silly song titled the stingray's revenge.
10. Her poem was printed in a literary magazine called fresh literary voices.
11. If you plan to visit the South Pacific, you should read the book basic canoeing tips.
12. Bring a copy of the cookbook Tropical island delights.
13. You should also rent the video documentary how to avoid electric eels.
14. I saw a short film titled exotic wildlife of Borneo.
15. It was based on the book wild creatures of Borneo.

Lesson 77 Underline the correct word in parentheses. If the word is a possessive, write *possessive*. If the word is a contraction, write the two words it was made from.

1. In 1994 a group of adventurers traveled the length of (Canada's/Canadas') largest island, Baffin Island. _____

2. Baffin Island is the (world's/worlds') fifth largest island. _____

3. The majority of the (island's/islands') landmass lies above the Arctic Circle. _____

4. Most of Baffin Island (is'nt/isn't) accessible by car. _____

5. The (men's/mens') journey required the use of skis, kayaks, and sleds. _____

6. The (explorer's/explorers') goal was to travel 1,800 miles in six months. _____

7. They knew such a journey (couldn't/could'nt) be done during winter. _____

8. They started in March, when (winter's/winters') icy grip had eased. _____

9. The travelers (weren't/were'nt) able to escape the cold weather entirely, however; they encountered temperatures of more than 40 degrees below zero. _____

10. On the (journey's/journeys') first leg, they skied more than 1,000 miles. _____

11. Maps (didn't/did'nt) prepare them for the reality of the rugged terrain. _____

12. The (mens'/men's) sleds weighed 200 pounds apiece, making travel difficult. _____

13. Next the explorers paddled 600 miles in kayaks, but their journey (wasn't/was'nt) over. _____

14. They hiked the final 230 miles to Baffin (Island's/Islands') southern tip. _____

15. The (adventurer's/adventurers') entire journey took 192 days. _____

Lesson 78 Add commas where they belong. Delete (⌿) commas that don't belong. Remember that a comma is not needed to separate two items, but it is needed to separate two adjectives of the same kind.

1. The three Aran Islands, are called Inishmore Inishmaan and Innishneer.

2. They lie, six miles off the coast, of Ireland.

3. The islands are isolated windswept and barren.

4. The islands had no running water electricity or telephones until 1970.

5. Then the islands gained rapid, popularity as a tourist destination.

6. Despite the damp windy weather, people from Europe and America began choosing the Aran Islands as a destination.

7. Visitors were fascinated by the Iron Age structures ancient monasteries and quaint villages.

8. Soon restaurants tour buses and inns became part of life in the Aran Islands.

9. Tourists visit the islands today to get a sense of traditional, Irish culture.

10. Permanent residents love the islands' ruggedness solitude and beauty.

11. Many islanders farm, or fish for a living.

12. Lobster crab and mackerel are harvested from the icy Atlantic.

13. The limestone cliffs are studded with small well-kept villages.

14. Aran Islanders keep traditions alive through music, and dancing.

15. The lively melodic music played by islanders is popular with natives and tourists alike.

Lesson 79 Add the missing comma to each sentence. Then decide why the comma is needed. Write *I* for introductory word, *D* for direct address, *T* for tag question, or *C* for compound sentence.

1. "Maya please show us your pictures of Puget Sound," we asked. _____

2. "I'd like to but I have so many!" Maya replied. _____

3. "We can see all of them can't we?" asked Mike. _____

4. Maya cleared a space on the table and then she took out her photographs. _____

5. She spread out the photographs and we crowded around. _____

6. "Wow this is you!" Sabrina said to Maya as she pointed to one photograph. _____

7. "It's a good picture isn't it?" Maya said. "It shows me on our kayaking trip." _____

8. "Maya weren't you scared out there in the sound?" Mike asked. _____

9. "Well we weren't exactly in the open sea," Maya responded. _____

10. "Puget Sound is protected by islands and a peninsula and the water is usually quite calm." _____

11. "I was nervous at first but I followed the leader's instructions," she continued. _____

12. "A seal swam up to my kayak and it looked right at me!" Maya said. _____

13. "You were at least a little frightened weren't you?" Mike asked. _____

14. "No the seal was just curious," Maya replied. _____

15. "Seals often approach kayakers and kayakers usually feel lucky to see them," she continued. _____

Lesson 80 If the boldfaced words are a nonrestrictive clause or phrase, add one or more commas to set off these words from the rest of the sentence.

1. The first Thanksgiving **an event that lives in American legend** was quite unlike the feast depicted in movies and TV.

2. Most of us picture a bountiful table **where friendly Pilgrims and Native Americans sit together.**

3. There is a giant turkey **roasted to perfection** in the center of the table.

4. Sweet cranberry sauce sits next to a pumpkin pie **that was baked in a Pilgrim oven.**

5. The real event **which is still somewhat mysterious** was very different.

6. There are only two known accounts of it; one is a letter by Edward Winslow **who was a leader of Plymouth Colony.**

7. It was actually a harvest celebration held **after the colonists had had successful crops.**

8. **Wanting to have a large feast** several men went hunting for the colony.

9. Nearby Wampanoag people heard the sounds **which rang throughout the woods.**

10. Chief Massasoit **suspecting that the colonists were preparing for a fight** visited the settlement.

11. The chief **relieved that the English were only hunting** sent his own men to hunt deer.

12. The colonists and Wampanoag spent three days eating the food **that they had hunted and harvested.**

13. Most of the Thanksgiving foods **that we prepare today** were not available.

14. Potatoes and pies were not served at the table **which likely held geese, mussels, grapes, and corn.**

15. The people also played games, sang, and danced **when they were done feasting.**

Lesson 81 Write a semicolon or a colon to separate the independent clauses in each sentence. Three sentences require a colon.

1. Sicily is the Mediterranean's largest island it lies off mainland Italy's southern tip.

2. The Greeks first settled Sicily 2,800 years ago they built temples and theaters.

3. Many peoples have claimed Sicily as their own Romans, Arabs, and Normans are among them.

4. Each culture left its mark Sicilian architecture reveals many influences.

5. Tourists may visit Norman castles and cathedrals they can also explore Greek ruins.

6. Sicily is prone to earthquakes and volcanic activity Mt. Etna, in northeastern Sicily, is Europe's tallest volcano.

7. Sicily's warm Mediterranean climate makes it possible for farmers to raise a variety of crops pistachios, lemons, melons, and oranges are just a few of those.

8. Family is an important part of Italian culture family members gather at mealtime.

9. Farmers produce much of the island's foods fresh pasta, olives, and sheep's cheese are among the delicacies.

10. Many traditional values and customs persist in Sicily some modern residents resist the old ways, though.

Write a colon where it should be in each item.

11. We brought home five souvenirs a leather purse, three T-shirts, and a book of postcards.

12. The plane will arrive from Sicily at 145 P.M.

13. Martinez, Iris A. *Italy's Volcanic Island*. Rome Dante Brothers, 1998.

14. The guide told us a good nickname for Sicily "One Island, Many Cultures."

15. **Michel** The view of the harbor is spectacular!
    Maria I wish we could see Rome from here.

Lesson 82 Add parentheses, dashes, and hyphens to these sentences where they are needed.

1. The island of New Guinea, which is in the western Pacific Ocean north of Australia, is the sec ond largest island in the world.

2. In 1963 Indonesia claimed the island's western half and named it *West Irian* victorious hot land.

3. After forty five years of Indonesian rule, much of this territory now known as Papua remains unchanged.

4. Out of the way villages are insulated from the modern world by dense forests and rugged mountains.

5. The highest mountain in Papua quite an impressive peak rises to a height of 16,503 feet.

6. The tropical highlands are home to many native groups collectively called Papuans PAP uh wuhns.

7. The native Asmat many say they are a fierce swamp dwelling people face a huge dilemma.

8. Their age old traditions are being challenged by the temptations and demands of the modern age.

9. Many Papuans still live as hunters or as sustenance farmers farmers who grow only enough for their families.

10. Until fairly recently, many had never seen an honest to goodness modern vehicle.

11. Ready to wear clothing is a rarity this is especially hard to imagine in rural New Guinea.

12. Most people they should count themselves lucky think of New Guinea as an exotic vacation.

13. For many workers, though, a trip to New Guinea is made in search of better than average wages.

14. New Guinea's mineral wealth copper, gold, petroleum has attracted both international corporations and fly by night operators.

15. Mineral resources create jobs and wealth, but they often spell the end of long established ways of life.

Lesson 83 Write *I* after each indirect quotation and *D* after each direct quotation. Then add quotation marks and other punctuation to the direct quotations. Draw three lines (≡) under each lowercase letter that should be capitalized.

1. Rick said that he visited San Francisco with his family. _____

2. Rick did you visit Alcatraz Island on your trip Jared asked. _____

3. Rick said yes, my family took a tour of Alcatraz. _____

4. Jared asked whether the island was still a federal prison. _____

5. Rick showed him a brochure that read it hasn't been used as a prison since 1963. _____

6. The brochure also said that Alcatraz is now part of the Golden Gate National Recreation Area. _____

7. Rick explained that the name *Alcatraz* comes from a Spanish word meaning "pelican." _____

8. More than a mile of cold, rough water separates Alcatraz from San Francisco Rick said. _____

9. Some of America's most dangerous criminals were held at Alcatraz he added. _____

10. Jared asked who lives on the island now? _____

11. Rick pointed again to the brochure, which said the island is inhabited mostly by birds. _____

12. He told us that the birds have become a real problem. _____

13. Jared asked if the tour was spooky. _____

14. It was a little spooky, but it was also fascinating Rick replied. _____

15. Jared said when I visit San Francisco, I'm going to take the first ferry in the morning out to Alcatraz.

_____

Lesson 84 Rewrite this business letter in correct letter form.

Western Sporting Goods 143 Arkansas Way Nacogdoches, TX 75961 Dear Sir or Madam I am interested in purchasing some snorkeling gear. Will you please send me a copy of your latest catalog? Sincerely yours Benjamin Ross 1434 Laughlin Road Derry, NH 03038 October 24, 20__

_____

_____

_____

_____

_____

_____

_____

_____

_____

_____

Read this text and answer the questions on the next page.

Now You See It

1   When it comes to helping you experience the world around you, the

2   eyes have it. These amazing sensory organs transform light into impulses that

3   your brain interprets as images. It sounds like a complicated process but the

4   basics of sight are, well, quite easy to see.

5   First you'll need to review the major components of the eye. The white

6   part is called the sclera! Blood vessels in the sclera carry blood throughout the

7   eye and sometimes show up as tiny red lines against the white. The iris is the

8   colored part of the eye, which can be blue, brown, green, or hazel? The iris is

9   actually a ring of muscles that open and close to control the amount of light

10   entering the eye. The pupil, the dark circle in the center of the iris, lets light

11   into the eye. When it is dark, your pupil becomes larger to allow more light in

12   and help you see better. Covering the pupil and iris is a clear protective shield

13   called the cornea, which also bends and focuses light to enable sight.

14   When you look at something, light bounces to the object and enters

15   the eye through the cornea and pupil. The light then passes through the lens a

16   curved, transparent structure behind the pupil. The lens refracts, or bends, the

17   light and projects an image onto a membrane at the back of the eye called the

18   retina. Millions of nerve cells in the retina, called rods and cones, change the

19   light into electrical impulses. The cones detect colors and bright light, the

20   rods perform when light is dim. These impulses then travel along the optic

21   nerve to the brain, which deciphers them and tells you what you are seeing.

22   After just a few simple steps, the power to observation is yours!

Read each item carefully. Fill in the circle next to the best answer.

1. What change, if any, should be made to the underlined words in lines 3–4?

   Ⓐ NO CHANGE
   Ⓑ process, the
   Ⓒ process, but the
   Ⓓ process and the

2. What change, if any, should be made to the underlined words in lines 5–6?

   Ⓐ NO CHANGE
   Ⓑ called the sclera?
   Ⓒ called the sclera:
   Ⓓ called the sclera.

3. What change, if any, should be made to the underlined words in lines 7–8?

   Ⓐ NO CHANGE
   Ⓑ or hazel.
   Ⓒ or hazel;
   Ⓓ or hazel!

4. What change, if any, should be made to the underlined words in lines 10–11?

   Ⓐ NO CHANGE
   Ⓑ the iris lets
   Ⓒ the iris; lets
   Ⓓ the iris: lets

5. What change, if any, should be made to the underlined words in lines 14–15?

   Ⓐ NO CHANGE
   Ⓑ bounces into the object
   Ⓒ bounces aboard the object
   Ⓓ bounces off the object

6. What change, if any, should be made to the underlined words in lines 15–16?

   Ⓐ NO CHANGE
   Ⓑ the lens. A
   Ⓒ the lens; a
   Ⓓ the lens, a

7. What change, if any, should be made to the underlined words in lines 19–20?

   Ⓐ NO CHANGE
   Ⓑ light, and the
   Ⓒ light the
   Ⓓ light but the

8. What change, if any, should be made to the underlined words in line 22?

   Ⓐ NO CHANGE
   Ⓑ power of observation
   Ⓒ power near observation
   Ⓓ power on observation

Read each item carefully. Fill in the circle next to the best answer.

9. Read the following sentences.

> Those puffy clouds in the distance <u>are cumulus clouds</u>. They likely have an altitude of less than 6,500 feet.

What part of the sentence is underlined?

Ⓐ complete subject
Ⓑ complete predicate
Ⓒ simple subject
Ⓓ simple predicate

10. Read the following sentences.

> Wheat has been an important staple crop since ancient times. The <u>world</u> now grows over 650 million tons of wheat each year.

What part of the sentence is underlined?

Ⓐ complete subject
Ⓑ complete predicate
Ⓒ simple subject
Ⓓ simple predicate

11. Read the following sentences.

> Meet me at the movie theater at 7:00. That should give us plenty of time to buy popcorn.

What is the simple predicate of the first sentence?

Ⓐ Meet
Ⓑ me
Ⓒ at
Ⓓ theater

12. Read the following sentences.

> William Howard Taft was our heaviest <u>president</u>. Legend says that he once got stuck in the White House bathtub.

What part of the sentence is underlined?

Ⓐ direct object
Ⓑ indirect object
Ⓒ predicate noun
Ⓓ predicate adjective

13. Read the following sentences.

> I'm on a roll! I've written nearly two <u>pages</u> of my story already!

What part of the sentence is underlined?

Ⓐ direct object
Ⓑ indirect object
Ⓒ predicate noun
Ⓓ predicate adjective

14. Read the following paragraph.

> [1] Both my mother and my uncle are meteorologists. [2] My uncle does research, and my mother gives weather reports for a local news station. [3] Uncle Tom collects and analyzes data related to global warming. [4] Mom warns the public when bad weather is coming.

Which sentence has a compound predicate?

Ⓐ Sentence 1
Ⓑ Sentence 2
Ⓒ Sentence 3
Ⓓ Sentence 4

335

Read each item carefully. Fill in the circle next to the best answer.

15. Read the following sentences.

> The phonograph was invented <u>in 1877</u> by Thomas Edison. It was the first device able to record and play back sounds.

What part of the sentence is underlined?

(A) adjectival prepositional phrase
(B) appositive
(C) complete predicate
(D) adverbial prepositional phrase

16. Read the following sentences.

> The shark, <u>a carnivore</u>, is at the very top of the ocean food chain. It feeds on smaller sharks, fish, and squid.

What part of the sentence is underlined?

(A) adjectival prepositional phrase
(B) appositive
(C) complete subject
(D) adverbial prepositional phrase

17. Read the following sentences.

> Mrs. Vargas is an excellent musician. She plays the clarinet and the oboe _____.

Which is a prepositional phrase that completes the second sentence?

(A) when she visits us
(B) a woodwind instrument
(C) in the symphony
(D) beautifully

18. Read the following paragraph.

> [1] Have you ever made a berry smoothie before? [2] It's really quite easy! [3] Then blend the ingredients in a blender.

Where is the best place to add the following sentence?

> First, wash and cut bananas, strawberries, and blueberries.

(A) Before sentence 1
(B) After sentence 1
(C) After sentence 2
(D) After sentence 3

19. Read the following paragraph.

> [1] Brianna wants to go to the soccer game with us. [2] She hasn't finished her homework. [3] Maybe she can join us next time.

What is the best way to combine sentences 1 and 2?

(A) Brianna wants to go to the soccer game with us, but she hasn't finished her homework.
(B) Brianna wants to go to the soccer game with us but she hasn't finished her homework.
(C) Brianna wants to go to the soccer game with us, and she also hasn't finished her homework.
(D) Brianna wants to go to the soccer game with us, she hasn't finished her homework.

20. Read the following sentences.

> <u>Hooray, our team has won the championship!</u> Did you ever think we would accomplish so much?

Which kind of sentence is underlined?

(A) exclamatory
(B) interrogative
(C) declarative
(D) imperative

Read this text and answer the questions on the next page.

Jefferson's Bones

1   Thomas Jefferson, who was a Founding Father and the third American president is

2   remembered for many things. He wrote the Declaration of Independence and

3   served as a governor, diplomat, secretary of state, and vice president. He

4   founded the University of Virginia; and designed his famous house, Monticello.

5   Many people also know that Jefferson was a scholar and an inventor. Who knew

6   several languages and made many scientific observations. Few have heard,

7   however, about his great passion for another pursuit—finding old bones.

8   Jefferson's America was a new country. Trying to prove itself. It had won

9   independence from England, but Europe was not impressed with this wild land

10   across the ocean. In fact, a French naturalist named Georges-Louis Leclerc had

11   declared that American land was so poor that its animal species were inferior

12   to those of the rest of the world. Jefferson took great offense at these words,

13   he wanted to show that America had creatures just as grand as the elephants

14   of Africa. Luckily, recent evidence was proving this to be true.

15   In 1705, a giant tooth had been found in New York. Then more teeth

16   were found, as well as bones and giant tusks. It seemed that a very large

17   elephant-like beast had roamed U.S. lands. Jefferson had proof of a great

18   American species, and he wanted more. He helped fund more digs to unearth

19   more of these animals, which were later called mastodons. He collected the

20   fossils in his house and even in the White House. And when he sent Lewis and

21   Clark on their journey west he hoped they might find live mastodons. America

22   would be known not only for its democracy, but for its elephants, too!

Read each item carefully. Fill in the circle next to the best answer.

1. What change, if any, should be made to the underlined words in lines 1–2?

   Ⓐ NO CHANGE
   Ⓑ president, is remembered,
   Ⓒ president is remembered,
   Ⓓ president, is remembered

2. What change, if any, should be made to the underlined words in lines 3–4?

   Ⓐ NO CHANGE
   Ⓑ Virginia and designed
   Ⓒ Virginia, and designed
   Ⓓ Virginia, designed

3. What change, if any, should be made to the underlined words in lines 5–6?

   Ⓐ NO CHANGE
   Ⓑ inventor, who, knew
   Ⓒ inventor who knew
   Ⓓ inventor; who knew

4. What change, if any, should be made to the underlined words in line 8?

   Ⓐ NO CHANGE
   Ⓑ country trying. To
   Ⓒ country; trying to
   Ⓓ country trying to

5. What change, if any, should be made to the underlined words in lines 8–10?

   Ⓐ NO CHANGE
   Ⓑ England but Europe
   Ⓒ England, or Europe
   Ⓓ England: Europe

6. What change, if any, should be made to the underlined words in lines 12–14?

   Ⓐ NO CHANGE
   Ⓑ words. Wanted
   Ⓒ words. He wanted
   Ⓓ words he wanted

7. What change, if any, should be made to the underlined words in lines 18–19?

   Ⓐ NO CHANGE
   Ⓑ animals which were
   Ⓒ animals which, were
   Ⓓ animals; which were

8. What change, if any, should be made to the underlined words in lines 20–21?

   Ⓐ NO CHANGE
   Ⓑ west. He hoped
   Ⓒ west, he hoped
   Ⓓ west; he hoped

Read each item carefully. Fill in the circle next to the best answer.

9. Read the following sentences.

> Yoshi's grandmother is celebrating her birthday, and he must fly to Japan to see her. <u>Although he is afraid of flying, he is willing to face his fear for her.</u>

What kind of sentence is underlined?

Ⓐ simple
Ⓑ compound
Ⓒ complex
Ⓓ compound-complex

10. Read the following sentences.

> <u>The day is very chilly, but it is quite pleasant when the sun peeks out.</u> I think we will enjoy our walk.

What kind of sentence is underlined?

Ⓐ simple
Ⓑ compound
Ⓒ complex
Ⓓ compound-complex

11. Read the following paragraph.

> [1] Galveston, Texas, was not prepared when a powerful hurricane struck in 1900. [2] Because weather forecasting was still imprecise, no one could predict the storm's path. [3] Waves washed away houses, and winds toppled telegraph poles. [4] After the storm had passed, the destruction left behind was overwhelming.

Which sentence does NOT have a dependent clause?

Ⓐ Sentence 1
Ⓑ Sentence 2
Ⓒ Sentence 3
Ⓓ Sentence 4

12. Read the following sentences.

> Hernando de Soto was a Spanish explorer <u>who led the first known European expedition across the Mississippi River.</u> He was searching for gold and a passage to Asia.

Which part of the sentence is underlined?

Ⓐ independent clause
Ⓑ adjective clause
Ⓒ adverb clause
Ⓓ nonrestrictive clause

13. Read the following sentences.

> Martin's school, <u>which is the oldest in town</u>, is on Berkley Street. It is only three blocks from his house.

Which part of the sentence is underlined?

Ⓐ nonrestrictive clause
Ⓑ restrictive clause
Ⓒ adverb clause
Ⓓ independent clause

14. Read the following sentences.

> Quinn loves to exercise at the new recreation center. <u>Swimming in the pool</u> is her favorite activity.

What kind of phrase is underlined?

Ⓐ appositive
Ⓑ infinitive
Ⓒ gerund
Ⓓ participial

Read each item carefully. Fill in the circle next to the best answer.

15. Read the following sentences.

> Many desert animals become active at night <u>to avoid the heat</u>. They sleep in cool underground burrows during the day.

What kind of phrase is underlined?

(A) appositive
(B) infinitive
(C) gerund
(D) participial

16. Read the following sentences.

> <u>Covered in flour,</u> Corey emerged from the kitchen. The cake was finally in the oven.

What kind of phrase is underlined?

(A) appositive
(B) infinitive
(C) gerund
(D) participial

17. Read the following sentences.

> Atoms, <u>which consist of protons, neutrons, and electrons</u>, are the building blocks of matter. Atoms bind together to form molecules.

Which part of the sentence is underlined?

(A) adjective phrase
(B) adverb phrase
(C) adjective clause
(D) adverb clause

18. Read the following sentences.

> Caused by collisions of gas particles in the _____ aurora borealis are colored lights in the northern sky. The colors are determined by the types of gas involved.

Which words and punctuation best complete the sentences?

(A) atmosphere. The
(B) atmosphere; the
(C) atmosphere, the
(D) atmosphere the

19. Read the following sentences.

> [1] Mr. Brooks enjoys restoring antique cars. [2] He has been doing this for years. [3] A Model T from the 1920s is his pride and joy.

What is the best way to combine sentences 1 and 2?

(A) Mr. Brooks enjoys restoring antique cars; he has been doing this for years.
(B) Mr. Brooks enjoys restoring antique cars, he has been doing this for years.
(C) Mr. Brooks enjoys restoring antique cars he has been doing this for years.
(D) Mr. Brooks enjoys restoring antique cars: he has been doing this for years.

20. Read the following paragraph.

> [1] When Julia first started playing, she could barely handle the basketball. [2] Now she can dribble the length of the court. [3] After weeks of practice, her shooting has improved, too.

Where is the best place to add the following sentence?

> All her shots bounced off the rim of the basket.

(A) Before sentence 1
(B) After sentence 1
(C) After sentence 2
(D) After sentence 3

Read this text and answer the questions on the next page.

Restoring a River

1   "I don't get it, Aunt Kathy," Theo said. "Why do they have to destroy

2 this dam? <u>Wasn't there a good reason for putting them up in the first place?"</u>

3   "Well, there was a reason," Kathy replied. <u>"In the 1930s, the town</u>

4 <u>wanted to create a reservoir of cooling water for it's power plant. Now that the</u>

5 <u>coal-burning, old plant is closed, the reservoir is no longer necessary."</u>

6   "And now they want to restore the river to its natural flow. Why

7 bother?" Theo had witnessed the demolition of the dam and the transformation

8 of the lake to a narrow, fast-moving stream. <u>Earth-moving various vehicles were</u>

9 <u>driven up and down the bank every day, piling dirt here and spreading it there.</u>

10   <u>"River restoration has quite a few advantages, both for local plants and</u>

11 <u>animals and for someone in town," Kathy said.</u> Theo felt a lecture coming on.

12   <u>"The dam has always prevented the salmons from swimming upstream</u>

13 <u>to spawn, or reproduce, which was an instinctive behavior for years.</u> Since the

14 1930s, the salmon population has been greatly reduced. And this isn't just a

15 problem for the salmon. <u>Other animals that rely on these fish for food, such</u>

16 <u>as wading birds, have been deprived of an energy source as well."</u>

17   "Okay, so the salmon will come back. What else will happen?"

18   <u>"The riverbed will have more water and nutrient-rich sediment, so</u>

19 <u>more species will have a healthier habitat.</u> The banks will become a wetland

20 where we can observe birds, reptiles, amphibians, and new vegetation."

21   Theo pictured herons fishing among cattails, croaking frogs, and trout

22 freely riding the swift current. "Maybe it is worth the trouble after all," he said.

Read each item carefully. Fill in the circle next to the best answer.

1. What change, if any, should be made to the underlined words in line 2?

   (A) NO CHANGE
   (B) putting those up
   (C) putting it up
   (D) putting him up

2. What change, if any, should be made to the underlined words in lines 3–4?

   (A) NO CHANGE
   (B) their power plant
   (C) its power plant
   (D) its' power plant

3. What change, if any, should be made to the underlined words in lines 4–5?

   (A) NO CHANGE
   (B) old coal-burning plant
   (C) old, coal-burning, plant
   (D) coal-burning old plant

4. What change, if any, should be made to the underlined words in lines 8–9?

   (A) NO CHANGE
   (B) Earth-moving, various vehicles
   (C) Various, earth-moving vehicles
   (D) Various earth-moving vehicles

5. What change, if any, should be made to the underlined words in lines 10–11?

   (A) NO CHANGE
   (B) something in town
   (C) anything in town
   (D) everyone in town

6. What change, if any, should be made to the underlined words in lines 12–13?

   (A) NO CHANGE
   (B) prevented the salmon
   (C) prevented the salmones
   (D) prevented the salmon's

7. What change, if any, should be made to the underlined words in lines 15–16?

   (A) NO CHANGE
   (B) animals which rely
   (C) animals whose rely
   (D) animals they rely

8. What change, if any, should be made to the underlined words in lines 18–19?

   (A) NO CHANGE
   (B) more species' will
   (C) more specieses will
   (D) more specis will

Read each item carefully. Fill in the circle next to the best answer.

9. Read the following sentences.

> How are we ever going to move this <u>piano</u>? It must weigh a thousand pounds!

What kind of noun is underlined?

(A) proper   (C) collective

(B) concrete   (D) abstract

10. Read the following sentences.

> Kayla encountered many creatures during her snorkeling adventure. She saw a stingray and a <u>school</u> of blue fish swim right in front of her.

What kind of noun is underlined?

(A) proper   (C) collective

(B) plural   (D) abstract

11. Read the following sentences.

> Deforestation, or removal of trees, destroys _____ habitats. It also causes more carbon dioxide to be trapped in the atmosphere.

Which word best completes the first sentence?

(A) animal's   (C) animals

(B) animals'   (D) animals's

12. Read the following sentences.

> Emma just got a Pekingese puppy. It is a cute puppy. It is a playful puppy.

What is the best way to combine these sentences?

(A) Emma just got a cute Pekingese playful puppy.

(B) Emma just got a cute, playful Pekingese puppy.

(C) Emma just got a Pekingese cute, playful puppy.

(D) Emma just got a playful cute Pekingese puppy.

13. Read the following paragraph.

> [1] He had made her a bracelet for her graduation, and she wanted to return the favor. [2] Yolanda carefully chose a color of yarn that would match Felipe's coat. [3] She worked on the scarf while he was at his daily soccer practice.

Where is the best place to add the following sentence?

> Yolanda decided to knit her brother a scarf for his birthday.

(A) Before sentence 1

(B) After sentence 1

(C) After sentence 2

(D) After sentence 3

14. Read the following sentences.

> The prospectors traveling to California in 1849 believed the arduous journey was worthwhile. They told <u>themselves</u> that they would make a fortune panning for gold.

What kind of pronoun is underlined?

(A) relative   (C) indefinite

(B) reflexive   (D) intensive

Read each item carefully. Fill in the circle next to the best answer.

15. Read the following sentences.

> In 1888, George Eastman developed a simple, inexpensive box camera. Suddenly <u>everyone</u> could take his or her own photographs.

What kind of pronoun is underlined?

Ⓐ relative
Ⓑ reflexive
Ⓒ indefinite
Ⓓ intensive

16. Read the following sentences.

> Wood and stone were often scarce on the Great Plains. Pioneers were sometimes forced to build <u>their</u> houses out of sod.

What kind of pronoun is underlined?

Ⓐ demonstrative
Ⓑ interrogative
Ⓒ possessive
Ⓓ relative

17. Read the following sentences.

> "<u>Who</u> will volunteer to help clean up the park?" asked Ms. Romero. "It will only take a few hours."

What kind of pronoun is underlined?

Ⓐ demonstrative
Ⓑ interrogative
Ⓒ possessive
Ⓓ relative

18. Read the following sentences.

> You should come to the bookstore to purchase that new book. The author _____ will be there signing autographs tonight.

Which pronoun best completes the second sentence?

Ⓐ he
Ⓑ him
Ⓒ his
Ⓓ himself

19. Read the following sentences.

> The Civil War's first major land battle was fought July 21, 1861. The conflict raged on for <u>several</u> years until peace was restored.

Which statement best describes the underlined adjective?

Ⓐ It tells what kind.
Ⓑ It tells how many.
Ⓒ It is an article.
Ⓓ It is a demonstrative adjective.

20. Read the following paragraph.

> [1] I thought the sudden downpour was bad enough. [2] But that was not the only unfortunate surprise of my morning. [3] When I got to school, I noticed my backpack was empty. [4] I had forgotten my history book!

Which sentence contains a demonstrative pronoun?

Ⓐ Sentence 1
Ⓑ Sentence 2
Ⓒ Sentence 3
Ⓓ Sentence 4

Read this text and answer the questions on the next page.

A New World

1   Mara and her crew were shaking with excitement as the sky rover

2   hovered over the rocky surface of the mysterious planet. Ever since the *Zeus II*

3   space probe had discovered this Earth-like sphere, the world had wanted to

4   know more. What was its atmosphere like? Was there water? Could something

5   grow in its soil? And, most importantly, may it support human life?

6   These anxious space explorers were about to find out. After weeks of

7   travel, they has made it halfway across the galaxy. In minutes, they would land,

8   put on their spacesuits, and step cautious onto an entirely new territory.

9   "Captain, where should I set this craft down?" asks Lieutenant Rice.

10   "Let's be patient," Mara replied. She will squint briefly at the horizon.

11   Yellow-gray clouds hung low in the sky, blocking light from this planet's sun. All

12   she could see was a barren expanse of gravel. Was there anything *to* explore?

13   Suddenly, in the distance, a dark spot appeared like a mirage in a desert.

14   Mara couldn't believe her eyes. As the sky rover moved closer, the crew can

15   see a hill covered in a green grass-like vegetation.

16   "I think we found our landing spot," Mara exclaimed. Soon the explorers

17   was wading through the waist-deep grass toward the top of the hill, where

18   another surprise awaited them. A lush valley lay below. A river snaked its way

19   through the bottom. Trees resembling pines stood tall along the bank. So there

20   was water and plant life. But would they find creatures of any sort?

21   "You might want to see this, Captain," Lieutenant Rice whispered. Mara

22   turned around slowly and got the shock of her life.

Read each item carefully. Fill in the circle next to the best answer.

1. What change, if any, should be made to the underlined words in lines 1–2?

   (A) NO CHANGE
   (B) were shaked
   (C) was shaking
   (D) will be shaking

2. What change, if any, should be made to the underlined words in line 5?

   (A) NO CHANGE
   (B) can it support
   (C) could it support
   (D) should it support

3. What change, if any, should be made to the underlined words in lines 6–7?

   (A) NO CHANGE
   (B) they have made it
   (C) they had made it
   (D) they will have made it

4. What change, if any, should be made to the underlined words in lines 7–8?

   (A) NO CHANGE
   (B) step cautiously onto
   (C) cautious step onto
   (D) step most cautious onto

5. What change, if any, should be made to the underlined words in line 9?

   (A) NO CHANGE
   (B) Lieutenant Rice is asking
   (C) Lieutenant Rice will ask
   (D) asked Lieutenant Rice

6. What change, if any, should be made to the underlined words in line 10?

   (A) NO CHANGE
   (B) She squints
   (C) She squinted
   (D) She has squinted

7. What change, if any, should be made to the underlined words in lines 14–15?

   (A) NO CHANGE
   (B) crew could see
   (C) crew can have seen
   (D) crew is seeing

8. What change, if any, should be made to the underlined words in lines 16–18?

   (A) NO CHANGE
   (B) explorers is wading
   (C) explorers are wading
   (D) explorers were wading

Read each item carefully. Fill in the circle next to the best answer.

9. Read the following sentences.

> Teresa <u>looked</u> anxious as she <u>stood</u> in line for the roller coaster. She <u>had</u> never <u>ridden</u> one before.

Which underlined word is a linking verb?

Ⓐ looked
Ⓑ stood
Ⓒ had
Ⓓ ridden

10. Read the following sentences.

> Ms. Asada received an advanced degree in business last year. Now she <u>works</u> for an insurance company.

What kind of verb is underlined?

Ⓐ linking
Ⓑ auxiliary
Ⓒ transitive
Ⓓ intransitive

11. Read the following sentences.

> Willis Tower _____ dominated the Chicago skyline since 1973. Originally called the Sears Tower, it was the tallest building in the world until 1998.

Which auxiliary verb best completes the first sentence?

Ⓐ have
Ⓑ will
Ⓒ has
Ⓓ was

12. Read the following sentences.

> Josh expects his team to qualify for the tournament final today. If they do, they _____ their rivals, the Monarchs, tomorrow night.

Which verb best completes the second sentence?

Ⓐ plays
Ⓑ played
Ⓒ playing
Ⓓ will play

13. Read the following paragraph.

> [1] The Great Pyramid of Giza, in Egypt, was built over 4,500 years ago. [2] The structure served as a tomb for the pharaoh Khufu. [3] Thousands of workers toiled for twenty years to complete this wonder. [4] They dragged huge stones from a quarry and set them in place.

Which sentence is written in the passive voice?

Ⓐ Sentence 1
Ⓑ Sentence 2
Ⓒ Sentence 3
Ⓓ Sentence 4

14. Read the following sentences.

> Anna is hard at work at a desk in the library. She _____ her research report on the effects of beach erosion.

Which verb best completes the second sentence?

Ⓐ had written
Ⓑ will have written
Ⓒ is writing
Ⓓ was writing

Read each item carefully. Fill in the circle next to the best answer.

15. Read the following sentences.

> Before my trip to Madrid, I <u>had
> learned</u> only a few Spanish words.
> Just two weeks in the city helped me
> improve my vocabulary immensely.

Which verb tense is represented by the
underlined words?

Ⓐ past progressive
Ⓑ past perfect
Ⓒ present
Ⓓ past

16. Read the following sentences.

> Gillian <u>hastily</u> got dressed and threw
> her books in her backpack. She was
> late for school again!

What does the underlined adverb describe?

Ⓐ when
Ⓑ where
Ⓒ how
Ⓓ to what extent

17. Read the following sentences.

> "Come back <u>to</u> me, Rex!" Amber
> shouted. Her energetic beagle had
> taken off after a squirrel.

What kind of word is underlined?

Ⓐ coordinating conjunction
Ⓑ transitive verb
Ⓒ subordinating conjunction
Ⓓ preposition

18. Read the following sentences.

> Neither the female _____ the male
> sea turtle tends to its young. The
> females lay their eggs on the beach
> and leave them unattended.

Which correlative conjunction best completes
the first sentence?

Ⓐ and   Ⓒ nor
Ⓑ but also   Ⓓ or

19. Read the following paragraph.

> [1] We can clean the garage this
> morning. [2] We can put it off until
> this afternoon. [3] It's really up to you.

What is the best way to combine sentences
1 and 2?

Ⓐ We can clean the garage this morning, or we
can put it off until this afternoon.
Ⓑ We can clean the garage this morning nor we
can put it off until this afternoon.
Ⓒ We can clean the garage this morning, and we
can put it off until this afternoon.
Ⓓ We can clean the garage this morning, but we
can put it off until this afternoon.

20. Read the following paragraph.

> [1] When Leo is in New York City,
> he likes to visit the Metropolitan
> Museum of Art. [2] He walks across
> Central Park until he sees the
> building's white columns. [3] After
> he enters and pays for his ticket,
> he heads straight for the exhibit of
> Greek and Roman art.

Where is the best place to add the following
sentence?

> Leo likes the objects in this collection
> because they are so old.

Ⓐ Before sentence 1   Ⓒ After sentence 2
Ⓑ After sentence 1   Ⓓ After sentence 3

Read this text and answer the questions on the next page.

Athena's Revenge

1   The ancient Greeks told a story about a young woman named Arachne.

2   She was known far and wide as the most gifted weaver in the land. <u>Every day</u>

3   <u>she would set at her loom creating the most exquisite and intricate tapestries.</u>

4   <u>Her work was so exceptional that many people were like, "This mortal has been</u>

5   <u>taught by Athena, goddess of the fabric arts."</u>

6   The smug Arachne took great pains to assure her admirers that the talent

7   was hers and hers alone. <u>She boldly announced that she, in fact, was a more</u>

8   <u>accomplished artist then the great Athena.</u> <u>The people gasped in horror when</u>

9   <u>foolish Arachne she uttered these words.</u> Regarding the deities with anything

10   but humility and respect was sure to result in the gravest consequences. The

11   silly woman should fear for her life if Athena ever heard her boastful talk.

12   The goddess did witness Arachne's arrogance and was duly angered. <u>She</u>

13   <u>wanted to confront Arachne, but she was compelled to give the woman a</u>

14   <u>chance to redeem herself, to.</u> Disguised as an old woman, Athena visited Arachne

15   and praised her lovely tapestries. <u>"Your work rivals that of Athena's,"</u> she said.

16   "Ha!" Arachne replied. "It is far better!" Athena could not contain her

17   fury. She rose to her full height, no longer an old hag, and challenged Arachne

18   to a contest. Goddess and girl got to work. <u>Their fingers flew across the looms.</u>

19   In minutes, a pair of magnificent tapestries filled the room. <u>Two more equally</u>

20   <u>wonderful weavings had not never been seen.</u> Then Arachne sealed her fate.

21   "My work is clearly superior," she said. Without another word, Athena

22   turned Arachne into a spider. Now her only tapestries would be humble webs.

Read each item carefully. Fill in the circle next to the best answer.

1. What change, if any, should be made to the underlined words in lines 2–3?

   (A) NO CHANGE
   (B) she would be setting
   (C) she would sat
   (D) she would sit

2. What change, if any, should be made to the underlined words in lines 4–5?

   (A) NO CHANGE
   (B) many people said
   (C) many people went
   (D) many people were all

3. What change, if any, should be made to the underlined words in lines 7–8?

   (A) NO CHANGE
   (B) them the great Athena
   (C) than the great Athena
   (D) that the great Athena

4. What change, if any, should be made to the underlined words in lines 8–9?

   (A) NO CHANGE
   (B) Arachne uttered she
   (C) Arachne they uttered
   (D) Arachne uttered

5. What change, if any, should be made to the underlined words in lines 12–14?

   (A) NO CHANGE
   (B) redeem herself, too
   (C) redeem herself, two
   (D) redeem herself, true

6. What change, if any, should be made to the underlined words in line 15?

   (A) NO CHANGE
   (B) Her work rivals
   (C) You're work rivals
   (D) You's work rivals

7. What change, if any, should be made to the underlined words in line 18?

   (A) NO CHANGE
   (B) Them's fingers
   (C) They're fingers
   (D) There fingers

8. What change, if any, should be made to the underlined words in lines 19–20?

   (A) NO CHANGE
   (B) had not ever been seen
   (C) never had not been seen
   (D) had not been never seen

Read each item carefully. Fill in the circle next to the best answer.

9. Read the following sentences.

> "_____test is this?" Mrs. Phelps asked, waving the paper in the air. "Someone forgot to write her name again!"

Which word best completes the first sentence?

(A) Who's
(B) Whom's
(C) Whose's
(D) Whose

10. Read the following sentences.

> Miguel _____ in the grass and looked up at the clouds. They looked like cotton balls drifting across the sky.

Which word best completes the first sentence?

(A) laid
(B) lay
(C) lied
(D) lain

11. Read the following sentences.

> Often an atom loses one of _____ electrons. When this happens, the atom becomes a positively charged ion.

Which word best completes the first sentence?

(A) it's
(B) its
(C) their
(D) they're

12. Read the following sentences.

> North Dakota has more citizens _____ ever before. This state has led the nation in population growth for the last several years.

Which word best completes the first sentence?

(A) that
(B) than
(C) then
(D) they

13. Read the following sentences.

> Kip suffers from allergies, so he can't have no dogs or cats in his house. He has to settle for a pet goldfish.

Which word should be deleted from the sentences?

(A) so
(B) can't
(C) no
(D) for

14. Read the following paragraph.

> [1] Helen is going to summer camp on Monday. [2] Before she leaves, she needs to talk to her friend Marla, too. [3] She hopes Marla isn't too busy to feed her rabbit while she is gone.

Where is the best place to add the following sentence?

> That means she has only two more days to pack!

(A) Before sentence 1
(B) After sentence 1
(C) After sentence 2
(D) After sentence 3

Read each item carefully. Fill in the circle next to the best answer.

15. Read the following sentences.

> Uri is an excellent local guitarist. Uri will entertain us at the party.

What is the best way to combine the sentences?

(A) Uri he is an excellent local guitarist and will entertain us at the party.

(B) Uri, he is an excellent local guitarist and will entertain us at the party.

(C) Uri, an excellent local guitarist, he will entertain us at the party.

(D) Uri, an excellent local guitarist, will entertain us at the party.

16. Read the following sentences.

> The quarterback _____ the ball to the receiver just in the nick of time. A second later, he was tackled by a defensive player.

Which word best completes the first sentence?

(A) throws

(B) throwed

(C) threw

(D) thrown

17. Read the following sentences.

> Japanese forces _____ the U.S. naval base at Pearl Harbor, Hawaii, on December 7, 1941. America entered World War II the next day.

Which word best completes the first sentence?

(A) striked

(B) struck

(C) strucked

(D) stricken

18. Read the following sentences.

> I caught Wesley playing video games when he should have been studying. Wesley _____, "Don't tell Mom!"

Which word or words best complete the second sentence?

(A) was like

(B) went

(C) was all

(D) said

19. Read the following paragraph.

> [1] The beautiful old mansion was crumbling around them. [2] The brick walls they were covered with creeping vines. [3] The front door was beginning to sag on its hinges. [4] A squirrel had made her nest in the attic.

Which sentence is incorrect because it has an extra pronoun?

(A) Sentence 1

(B) Sentence 2

(C) Sentence 3

(D) Sentence 4

20. Read the following sentences.

> Spanning the channel between San Francisco Bay and the Pacific Ocean, the Golden Gate Bridge is one of the most well-known and famous structures in America. The bridge was completed in 1937 and cost more than $35 million to construct.

Which underlined words are unnecessary?

(A) and the Pacific Ocean

(B) and famous

(C) in America

(D) more than

Read this text and answer the questions on the next page.

An Unfair Advantage

1   "Where did you get that, Jason?" Deshawn asked. Heading down the

2   hall to gym class, he had spied his friend huddled with three other boys from

3   English class. They were studying a piece of paper and talking with hushed

4   excitement. Deshawn thought it strange that they kept stealing glances behind

5   their shoulders, as if they were engaged in some top-secret activity.

6   "Taylor and me found this test on the floor outside the teachers' lounge,"

7   Jason said. "We don't know whom left it there, but it looks like a copy of

8   tomorrow's test. This is the luckiest break ever! Now we know exactly which

9   questions Mr. Sumner is going to ask!"

10   "Wait a minute," Deshawn cautioned. "Nobody have the right to see

11   the test questions beforehand. That's kind of like cheating, isn't it?"

12   Jason and Taylor looked at each other. Then he rolled his eyes. "What

13   do you mean, Deshawn? This test just fell in our laps. I wouldn't call this

14   cheating; I'd just call it extremely good fortune," he said.

15   Deshawn shook his head. "I know you wasn't *trying* to cheat," he

16   replied. "But having those questions give you an unfair advantage. And how

17   are you supposed to learn all the material if you only memorize the answers

18   to these ten questions? I think we should go to Mr. Sumner and tell them you

19   found the test. It's the right thing to do."

20   "I don't know," said Jason. "It's a shame to give up the chance to finally

21   get a good grade for once."

22   "Try studying," Deshawn said as he confiscated the stolen paper.

Read each item carefully. Fill in the circle next to the best answer.

1. What change, if any, should be made to the underlined words in lines 6–7?

   Ⓐ NO CHANGE
   Ⓑ Me and Taylor
   Ⓒ Myself and Taylor
   Ⓓ Taylor and I

2. What change, if any, should be made to the underlined words in lines 7–8?

   Ⓐ NO CHANGE
   Ⓑ know who left it
   Ⓒ know whose left it
   Ⓓ know whom's left it

3. What change, if any, should be made to the underlined words in line 8?

   Ⓐ NO CHANGE
   Ⓑ the luckier break
   Ⓒ the more lucky break
   Ⓓ the most luckiest break

4. What change, if any, should be made to the underlined words in lines 10–11?

   Ⓐ NO CHANGE
   Ⓑ Nobody is having
   Ⓒ Nobody had
   Ⓓ Nobody has

5. What change, if any, should be made to the underlined words in line 12?

   Ⓐ NO CHANGE
   Ⓑ Then they rolled
   Ⓒ Then Jason rolled
   Ⓓ Then Deshawn rolled

6. What change, if any, should be made to the underlined words in lines 15–16?

   Ⓐ NO CHANGE
   Ⓑ you weren't
   Ⓒ you isn't
   Ⓓ you was not

7. What change, if any, should be made to the underlined words in line 16?

   Ⓐ NO CHANGE
   Ⓑ given you
   Ⓒ gives you
   Ⓓ giving you

8. What change, if any, should be made to the underlined words in lines 18–19?

   Ⓐ NO CHANGE
   Ⓑ and tell him
   Ⓒ and tell us
   Ⓓ and tell himself

Read each item carefully. Fill in the circle next to the best answer.

9. Read the following sentences.

> Ming had collected a pile of shirts and pants she no longer wore. "To _____ should I give these old clothes?" she asked herself.

Which word best completes the second sentence?

Ⓐ what
Ⓑ whose
Ⓒ who
Ⓓ whom

10. Read the following sentences.

> Troy is visiting his aunt and uncle to help celebrate their anniversary. He has even brought them a thoughtful gift.

Which underlined word is an object pronoun?

Ⓐ his
Ⓑ their
Ⓒ He
Ⓓ them

11. Read the following sentences.

> [1] Kelly can be found at the skating rink most Saturdays. [2] She loves to glide across the ice. [3] Her sisters love to glide across the ice too.

What is the best way to combine sentences 2 and 3?

Ⓐ She and her sisters love to glide across the ice.
Ⓑ Her and her sisters love to glide across the ice.
Ⓒ Her sisters and she loves to glide across the ice.
Ⓓ She and her sisters loves to glide across the ice.

12. Read the following sentences.

> In 1837, John Deere invented a plow with a steel blade. _____ sold his plow to settlers arriving in Illinois to cultivate the soil.

Which pronoun best completes the second sentence?

Ⓐ It
Ⓑ He
Ⓒ They
Ⓓ You

13. Read the following paragraph.

> [1] The North American grizzly bear can be found in Canada, Alaska, and several other northwestern U.S. states. [2] The average grizzly weighs 800 pounds and stands up to eight feet tall. [3] It eats mostly nuts, berries, and leaves. [4] They can also be spotted fishing for salmon in Alaska.

Which sentence contains an incorrect pronoun?

Ⓐ Sentence 1
Ⓑ Sentence 2
Ⓒ Sentence 3
Ⓓ Sentence 4

14. Read the following sentences.

> The leafy oak grew right next to a rustic stone cottage. It was the most beautiful one I had ever seen.

Which word or words should replace the vague pronoun underlined in the second sentence?

Ⓐ That
Ⓑ This
Ⓒ The tree
Ⓓ This sight

Read each item carefully. Fill in the circle next to the best answer.

15. Read the following sentences.

> When my dad or my older sister _____ dinner, I know I am in for a treat. But when Mom cooks, I try to eat at my friend's house.

Which verb best completes the first sentence?

(A) makes
(B) make
(C) made
(D) have made

16. Read the following sentences.

> Ms. Olenska was a ballerina on the New York stage for many years. Now she _____ dance at my school.

Which verb best completes the second sentence?

(A) teach
(B) teaches
(C) taught
(D) had taught

17. Read the following paragraph.

> [1] Tired after his morning run, Jerrod decided to rest in the hammock. [2] Loaned to him by his cousin, he started reading a book. [3] Struggling to keep his eyes open, Jerrod realized the book was boring. [4] His brother later found Jerrod napping in the sun.

Which sentence contains a misplaced modifier?

(A) Sentence 1
(B) Sentence 2
(C) Sentence 3
(D) Sentence 4

18. Read the following paragraph.

> [1] The South American country of Brazil is the fifth-largest country in the world. [2] This expansive nation has one of the most diverse arrays of land features as well. [3] It also contains many waterways, including the Amazon, the world's widest river.

Where is the best place to add the following sentence?

> Tropics, mountains, plains, and scrublands can all be found in Brazil.

(A) Before sentence 1
(B) After sentence 1
(C) After sentence 2
(D) After sentence 3

19. Read the following sentences.

> Frozen from head to toe, we finally made it back to the ski lodge. Warming ourselves by the fire, it was time for a hearty meal in the dining room.

Which underlined phrase is a dangling modifier?

(A) Frozen from head to toe
(B) to the ski lodge
(C) Warming ourselves by the fire
(D) in the dining room

20. Read the following sentences.

> There are about twenty geese living at the pond in City View Park. Every year, this flock _____ in from Canada for the winter.

Which verb best completes the second sentence?

(A) fly
(B) flew
(C) flown
(D) flies

Read this text and answer the questions on the next page.

New Book Takes on a Hurricane

1   "Storm surge in Galveston" is a book in Preston Morer's historical

2   fiction series featuring young heroes and heroines caught in the drama of

3   America's worst disasters. It introduces us to Tom, a thirteen-year-old newsboy

4   who sells papers on the street corner but dreams of someday becoming a doctor.

5   It is 1900, and Tom and his family have lived in Galveston, Texas, for only a year.

6   His father, Thomas H Purdy Sr, owns a general store downtown. Tom's father,

7   mother, and three sisters all live in a modest apartment above the store.

8   The Purdy family knows that a major storm has been predicted for the

9   Gulf Coast: Tom can see large swells out in the water. But the weather has been

10   pleasant this first week of September. A deadly hurricane is the last thing they

11   expect. Days later, however, their world and their city are turned upside down.

12   Morer's descriptions of the devastation caused by the Galveston hurricane

13   are vivid and compelling. He writes "The streets were filled with piles of debris,

14   small mountains of broken lives, made up of front doors, fence posts, chair legs,

15   kitchen sinks, and smashed staircases." The reader really experiences the surge

16   of water through the town and the destruction of the buildings along with Tom.

17   The only weakness of the book, which does not take away from Morer's

18   striking images is that Tom is not a fully developed character. He shows bravery

19   when he rescues a neighbor in one important scene. And his ambition to go to

20   medical school is interesting. But Morer does little to describe Tom's feelings

21   about his ordeal. Knowing this boys thoughts would involve the reader even

22   more. Such details would also turn a very good book into a great one.

Read each item carefully. Fill in the circle next to the best answer.

1. What change, if any, should be made to the underlined words in lines 1–3?

   (A) NO CHANGE
   (B) "Storm Surge in Galveston"
   (C) *Storm Surge In Galveston*
   (D) *Storm Surge in Galveston*

2. What change, if any, should be made to the underlined words in lines 3–4?

   (A) NO CHANGE
   (B) thirteen—year—old newsboy
   (C) thirteen year old newsboy
   (D) (thirteen year old) newsboy

3. What change, if any, should be made to the underlined words in line 6?

   (A) NO CHANGE
   (B) Thomas H. Purdy sr
   (C) Thomas H. Purdy Sr.
   (D) Thomas H Purdy Sr.

4. What change, if any, should be made to the underlined words in lines 6–7?

   (A) NO CHANGE
   (B) father mother and three sisters
   (C) father mother, and three sisters
   (D) father, mother, and, three sisters

5. What change, if any, should be made to the underlined words in lines 8–9?

   (A) NO CHANGE
   (B) Gulf Coast; Tom can
   (C) Gulf Coast Tom can
   (D) Gulf Coast, Tom can

6. What change, if any, should be made to the underlined words in lines 13–15?

   (A) NO CHANGE
   (B) He writes The streets
   (C) He writes, The streets
   (D) He writes, "The streets

7. What change, if any, should be made to the underlined words in lines 17–18?

   (A) NO CHANGE
   (B) images; is that
   (C) images, is that
   (D) images. Is that

8. What change, if any, should be made to the underlined words in lines 21–22?

   (A) NO CHANGE
   (B) boy's thoughts
   (C) boys' thoughts
   (D) boys's thoughts

Read each item carefully. Fill in the circle next to the best answer.

9. Read the following sentences.

> The _____ was founded in 1954 to oversee animal welfare. Today it has millions of members and supporters.

Which words best complete the first sentence?

Ⓐ Humane society of the United States
Ⓑ humane society of the United States
Ⓒ Humane Society Of The United States
Ⓓ Humane Society of the United States

10. Read the following sentences.

> When did the british passion for drinking tea begin? England's wealthiest citizens began importing it from China in the 1600s.

Which underlined word should be capitalized?

Ⓐ british
Ⓑ tea
Ⓒ citizens
Ⓓ importing

11. Read the following heading from a friendly letter.

> _____
> Santa Fe, NM 87501
> November 5, 20__

Which address that completes the heading is written correctly?

Ⓐ 1124 Aspen Blvd
Ⓑ 1124 Aspen Blvd.
Ⓒ 1124 Aspen BLVD
Ⓓ 1124 Aspen B.l.v.d.

12. Read the following sentences.

> My favorite book of short stories is *In the Country,* by Roberta C. Ingold. It contains a thrilling story called _____.

Which words best complete the second sentence?

Ⓐ *Falling-from the Sky*
Ⓑ *Falling From The Sky*
Ⓒ "Falling From the Sky"
Ⓓ "Falling from the sky"

13. Read the following sentences.

> Tara wandered into my room with a confused look on her face. "You haven't seen my science book have you?" she asked.

Where should a comma be placed in the sentences?

Ⓐ after *room*
Ⓑ after *look*
Ⓒ after *book*
Ⓓ after *you?*

14. Read the following paragraph.

> [1] Well, I'm having another Independence Day party this year. [2] Jake will you be able to come and bring your guitar? [3] We will eat and play games, but I would also like to have some music. [4] You know quite a few songs, don't you?

Which sentence is missing a comma?

Ⓐ Sentence 1
Ⓑ Sentence 2
Ⓒ Sentence 3
Ⓓ Sentence 4

Read each item carefully. Fill in the circle next to the best answer.

15. Read the following sentences.

> I have an idea for our presentation ____ let's act out the signing of the Constitution. That will really get the audience's attention!

Which punctuation mark best completes the first sentence?

Ⓐ colon   Ⓒ comma

Ⓑ semicolon   Ⓓ no punctuation

16. Read the following sentences.

> You should try to see *Beyond the Sunat* at the theater this weekend. This film takes you on a ____ ride through the universe.

Which words and punctuation best complete the second sentence?

Ⓐ thrilling mind bending

Ⓑ thrilling, mind bending

Ⓒ thrilling mind-bending

Ⓓ thrilling, mind-bending

17. Read the following sentences from a business letter.

> We have received your submission and are hoping to publish it in our next edition. Our editors will be contacting you shortly.

Which greeting should be used in this letter?

Ⓐ Dear Ms. Nelson,   Ⓒ Dear Ms. Nelson:

Ⓑ Dear Cindy,   Ⓓ Dear Ms Nelson:

18. Read the following sentences.

> My dentist, who just moved into a new office, is very pleasant. I never feel nervous during my checkup.

What do the commas show in the first sentence?

Ⓐ a direct address   Ⓒ an independent clause

Ⓑ an appositive   Ⓓ a nonrestrictive clause

19. Read the following sentences.

> [1] The best ride at the fair is the Ferris wheel. [2] I wouldn't recommend it if I didn't really love it. [3] From the top, you can see the entire fairgrounds.

What is the best way to combine sentences 1 and 2?

Ⓐ The best ride at the fair, I wouldn't recommend it if I didn't really love it, is the Ferris wheel.

Ⓑ The best ride at the fair—I wouldn't recommend it if I didn't really love it—is the Ferris wheel.

Ⓒ The best ride at the fair—(I wouldn't recommend it if I didn't really love it)—is the Ferris wheel.

Ⓓ The best ride at the fair-I wouldn't recommend it if I didn't really love it-is the Ferris wheel.

20. Read the following paragraph.

> [1] "I'm not sure of that name, so I'll look it up in the encyclopedia," Noelle said to herself. [2] She was writing the first draft of her report about the moon's phases. [3] The entry said, "The phase after the full moon is the waning gibbous."

Where is the best place to add the following sentence?

> Noelle discovered she had misspelled *gibbous,* and she made the correction.

Ⓐ Before sentence 1   Ⓒ After sentence 2

Ⓑ After sentence 1   Ⓓ After sentence 3

Grammar, Usage, and Mechanics Handbook
Table of Contents

Mechanics

Sentence Structure and Parts of Speech

(Continued on page 362)

(Continued from page 361)

Usage

Letters and E-mails

Research

Guidelines for Listening and Speaking

(you) | Diagram | sentences

Mechanics

- Capitalize the first word in a sentence.

  <u>T</u>he kangaroo rat is an amazing animal.

- Capitalize all *proper nouns,* including people's names and the names of particular places.

  <u>G</u>regory <u>G</u>ordon   <u>W</u>ashington <u>M</u>onument

- Capitalize titles of respect.

  <u>M</u>r. Alvarez   <u>D</u>r. Chin   <u>M</u>s. Murphy

- Capitalize family titles used just before people's names and titles of respect that are part of names.

  <u>U</u>ncle Frank   <u>A</u>unt Mary   <u>G</u>overnor Adamson

- Capitalize initials of names.

  Thomas Paul Gerard (<u>T.P.</u> Gerard)

- Capitalize place names.

  <u>F</u>rance   <u>U</u>tah   <u>C</u>hina   <u>B</u>altimore

- Capitalize *proper adjectives,* adjectives that are made from proper nouns.

  <u>C</u>hinese   <u>I</u>celandic   <u>F</u>rench   <u>L</u>atin <u>A</u>merican

- Capitalize the months of the year and the days of the week.

  <u>F</u>ebruary   <u>A</u>pril   <u>M</u>onday   <u>T</u>uesday

- Capitalize important words in the names of products and companies.

  <u>B</u>lue <u>B</u>rook <u>C</u>heese Spread   <u>H</u>eart of <u>G</u>old <u>A</u>pplesauce

  <u>L</u>ittle <u>H</u>ills <u>B</u>akery   <u>A</u>nderson and <u>M</u>umford, <u>I</u>nc.

- Capitalize important words in the names of organizations.

  <u>A</u>merican <u>L</u>ung <u>A</u>ssociation   <u>V</u>eterans of <u>F</u>oreign <u>W</u>ars

- Capitalize important words in the names of holidays.

  <u>V</u>eterans <u>D</u>ay   <u>F</u>ourth of <u>J</u>uly

- Capitalize the first word in the greeting or closing of a letter.

  <u>D</u>ear Edmundo,   <u>Y</u>ours truly,

- Capitalize the word *I.*

  Frances and <u>I</u> watched the movie together.

- Capitalize the first, last, and most important words in a title. Be sure to capitalize all verbs, including *is* and *was.*

  <u>I</u>sland of the <u>B</u>lue <u>D</u>olphins   *<u>A</u>way <u>I</u>s a <u>S</u>trange <u>P</u>lace to <u>B</u>e*

- Capitalize the first word in a direct quotation.

  Aunt Rose said, "<u>P</u>lease pass the clam dip."

Abbreviations are shortened forms of words. Many abbreviations begin with an uppercase letter and end with a period.

- You can abbreviate words used in addresses when you write.

  Street (**St.**)   Avenue (**Ave.**)   Route (**Rte.**)   Boulevard (**Blvd.**)   Road (**Rd.**)   Drive (**Dr.**)

- **Use postal abbreviations for names of states in addresses.**

  Note: State names are abbreviated as two uppercase letters with no periods.

Alabama (AL)	Idaho (ID)	Missouri (MO)	Pennsylvania (PA)
Alaska (AK)	Illinois (IL)	Montana (MT)	Rhode Island (RI)
Arizona (AZ)	Indiana (IN)	Nebraska (NE)	South Carolina (SC)
Arkansas (AR)	Iowa (IA)	Nevada (NV)	South Dakota (SD)
California (CA)	Kansas (KS)	New Hampshire (NH)	Tennessee (TN)
Colorado (CO)	Kentucky (KY)	New Jersey (NJ)	Texas (TX)
Connecticut (CT)	Louisiana (LA)	New Mexico (NM)	Utah (UT)
Delaware (DE)	Maine (ME)	New York (NY)	Vermont (VT)
District of	Maryland (MD)	North Carolina (NC)	Virginia (VA)
Columbia (DC)	Massachusetts (MA)	North Dakota (ND)	Washington (WA)
Florida (FL)	Michigan (MI)	Ohio (OH)	West Virginia (WV)
Georgia (GA)	Minnesota (MN)	Oklahoma (OK)	Wisconsin (WI)
Hawaii (HI)	Mississippi (MS)	Oregon (OR)	Wyoming (WY)

- **You can abbreviate titles of address and titles of respect when you write.**

  Mister (**Mr.** Brian Davis) Mistress (**Miss** or **Mrs.** Maria Rosario) General (**Gen.** Robert E. Lee)

  Doctor (**Dr.** Emily Chu) Junior (Everett Castle **Jr.**) Saint (**St.** Andrew)

  Note: *Ms.* is a title of address used for women. It is not an abbreviation, but it requires a period. (**Ms.** Anita Brown).

- **You can abbreviate certain words in the names of businesses when you write.**

  Pet Helpers, Incorporated (Pet Helpers, **Inc.**) River Corporation (River **Corp.**)

- **You can abbreviate days of the week when you take notes.**

  Sunday (**Sun.**) Wednesday (**Wed.**) Friday (**Fri.**)

  Monday (**Mon.**) Thursday (**Thurs.**) Saturday (**Sat.**)

  Tuesday (**Tues.**)

- **You can abbreviate months of the year when you take notes.**

  January (**Jan.**) April (**Apr.**) October (**Oct.**)

  February (**Feb.**) August (**Aug.**) November (**Nov.**)

  March (**Mar.**) September (**Sept.**) December (**Dec.**)

  (May, June, and July do not have abbreviated forms.)

- **You can abbreviate directions when you take notes.**

  North (**N**) East (**E**) South (**S**) West (**W**)

An *initial* is the first letter of a name. An initial is written as an uppercase letter and a period. Sometimes initials are used in the names of countries or other places.

Michael Paul Sanders (**M.P.** Sanders) United States of America (**U.S.A.**)

Washington, District of Columbia (Washington, **D.C.**)

Section 3 Titles

- **Underline titles of books, newspapers, TV series, movies, and magazines.**

  Island of the Blue Dolphins Miami Herald I Love Lucy

  Note: These titles are written in italics in printed text.

- **Use quotation marks around articles in magazines, short stories, chapters in books, songs, and poems.**

  "This Land Is Your Land" "The Gift" "Eletelephony"

- Capitalize the first, last, and most important words in titles. Articles, short prepositions, and conjunctions are usually not capitalized. Be sure to capitalize all verbs, including forms of the verb *be* (*am, is, are, was, were, been*).

   A Knight in the Attic   *My Brother Sam Is Dead*

Section 4 Quotations and Quotation Marks

- Put quotation marks (" ") around the titles of articles, short stories, book chapters, songs, and poems.
   My favorite short story is "Revenge of the Reptiles."
- Put quotation marks around a *direct quotation,* or a speaker's exact words.
   "Did you see that alligator?" Max asked.
- Do not put quotation marks around an *indirect quotation,* a person's words retold by another speaker. An indirect quotation is often signalled by *whether* or *that.*
   Max asked Rory whether he had seen an alligator.

Writing a Conversation

- Put quotation marks around the speaker's words. Begin a direct quotation with an uppercase letter. Use a comma to separate the quotation from the rest of the sentence.
   Rory said, "There are no alligators in this area."
- When a direct quotation comes at the end of a sentence, put the end mark inside the last quotation mark.
   Max cried, "Look out!"
- When writing a conversation, begin a new paragraph with each change of speaker.
   Max panted, "I swear I saw a huge, scaly tail and a flat snout in the water!"

   "Relax," Rory said. "I told you there are no alligators around here."

- Put quotation marks around a quotation from a text. Include information on the source of the quotation.

   In his letter from the Birmingham jail which was reprinted in *Atlantic Monthly* (August, 1963), the great civil rights leader Martin Luther King Jr. wrote, "Injustice anywhere is a threat to justice everywhere."

Writing a Long Quotation from a Text

- Set off a lengthy quotation from the rest of an essay or report, either by indenting the whole block of text or by printing it in smaller type. Do not use quotation marks at the beginning and end of the quotation.
- Give source information either in the sentence that precedes the quotation or in indented lines below the quotation.

   And then as the little plane climbed higher and Olive saw spread out below them fields of bright and tender green in this morning sun, farther out the coastline, the ocean shiny and almost flat, tiny white wakes behind a few lobster boats—then Olive felt something she had not expected to feel again: a sudden surging greediness for life. She leaned forward, peering out the window: sweet pale clouds, the sky as blue as your hat, the new green of the fields, the broad expanse of water—seen from up here it all appeared wondrous, amazing. She remembered what hope was, and this was it. That inner churning that moves you forward, plows you through life the way the boats plowed the shiny water, the way the plane was plowing forward to a place new, and where she was needed.

   —Elizabeth Strout
   Olive Kitteridge

Section 5 Spelling

Use these tips if you are not sure how to spell a word you want to write:
- Say the word aloud and break it into syllables. Try spelling each syllable. Put the syllables together to spell the whole word.
- Write the word. Make sure there is a vowel in every syllable. If the word looks wrong to you, try spelling it other ways.
- Think of a related word. Parts of related words are often spelled the same.

When you use the word-processing function of a computer to write something, you can use the spell-check feature to identify possible spelling errors. But a spell checker will not catch errors with homophones. For example, if you type *break* instead of *brake*, the spell checker will not catch the mistake because the word is spelled correctly.

Section 6 End Marks

Every sentence must end with a period, an exclamation point, or a question mark.
- Use a *period* at the end of a declarative sentence (statement) or an imperative sentence (command).

  Dad and I look alike. (*declarative*)   Step back very slowly. (*imperative*)
- Use an *exclamation point* at the end of a firm command (imperative sentence) or at the end of an exclamatory sentence (a sentence that shows great feeling or excitement).

  Get away from the cliff! (*imperative*)   What an incredible sight! (*exclamatory*)
- Use a *question mark* at the end of an interrogative sentence (asking sentence).

  How many miles is it to Tucson? (*interrogative*)

Section 7 Apostrophes

An apostrophe (') is used to form the possessive of a noun or to join words in a contraction.
- Possessives show ownership. To make a singular noun possessive, add *'s*.

  The bike belongs to Carmen. It is Carmen's bike.
- To form a possessive from a plural noun that ends in *-s*, add only an apostrophe.

  Those books belong to my sisters. They are my sisters' books.
- Some plural nouns do not end in *-s*. To form possessives with these nouns, add *'s*.

  The children left their boots here. The children's boots are wet.
- Use an apostrophe to replace the dropped letters in a contraction.

  it's (it is)   hasn't (has not)

Section 8 Commas, Semicolons, and Colons

Commas in Sentences
- Use a comma after an introductory word in a sentence.

  Yes, I'd love to go to the movies.   Actually, we had a great time.
- Use a comma after an introductory element in a sentence.

  According to the weather report, we are in for some chilly temperatures.
- Use a comma after a mild interjection at the beginning of a sentence.

  Oh, it has started raining.   Hey, just grab an umbrella!
- Use a comma to separate items in a series. A series is a list of three or more items. Put the last comma before *and* or *or*. A comma is not needed to separate two items.

  Shall we eat cheese, bread, or fruit?   Let's eat cheese and fruit.
- Use a comma to separate a noun of direct address from the rest of a sentence.

  Akila, will you please stand up?   We would like you to sing, Akila.
- Use a comma to separate a tag question from the rest of a sentence.

  "It's a hot day, isn't it?" remarked Jill.
- Use a comma to separate a direct quotation from the rest of a sentence.

  Joe asked, "How long must I sit here?"   "You must sit there for one hour," Vic said.

- Use a comma with the conjunction *and, or,* or *but* when combining independent clauses in a compound sentence.
  Lisa liked the reptiles best, but Lyle preferred the amphibians.
- Use a comma to separate a dependent clause at the beginning of a sentence from the rest of the sentence.
  Because Lisa likes reptiles, she is considering a career as a herpetologist.
- Use a comma to separate coordinate adjectives —a pair of adjectives of a similar kind.
  To decide whether to put a comma between adjectives, try reading the sentence with the word *and* inserted between the adjectives. If the word *and* sounds natural there, you should use a comma.
  Reptiles have dry, scaly skin. (*needs a comma*)
  Look at that big green lizard! (*does not need a comma*)
- Use commas to set off a clause or phrase that presents information that is not necessary for understanding the main idea of a sentence.
  Alaska, the largest state in the Union, offers summer visitors the opportunity to see the midnight sun.
- Use commas to set off a nonrestrictive adjective clause. A nonrestrictive clause is one that adds information about the word it modifies but is not essential to the meaning of the sentence.
  Walt Jackson, **who sold me a turtle last year,** has a new pet gecko. (*The adjective clause just tells more about the noun it modifies. Because the information in the clause is not essential, the clause is nonrestrictive. Commas are needed.*)

  The woman **who runs the pet store** offered me a job. (*The adjective clause tells which woman is being talked about. Because the information in the clause is essential, no commas are used.*)

Semicolons and Colons in Sentences

- You may use a semicolon in place of a comma and a conjunction when combining independent clauses.
  Lisa likes reptiles; Lyle prefers amphibians.
- A colon can be used when the second clause states a direct result of the first or explains the first.
  Lisa owns reptiles: she has two pet snakes.
- Use a colon to introduce a list or series.
  I like three kinds of cheese: cheddar, Swiss, and colby.
- Use a colon to introduce a quotation.
  Cory always follows this motto: "A penny saved is a penny earned."
- Use a colon after the speaker's name in a play.
  LOGAN: Where were you on the night of October 5th, when the gold bullion was stolen?

  BLAKE: I was attending the opening night of *Carmen* at the opera house.
- Use a colon to separate hours and minutes in an expression of time.
  8:15 P.M.   11:45 A.M.
- Use a colon between the city of publication and the publisher in a bibliographical reference.
  O'Dell, Scott. *The Cruise of the Arctic Star.* Boston: Houghton Mifflin, 1973.

Commas with Dates and Place Names

- Use a comma to separate the day from the date and the date from the year.
  We clinched the division championship on Saturday, September 12, 2015.
- Use a comma to separate the name of a city or town from the name of a state.
  I visited Memphis, Tennessee.

Commas and Colons in Letters

- Use a comma after the greeting and the closing of a friendly letter.
  Dear Reginald,   Your friend, Deke
- Use a colon after the greeting of a business letter. Use a comma after the closing.
  Dear Ms. Brocklehurst: Sincerely,

Hyphens in Sentences

- **When you break a word at the end of a line, use a hyphen to separate the syllables.**
  There is no single "perfect food." Milk, for example, contains most of the nutrients needed by the human body, but it lacks enough iron.

- **Use hyphens to link the parts of some compound words.**
  <u>son-in-law</u>   <u>city-state</u>

- **Use hyphens to link some pairs or groups of words that precede a noun and act as an adjective.**
  a <u>**family-style**</u> meal   a <u>**horse-drawn**</u> carriage   an <u>**up-to-date**</u> schedule

- **Use hyphens to link the parts of numbers between twenty-one and ninety-nine.**
  eighty-two   fifty-seven   seventy-six   thirty-five

Parentheses in Sentences

- **Use parentheses to set off an explanation.**
  I interviewed my uncle <u>**(he raises goats for a living)**</u> for my report on animal husbandry.
  Rolf and Dana's farm is 100 miles <u>**(160 km)**</u> outside of Chicago.

- **Use parentheses to set off an example.**
  Many types of cheese <u>**(chèvre, for example)**</u> are made with goats' milk.

Dashes in Sentences

- **Use long dashes to set off some types of nonessential information from the other parts of a sentence. An authorial comment may be set off with long dashes.**
  Tall sunflowers—my personal favorite among American wildflowers—grow on prairies
  across much of the United States.

- **Use a long dash to mark an unfinished sentence.**
  The door slowly opened, and—

- **Use a long dash to stress a word or phrase at the end of a sentence.**
  Only one thing can make me happy—a victory.

Sentence Structure and Parts of Speech

Section 10 The Sentence

A *sentence* is a group of words that tells a complete thought. A sentence has two parts: a *subject* and a *predicate*.

- The subject tells *whom* or *what* the sentence is about.   <u>The swimmers</u> race.
- The predicate tells what the subject *is* or *does*.   The judges <u>watch carefully</u>.

There are four kinds of sentences: *declarative, interrogative, imperative,* and *exclamatory.*

- A *declarative sentence* makes a statement and ends with a period.
  Jake swam faster than anyone.
- An *interrogative sentence* asks a question and ends with a question mark.
  Did Sammy qualify for the finals?
- An *imperative sentence* gives a command and usually ends with a period; a firm command can end with an exclamation point.
  Keep your eyes on the finish line.   Watch out for that bee!
- An *exclamatory sentence* ends with an exclamation point.   Jake has won the race!

Section 11 Subjects

The *subject* of a sentence tells whom or what the sentence is about.

- A sentence can have one subject.   <u>Mary</u> wrote a book.
- A sentence can have a *compound subject,* two or more subjects that are joined by a conjunction (*and, or*) and that share the same predicate.   <u>Alex and Mark</u> have already read the book.
- Imperative sentences have an unnamed *understood subject,* the person being spoken to. This subject is referred to as "understood *you.*"   Give me the book, please.
- The *complete subject* includes all the words that name and tell about the subject.
  <u>Many students</u> have borrowed the book.
- The *simple subject* is the most important noun or pronoun in the complete subject.
  Many <u>students</u> have borrowed the book.   <u>They</u> discussed the book yesterday.

  Note: Sometimes the simple subject and the complete subject are the same.
          <u>Ricardo</u> is writing a book.

Section 12 Predicates

The *predicate* of a sentence tells what happened. The *complete predicate* includes a verb and all the words that tell what happened or tell more about the subject.

- A complete predicate can include an action verb to tell what the subject of the sentence did.
  Mary <u>*won an award*</u>.
- A complete predicate can include a linking verb to tell more about the subject.
  Mary <u>*is a talented writer*</u>.

The *simple predicate* is the verb that goes with the subject. It generally tells what the subject did, does, or will do.

     Celia <u>won</u> an award for her performance.
     She <u>will receive</u> a trophy next week.

A *compound predicate* is two or more predicates that share the same subject. Compound predicates are often joined by the conjunction *and* or *or.*

     Ramon <u>sang</u> and <u>danced</u> in the play.
     Mary <u>wrote</u> the play and <u>directed</u> it.

A *predicate noun* follows a linking verb and renames the subject.
     Mary is a <u>writer</u>.   Ramon is a <u>singer</u>.

A *predicate adjective* follows a linking verb and describes the subject.
     Mary is <u>talented</u>.   Ramon is <u>clever</u>.

Section 13 Kinds of Sentences

A *simple sentence* tells one complete thought.

> Arthur has a rock collection.

A *compound sentence* is made up of two simple sentences (or *independent clauses*) whose ideas are related. The clauses can be joined by a comma and a coordinating conjunction (*and, or, but*).

> Arthur has a rock collection**, and** Mary collects shells.

The two independent clauses in a compound sentence can also be joined by a semicolon.

> Arthur collects rocks**;** Mary collects shells.

Two clauses in a compound sentence can be separated by a colon when the second clause is a direct result of the first clause.

> Arthur enjoys visiting new places**:** he can hunt for rocks to add to his collection.

A *complex sentence* is made up of one independent clause and at least one dependent clause. A *dependent clause* is a group of words that has a subject and a predicate, but it cannot stand on its own.

> Dependent Clause: when Arthur visited Arizona
> Independent Clause: He learned a lot about desert plants.
> Complex Sentence: When Arthur visited Arizona, he learned a lot about desert plants.

A *compound-complex sentence* includes two or more independent clauses and at least one dependent clause.

> Independent Clauses: Arizona is proud of its saguaro cactus.
>   The saguaro cactus can grow up to sixty feet tall.
> Dependent Clause: which is also called the giant cactus
> Compound-Complex Sentence: Arizona is proud of its saguaro cactus; the saguaro,
>   which is also called the giant cactus, can grow up to sixty feet tall.

An *adjective clause* is a dependent clause that describes a noun or pronoun. An adjective clause always follows the word it describes and begins with a relative pronoun such as *who, whom, whose, which*, or *that*.

> My cousin Arthur, **who has a rock collection**, visited the Arizona desert. (*describes* Arthur)
> He studied the interesting rock formations **that rise above the desert floor**. (*describes* formations)

An *adverb clause* is a dependent clause that tells more about a verb, an adjective, or an adverb. Adverb clauses tell *where, when, why*, or *how much*. They often begin with a subordinating conjunction such as *after, since, where, than, although, because, if, as, as if, while, when*, or *whenever*.

> **Whenever Arthur came across an unfamiliar rock,** he took a photograph of it.
> (*tells* when *Arthur* took *a photograph*)
> Arthur didn't take any rocks away **because the desert environment is fragile**.
> (*tells* why *Arthur* didn't take *rocks away*)

Section 14 Fragments, Run-ons, Comma Splices, and Ramble-ons

A *fragment* is an incomplete sentence that does not tell a complete thought.

> Sumi and Ali. (*missing a predicate that tells what happened*)
> Went hiking in the woods. (*missing a subject that tells who went hiking*)

A *run-on sentence* is two complete sentences that are run together. To fix a run-on sentence, use a comma and a conjunction (*and, or, but*) to join the two sentences. (You may also join the sentences with a semicolon.)

> Incorrect: Sumi went hiking Ali went swimming.
> Correct: Sumi went hiking**, but** Ali went swimming.

A *comma splice* is two complete sentences that have a comma between them but are missing a conjunction (*and, or, but*). To fix a comma splice, add *and, or*, or *but* after the comma.

> Incorrect: Sumi went hiking yesterday, Ali went swimming.
> Correct: Sumi went hiking yesterday, **and** Ali went swimming.

A *ramble-on sentence* is grammatically correct but contains extra words that don't add to its meaning.

| Incorrect: | Hiking through the wilderness to enjoy nature is my favorite outdoor sports activity, probably because it is so enjoyable and such good exercise, and because I enjoy observing wild animals in the wilderness in their natural environment. |
| Correct: | Hiking through the wilderness to enjoy nature is my favorite outdoor sports activity. I enjoy observing wild animals in their natural environment. |

Try not to string too many short sentences together when you write. Instead, combine sentences and take out unnecessary information.

| Incorrect: | I stared at him and he stared at me and I told him to go away and he wouldn't so then I called my big sister. |
| Correct: | We stared at each other. I told him to go away, but he wouldn't. Then I called my big sister. |

Section 15 Nouns

A *common noun* names any person, place, thing, or idea.

Ira visited an auto **museum** with his **friends**. Ira has always had an **interest** in **cars**.

A *proper noun* names a certain person, place, thing, or idea. Proper nouns begin with an uppercase letter. A proper noun that is made up of two or more words is considered one noun.

Ira wants to visit the **Sonoran Desert** in **Mexico** in **April**.

He is reading a guidebook about the region entitled *The Undiscovered Desert*.

A *collective noun* names a group of people or things that act as one unit.

| jury | family | committee | audience | crowd |

A *concrete noun* names something you can see, touch, hear, smell, or taste.

| dog | meadow | pebble | stove |

An *abstract noun* names an idea, a quality, or a characteristic.

| freedom | bravery | freshness | excellence |

Section 16 Adjectives

An *adjective* is a word that tells more about a noun or a pronoun.

- Some adjectives tell what kind.
  Jim observed the **huge** elephant. The **enormous** beast towered above him.
- Some adjectives tell how many. The elephant was **twelve** feet tall. It weighed **several** tons.
- A *predicate adjective* follows a linking verb and describes the subject.
  Jim was **careful** not to anger the elephant. He was **happy** when the trainer led it away.
- *A, an,* and *the* are special kinds of adjectives called *articles*. Use *a* and *an* to refer to any person, place, thing, or idea. Use *the* to refer to a specific person, place, thing, or idea. Use *a* before a singular noun that begins with a consonant sound. Use *an* before a singular noun that begins with a vowel sound.
  An elephant is heavier than **a** rhino. **The** elephant in this picture is six weeks old.
- A *demonstrative adjective* tells which one. *This, that, these,* and *those* can be used as demonstrative adjectives. Use *this* and *these* to talk about things that are nearby. Use *that* and *those* to talk about things that are farther away.

  This book is about rhinos.   **These** rhinos just came to the zoo.

  That rhino is enormous!   **Those** funny-looking creatures are wildebeests.

  Note: Never use *here* or *there* after the adjectives *this, that, these,* and *those*.

- A *proper adjective* is made from a proper noun. Capitalize proper adjectives.
  Italian cooking   **Democratic** convention   **Apache** legend
- Two or more adjectives can be used to describe a noun. When you use two or more adjectives to describe a noun, put the adjectives in an order that sounds natural. This chart can help you.

how many	what quality	how big	how old	what shape	what color	what material	→	noun
three	*beautiful*	*small*	*new*	*round*	*pink*	*silken*	→	*petals*

A *pronoun* can replace a noun.

17a Personal Pronouns

Personal pronouns include *I, me, you, we, us, he, she, it, they, him, her,* and *them*. Personal pronouns can be used to stand for the person speaking, the person spoken to, or the person spoken about.

- *First person pronouns* refer to the speaker (*I, me*) or include the speaker (*we, us*).
  Let <u>me</u> know when <u>I</u> am next at bat.   It took <u>us</u> hours, but <u>we</u> managed to get to the stadium.

- *Second person pronouns* refer to the person or people being spoken to (*you*).
  Are <u>you</u> going to the game?   I asked Marisa to give the bases to <u>you</u>.

- *Third person pronouns* refer to the person, people, or thing(s) being spoken about (*he, him, she, her, it, they, them*).
  <u>They</u> played well.   Pass the ball to <u>him</u>.   Kick <u>it</u> to <u>her</u>.

- The third person pronoun *he* (with *him* and *his*) was once accepted as a universal pronoun that could refer to anyone, male or female, if a generalization about people was being made. Now most writers try to avoid the use of universal *he*.

  One solution to this pronoun problem is to make the pronoun and the word it refers to plural.

  When a chef cooks, <u>he</u> displays creativity. **becomes:** When chefs cook, <u>they</u> display creativity.
  Each player should bring <u>his</u> own racket. **becomes:** Players should bring <u>their</u> own rackets.

  Another solution is to replace *he* with *he or she,* or replace *his* with *his or her*.

  Each player should bring <u>his</u> own racket. **becomes:** Each player should bring <u>his or her</u> own racket.

17b Subject and Object Pronouns

A *subject pronoun* takes the place of the subject of a sentence. Subject pronouns are said to be in the *nominative case*. Subject pronouns include *I, you, he, she, it, we,* and *they*.

Incorrect: Rita is an excellent soccer player. <u>Rita she</u> made the team.
Correct: Rita plays goalie. <u>She</u> never lets the other team score.

An *object pronoun* replaces a noun that is the object of a verb or a preposition. Object pronouns are said to be in the *objective case*. Object pronouns include *me, him, her, us,* and *them*.

Rita's team played the Bobcats. Rita's team beat <u>them</u>.

The pronouns *it* and *you* can be either subjects or objects.

<u>It</u> was a close game. (*subject pronoun*)   The Bobcats almost won <u>it</u>. (*object pronoun*)

- Use a subject pronoun as part of a compound subject. Use an object pronoun as part of a compound object. To test whether a pronoun is correct, say the sentence <u>without</u> the other part of a compound subject or object.
  Incorrect: Rita told Ellen and <u>I</u> it was a close game. (Rita told <u>I</u> it was a close game.)
  Correct: Rita told Ellen and <u>me</u> it was a close game. (Rita told <u>me</u> it was a close game.)

- When the pronouns *I* and *me* are used in a compound with a noun or another pronoun, *I* or *me* always comes second in a pair or last in a series of three or more.
  Incorrect: The coach gave the Most Improved Players awards to <u>me and Carlos</u>.
  Correct: The coach gave the Most Improved Players awards to <u>Carlos and me</u>.

17c Pronoun Antecedents

An *antecedent* is the word a pronoun refers to. The antecedent is almost always a noun.
The <u>Bobcats</u> are excellent players. They won every game last season.

- A pronoun must agree with its antecedent. An antecedent and a pronoun agree when they have the same *number* (singular or plural) and *gender* (male or female).
  Nick's <u>mother</u> cheered. <u>She</u> was very excited.

17d Possessive Pronouns

Possessive pronouns show ownership.
- The possessive pronouns *my, your, his, her, its, their,* and *our* replace possessive nouns.
  Those skates belong to <u>my</u> brother Jorge.
  Those are <u>his</u> kneepads, too. (*The pronoun* his *replaces the possessive noun* Jorge's.)
- The possessive pronouns *mine, ours, yours, hers, his, its,* and *theirs* replace both a possessive noun and the noun that is possessed.
  Alisha's kneepads are blue. <u>Mine</u> are red, and <u>hers</u> are blue.
  (*The possessive pronoun* hers *replaces both the possessive noun* Alisha's *and the noun* kneepads.)
- *Whose* is the possessive form of the relative pronoun *who*. It is also used as the possessive form of the relative pronoun *which*.
  The skaters <u>whose</u> parents cannot pick them up at 6 P.M. must wait inside the office.
  (Whose *indicates that the parents belong to the skaters.*)

17e Compound Personal Pronouns

Compound personal pronouns can be used as *reflexive pronouns* or *intensive pronouns*. Compound personal pronouns include *myself, herself, himself, itself, yourself, ourselves,* and *themselves.*

- A *reflexive pronoun* refers to the subject of a sentence.
  My brother bought <u>himself</u> a new puck.   We cheered for <u>ourselves</u>.
- An *intensive pronoun* emphasizes the identity of the sentence subject.
  She made the winning goal <u>herself</u>.   I <u>myself</u> am not a hockey fan.

17f Indefinite Pronouns

Indefinite pronouns refer to persons or things that are not identified as individuals. These pronouns include *all, anybody, both, anything, few, most, no one, either, nothing, everyone, one, several, none, everybody, nobody, someone, everything, something, anyone,* and *somebody.*

<u>Somebody</u> lost the ball.   We can't play <u>anything</u> until we find it.

17g Relative Pronouns

When the pronouns *who, whom, whose, which,* and *that* are used to introduce an adjective clause, they are called *relative pronouns*. A relative pronoun always follows the noun it refers to.

The player <u>who brought the volleyball</u> can serve first.
I joined the team <u>that chose me</u>.
This net, <u>which I found in my closet</u>, will be perfect for our volleyball game.

Note: For more information on using *who, whom, which,* and *that,* see **G.U.M. Handbook** section 32.

17h Interrogative Pronouns

When the pronouns *who, whom, which,* and *what* are used to begin a question, they are called *interrogative pronouns.*

<u>Who</u> has brought the volleyball?   <u>What</u> is a wicket used for?

<u>Which</u> is the net for volleyball?   To <u>whom</u> did you hit the ball?

17i Demonstrative Pronouns

This, that, these, and *those* can be used as *demonstrative pronouns.*
- Use *this* and *these* to talk about one or more things that are nearby.
  <u>This</u> is a soft rug.   <u>These</u> are sweeter than those over there.
- Use *that* and *those* to talk about one or more things that are far away.
  <u>That</u> is where I sat yesterday.   <u>Those</u> are new chairs.

18a Action and Linking Verbs

An *action verb* shows action.

Scientists <u>study</u> the natural world.   They <u>learn</u> how the laws of nature work.

A *linking verb* does not show action. It connects the subject of a sentence to a word or words in the predicate that tell about the subject. Linking verbs include *am, is, are, was, been,* and *were. Seem, appear,* and *become* can be used as linking verbs, too.

Explorers <u>are</u> brave.   That route <u>seems</u> long and dangerous.

Some verbs, such as *appear, look, smell, feel, grow, sound,* and *taste,* can be either action verbs or linking verbs. You can test whether a verb is a linking verb by substituting a form of the verb *be* (*am, is, are, was,* or *were*) in its place. If the form of *be* makes sense, the verb is probably a linking verb.

I <u>looked</u> at the bear. (*"I <u>was</u> at the bear" does not make sense:* looked *is an action verb.*)
The bear <u>looked</u> hungry. (*"The bear <u>was</u> hungry" makes sense:* looked *is a linking verb.*)

18b Transitive and Intransitive Verbs

A *transitive verb* is an action verb that transfers its action to a direct object.

The polar bear <u>watched</u> a seal's air hole in the ice.   The polar bear <u>caught</u> the seal.

An *intransitive verb* does not have a direct object. An intransitive verb shows action that the subject does alone.

The bear <u>waited</u> patiently.   Suddenly the bear <u>struck</u>.

Many verbs can be either transitive or intransitive, depending on whether or not there is a direct object.

The bear <u>ate</u> the seal. (Seal *is the direct object:* ate *is a transitive verb.*)

The bear <u>ate</u> hungrily. (Hungrily *is an adverb, and there is no direct object:* ate *is an intransitive verb.*)

18c Main Verbs and Auxiliary Verbs

A *main verb* is the most important verb in a sentence. An *auxiliary verb,* or helping verb, comes before the main verb to help it show action. Auxiliary verbs such as *had, are,* and *will* indicate the tense of the main verb. Others, such as *could, might,* and *may,* show how likely it is that something will happen.

Scientists *are* <u>studying</u> glaciers.   The studies *may* <u>help</u> us learn more about Earth.

Certain auxiliary verbs have special functions. The auxiliary verbs *may* and *might* can be used to ask or give permission. The auxiliary verbs *can* and *could* can be used to indicate ability. The auxiliary verbs *should* and *must* can be used to communicate a duty or an obligation. The auxiliary verbs *may, might, could, should,* and *will* can be used to indicate possibility—how likely something is to happen. Auxiliary verbs that have these special functions are called *modal auxiliaries.*

18d The Principal Parts of a Verb

Each verb has three *principal parts:* its *present form,* its *past form,* and its *past participle form.*

- Most verbs add *-ed* to the present form to create both the past form and the past participle form. These verbs are called *regular verbs.*
- *Irregular verbs* form their past and past participle forms in other ways. The chart below shows the principal parts of several common irregular verbs.

Present	Past	Past Participle
arise	arose	arisen
(be) is	was	been
blow	blew	blown
bring	brought	brought
build	built	built
cut	cut	cut
drive	drove	driven
eat	ate	eaten
fall	fell	fallen
fly	flew	flown
give	gave	given
go	went	gone
grow	grew	grown
have	had	had
hear	heard	heard
hide	hid	hidden
hold	held	held
know	knew	known
lay	laid	laid
leave	left	left
lie	lay	lain
light	lit	lit
make	made	made
ring	rang	rung
run	ran	run
say	said	said
see	saw	seen
shake	shook	shaken
sing	sang	sung
swim	swam	swum
take	took	taken
tell	told	told
think	thought	thought
throw	threw	thrown
wear	wore	worn
write	wrote	written

- The ending *-ing* is added to the present form of almost all verbs to create the *present participle* form: *sing/singing; talk/talking.*

18e Verb Tense

Verb tense places an action in time.

- The *present tense* is used to show that something happens regularly or is true now.
  Squirrels <u>bury</u> nuts each fall.

  Add *-s* to most verbs to show present tense when the subject is *he, she, it,* or a singular noun. Add *-es* to verbs ending in *s, ch, sh, x,* or *z*. Do not add *-s* or *-es* if the subject is a plural noun or *I, you, we,* or *they.*

add *-s*	add *-es*	change *y* to *i*
speak/speak<u>s</u>	reach/reach<u>es</u>	carry/carr<u>ies</u>

- The *past tense* shows past action. Add *-ed* to most verbs to form the past tense. Verbs that do not add *-ed* are called *irregular verbs.*
  reach/reach<u>ed</u> (regular)   speak/<u>spoke</u> (irregular)
- The *future tense* shows future action. Use the verb *will* to form the future tense.
  Mom <u>will visit</u> Antarctica next year.   She <u>will photograph</u> penguins.
- The *present perfect tense* shows action that began in the past and may still be happening. To form the present perfect tense, add the helping verb *has* or *have* to the past participle of a verb.
  Mom <u>has studied</u> Antarctica for years.   Her articles <u>have appeared</u> in science journals.
- The *past perfect tense* shows action that was completed by a certain time in the past. To form the past perfect tense, add the helping verb *had* to the past participle of a verb.
  Before she visited Antarctica, Mom <u>had imagined</u> it as a wasteland.
- The *future perfect tense* shows action that will be complete by a certain time in the future. To form the future perfect tense, add the helping verbs *will have* to the past participle form of a verb.
  By the end of next year, Mom <u>will have published</u> a book on Antarctic wildlife.
- *Progressive forms* of verbs show continuing action. To form a present progressive verb, add *am, is,* or *are* to the present participle of a verb (usually the present form + *-ing*). To form the past progressive verb, add *was* or *were* to the present participle. To form a future progressive verb, add *will be* to the present participle.
  Scientists <u>are learning</u> new facts about Antarctica every day. (*present progressive*)
  When Mom <u>was traveling</u> in Antarctica, she saw its beauty. (*past progressive*)
  Someday soon I <u>will be visiting</u> Antarctica with Mom. (*future progressive*)
- Choose verb tenses carefully so that the verb forms you use work together to indicate time accurately and consistently. When you describe events that happen in the same time frame, do not shift tenses. When you describe events that happen at different times, use verbs in different tenses to indicate the order in which the events happened.
  Malcolm wanted to stay dry on the hike, so he <u>packed</u> a poncho. (not <u>packs</u>)
  The doves begin their calls early in the morning, and they <u>continue</u> them past noon.
  (not <u>continued</u>)

18f Subject-Verb Agreement

The subject and its verb must agree in number. Be sure that the verb agrees with its subject and not with the object of a preposition that comes before the verb.

An Antarctic explorer needs special equipment.

(*singular subject:* **An Antarctic explorer;** *singular verb* [*verb* + *-s* or *-es*]: **needs**)
Explorers in Antarctica carry climbing tools and survival gear.
(*plural subject:* **Explorers;** *plural verb* [*verb without -s or -es*]: **carry**)

A *compound subject* and its verb must agree.

- Compound subjects joined by *and* are plural.
  Snow and ice <u>make</u> exploration difficult.
- If a compound subject is joined by *or,* the verb must agree with the last item in the subject.
  Either the helpers or the leader <u>checks</u> the weather report.

There are special rules for agreement with certain kinds of subjects.

- Titles of books, movies, magazines, newspapers, stories, and songs are always considered singular, even if they end in *s*.
  The Secret Life of Penguins is the title of Mom's book.
  "Ice and Darkness" is the name of a poem I wrote.
- A collective noun, such as *collection, group, team, country, kingdom, family, flock*, and *herd*, names more than one person or object acting as a group. These nouns are usually considered singular.
  My <u>family</u> lives in southern Australia.   A <u>flock</u> of seagulls is flying overhead.
- Most indefinite pronouns, including *everyone, nobody, nothing, everything, something*, and *anything*, are considered singular.
  <u>Somebody</u> has left the tent flap open.   Is <u>anything</u> missing?   <u>Everything</u> is fine.
- Some indefinite pronouns that clearly refer to more than one, such as *many, most, few*, and *both*, are considered plural.
  <u>Many</u> are interested in Antarctica, but <u>few</u> are able to make the journey there.

18g Active and Passive Voice

A verb is in *active voice* if its subject performs an action. A verb is in *passive voice* if its subject is acted upon by something else. Many sentences in the passive voice have a prepositional phrase that begins with the word *by* and follows the verb.

Explorers <u>plan</u> trips months in advance. (*active voice*)
Trips <u>are planned</u> by explorers months in advance. (*passive voice*)

The active voice can communicate action briefly and powerfully. In most cases, the active voice is stronger and clearer than the passive voice. Try to write most of your sentences in the active voice.

Strong active voice: The penguin <u>snapped</u> up the fish.
Weak passive voice: The fish was <u>snapped up</u> by the penguin.

Some writers believe that the passive voice should be used only when an action is done by an unknown or unimportant agent.

The tent flap <u>was left</u> open. (*The agent who left the tent flap open is unknown.*)

Section 19 Adverbs

An *adverb* describes a verb, an adjective, or another adverb. Adverbs tell how, when, where, or to what extent.

- Many adverbs end in *-ly*. Some adverbs do not end in *-ly*. These include *now, then, very, too, often, always, again, sometimes, soon, later, first, far, now*, and *fast*.
  Andrew approached the snake cage <u>slowly</u>. He knew that snakes can move <u>fast</u>.
- Some adverbs tell *how*.
  She spoke <u>confidently</u>. He <u>eagerly</u> bit into the sandwich.
- Some adverbs tell *when*.
  <u>Then</u> the bell rang.   School ended <u>yesterday</u>.   I eat pizza <u>only</u> on Friday.
- Some adverbs tell *where*.
  We went <u>inside</u>.   They built a house <u>there</u>.   Come <u>here</u>.
- Some adverbs tell *to what extent*.
  It is <u>very</u> quiet.   I am <u>almost</u> finished.
- When the word *when, where*, or *why* begins a dependent clause that tells about a place, a time, or a reason, it is called a *relative adverb*.
  Tucker Avenue is a street <u>where</u> many accidents happen. (place)
  Friday is the day <u>when</u> my report is due. (time)
  This article gives five reasons <u>why</u> you should drink water instead of soda. (reason)

Note: A relative adverb can also be classified as a subordinating conjunction.

Section 20 Prepositions

A *preposition* shows a relationship between a word in a sentence and a noun or pronoun that follows the preposition. Prepositions tell when, where, what kind, how, or how much.

- Prepositions include the words *after, in front of, without, above, down, among, with, of, from, for, about, such as, throughout, into, onto, inside, in, at, under, over, on, through, to, across, around, by, beside, during, off,* and *before.*
  Jeff left the milk **on** the table.   He knew it belonged **in** the refrigerator.

- A *prepositional phrase* is a group of words that begins with a preposition and ends with its object. The object of a preposition is a noun or a pronoun. A prepositional phrase can be at the beginning, middle, or end of a sentence.
  Jeff's mom would be home **in five minutes**. **Within three minutes** he had put it away.

- Prepositional phrases that modify (or tell more about) nouns or pronouns are called *adjectival prepositional phrases*. An adjectival prepositional phrase usually comes after the noun or pronoun it modifies. Adjectival prepositional phrases often tell *which*.
  The milk **in the refrigerator** is spoiled. (*modifies the noun* milk *and tells* which milk)
  I can't stand the odor **of spoiled milk**! (*modifies the noun* odor *and tells* which odor)

- *Adverbial prepositional phrases* modify a verb, an adverb, or an adjective. Many adverbial prepositional phrases tell *when, where, how,* or *how long* something was done.
  Jeff usually drinks orange juice **before breakfast**. (*modifies the verb* drinks *and tells* when)

  He says his mom's fresh-squeezed orange juice is the best **in the world**.
  (*modifies the adjective* best *and tells* where)
  Late **in the evening** I heard a knock at my door. (*modifies the adverb* late *and tells* when)

Section 21 Direct Objects and Indirect Objects

A *direct object* is the noun or pronoun that receives the action of the verb. Direct objects follow action verbs. To find the direct object, say the verb and then "Whom?" or "What?"

Jacques painted a **picture**. (Painted whom or what? Picture. *Picture* is the direct object.)

- A *compound direct object* occurs when more than one noun receives the action of the verb.
  He used a **brush** and oil **paints**. (*Brush* and *paints* compose the compound direct object.)

A sentence with a direct object may also have an *indirect object*. An indirect object is a noun or pronoun and usually tells to whom something is given, told, or taught.

Jacques gave his **mom** the painting.

Section 22 Conjunctions

The words *and, or,* and *but* are *coordinating conjunctions*.
- Coordinating conjunctions may be used to join words within a sentence.
  My favorite reptiles are snakes **and** lizards.   Najim doesn't like snakes **or** lizards.

- A comma and a coordinating conjunction can be used to join two or more simple sentences. (The conjunction *and* does not need a comma if both sentences are short.)
  I like snakes, **but** he says they're creepy.   We can get a snake, **or** we can get a lizard.

A *subordinating conjunction* relates one clause to another. Dependent clauses begin with a subordinating conjunction. Subordinating conjunctions include *because, if, although, when, where, as, while, though, than, as if, whenever, since, wherever, after, often, over,* and *before.*

Before his mom left, Bo cleaned his room.

Correlative conjunctions always appear in pairs. They connect words or groups of words and provide more emphasis than coordinating conjunctions. Some common correlative conjunctions are *both...and, either...or, neither...nor, not only...but (also),* and *whether...or.*

She is **not only** a good singer **but also** an excellent athlete.

Neither Raj **nor** Chris came to the concert.

Section 23 Interjections

An *interjection* expresses emotion and is not part of any independent or dependent clause.

<u>Wow</u>! This bread is delicious.   <u>Mmmm</u>, this bread tastes good!

Section 24 Appositives

An *appositive* is a phrase that identifies a noun.

My favorite snack, <u>cornbread with honey</u>, is easy to make.

- Most appositives are separated from the rest of a sentence by commas. These appositives just give more information about the nouns they describe.
  Tara<u>, my friend who figure skates,</u> is traveling to Dallas for a competition.

- Some appositives should not be set off by commas. If an appositive is vital to the meaning of the sentence, it should not be set off by commas.
  His book <u>*The Basics of Automobile Maintenance*</u> tells how to take care of a car.

  My sister <u>Katie</u> likes to read on the porch.

Section 25 Verbals and Absolutes

25a Verbals

Sometimes a verb does not act as a predicate. *Verbals* are forms of verbs that play other roles in sentences.

- One type of verbal, a *participle,* acts as an adjective. A participle may be the present participle or the past participle form of a verb. (See G.U.M. Handbook section 18d.)
  George heard the bell <u>ringing</u>. (*acts as an adjective describing the noun* bell)

  A <u>shivering</u> child stood at the door. (*acts as an adjective describing the noun* child)

  A *participial phrase* is made up of a participle and other words that complete its meaning.
  <u>Filled</u> with pride, Angela accepted her medal. (*acts as an adjective modifying the noun* Angela)

  Matt noticed a skunk <u>waddling</u> through the bushes. (*acts as an adjective modifying the noun* skunk)

- An *infinitive* is a phrase made up of the word *to* followed by the present form of a verb (*to defend*). Infinitives may act as adjectives, adverbs, or nouns. An *infinitive phrase* is made up of an infinitive and other words that complete its meaning.
  I like <u>to walk</u> in the woods. (*acts as a noun; the direct object of the verb* like)

  This is a good way <u>to appreciate</u> nature. (*acts as an adjective modifying the noun* way)

  I listen carefully <u>to hear</u> the sounds of woodland creatures. (*acts as an adverb modifying the verb* listen)

- A *gerund* is a verbal that acts as a noun. All gerunds are present participles. (See Handbook Section 18d.)
  My brother enjoys <u>swimming</u>. (*acts as a noun; the direct object of the verb* enjoys)

  A *gerund phrase* is made up of a gerund and the other words that complete its meaning.
  <u>Riding</u> the waves on a surfboard is his great ambition. (*acts as the subject of the sentence*)

25b Absolutes

An *absolute phrase* consists of a noun or noun phrase followed by a descriptive word or phrase.
- An absolute phrase may contain a present or past participle.
  <u>Her face</u> <u>**glowing**</u>, Sue looked as happy as she felt. (*noun phrase plus a present participle*)

  The general, <u>his army</u> <u>**defeated**</u>, prepared to surrender. (*noun phrase plus a past participle*)

- An absolute phrase may also contain an adjective, a noun, or a prepositional phrase.
  Teri woke from a deep sleep, <u>her mind and body</u> <u>**alert**</u>. (*noun phrase plus an adjective*)

  Melissa, <u>good grades</u> <u>**her prime objective**</u>, never went out on a school night. (*noun phrase plus a noun phrase*)

  Teri rode home, <u>her guitar</u> <u>**across her back**</u>. (*noun phrase plus a prepositional phrase*)

Usage

Section 26 Negatives

A *negative word* means "no" or "not."

- The words *no, not, nothing, none, never, nowhere,* and *nobody* are negatives.

  The notebook was **nowhere** to be found.   **Nobody** wanted to miss the party.

- Often negatives are in the form of contractions.

  Do **not** enter that room.   **Don't** even go near the door.

- In most sentences it is not correct to use two negatives.

Incorrect	Correct
We **can't** see **nothing**.	We **can't** see anything.
We **haven't** got **no** solution.	We **haven't** got a solution.

- Some sentences express ideas that require the use of two negative words.

  No one will work for you for **nothing**. (*In other words, anyone who works will expect to be paid.*)

  I **couldn't** *not* say hello to her. (*In other words, the speaker had to say hello, even if the speaker might not have wanted to.*)

- Do not use the word *ain't.*

Section 27 Comparisons

- The *comparative form* of an adjective or an adverb compares two people, places, or things. The comparative form is often followed by "than." To compare two people, places, or things, add *-er* to short adjectives and adverbs.

  An elephant is **tall**. A giraffe is **taller** than an **elephant**. (Giraffe *is compared with* elephant.)

  A lion runs **fast**. A cheetah runs **faster** than **any other land animal**. (Cheetah *is compared with* any other land animal.)

- The *superlative form* of an adjective or an adverb compares three or more people, places, or things. The article *the* usually comes before the superlative form. To compare three or more items, add *-est* to short adjectives and adverbs.

  The giraffe is the **tallest** land animal.   The cheetah runs the **fastest** of any land animal.

- When comparing two or more persons, places, or things using the ending *-er* or *-est,* never use the word *more.*

Incorrect	Correct
She is **more faster** than he is.	She is **faster** than he is.

- The word *more* is used with longer adjectives to compare two persons, places, or things. Use the word *most* to compare three or more persons, places, or things.

  Mario is **excited** about the field trip.   Duane is **more excited** than Mario.

  Kiki is the **most excited** student of all.

- Sometimes the words *good* and *bad* are used to compare. These words change forms in comparisons.

  Mario is a **good** athlete.   The basketball court is in **bad** shape.

  Kiki is a **better** athlete.   The pool is in **worse** shape than the court.

  Bill is the **best** athlete of all.   The ice rink is in the **worst** shape of all.

  Note: Use *better* or *worse* to compare two things. Use *best* or *worst* to compare three or more things.

Section 28 Contractions

When two or more words are combined to form one word, one or more letters are dropped and replaced by an apostrophe. These words are called *contractions*. For example, when *he will* becomes the contraction *he'll,* the apostrophe replaces *wi.*

- Here are some other common contractions.

  can't (cannot)   **haven't** (have not)   **she'd** (she would)
  couldn't (could not)   **I'll** (I will)   **they've** (they have)
  doesn't (does not)   **it's** (it is, it has)   **we're** (we are)

Section 29 Plural Nouns

- A *singular noun* names one person, place, thing, or idea.
  girl   pond   arrow   freedom
- A *plural noun* names more than one person, place, thing, or idea. To make most singular nouns plural, add -*s*.
  girl<u>s</u>   pond<u>s</u>   arrow<u>s</u>   freedom<u>s</u>
- For nouns ending in *sh, ch, x* or *z*, add -*es* to make the word plural.
  bush/bush<u>es</u>   box/box<u>es</u>
  lunch/lunch<u>es</u>   buzz/buzz<u>es</u>
- For nouns ending in a consonant and *y*, change the *y* to *i* and add -*es*.
  penny/penn<u>ies</u>   army/arm<u>ies</u>
- For some nouns that end in *f* or *fe*, replace *f* or *fe* with *ves* to make the noun plural.
  shelf/shel<u>ves</u>   wife/wi<u>ves</u>   (Exceptions: cliff/cliff<u>s</u>; reef/reef<u>s</u>; cafe/cafe<u>s</u>)
- Some words change spelling when the plural is formed. These plurals are called *irregular plurals*.
  man/m<u>e</u>n   woman/wom<u>e</u>n   mouse/m<u>ice</u>   goose/g<u>ee</u>se
- Some words have the same singular and plural form. These are also called *irregular plurals*.
  deer   sheep   offspring   scissors

Section 30 Possessive Nouns

A *possessive* shows ownership.
- To make a singular noun possessive, add an apostrophe and -*s*.
  John<u>'s</u> bat   the girl<u>'s</u> bike
- When a singular noun ends in *s*, add an apostrophe and -*s*.
  Ross<u>'s</u> project   James<u>'s</u> glasses
- To make a plural noun that ends in -*s* possessive, add an apostrophe.
  the soldiers<u>'</u> songs   the girls<u>'</u> bikes
- When a plural noun does not end in -*s*, add an apostrophe and -*s* to show possession.
  the men<u>'s</u> ideas   the children<u>'s</u> shoes

Section 31 Dangling Modifiers and Misplaced Modifiers

A verbal phrase acting as an adjective must modify, or refer to, a specific word in the main part of a sentence. A *dangling modifier* is a phrase that does not refer to any particular word in the sentence.

    Incorrect: <u>Walking down the street</u>, deep thoughts come to mind.

    (*Are deep thoughts walking down the street? No. This verbal phrase does not refer to any particular word in the main part of the sentence: it is a dangling modifier.*)

Dangling modifiers make your writing unclear, so avoid them. When you begin a sentence with a verbal phrase such as "Walking down the street," make sure that the question "Who is walking down the street?" is answered clearly in the first part of the rest of the sentence.

    Correct: <u>Walking down the street</u>, I often think deep thoughts.

    (*Who is walking down the street? I am. This verbal phrase clearly relates to the pronoun* I.)

A *misplaced modifier* is a word, phrase, or clause that does not appear near the word or phrase that it modifies.

    Incorrect: <u>Containing the tickets to the baseball game,</u> Ervin hurriedly opened the envelope.

When you proofread your work, check to make sure you have not written any sentences with misplaced modifiers. If you have, rewrite those sentences so modifiers appear near the words they describe.

    Correct: Ervin hurriedly opened the envelope <u>containing the tickets to the baseball game.</u>

These words are often misused in writing.

---

sit	*Sit* means "rest or stay in one place." <u>Sit</u> down and relax for a while.
sat	*Sat* is the past tense of *sit*. I <u>sat</u> in that chair yesterday.
set	*Set* is a verb meaning "put." <u>Set</u> the chair here.

---

lay	*Lay* means "to put something down somewhere." It takes a direct object. The past tense form of *lay* is *laid,* and the past participle form of *lay* is also *laid.* Each day I <u>lay</u> a tablecloth on the table. Yesterday I <u>laid</u> the yellow tablecloth. I had never <u>laid</u> that one on the table before.
lie	*Lie* means "to recline." It can also mean "to occupy a certain place." *Lie* does not take a direct object. The past tense form of *lie* is *lay,* and the past participle form of *lie* is *lain.* Most mornings I <u>lie</u> half awake just before the alarm rings. Early this morning I <u>lay</u> with my eyes open, waiting for the alarm. I had <u>lain</u> there for a few minutes before I realized that it was Saturday. Ohio <u>lies</u> east of Indiana.

---

may	*May* is used to ask permission or to express a possibility. <u>May</u> I have another hot dog? I <u>may</u> borrow that book someday.
can	*Can* shows that someone is able to do something. I <u>can</u> easily eat three hot dogs.

---

learn	*Learn* means "to get knowledge." Who will help you <u>learn</u> Spanish?
teach	*Teach* means "to give knowledge." Never use *learn* in place of *teach.* Incorrect: My sister will <u>learn</u> me to speak Spanish. Correct: My sister will <u>teach</u> me to speak Spanish.

---

is	Use *is* to tell about one person, place, or thing. Alabama <u>is</u> warm during the summer.
are	Use *are* to tell about more than one person, place, or thing. Also use *are* with the word *you.* Seattle and San Francisco <u>are</u> cool during the summer. You <u>are</u> welcome to visit me anytime.

---

doesn't	The contraction *doesn't* is used with the singular pronouns *he, she,* and *it.* He <u>doesn't</u> like sauerkraut. It <u>doesn't</u> agree with him.
don't	The contraction *don't* is used with the plural pronouns *we* and *they.* *Don't* is also used with *I* and *you.* They <u>don't</u> like Swiss cheese. I <u>don't</u> care for it, either.

I	Use the pronoun *I* as the subject of a sentence. When using *I* or *me* with another noun or pronoun, always name yourself last. <u>I</u> am going to basketball camp. Renée and <u>I</u> will ride together.
me	Use the pronoun *me* after action verbs. Renée will call <u>me</u> this evening. **Also use *me* after a preposition, such as *to, at,* and *with.*** Pass the ball to <u>me</u>. Come to the game with Renée and <u>me</u>.

---

good	*Good* is an adjective.
well	*Well* is an adverb. These words are often used incorrectly. Incorrect: Renée plays <u>good</u>. Correct: Renée is a <u>good</u> basketball player. She plays <u>well</u>.

---

raise	*Raise* must be followed by a direct object. I <u>raise</u> the flag every morning.
rise	*Rise* is not used with a direct object. I <u>rise</u> at dawn every morning.
like	*Like* means "similar to" or "have a fondness for." Do not use *is like* to indicate a pause or to mean "says." Incorrect: I enjoy, <u>like</u>, all kinds of water sports. He was <u>like</u>, "Swimming is fun." Correct: I <u>like</u> swimming and water polo. He said, "I <u>like</u> the water."
go	*Go* means "move from place to place." Don't use *go* or *went* to mean "says" or "said." Incorrect: She <u>went</u>, "The swim meet was yesterday." Correct: She said, "I <u>went</u> to the swim meet."
all	*All* means "the total of something." Avoid using *was all* to mean "said." Incorrect: He <u>was all</u>, "Everyone likes swimming." Correct: He said, "Everyone likes swimming."
you know	Use the phrase *you know* only when it helps a sentence make sense. Try not to use it in places where it does not belong. Incorrect: We can, <u>you know</u>, go canoeing. Correct: Did <u>you know</u> that my family has a canoe?
let	*Let* is a verb that means "allow." Please <u>let</u> me go to the mall with you.
leave	*Leave* is a verb that means "go away from" or "let stay." We will <u>leave</u> at noon. <u>Leave</u> your sweater here.
was	*Was* is a past tense form of *be*. Use *was* to tell about one person or thing. Hana <u>was</u> sad yesterday.
were	*Were* is also a past tense form of *be*. Use *were* to tell about more than one person or thing. Also use the word *were* with *you*. Hana and her friend <u>were</u> both unhappy. <u>Were</u> you home yesterday?
has	Use *has* to tell about one person or thing. Rory <u>has</u> a stamp collection.
have	Use *have* to tell about more than one. Also use *have* with the pronoun *I*. David and Lin <u>have</u> a rock collection. I <u>have</u> a bottle cap collection.
who	*Who* is in the nominative case and should be used as the subject of a clause. Use *who* to refer to people. The man <u>who</u> picked me up is my father.
whom	*Whom* is in the objective case and should be used as a direct or indirect object or as the object of a preposition. Use *whom* to refer to people. To <u>whom</u> am I speaking?
which	Use *which* to refer to things. His rear tire, <u>which</u> was flat, had to be repaired.
that	*That* can refer to people or things. Use *that* instead of *which* to begin a clause that is necessary to the meaning of the sentence. The picture <u>that</u> Stephen drew won first prize.
very	*Very* is an adverb. It means "extremely." I was <u>very</u> tired after the hike.
real	*Real* is an adjective. It means "actual." Never use *real* in place of *very*. Incorrect: The hike was <u>real</u> long. Correct: I used a <u>real</u> compass to find my way.

Homophones sound alike but have different spellings and meanings.

are	*Are* is a form of the verb *be*.	We **are** best friends.
our	*Our* is a possessive pronoun.	**Our** favorite color is green.
hour	An *hour* is sixty minutes.	Meet me in an **hour**.

its	*Its* is a possessive pronoun.	The horse shook **its** shaggy head.
it's	*It's* is a contraction of *it is* or *it has*.	**It's** a beautiful day for a ride.

there	*There* is an adverb that usually means "in that place." It can also be used in the expressions *there is* and *there are*.
	Please put the books **there**. **There** are three books on the table.
	There is an aquarium nearby.
their	*Their* is a possessive pronoun. It shows something belongs to more than one person or thing.
	Their tickets are in my pocket.
they're	*They're* is a contraction made from the words *they are*.
	They're waiting for me inside.

two	*Two* is a number. Apples and pears are **two** fruits I like.
to	*To* can be a preposition meaning "toward." *To* can also be used with a verb to form an infinitive.
	I brought the pot **to** the stove. (preposition) I like **to** cook. (infinitive)
too	*Too* means "also." I'd like some lunch, **too**.
	Too can mean "more than enough." That's **too** much pepper!

your	*Your* is a possessive pronoun.
	Where are **your** socks?
you're	*You're* is a contraction made from the words *you are*.
	You're coming with us, aren't you?

whose	*Whose* is a possessive pronoun. It can refer to people or things.
	Whose raincoat is this? The raincoat whose buttons are blue is mine.
who's	*Who's* is a contraction made from the words *who* and *is* or *who* and *has*.
	Who's at the front door? **Who's** taken my book?

than	*Than* is used to make comparisons.
	We waited for more than an hour. She is taller than you.
then	*Then* can be an adverb that tells about time. It can also mean "therefore."
	Then I went home.
	If you like mangoes, **then** you should try this mango ice cream.

principal	A *principal* is a person with authority.
	The **principal** made the rule.
principle	A *principle* is a general rule or code of behavior.
	He lived with a strong **principle** of honesty.

waist	The *waist* is the middle part of the body.
	She wore a belt around her **waist**.
waste	To *waste* something is to use it in a careless way.
	She would never **waste** something she could recycle.

aloud	*Aloud* means "out loud" or "able to be heard."	He read the poem **aloud**.
allowed	*Allowed* is a form of the verb *allow*.	We were not **allowed** to swim after dark.

Letters and E-mails

Section 34 Letters

A *friendly letter* is an informal letter written to a friend or a family member. In a friendly letter, you might send a message, invite someone to a party, or thank someone for a gift. A friendly letter has five parts.

- The *heading* gives your address and the date.
- The *greeting* includes the name of the person you are writing to. It begins with an uppercase letter and ends with a comma.
- The *body* of the letter gives your message.
- The *closing* is a friendly or polite way to say good-bye. It ends with a comma.
- The *signature* is your name.

> 35 Rand Street
> Chicago, IL 60606
> July 15, 20___
>
> Dear Kim,
>
>   Hi from the big city. I'm spending the summer learning to skateboard. My brother Raj is teaching me. He's a pro.
>
>   I have one skateboard and hope to buy another one soon. If I can do that, we can practice together when you come to visit.
>
>   Your friend,
>   *Art*

A *business letter* is a formal letter. You would write a business letter to a company, an employer, a newspaper, or any person you do not know well. A business letter looks a lot like a friendly letter, but a business letter also includes the name and address of the business you are writing to. The *greeting* of a business letter begins with an uppercase letter and ends with a colon (:). A business letter omits paragraph indentations and aligns all of the letter parts along the left-hand margin.

> 35 Rand Street
> Chicago, IL 60606
> July 15, 20___
>
> Swenson Skateboard Company
> 10026 Portage Road
> Lansing, MI 48091
>
> Dear Sir or Madam:
>
> Please send me your latest skateboard catalog. I am particularly interested in your newest models, the K-7 series.
>
> Thank you.
>
> Sincerely yours,
> *Arthur Quinn*
> Arthur Quinn

The envelope below shows how to address a letter. A friendly letter and a business letter are addressed the same way.

> ARTHUR QUINN
> 35 RAND ST
> CHICAGO IL 60606
>
>   KIM LEE
>   1555 MONTAGUE BLVD
>   MEMPHIS TN 38106

An *e-mail* is a note sent from one person to another person, a group, or a company through a computer network. Many people use e-mail to stay in touch with friends and family. An e-mail should contain four parts.

- An e-mail contains a *greeting*, a *body*, a *closing*, and your *name*.
- An e-mail *header* contains your e-mail address, the e-mail address of the person you are writing to, the date, and a subject line.

| Send | Save as a Draft | Cancel |

From:	arthur_quinn@communicago.net
To:	info@swenskate.com
Date:	July 15, 20__
Subject:	Skateboard catalog

Attach Files

Dear Sir or Madam:

Please send me your latest skateboard catalog. I am particularly interested in your newest models, the K-7 series.

My address is 35 Rand Street, Chicago, IL 60606. Thank you.

Sincerely,
Arthur Quinn

Research

Section 36 | Library Research

You can find information for a report or a project in a library.

- Many libraries have an information desk. The person at the desk can help you look for information.
- Libraries have many reference books, including dictionaries, thesauruses, and encyclopedias. You can use these to find information about words and basic information about topics.
- Libraries have nonfiction books about all kinds of subjects. You can find books on a particular subject by entering that subject into a computer connected to the library's database. This database lists all the publications in the library. The computer will usually list several books on the subject you entered. Each listing will have a code that tells where in the library that book can be found.

Section 37 | Internet Research

You can use online dictionaries, thesauruses, and encyclopedias to find basic information about words and topics. You can also find information for a report or a project by using an Internet *search engine*.

- Think of **key words** that describe what you are looking for. For example, if you need information on animals that live in the rain forest, you might use the key words **rain forest animals.** Type these words into the search engine's text box.
- The search engine will provide you with links to **websites.** You can click on a link to visit a website.
- When you get to the website, you need to judge whether it will be a good source of information.
  —Notice the last three letters of the website's Internet address. Sites with **.gov** and **.edu** are usually more reliable than sites with **.com**.
  —Think about who has written the information. Is the writer an expert on the topic? Is the writer giving facts, or just expressing opinions?
  —Check to see if the information is up-to-date. The site should tell you when it was last updated.

Internet Safety

Be sure to follow safety rules whenever you use the Internet. These rules will help you keep personal information private.

- When you log on to a school computer, you may type your own name as a username. However, when you go on the Internet, you use a screen name. That should never be your real name or nickname. You will also use a password, a secret word or symbol that identifies who you are. Keep your password safe. Do not share it with anyone. Never use your address, birthday, phone number, or pet's name as a password. Those are too easy for someone else to figure out.
- Have you ever received e-mail with an attachment? Usually you must click the attachment to load it into your computer. Never download attachments from strangers. These may harm your computer.

Guidelines for Listening and Speaking

Section 38 Listening

These steps will help you be a good listener:

- **Listen carefully** when others are speaking.
- **Keep in mind your reason for listening.** Are you listening to learn about a topic? To be entertained? To get directions? Decide what you should get out of the listening experience.
- **Look directly at the speaker.** Doing this will help you concentrate on what he or she has to say.
- **Do not interrupt** the speaker or talk to others while the speaker is talking.
- **Ask questions** when the speaker is finished talking if there is anything you do not understand.

Section 39 Speaking

Being a good speaker takes practice. These guidelines can help you become an effective speaker:

Giving Oral Reports

- **Be prepared.** Know exactly what it is that you are going to talk about and how long you will speak. Have your notes in front of you.
- **Speak slowly** and **clearly.** Speak **loudly** enough so everyone can hear you.
- **Look** at your audience.

Taking Part in Discussions

- **Listen** to what others have to say.
- **Disagree politely.** Let others in the group know you respect their point of view.
- **Try not to interrupt** others. Everyone should have a chance to speak.

(you)|Diagram|sentences

A sentence diagram is a map of a sentence. It shows how the parts of a sentence fit together and how the individual words in a sentence are related. Sentence diagrams can represent every part of speech and every type of sentence. The models below demonstrate how to create sentence diagrams, beginning with the simplest kinds of sentences.

- In a sentence consisting of a subject and an action verb, the subject and the verb are separated by a vertical line that bisects the horizontal line.
  Rain fell.

  Rain | fell

- An adjective (or article) that modifies a noun or pronoun belongs on a slanted line below the word it modifies.
  A **cold** rain fell.

- An adverb that modifies a verb belongs on a slanted line below the verb it modifies.
  A cold rain fell **steadily**.

  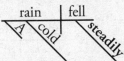

- A direct object is placed on the horizontal line to the right of the verb. It is separated from the verb by a short vertical line that does not bisect the horizontal line.
  The downpour drenched the **land**.

  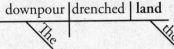

- An indirect object goes below the verb to show *who* or *what* receives something.
  It gave the **crops** a welcome soaking.

  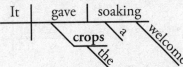

- Two separate horizontal lines show a compound predicate. The conjunction joins the verbs.
  Seedlings **uncurled** and **grew**.

  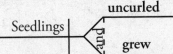

- A compound subject is placed on two horizontal lines with a conjunction joining the subjects.
  Leaves and **flowers** glistened.

  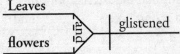

- A compound sentence is diagrammed as two sentences with a conjunction joining them.
  The rain stopped and the sun appeared.

  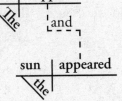

389

- **A demonstrative pronoun takes the place of a noun. It belongs wherever the noun it replaces would go in the diagram.**
  This prompted a collective cheer.

  This | prompted | cheer
  a / collective

- **A possessive pronoun belongs on a slanted line under the noun that is the possession.**
  The children left **their** homes gleefully.

  children | left | homes
  The / gleefully / their

- **An indefinite pronoun, a subject pronoun, or an object pronoun also belongs wherever the noun it replaces would go.**
  Someone started a soccer game.

  Someone | started | game
  a / soccer

  I watched **it**.

  I | watched | it

- **The understood** *you* **belongs where the subject of the sentence would go. It is written in parentheses.**
  Remove your muddy shoes.

  (you) | Remove | shoes
  your / muddy

- **A linking verb has the same position in a diagram that an action verb has, but the linking verb is separated from the predicate adjective or predicate noun by a diagonal line instead of by a vertical line.**
  Your clothes **are** incredibly muddy.

  clothes | are \ muddy
  Your / incredibly

  Soccer **is** a rough sport.

  Soccer | is \ sport
  a / rough

- **An adverbial prepositional phrase that modifies a verb is connected to that verb.**
  Leave your shoes **on the porch.**

  (you) | Leave | shoes
  on porch / your
  the

- **An adjectival prepositional phrase that modifies a noun is connected to that noun.**
  The mud **in the field** is quite deep.

  mud | is \ deep
  The / in field / quite
  the

- **When** *there* **begins a sentence, it is placed on a separate line above the rest of the diagram.**
  There are fresh towels inside the house.

  There
  towels | are
  fresh / inside house
  the

- An adjective or an adverb is written on a slanted line and is connected to the word it modifies.
The **bright** green towel is mine.

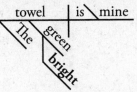

You must clean your shoes **very** carefully.

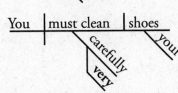

- To diagram a sentence containing an adjective clause, first identify the independent clause and diagram it. Then place the dependent clause below the first diagram. Connect it to the first diagram with a slanted, dashed line that joins the clause to the noun it modifies. Write the relative pronoun or relative adjective on the dashed line.
The new shoes **that you bought** are very wet.

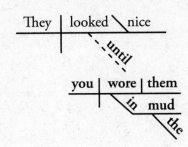

- Diagram a sentence containing an adverb clause in a similar way, but connect the dependent clause to the independent clause with a slanted, dashed line connecting to the verb.
They looked nice **until you wore them in the mud.**

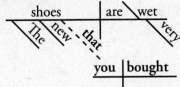

Language Index

Conventions of Standard English